THE TECHNICAL INTELLIGENTSIA
AND THE EAST GERMAN ELITE

The Technical Intelligentsia and the East German Elite

Legitimacy and Social Change in Mature Communism

by THOMAS A. BAYLIS

UNIVERSITY OF CALIFORNIA PRESS

Berkeley / Los Angeles / London

University of California Press
Berkeley and Los Angeles, California
University of California Press, Ltd.
London, England
Copyright © 1974, by
The Regents of the University of California
ISBN: 0-520-02395-1
Library of Congress Catalog Card Number: 72-95306
Printed in the United States of America

To my parents

CONTENTS

PREFACE

The bourgeois revolutions of the past demanded only lawyers from the universities as the best raw material for politicians; the liberation of the working class requires in addition doctors, engineers, chemists, agronomists, and other specialists; for it is not only a question of taking over the directing of the political machinery, but equally that of all social production, and that requires solid knowledge instead of high-sounding phrases.

FRIEDRICH ENGELS, 1893[1]

THIS BOOK explores the political profile of a new social stratum in a European Communist society and of those members of the political elite recruited from it. It seeks to relate the emergence of both to the troubled process of authority building in such a society. More broadly, it attempts to assess their influence in shaping the course of change in Communist polities.

The technical intelligentsia in the German Democratic Republic (DDR) is an example of an infrequent but fascinating social phenomenon: a stratum consciously created by a political regime as an instrument for furthering its goals for remaking society. The term itself is of Russian origin; it refers to those individuals with specialized technical, scientific, and managerial skills who directly or indirectly do the brain work of the process of material production. The boundaries of the stratum are generously drawn and encompass a much wider group than the Western term "intellectuals." With exceptions, membership in the technical intelligentsia implies an advanced formal education in engineering, economics, or science, and work either in these fields or in related manage-

---

[1] "An den Internationalen Kongress sozialistischer Studenten," cited in Richard Herber and Herbert Jung, *Wissenschaftliche Leitung und Entwicklung der Kader* ([Berlin]: Staatsverlag der DDR, [1964]), p. 12.

ment, planning, administrative, or educational positions. This is the sense in which I shall use the term in this book, as well as the substitute terms "technicians" and "technical specialists."

The creation of a technical intelligentsia is part of a larger process of the manipulation of social structure by a self-conscious political elite which sees itself as a revolutionary vanguard engaged in the task of creating a radically different and better society. We shall observe, however, that social structure in Communist systems (as elsewhere) is not simply a docile and dependent variable; as it is molded, it works its own influence—often in unanticipated ways—on the character of society and indeed on the characteristics and performance of the molding elite itself. The Promethean ambitions of the elite are subtly and gradually revised by the cunning of the clay it seeks to shape. What I am undertaking, then, is a study of the interaction—one might say, dialectic—of conscious social engineering, in the name of a higher ideological purpose, with a varied set of social actors, structures, and relationships, both responsive and resistant, manipulable and voluntaristic, long established and newly called into being. This is a political study, for its purpose is to explore the ways in which this interaction may affect and change the distribution of power, the conditions and assumptions of decision making, and the development of authority in Communist polities.

There are two major expository sections in this book. The first of these (Part I) investigates the political characteristics of the stratum of technical intelligentsia as a whole. It records the history of its development under the Communist regime established in East Germany after World War II and examines the process of conscious socialization by which the regime seeks to implant in it appropriate political values. It explores the politicalization of the workplace and its effects and seeks to establish some rough generalizations about the resulting political and politically related attitudes of the technical intelligentsia.

The second expository section (Part II) turns to the question of recruitment into the political elite from this stratum: It seeks to discover who is recruited, according to what principles and practices of selection, how their membership in (and relationship to) the stratum may condition their performance as an elite, and what typical career patterns they follow. It then examines in some detail the growth in numbers and education of technical specialists in positions of political influence over the years. Finally, it seeks to present what evidence is available of their effect on specific policy decisions and the more general contours of regime policy.

As this brief account suggests, the book is written against the background of recurring discussions of "technocracy." The technocracy thesis in one form or another argues that modern industrial societies thrust forward their own characteristic ruling elites of specialists or "managers" and explains their growing power not on the basis of traditional forms of political legitimation but on their very indispensability to such societies. One of my central purposes is to contribute to the critical exploration of these propositions through the analysis of the East German case. To do that, it is necessary to define the problem in more precise terms than is customary and to refine a good many of the conceptions underlying the idea of technocratic rule. In its crude form the thesis of "managerial revolution" or technocratic rule is not easily amenable to precise justification through systematic argument and evidence; it has accordingly provided an easy target for a great number of critics. I will argue, however, that, more subtly and less spectacularly understood, the phenomenon of technocratic power is real, if elusive, and worthy of serious attention from political scientists.

Thus, a broader comparative dimension underlies this study. In particular, I have devoted the introduction and parts of the last chapter to problems of definition, clarification, the formation of propositions and analysis. While I have not sought to go beyond the data for the DDR in this study, I have tried to formulate the problem of technocracy in such a way as to encourage future comparison. I argue that the rise of the technical stratum and elite is intimately bound up with the question of legitimacy in mature Communist societies and that their ultimate success or failure in obtaining substantial, institutionalized influence rests in great part on the shifting bases of regime authority. In addition, I suggest that at least some of the elements encouraging or restraining the development of the technocratic phenomenon in Communist systems also have application in Western industrial societies.

A study of an emerging stratum and elite is perforce a study of social change, and while it would be beyond the scope of this book to elaborate a full-scale analysis of the character of present East German society, it is well to make explicit some of the more basic assumptions with which I approach it. The totalitarian model of Communist societies has come in for a great deal of generally justified criticism in recent years,[2] so much so that I, with many other writers, have generally sought to avoid the use of the term. Yet it is essential to remark that while totalitarianism itself is surely dead, the totalitarian aspiration continues to live in the way in which the leaders of the DDR envisage the organization of their society. The aspiration toward total mobilization and control coexists rather illogically with a growing awareness of the demands of diverse social forces in East German society and the operational advantages of some deconcentration of decision making and deferral to expertise. While the balance between them has shifted from an emphasis on the one to an emphasis on the other and back again, it is hard to imagine that either will obtain exclusive hegemony in the near future. This is only to say that the leaders of the DDR —in differing mixes—seek to follow both the codified official wisdom of Marx and Lenin and the newer logic of a complex industrial order. This simultaneous adherence to inconsistent if not contradictory visions of society should surprise no one acquainted with the psychological dimensions of political belief and ideology.[3]

A number of terms have been offered to characterize contemporary Communist societies sharing the characteristics of the DDR and the Soviet Union: "consultative authoritarianism" (Ludz[4]), the "administered society" (Kassof[5]), "USSR, Incorporated" (Meyer[6]), and "cooptative" system (Fleron[7]). All these seek to con-

---

[2] See Chalmers Johnson, ed., *Change in Communist Systems* (Stanford: Stanford University Press, 1970); Carl J. Friedrich, Michael Curtis, and Benjamin Barber, *Totalitarianism in Perspective* (New York: Praeger, 1969).

[3] See Ralf Dahrendorf, *Society and Democracy in Germany* (Garden City, N.Y.: Anchor Books, 1967), pp. 401–403.

[4] Peter Christian Ludz, *Parteielite im Wandel* (Köln and Opladen: Westdeutscher Verlag, 1968), pp. 35–37. The Ludz book has been translated as *The Changing Party Elite in East Germany* (Cambridge: MIT Press, 1972). All my references to it, however, are to the German version.

[5] Allen Kassof, "The Administered Society," *World Politics*, XVI (July 1964), 558–575.

[6] Alfred G. Meyer, "USSR, Incorporated," *Slavic Review*, XX (October 1961), 369–376. See also his *The Soviet Political System* (New York: Random House, 1965).

[7] Frederic J. Fleron, Jr., "Toward a Reconceptualization of Political Change in the Soviet Union," *Comparative Politics*, I (January 1969), 228–244. Reprinted in Fleron,

vey a form of conservative, bureaucratized rule, authoritarian in essence and yet sufficiently adaptive to the forces of modernity to maintain social stability and popular acquiescence. With the crushing of reform Communism in Czechoslovakia, the consolidation of Brezhnev's leadership in the Soviet Union, and the successful transference of power from Ulbricht to a successor *apparatchik* regime in East Berlin, the viability of what I will call "bureaucratic Communism" would seem resistant to challenge. Yet it is no longer possible to consider these systems in isolation from an alternative Communist model now presented for advanced industrial societies which, in the absence of a better term, may be called "pluralistic Communism." [8] This is the Communism of Yugoslavia, of the Czechoslovak Action Program, of much of Western Communist revisionism. Both bureaucratic and pluralistic Communism are modernizing departures from Stalinism; neither, I suggest, is an inherently stable form of rule. Both forms are still fluid and ambiguous in their ideological underpinnings, their social structures, and their organizational principles and, therefore, admit of a potential for far-reaching transformation. Within bureaucratic Communism lies the potential for change to pluralistic Communism, just as pluralistic Communism might plausibly harden into bureaucratic Communism or become something not very different from Western social democracy, precisely as the Soviet leaders feared in the case of Czechoslovakia. I have suggested elsewhere that the ambiguous role of participation in Communist systems is an important potential source of change.[9] In this book I am primarily con-

---

ed. *Communist Studies and the Social Sciences* (Chicago: Rand McNally, 1969), pp. 222–243.

[8] H. Gordon Skilling suggests the term "democratizing and pluralistic authoritarianism" while remarking that such regimes are "neither fully democratic nor fully pluralistic." He uses Ludz's term "consultative authoritarianism" for my "bureaucratic communism" and adds a transitional type, "quasi-pluralistic authoritarianism." Skilling, "Group Conflict and Political Change," in Johnson, ed., *op. cit.*, pp. 222–229. The term "mature Communism" in the subtitle of the present book is borrowed from Meyer and refers to the phase of Communst development in which the initial consolidation of party power has been completed and at least the basic apparatus of an advanced industrial society is present. See Alfred G. Meyer, "Authority in Communist Political Systems," in Lewis J. Edinger, ed., *Political Leadership in Industralized Societies* (New York: Wiley, 1967), pp. 84–107.

[9] Thomas A. Baylis, "East Germany: In Quest of Legitimacy," in *Problems of Communism* (March–April 1972), pp. 46–55.

cerned with the consequences of elite development and social structure for such change.

There is, however, nothing deterministic about the change process. A study like this one falls easy prey to charges of technological determinism, of investing the forces of technical innovation and organizational science with a power to order men's lives as great as that Marx attributed to the forces of production. I wish explicitly to disavow any such intent, except in the broad and banal sense that science must assume that behavior is ultimately "determined" and not random.[10] Technology and organization often do appear to have a compelling logic of their own, once men accept the premises and definitions behind that logic. It is characteristic of contemporary Eastern and Western industrial societies that both do accept, or claim to accept, much of it. But their political and social decisions continue to reflect ancient dogmas, psychological and physiological drives, idiosyncratic perceptions of self-interest, cultural biases, and much else in addition to economic and technical "rationality." [11] Undoubtedly, technology and organization have imparted a rough sort of common *direction* to social development in advanced societies. But the differences of "detail" remain enormous; and we could even reverse the direction, if we wanted.[12]

Only the writer of a book such as this one can be fully aware of the limitations of some of the evidence on which the argument rests. It would be pretentious to claim more scientific demonstrability or to use a more rigorous vocabulary than the character of the materials I have used warrants. The imaginative use of aggregate data, elite social background analysis, content analysis, and other empirical techniques has introduced a whole new dimension to Communist studies in the last several years.[13] The obstacles to

[10] See Alfred G. Meyer, "Theories of Convergence," in Johnson, ed., *op. cit.*, pp. 337–338.
[11] See Skilling, "Group Conflict," pp. 229–232.
[12] "Technology conditions civilizations and explains much about them but never completely determines them or acts in isolation or independent of human choosing." Victor Ferkiss, *Technological Man* (New York: Braziller, 1969), pp. 29–30.
[13] See, for example, Fleron, ed., *op. cit.*; Roger E. Kanet, ed., *The Behavioral Revolution and Communist Studies* (New York: Free Press, 1971); R. Barry Farrell, ed., *Political Leadership in Eastern Europe and the Soviet Union* (Chicago: Aldine, 1970); Milton C. Lodge, *Soviet Elite Attitudes Since Stalin* (Columbus, Ohio: Merrill, 1969).

effective data collection remain formidable in most Communist polities, however, and studies as broad as the present one must still rely largely on the laborious mining and the informed interpretation of official documents and publications. This study, for example, would benefit most greatly from the use of survey data and intensive interviews. A good deal of data of this sort exists in the DDR, collected by the Central Committee's Institut für Meinungsforschung, the Zentralinstitut für Jugendforschung, and other agencies, but it is utilized for purposes of feedback and social control and remains in large measure unpublished.[14]

I have been able to use some refugee data, but it suffers from twin disabilities: It was collected before the erection of the Berlin Wall in 1961 and, thus, is often outdated, and much of it is methodologically suspect. The most valuable source of information on the refugee intelligentsia is the study carried out in late 1958 by the Infratest Institute in Munich.[15] In spite of its date and its severe methodological limitations, it offers some compelling in-

[14] Empirical studies are sometimes published in such journals as the *Deutsche Zeitschrift für Philosophie, Wirtschaftswissenschaft,* and *Jugendforschung.* Unfortunately, accounts of both findings and method are often sketchy, and studies directly concerning the technical intelligentsia are rare. Examples of some of the best DDR sociological studies have been reprinted in Peter Christian Ludz, ed., *Soziologie und Marxismus in der Deutschen Demokratischen Republik,* 2 vols. (Neuwied and Berlin: Luchterhand, 1972).

[15] *Die Intelligenzschicht in der Sowjetzone Deutschlands,* 3 vols. (München: Infratest GmbH & Co., November 1960), mimeographed. The study was carried out between October and December 1958 at the refugee camp in Berlin-Marienfelde. A sample of 80 members of the intelligentsia was selected: 24 from the "economic-technical" intelligentsia, 27 from the "scientific" (that is, scholarly) and pedagogical, 10 from the medical, 9 from the "cultural," and 10 from the administrative. These numbers were intended to correspond to the proportion of the groups concerned among the entire DDR intelligentsia; it was also sought, somewhat less successfully, to have the sample mirror the distribution of other sociological characteristics such as age, sector of work, and geographical location of job. Each subject was interviewed in depth for an average of eight hours; questions were by and large open-ended, and thus the authors' statistical summarizations were based on their own categorization of the answers. They do, however, reproduce many representative responses verbatim.

The most serious difficulties of the study are imposed by the size of the sample, the failure in most cases to distinguish among results from different intelligentsia groups (roughly half of the total would appear to belong to the *technical* intelligentsia as I define it), the unsophisticated methods employed in interviews and analysis, and the inherent unrepresentativeness of *any* refugee group. Yet the answers reproduced reflect an uncommon subtlety and thoughtfulness, and only a handful of those interviewed were dogmatic and undiscriminating opponents of the regime; the majority saw positive as well as negative features in the DDR's social system.

sights into the work environment and the political perspectives of the technical intelligentsia, and I have made considerable, though cautious, use of it. A second study, Karl Valentin Müller's *Die Manager in der Sowjetzone,* is more dubious; I regard Müller's absolute results as often unreliable, but useful information can sometimes be extracted from his comparative findings dealing with groups within the technical intelligentsia.[16]

My principal sources have been East German publications: party and government documents, specialized publications aimed at specific intelligentsia and party groups, and other products of the official press. There is no need to exercise here the familiar difficulties of using such materials. I am aware that the subjective criteria of selection used by the author is all-important in a study of this sort; the nonspecialist reader must take it largely on faith mixed with limited internal evidence that the author has selected representative rather than exceptional data. Unfortunately, the extensive use of content analysis, the alternative, is too costly and time-consuming (and sometimes too methodologically problematical) to be feasible in a study of this scope.

The breadth of my subject has also made it necessary and desirable to use a good deal of secondary material, most of it collected by West German scholars. The wealth of information and insight in the work of Peter Christian Ludz and Ernst Richert, and the high intellectual quality of the numerous special studies regularly appearing in *Deutschland Archiv* have been of special value. In addition I have been able to make use of informal interview materials gathered on visits to the DDR and in conversation with journalists and others with extensive contacts there. Such information generally cannot be attributed directly but add confirmation and human depth to the printed sources.

Many of my East German informants will disagree with much of what is written here. The epistemological distance between bourgeois social science and Marxism-Leninism as understood in the DDR will explain a large part of the disagreement, but there

---

[16] (Köln and Opladen: Westdeutscher Verlag, 1962). One problem with this study is the intense anti-Communist bias of the late author. A more serious one is the source of the data: brief questionnaires given to refugees at reception camps and "third-person" reports of refugees and visitors to West Berlin on managers still in the DDR. The samples here are very large, running into the thousands, but there are none of the checks provided by Infratest's long and probing interviews.

are simpler problems of fact and interpretation introduced by the necessity of writing at a physical distance from the object of study. The weight to be assigned new ideological pronouncements, the relative importance of technological innovation and organizational inertia, the impact of formal norms on informal behavior can seldom be measured so well from outside a society as from within it. Thus, the possibility that the new international recognition of the DDR will bring new opportunities for direct scholarly exchange is to be welcomed. Research by Western social scientists in the DDR and by DDR scholars in the West will not eliminate ideological divergence but, at least, may serve to separate it from simple misunderstanding.

The greatest portion of the research for this book was carried out at the Institut für politische Wissenschaft of the Free University of Berlin. I am particularly grateful to the past and present directors of the Institute's DDR division, Peter Christian Ludz and Hartmut Zimmermann, and to Jean-Paul Picaper, Peter Brokmeier, and the several other staff members who assisted me and whose ideas stimulated my research. In ways only indirectly reflected in the manuscript, my conversations with diverse officials, scholars, and other citizens of the DDR, as well as with Western journalists and others who have traveled extensively there, have also deepened and broadened my understanding.

This book began as a dissertation written under Professors Sheldon S. Wolin, now of Princeton University, and Reinhard Bendix and Andrew Janos, of the University of California at Berkeley. All three were extraordinarily generous of their time and criticism during the writing of the original manuscript; Professor Bendix also opened several important doors to me in Berlin. Sections of the present manuscript were read and criticized by several of my colleagues at the State University of New York at Albany, including Walter Goldstein, Leigh Stelzer, Clifford Brown, Erik Hoffmann, and Melvin Whartnaby, as well as by my wife, Helen Ullrich Baylis. I am grateful to all of them.

Part of Chapter 10 originally appeared in different form as an article in *Comparative Politics* in January 1971; I thank the editors for allowing me to use it here. I also thank the Center for Slavic and East European Studies at Berkeley and the Duke University Research Council, which provided support for part of my research, and the staff of the archive of the Bundesanstalt für gesamtdeutsche Angelegenheiten, who assisted me in finding biographical data. Finally, I am especially grateful to Ann Wright, Helen Ecker, Ada Bradley, Linda Varriale, Betty Jones, and Betty MacIntosh, who typed and retyped the manuscript with only occasional carping at the long German titles in the footnotes.

ABBREVIATIONS

CC (ZK)	Zentralkomitee	Central Committee
COMECON	Rat für Gegenseitige Wirtschaftshilfe	Council for Mutual Economic Assistance
DDR	Deutsche Demokratische Republik	German Democratic Republic
DWK	Deutsche Wirtschaftskommission	German Economic Commission
FDGB	Freier Deutscher Gewerkschaftsbund	Free German Trade Union Federation
FDJ	Freie Deutsche Jugend	Free German Youth
KDT	Kammer der Technik	Chamber of Technology
KPD	Kommunistische Partei Deutschlands	Communist Party of Germany
LPG	Landwirtschaftliche Produktionsgenossen-schaft	Collective farm

NES	Neues ökonomisches System der Planung und Leitung der Volkswirtschaft	New Economic System for the Planning and Direction of the Economy
SED	Sozialistische Einheitspartei Deutschlands	Socialist Unity Party of Germany
SPC	Staatliche Plankommission	State Planning Commission
SPD	Sozialdemokratische Partei Deutschlands	Social Democratic Party of Germany
VdgB	Verein der gegenseitige Bauernhilfe	Union of Mutual Agricultural Assistance
VEB	Volkseigener Betrieb	Publicly owned factory
VVB	Vereinigung Volkseigener Betriebe	Union of Publicly Owned Factories
VWR	Volkswirtschaftsrat	National Economic Council

INTRODUCTION: OF TECHNOCRATS AND INDUSTRIAL SOCIETY

> From the political, social, and human points of view, this con-
> junction of state and technique is by far the most important
> phenomenon of history.
>
> JACQUES ELLUL, *The Technological Society*[1]

T HE TECHNOCRAT has become one of the myth figures of contemporary popular social analysis and political invective. He
is a shadowy and misunderstood being, to my mind, sometimes
calling forth extravagant hopes for a more rational and just social
order but more frequently inspiring fears of the impersonal op-
pression and alienation of men by complex machinery and organization tables. Whether viewed positively or with abhorrence, he is
regarded as the symbolic product of the forces of production in a
post-Marxian world, in which the visibility of the class struggle has
given way to the subtle determinism of advanced technology.
Theodore Roszak writes:

In the technocracy, nothing is any longer small or simple or readily apparent to the non-technical man. Instead, the scale and intricacy of all human activities—political, economic, cultural—tran-
scends the competence of the amateurish citizen and inexorably
demands the attention of specially trained experts. Further, around
this central core of experts who deal with large-scale public necessi-
ties, there grows up a circle of subsidiary experts who, battening on
the general social prestige of technical skill in the technocracy, assume authoritative influence over even the most seemingly personal
aspects of life: sexual behavior, child-rearing, mental health, recrea-

[1] (New York: Vintage, 1964), p. 233.

tion, etc. In the technocracy everything aspires to become purely technical, the subject of professional attention. The technocracy is therefore the regime of experts—or of those who can employ the experts. . . .

. . . the distinctive feature of the regime of experts lies in the fact that, while possessing ample power to coerce, it prefers to charm conformity from us by exploiting our deep-seated commitment to the scientific world-view and by manipulating the securities and creature comforts of the industrial affluence which science has given us.[2]

To the extent that, as here, the technocrat becomes the personified target of a broad, polemical critique of contemporary society, any precision in the definition of his character and role is likely to dissolve. Serious studies of the technocratic phenomenon remain relatively rare, even though there are few societies which do not purport to have found a band of technocrats in their midst exercising or seeking to exercise political power. "Technocratic" is used to refer to the influence of expertise in virtually any field and on some occasions seems hardly to mean more than "pragmatic," "efficient," or even "sensible." As a political doctrine, however, technocracy in any strict sense would seem to include two principal tenets: (1) that political authority ought to be given to those elites of talent and specialized education which are produced by and are essential to the operation of the advanced industrial order, and (2) that politics can and ought to be reduced to a matter of technique, that is, that political decisions should be made on the basis of technical knowledge, not the parochial interests or untutored value preferences of politicians.[3] "The fundamental assumption," in the words of Ridley and Blondel, "is that disagreements occur not because people are bound to differ but because they are misinformed."[4]

The technocrat characteristically regards himself as an agent of

[2] *The Making of a Counter Culture* (Garden City, N.Y.: Anchor Books, 1969), pp. 6–7, 9.

[3] Roszak defines technocracy as "that society in which those who govern justify themselves by appeal to technical experts who, in turn, justify themselves by appeal to scientific forms of knowledge. And beyond the authority of science, there is no appeal" (pp. 7–8). See also Jean Meynaud, *Technocracy* (London: Faber & Faber, 1968), pp. 29–33.

[4] F. Ridley and J. Blondel, *Public Administration in France* (New York: Barnes and Noble, 1965), p. 322, cited in Anthony Sampson, *The New Europeans* (London: Hodder & Stoughton, 1968), p. 340.

progress and humanism. He says, in effect, that there are desirable, progressive social objectives that all men of good will ought to agree upon. The problem of politics is not to dispute over these goals or their ideological sanctification but rather to devise the most appropriate, direct, and efficient means of obtaining them. It is to those with special training and ability in manipulating the technical and organizational apparatus of modern societies that this responsibility must be assigned.

It follows that all technical specialists are not technocrats; in many instances they may have no distinctive political posture at all.[5] Managers and engineers in Western capitalist societies have frequently adopted the customary political stance of property, aligning themselves with large stockholders and old-fashioned entrepreneurs.[6] In the Soviet bloc states, as we shall observe, many technical specialists gratefully identify with the regime that made possible their relative prosperity and status. It is equally conceivable that a technician might hold dissenting opinions entirely at variance with a "technocratic" perspective. This book, accordingly, does not investigate the role of "technocrats" in East German politics, but rather that of the technical intelligentsia. However, one of the central questions it seeks to answer is the degree to which, and the ways in which, the members of the technical intelligentsia can be said to have adopted a distinctively "technocratic" outlook.

Five Theories of Technocracy

Suppose, Saint-Simon wrote in 1819, that France were to lose 3,000 of its "most essential producers, those who make the most important products, those who direct the enterprises most useful to the

[5] "Technologists are potential technocrats—the extent of their ultimate powers of intervention depends especially on their professional status. But the transition must not be thought necessary or inevitable." Meynaud, *op. cit.*, p. 29.

[6] Hans H. Gerth and C. Wright Mills attack the possibility of an American "Soviet" of technicians on the grounds that it would be "as politically and socially conservative as any businessman's service club." "A Marx for Managers," in Robert K. Merton *et al.*, eds., *Reader in Bureaucracy* (Glencoe, Ill.: Free Press, 1952), p. 171. In England, G. D. H. Cole reports that the "upper managerial" group identifies socially with the professionals while the "general run of factory managers" identifies with the class of shopkeepers and the like. *Studies in Class Structure* (London: Routledge & Kegan Paul, 1955), p. 123.

nation, those who contribute to its achievements in the sciences, the fine arts, and professions." Instantly, he suggested, the nation would become a "lifeless corpse," and at least a generation would be required to repair the damage, "for men who are distinguished in work of positive ability are exceptions, and nature is not prodigal of exceptions, particularly in this species."

Or suppose, on the other hand, that the loss were that of 30,000 officers of the royal household, nobles, ministers, clergy, public officials, and wealthy proprietors. "This mischance," wrote Saint-Simon, "would certainly distress the French, because they are kind-hearted"; but nothing of the smooth functioning of the polity would really be impaired. All could be replaced by humble and ordinary citizens, if indeed they needed to be replaced at all.

Yet, "society is a world upside down," and "in every sphere men of greater ability are subject to the control of men who are incapable." Saint-Simon saw with bitterness that an age of science and industry, whose progress rested on the services of its producing classes, remained under the dominance of the unproductive and indolent remnants of the past. Elsewhere, however, he had written more optimistically: "I conclude that the industrial class is bound to continue its progress and finally to dominate the whole community." Such a development, he asserted, was "inevitable." [7]

Saint-Simon is frequently, and quite properly, identified as the prophet of technocracy.[8] He foresaw a new political elite of scientists and industrialists (in one formulation, the first were to hold "spiritual" powers, the second "temporal" ones), joined by artists and engineers, as the logical rulers of modern society.[9] But Saint-Simon and the other writers who agree that modern industrial society does tend to thrust forward its own characteristic ruling elite, or at least a potential elite, agree on little else. They do not agree, first of all, on who constitutes the elite, and this reflects a deeper disagreement over what the salient characteristics of such a society in fact are. Nor do they agree on the crucial questions of how such an elite acquires consciousness and cohesiveness and what mecha-

[7] F. M. H. Markham, ed., *Henri Comte de Saint-Simon: Selected Writings* (Oxford: Basil Blackwell, 1952), pp. 72–75, 70.
[8] See Sheldon S. Wolin, *Politics and Vision* (Boston: Little, Brown, 1960), pp. 376–379; Daniel Bell, "Notes on the Post-Industrial Society," in Jack D. Douglas, ed., *The Technological Threat* (Englewood Cliffs, N.J.: Prentice-Hall, 1971), pp. 9–10.
[9] Markham, ed., *op. cit.*, pp. xxvi–xxvii, 11.

nisms serve to bring it to power and to exclude its rivals. There is no unambiguous case of such an elite's anywhere having seized power, and the possibility of its doing so remains in great part in the realm of speculation. If we are to throw any empirical light whatever on the problem of technocracy, it is necessary that we first deal with these definitional and conceptual questions. It will be useful to begin by examining the answers suggested by several of the "classical" theorists of technocracy.

Saint-Simon, as we have just seen, began the definition of his ruling elite by separating the "producers" from the "idlers," but among the former included workmen, artisans, farmers, and businessmen, as well as scientists, engineers, and artists. The elite itself was to be constituted of those among the producing group who had distinguished themselves by talent, training, and economic power—the scientists, industrialists, artists, and engineers—whereas the broad masses were expected to follow out of enlightened self-interest. Saint-Simon denied the legitimacy of an exclusively political class, resting its claims to power on political rather than productive talents.[10]

Among the "idlers" of society Saint-Simon included the bureaucrats. It was one of Max Weber's major contributions to social science to suggest that, on the contrary, the very indispensability under modern conditions of a centralized bureaucratic structure manned by an expert officialdom posed the threat of a "new despotism." For Weber, the development of a hierarchical, impersonal bureaucracy subject to fixed rules and procedures was part of the inexorable process of rationalization in Western societies; bureaucracy, he argued, stands in the same relation to earlier organizational forms as does the machine to nonmechanical modes of production. This analogy should not conceal the fact that Weber's classical bureaucracy differed in important respects—for example, in its rigid rule boundedness and sharp demarcation of responsibilities—from the more flexible economic and technical bureaucracies we might call "technocracies." [11] But Weber's forebodings apply equally to either: that the bureaucracy might not

[10] See *Ibid.*, esp. pp. 1–11.
[11] See Warren Ilchman, "Productivity, Administrative Reform, and Anti-Politics," in Ralph Braibanti, ed., *Political and Administrative Development* (Durham: Duke University Press, 1969), pp. 474–479.

function—as ideally it was expected to—as the disinterested and impersonal instrument of elected politicians. The very conditions making for the efficiency of bureaucracy might permit it to usurp decision-making powers. The bureaucrat's technical and organizational knowledge, combined with his penchant for secrecy, were the potential roots of a "bureaucratic absolutism." [12]

Thorstein Veblen, and, following him, the "technocrats" who enjoyed a considerable vogue in the 1930s,[13] contemplated with anticipation rather than fear the possible ascendancy of another offspring of the rationalization of industrial society: the engineers. In his *The Engineers and the Price System,* first published in 1921, Veblen argued that the modern community was dependent upon the effectual day-to-day working of the industrial system and that the "technicians" constituted the "General Staff" of that system. Any question of overthrowing the greed-ridden and grossly inefficient profit system along with the "Vested Interests" controlling it "resolves itself in practical fact into a question of what the guild of technicians will do." To show, as he sardonically put it, "how remote any contingency of this nature still is," Veblen outlined a strategy of revolution—centering on a general strike of engineers, which would paralyze the country—and described some of the economic features of an engineer-run utopia. In spite of his ostensible pessimism, he even seems to have nourished the mistaken hope that a contemporary ferment within the American Society of Mechanical Engineers was the first sign of developing class-consciousness.[14]

Another prophet of revolution, James Burnham, saw the "managers," a group defined none too carefully,[15] as the coming ruling class. Burnham's reasoning took the form of a syllogism, resting on

[12] Max Weber, *Wirtschaft und Gesellschaft,* Studienausgabe (Köln: Kiepenheuer & Witsch, 1964), II, 703–738. Translated in Weber, *From Max Weber,* eds. Hans H. Gerth and C. Wright Mills (New York: Oxford University Press, 1958), pp. 196–244. See also Reinhard Bendix, *Max Weber* (Garden City, N.Y.: Anchor Books, 1963), pp. 383–384, 423–457.

[13] See Henry Elsner, Jr., *The Technocrats: Prophets of Automation* (Syracuse: Syracuse University Press, 1967).

[14] Thorstein Veblen, *The Engineers and the Price System* (New York: Harcourt, Brace, 1963), pp. 97–99, 127–130, 133ff.; also see the introduction by Daniel Bell, esp. p. 22.

[15] It is a frequent criticism of Burnham that he shifts his definition of "manager" to fit the argument of the moment. See Cole, *op. cit.;* Gerth and Mills, "A Marx for Managers," pp. 173–174.

a revision of the Marxist premise. The source of political power, he contended, was not the legal ownership of the means of production but rather their control. Berle and Means had shown the tendency in the large American corporation for control to be separated from formal ownership, and Burnham saw a comparable development in the totalitarian pattern of state ownership. It followed that the managers, who by virtue of their skills in "direction and co-ordination" had effectively come to control industry, would constitute the new ruling class. Whatever the superficial differences in their ideologies, both capitalist and totalitarian societies had already "turned the corner" toward becoming in fact managerial societies characterized by new forms of domination and exploitation.[16]

The contemporary French sociologist Jacques Ellul gives only passing attention to a putative new ruling class but pessimistically warns of the phenomenon which must create it: the inexorable march of "technique" to domination over every element of human existence. "Technique" is defined broadly as *"means* and the *ensemble of means,"* comprising not merely mechanical techniques but also techniques of production and organization and "human techniques," which range, as he says, "from medicine and genetics to propaganda." Politics is not exempt from penetration by technique, and indeed the state must finally become "an enormous technical organism," which makes the politician its "impotent satellite" instead of its master. The struggle between politician and technical specialist in government rapidly becomes an uneven one,

[16] James Burnham, *The Managerial Revolution* (Bloomington: Indiana University Press, 1960), pp. 71–95 and *passim*. One might compare Burnham's scenario with that of Engels, who argued that once private property and attendant class domination had been abolished, political rule would be displaced entirely by the "administration of things." He admitted that even in the classless society authority—especially industrial authority—would persist, and it might be argued that in practice his "administration of things" could only mean rule by experts. Elsewhere, he suggested that the proletarian revolution would call forth "doctors, engineers, chemists, agronomists, and other specialists" as political and social leaders, "for here solid knowledge instead of high-sounding phrases is necessary." These brief assertions do not suffice to make Engels a full-blown theorist of technocracy. They do suggest, as Azrael puts it, that classical Marxism agrees "that extensive managerial authority is endemic to modern production," even under socialism; they further hint that this fact has implications for political rule. See Engels, "On Authority," *Marx and Engels on Politics and Philosophy*, ed. Lewis Feuer (New York: Anchor Books, 1959), pp. 481–485; Engels, "An den Internationalen Kongress Sozialistischer Studenten," cited in Herber and Jung, *Wissenschaftliche*, p. 12; Jeremy R. Azrael, *Managerial Power and Soviet Politics* (Cambridge: Harvard University Press, 1966), pp. 15–17.

the latter winning the applause of public opinion for alone seeming competent to deal with technological reality. The politician can only save himself by becoming a "political technician" on the model of Lenin and, thereby, a great synthesizer of all technique and all social relationships. The logic of technique, permeating all aspects of society, leads to the totalitarian state, under the dominance of a "new aristocracy" of skilled political managers; political equality, parliamentary government, liberty, all the doctrines of traditional democracy, become illusory. "Unfortunately," remarks Ellul, "efficiency is a fact and justice a slogan." [17]

The theories of Saint-Simon, Weber, Veblen, Burnham, and Ellul point up the three problems we must deal with before proceeding to the discussion of the political significance of technical specialists in concrete situations. First, since it is proposed that certain special characteristics of contemporary industrial society may produce a distinctive political elite, those characteristics must be briefly explored. Second, we must define the contours of this potential technological elite, subject to further refinement in the light of empirical findings. Finally, the conditions under which a technical elite may become the ruling political elite must be considered. As Hans H. Gerth and C. Wright Mills have pointed out in criticizing Burnham's thesis, it is an error to assume "that the technical indispensability of certain functions in a social structure are [to be] taken ipso facto as a prospective claim to political power." [18] Of the five writers we have considered, neither Saint-Simon nor Veblen seriously attempt to bridge the gap between technical indispensability and political power; they say merely that it ought to be bridged but are not fully confident that it will be. Burnham rests his argument on his dubious premise: that the control of property automatically brings political power in its train. Weber's suggestion deserves more serious attention: that power may gravitate into the hands of the bureaucracy silently and almost unobserved, that the line between political and administrative decisions may become so blurred as to permit the taking of the first

[17] Ellul, *The Technological Society* (New York: Vintage, 1964), pp. 19–22, 228ff. Emphasis his. The "new aristocracy" is discussed on pp. 274–275.
[18] Gerth and Mills, "A Marx for Managers," p. 168. Weber acidly remarks that if the "indispensability" of a group automatically lent it social or political power, then in slave-holding periods the slaves themselves should have ruled. *Wirtschaft und Gesellschaft*, II, 729–730.

in the form of the second. Ellul's theory may be regarded as a rather apocalyptic extension of Weber's: The logic of modern technique is such that political decisions must become technical ones, and politicians must either become powerless figureheads, abdicating their authority to technical specialists, or become technicians themselves, adopting rationality and efficiency as their decision-making criteria.

All five theorists largely neglect the difficult, related question of how the technicians are to acquire the sense of common interests and goals requisite to making them a cohesive and conscious political force.[19] Veblen asserts that the engineers are lamentably unconscious of their exploitation and their indispensability, although his book might be regarded as a manifesto intended to rouse the slumberers.[20] Burnham frankly insists that "the question whether the managers are conscious and critical . . . is not really at issue"; like the bourgeoisie before them, they are thrust forward by history independent of their own volition.[21] Weber suggests, somewhat more helpfully, that advanced specialized education is the basis of high bureaucratic status and resultant group solidarity.[22] His insight, however, furnishes us with only the beginning of an answer to a question we shall have to return to at length.

The theory of technocracy is provided its defining context by the notion that advanced industrial societies all share a number of economic, technical, and organizational characteristics which taken together call forth the new elite. This is not the place for an extended examination of the contours of such societies, but a composite list of eight of their major features, drawn from a selection of contemporary writing on the subject, may be usefully presented.[23] First, advanced industrial societies are said to be strongly

[19] T. B. Bottomore points to the absence of cohesion and a collective "elite-consciousness" as the most serious weakness of theories seeing intellectuals, managers, or bureaucrats as a potential ruling class. *Elites and Society* (Harmondsworth: Penguin Books, 1964), pp. 89–90.

[20] Veblen, *op. cit.*, pp. 128–130.

[21] Burnham, *op. cit.*, pp. 73–74.

[22] Bendix, *Max Weber*, p. 437.

[23] This discussion is based in part on John Kenneth Galbraith, *The New Industrial State* (New York: Signet, 1967); Andrew Schonfield, *Modern Capitalism* (New York: Oxford University Press, 1965); Harold D. Lasswell, "Political Systems, Styles, and Personalities," in Edinger, ed., *Political Leadership*, pp. 329–334; Edinger, "Editor's Introduction," in *ibid.*, pp. 15–18; Clark Kerr, John T. Dunlop, Frederick H. Harbison, and Charles A. Myers, *Industrialism and Industrial Man* (Cambridge:

oriented to continual, steady, and disciplined material progress, measured not only by the gross rate of increase in the GNP, but also by the diffusion of material benefits throughout society. Second, such societies depend upon continual, regularized scientific discovery and technological innovation as the principal source of material progress.[24] Third, there exists a high degree of functional differentiation and specialization which brings with it, fourth, an extensive, intricate, and unavoidable social and economic interdependence among actors in the society. Fifth, the very intricacy of modern industrial societies requires new and elaborate structures of administration throughout them.[25] Concomitantly (sixth), there emerges a need for detailed planning, long as well as short term, private as well as public, social as well as economic. Seventh, a vast increase in the scale of major economic undertakings implies transnational interdependencies and calls forth pressures for various types of international economic arrangements. Finally (eighth), the fulfillment of the requirements of the first seven characteristics demands appropriate staffing and, consequently, a highly developed system of mass education capable of producing personnel in adequate numbers with the requisite, often highly sophisticated, skills.[26]

This list does not in itself furnish a well-rounded portrait of advanced industrial society. For example, it ignores the psychic and emotional dimensions of economic modernity and suggests little of its impact upon popular culture.[27] It is arguable that the

Harvard University Press, 1960), Introduction and Chap. 2; Ralf Dahrendorf, *Class and Class Conflict in Industrial Society* (Stanford: Stanford University Press, 1959), Chap. 2; Peter F. Drucker, *The New Society* (New York: Harper and Bros., 1950); Jean-Jacques Servan-Schreiber, *The American Challenge* (New York: Atheneum, 1968); Raymond Aron, *The Industrial Society* (New York: Praeger, 1967); Ferkiss, *Technological Man*; Bell, "Notes"; Ilchman, "Productivity"; Ellul, *op. cit.*

[24] Bell puts it more broadly: "Perhaps the most important social change of our time is the emergence of a process of direct and deliberate contrivance of change itself. Men now seek to anticipate change, measure the course of its direction and impact, control it, and even shape it for predetermined ends" (*op. cit.*, p. 9).

[25] "It is the organization rather than the individual which is productive in our industrial system" (Drucker, *op. cit.*, p. 6).

[26] Galbraith remarks that "trained and educated manpower" is the "decisive factor of production" in the modern industrial system (*op. cit.*, p. 377).

[27] Ellul's broad definition of "technique" allows him to capture some of these additional dimensions and gives his account of modern societies a greater comprehensiveness than others. But the very breadth of his conception and of his insistence that mechanical and human "means" present a common threat to civilized existence vitiates the force of his argument.

psychiatrist and the media idol are at least as "indispensable" to modern industrial society as the scientist and engineer. Yet the theory of technocracy as it is customarily presented depends on a vision of modern society thus limited to its economic, technical, and organizational characteristics. It is the groups which are said to be indispensable to a society so defined who compose the classic "technocratic" stratum.

Accepting these limitations for the purposes of identification, I have singled out six major occupational groups for investigation in this book. I have drawn the boundaries of the six rather generously and chosen terms not specific to any particular type of social system. Unfortunately, there is no very tidy way of delimiting the subject matter of "technology" once one moves beyond loose dictionary references to the "industrial and mechanical arts." But all the groups I have chosen are concerned either with the organization and planning of the economy and its parts, the discovery and use of scientific and technical equipment, the production of the skills necessary to both, or some combination of these. They include: (1) the chief governmental planners and economists; (2) bureaucrats with important economic, technical, or scientific responsibilities; (3) industrial managers on all levels; (4) physical scientists and mathematicians; (5) engineers; and (6) educators and journalists in scientific, technical, and economic fields.

The first group is intended also to include such specialists in ruling political parties which carry out governmental functions. The second includes officials in party and private as well as government bureaucracies, and regional as well as centralized administrators. There is, of course, a degree of arbitrariness in the choice of all six categories; certain marginal groups, like agronomists and doctors, are excluded. Lower-ranking categories included in the Soviet-East German conception of the technical intelligentsia, such as "technologists" (*Techniker*) and foremen, are also excluded; in general, however, the Soviet term conforms well to the group I wish to investigate.[28] It is important to add that the present listing remains provisional; further investigation may reveal that only certain segments of the technical intelligentsia have substantial relevance to the question of political influence.

[28] See also Chap. 3, below.

To say that the technical intelligentsia is the characteristic product of contemporary industrial society and is of decisive importance in its operation is not to assert that it will or can take power
or even that it can properly be identified as a coherent stratum.
I have used the "objective" criterion of occupation (and, underlying it, function) to separate the technical intelligentsia from the
rest of society. If the technical intelligentsia is, however, to serve
as the source of a potential political elite, we must also consider
its "subjective" status.[29]

It is conceivable, but hardly likely, that members of a technical
elite might silently assume power without themselves or the rest
of the society identifying them as any sort of coherent unit, much
less evaluating them. Under such improbable circumstances, however, they would be unlikely to act in any distinguishable way on
having attained power and would thus be of little interest to us.
If we view the technical intelligentsia as the recruiting ground for
a dynamic, innovating political elite, it is important to ask whether
the relevant population regards them as a distinct social stratum
and, if so, what ranking is assigned to them. It is still more important to ask whether they regard themselves as in some measure
a unified and coherent group and whether they believe themselves
to share common interests and goals. The question, in other words,
is the one raised earlier—the degree to which the technical intelligentsia is "stratum conscious."

The question of how the technical intelligentsia might acquire
some form of political power on the basis of the undoubted critical
importance of its professional functions also demands that we consider the mechanisms it might use. "Power" is understood here in
the broad sense of the ability of an actor to affect another's behavior, with or without his consent. Thus, it may be exercised even
in roles without formal prerogatives attached to them. As a rule,
other forms of power may be utilized in order to gain political
power.[30] The control or ownership of property, high status, and
technical skills or knowledge are all generally recognized as forms

[29] For the distinction between "objective" and "subjective" standards of social
stratification see Seymour M. Lipset and Reinhard Bendix, "Social Status and Social
Structure: A Reexamination of Data and Interpretations," *British Journal of Sociology,* II (June–September 1951), 153.

[30] See Harold D. Lasswell and Abraham Kaplan, *Power and Society* (New Haven:
Yale University Press, 1950), pp. 83–92.

of power and as such are presumably convertible to political uses. The ease of such a conversion, however, depends on the mechanisms available and employed. Scientists, for example, might attempt to utilize their social prestige to win votes; technicians might halt vital services until their political demands were heeded. More subtly, economists might suggest that their professional counsel can be implemented only when accompanied by related political reforms. None of the three, however, would be likely to succeed without some sort of organization, which is my second point. The influence of a single individual is usually insignificant in the political world; organization makes possible the combining and mobilizing of the influence of numerous like-minded individuals into a political force.[31] It would seem to follow that the possibility of organization—which may be limited by law, geography, inclination, or other factors—strongly conditions the acquisition of political power.

Third, and perhaps most important, the individual or group may not actually utilize their "power resources." Potential power may not be converted into actual power either because the actor does not choose to do so or because he is ignorant of his ability to do so.[32] Thus, the fact that by virtue of its professional functions the technical intelligentsia has the power to strangle the economy does not mean it will use that power for political purposes. Whether it will would seem to depend on several factors, among them: (1) its interest in politics and its awareness of the power realities of the political system; (2) its consciousness of its own potential power—including, for example, the size of its potential constituency and the means for organizing it; (3) the extent to which the perceived interests of its members coincide; and (4) the degree of its satisfaction with the performance of the existing political elite. Clearly, where the technical intelligentsia is in agreement with the objectives and respects the competence of the incumbent ruling stratum, upheaval is not to be expected.

The sober student of the possibilities of technocratic influence is not in any case well advised to anticipate an overt coup d'etat or

---

[31] See Bernard Barber, *Social Stratification* (New York: Harcourt, Brace, 1957), p. 252.

[32] See Robert A. Dahl, *Modern Political Analysis* (Englewood Cliffs, N.J.: Prentice-Hall, 1963), pp. 47–49.

a sudden wholesale replacement of elite personnel. What is more likely to take place is what Meynaud calls the "slipping sideways of power," [33] the quiet absorption of decision-making functions by men ostensibly in advisory roles or the subtle alteration in the balance of "policy" and "administration" so as to expand the discretion of those charged with the latter. The criteria guiding decisions and the framework of assumptions within which they are made may shift to meet the outlook and style of the "technocrats" without any immediate and obvious turnover of personnel. Such a shift will not require formal organization of the technicians although to be meaningful it will require the development of sufficient communications among them to build some sense of a common outlook and consciousness. Here we are dealing with a phenomenon far more difficult to measure or evaluate than an open "managerial revolution," yet much more plausible; it demands our close attention.

ELITES AND LEGITIMACY IN COMMUNIST SYSTEMS

Ultimately, the question of whether and in what ways the potential influence of the technical intelligentsia may become transformed into actual power turns on the question of legitimacy.[34] Communist elites, as Alfred G. Meyer has argued, are characteristically preoccupied with the problem of authority and indeed "strain their systems" in the effort to "accumulate" it. Nowhere has this been more true than in the DDR, whose search for legitimacy has been persistent, troubled, and punctuated by crisis since 1945.[35]

In any type of political system, both the degree and type of legitimacy attributed to a regime are likely to have an important

[33] Meynaud, *Technocracy*, p. 30.
[34] By "legitimacy" I mean the free acceptance of communications and/or compliance with decisions issued by one actor on the part of a second actor, based on the perception by both of the propriety and the continuing nature of the relationship between them. This is a modification of the definition of authority of Alfred G. Meyer, in "Authority," p. 84. The two terms are very close in my usage; "authority," however, refers to the *relationship* while "legitimacy" refers to the *willingness* to accept/comply. "Authority" is sometimes also used in the sense of ability to rule, whether "legitimately" or not; I have tried to avoid that usage. See also Zvi Gitelman, "Power and Authority in Eastern Europe," in Johnson, ed., *Change in Communist Systems*, esp. pp. 237–238.
[35] Meyer, "Authority," p. 84; Baylis, "East Germany," pp. 46–55.

impact on the posture of potential elites. A democratic society rests its claim to legitimacy partly on what Weber called a "rational" or "legal" form of rule, in which regularized laws and procedures assure the citizen of predictable political treatment applied within defined limitations.[36] I would suggest that like other modern regimes a democratic system is legitimized as well by performance criteria—how adequately it produces the goods, services, and less tangible satisfactions its population demands—a category which may be usefully distinguished from rational-legal legitimation. While long-established democratic systems (for example, Great Britain) rely heavily upon formal rational-legal criteria, newer ones (for example, the German Federal Republic)[37] often owe their support primarily to their successful performance.[38] This distinction may have important implications for an aspiring political elite; so long as certain regularized procedures—for example, political party competition and balloting—are viewed as the exclusive appropriate means of change, its freedom of action is considerably restricted. Where concrete political output is the primary basis of legitimacy, however, it may seek a greater variety of routes to political power and, should output fall, have more immediate prospects of success. This reflects the fact that performance-based (in Weber's terms, *zweckrational*) legitimacy is less apt to be stable and enduring than other, *wertrational* forms which, however, are more difficult to acquire. At best, legitimacy originating in performance may purchase a democratic regime the time for building other, more permanent foundations for its authority.

The legitimacy underlying a Communist regime is still more ambiguous and may, consequently, offer additional opportunities

[36] Weber, *Wirtschaft und Gesellschaft*, I, 157–167.

[37] See Gabriel Almond and Sidney Verba, *The Civic Culture* (Boston: Little, Brown, 1965), pp. 362–363.

[38] It may be, however, that performance-based legitimacy is the only type most advanced societies will be able to enjoy. John Schaar argues that "the philosophical and experiential foundations of legitimacy in modern states are gravely weakened, leaving obedience a matter of lingering habit, or expediency, or necessity, but not a matter of reason and principle, and of deepest sentiment and conviction." This is because "the crisis of legitimacy is a function of some of the basic, defining orientations of modernity itself; specifically, rationality, the cult of efficiency and power, ethical relativism, and equalitarianism." "Legitimacy in the Modern State," in Philip Green and Sanford Levinson, eds., *Power and Community* (New York: Vintage, 1970), p. 279.

to a challenging elite.[39] Hans Gerth has written that the German Nazi Party could be described only as a "fusion" of two Weberian types of domination: the charismatic and the rational-legal.[40] I would suggest that in Communist systems charismatic legitimacy is joined to rational-legal and performance-based authority; rather than being "fused," however, they coexist somewhat tenuously with considerable tension among them.

Weber did not anticipate the phenomenon of mature Communism, and, therefore, his categories must be used with caution —the fit is far from exact. They do point up, however, some basic dilemmas of legitimacy in a Communist system. Charismatic leadership within a radical movement generally appears at a time of social crisis, claiming extraordinary powers of insight into the secrets of history, society, and human nature; the movement uses these claimed powers as justification for overthrowing the existing order and establishing a new one. Charisma may be said to reside either in the providential leader or the elite party, or both; often there is an attempt to transfer it from leader to party, a process analogous to Weber's "institutionalization of charisma." [41] In another sense, charisma may be said to reside in the official ideology, the charismatic "message."

Weber, however, suggested that charismatic authority is by its nature unstable and difficult to perpetuate and that, consequently, there is a tendency for it to be transformed into either traditional or rational-legal authority. He explicitly regarded a rational-legal order as resting on representative institutions, which served to safeguard the rule of law against the arbitrary acts of an entrenched authority.[42] As a Communist regime accomplishes over a shorter or longer period its most violent and revolutionary changes

[39] Ralf Dahrendorf notes: "Political communities organized in a plan-rational manner are under all conditions more strongly exposed to crises of legitimacy than those organized in market-rational ways." *Society and Democracy in Germany,* p. 410.

[40] Hans H. Gerth, "The Nazi Party: Its Leadership and Composition," in Merton *et al.,* eds., *Reader in Bureaucracy,* p. 100. See also Alex Simirenko, "Ersatz Charisma: A Sociological Interpretation of Communist Countries," *Newsletter on Comparative Studies of Communism,* IV (August 1971), 3–15.

[41] See Bendix, *Max Weber,* pp. 308–328. Meyer's argument in "Authority in Communist Political Systems" (pp. 88ff.) generally resembles mine. See also Robert C. Tucker, "The Theory of Charismatic Leadership," in *Philosophers and Kings: Studies in Leadership, Daedalus* (Summer 1968), pp. 731–756.

[42] Bendix, *op. cit.,* pp. 417–418 and *passim.*

and turns to the more prosaic tasks of day-to-day government, charisma is likely to wane and the resentments arising from its accompanying arbitrariness and frenzy may grow.[43] The regime may then seek to adapt to these changing circumstances by introducing a sort of ersatz rational-legal order and increasing concrete rewards to its population. It may regularize its law to the extent that the average citizen can expect reasonably stable and predictable treatment (an example is the Soviet Union's post-Stalin concern over "socialist legality"), rationalize its economic system, and expand the production of consumer goods.

The compulsion to follow such an approach to authority building is especially great in a state like the DDR, initially dependent for its existence on the armed forces of its Soviet parent. Such a regime must confront the ambiguity arising from the simultaneous presence of quasi-charismatic, rational-legal and performance-based legitimacy claims almost from its inception. Its claims to legitimacy on the basis of the received ideology and a largely borrowed revolutionary tradition are apt to find little resonance among the general population; it has hardly any choice but to supplement such claims with tangible evidence of performance and some elements of a reliable political and legal order. The dilemma which then confronts it, however, is twofold. First, the "natural" beneficiaries of a legitimacy based on economic performance might appear to be the experts who created it rather than the incumbent nonspecialist party leaders. Second, the logic of a rationalized legal and economic system seems to point toward some form of constitutional government: If the elite qualifies its arbitrary power in some respects in the interest of rationalization, why not in all? Yet to permit such an institutionalization of constraints would threaten the leaders' own position and inhibit their drive toward completion of the remaining, long-term revolutionary goals specified by the ideology.

In response to these irreconcilable imperatives, the regime is apt to steer an equivocal course between the alternative types of legitimacy claims, resorting in turn to whichever seems best to meet the pressures of the moment. Moreover, the established party bureau-

[43] See Samuel P. Huntington, "Social and Institutional Dynamics of One-Party Systems," in Huntington and Clement H. Moore, eds., *Authoritarian Politics in Modern Society* (New York: Basic Books, 1970), pp. 26–27.

cratic elite will seek to appropriate the symbols and tangible manifestations of performance-based legitimacy for its own profit. It
will attempt to identify economic successes and social achievements
as closely as possible with its own leadership. Such a strategy seeks
to offset the advantages the specialist is sometimes assumed to enjoy
as a legitimacy claimant in contemporary industrial societies. The
near-mystical authority of "science," the technician's claim to objectivity and disinterest and to being "above" petty personal and
political motivations, the presumption that his special training and
skills especially suit him for decision making in complex societies
—all might seem to promise popular support of his claims to political influence.[44] The transfer of legitimacy from politician to
expert is, however, inhibited in Communist polities by the undoubted fact that their citizens are not in a position directly to
choose those who rule them. Even granting the population considerable indirect influence, its view of the leadership will often
be too distant and clouded to allow it to distinguish clearly between experts and *apparatchiki*. Popular distrust of the latter is
likely to spill over to the former; in the same way, regime accomplishments may not be clearly assigned to either group. Insofar as
the party bureaucratic elite succeeds in blurring the perception
of such distinctions and cloaks itself in the rhetoric of modernization and reform, it may successfully obscure the possibility of leadership alternatives.

On the other hand, a shift in the basis of legitimacy claims may
profoundly affect power relationships within the elite itself. Insofar as economic growth and technological rationalization become
the foci of policy, the internal influence of technical experts is
likely to expand.[45] Not only must the existing leadership coopt

[44] Ellul argues: "Public opinion, which counts for a great deal even in authoritarian regimes, is almost unanimously favorable to technical decisions as opposed to
political ones, which are usually described as either 'partisan' or 'idealistic.' . . . In
case of a conflict between politician and technician, the technician has public opinion behind him" (*The Technological Society*, pp. 262–263). Robert Wood lists
among the sources of influence for scientists in American politics the media
image of the "scientist as disinterested party," the public image of the "scientist as
miracle worker," and the scientist's self-image as "nature's agent." See "Scientists
and Politics: The Rise of an Apolitical Elite," in Robert Gilpin and Christopher
Wright, eds., *Scientists and National Policy-Making* (New York: Columbia University Press, 1964), pp. 52–70.

[45] Cf. Victor A. Thompson's argument that in modern organizations "the growing
imbalance between the rights of authority positions, on the one hand, and the

specialists into its ranks as visible evidence of its modernizing priorities, but it finds it cannot ignore their advice without imperiling its own success. Virtually all contemporary Communist regimes place economic development at the top of their political-ideological agenda.[46] The more seriously they pursue this goal, the more at least some "slipping sideways of power" is likely to occur.

To be sure, it must be recalled that the general population is not the only salient "legitimacy audience" for most regimes. In the case of the DDR, there are at least three others whose approval the regime must seek: the strategic intellectual and professional groups of society, the Soviet Union, and the party itself. They provide a complex mix of reinforcement and opposition to performance-oriented legitimacy. The largest and most significant component of the first group is the technical intelligentsia itself, a stratum whose support the regime is especially anxious to enjoy. We might expect it to be the most sympathetic of the three to rational economic values and thus to performance-based legitimacy. The Soviet Union, a particularly powerful and attentive "audience," has a strong interest in the economic viability of its most important trading partner, but its interest is probably even stronger in maintaining the traditional ideological verities and the quasi-charismatic basis of rule. To a considerable extent, of course, the Soviet state's influence on the DDR's approach to legitimation will depend on the evolution of its own elite. Within the Socialist Unity Party of Germany (*Sozialistische Einheitspartei Deutschlands,* SED), considerations of *self*-legitimation both among the predominant sector of the present leadership and older members of the rank-and-file point, unsurprisingly, to the retention of quasi-charismatic ideological claims. Even here, however, the party's devotion to realizing the principle that socialism means a more abundant

---

abilities and skills needed in a technological age, on the other, generates tensions and insecurities in the system of authority." *Modern Organization* (New York: Knopf, 1961), p. 23.

[46] Lenin's own conviction appears to have been that economic success was indispensable to mass conversion to the world view of Marxism-Leninism. "We must see to it that every factory and every power station becomes a centre of enlightenment; if Russia is covered with a dense network of electric power stations and powerful technical installations our communist economic development will become a model for a future socialist Europe and Asia." "Report on the Work of the Council of People's Commissars," December 22, 1920, in *Selected Works* (New York: International Publishers, 1967), III, 514.

and happy life for all lends support to the strengthening of concrete output as a mark of legitimacy. Thus, not even the influence of the Soviet Union and the SED's own ideological self-image are entirely inimical to a larger legitimating role for the technical specialists.

It is not possible to assign precise quantitative weights to the influence of diverse legitimacy audiences or to the competing criteria to which they respond. It is apparent that the relationship between shifting determinants of legitimacy and the character of Communist elites is extraordinarily complex and by no means unidirectional. Legitimacy, after all, is a subjective phenomenon dependent on the perceptions of political actors both within the elite and outside of it, and within limits it is responsive to elite manipulation. The "objective" conditions of power rest in the last analysis on such subjective foundations. On balance and over time, however, there is considerable historical as well as logical plausibility to the simple assertion that *those who are perceived as the creators or guardians of legitimacy in a political system are likely to be its beneficiaries.* The long sway of the dogma of divine right, the political rise of the bourgeoisie in nineteenth-century Europe, and the assumption of power by the military in contemporary developing states, all admit of interpretation in such terms. To the extent that economic development and accomplishment become the primary sources of legitimacy in Communist systems and insofar as the strategic elite of technical intelligentsia is perceived as being responsible for them, we should expect its influence in the leadership to increase. When, however, the sources of legitimacy remain ambiguous and perceptions of the role of the technical intelligentsia remain clouded, we should expect resistance to such a rise in influence. The interplay between legitimacy and elite influence is a subtle and multidimensional phenomenon in all modern societies. Its operation in the German Democratic Republic will be a major theme of this book.

PART I

The Technical Intelligentsia
as a New Social Stratum

1

IMPROVISATION AND STRATUM BUILDING

> Don't you believe that I therefore went over to socialism with
> wild enthusiasm . . . the things one didn't like became clearer
> again. The cord that wasn't there, the silly piece of tubing that
> couldn't be obtained. Political meetings instead of concerts. . . .
> And the emptiness you felt around you. Old friends, fellow art-
> lovers, went one after the other. After all, it was so easy. But our
> products were needed, Lord knows, you could see it. Just as we
> were without our piece of tubing, others were without our nitrog-
> enous fertilizer, our medicines, our gasoline. And it wasn't true
> that nothing at all was there. Has that destroyed factory been
> rebuilt? There was just nothing else, besides the main job.
>
> Chemist at Leuna works, speaking of first years after war[1]

THE PHYSICAL devastation which greeted Walter Ulbricht and
the first group of émigré Communists on their return to Germany in the train of the Red Army was equaled by the organizational devastation of the Nazi administrative and economic apparatus. The "overwhelming majority" of the executives and directors
and of "other leading personnel" in the large capitalist firms had
fled West, East German sources tell us,[2] presumably in the hope
of escaping harsh treatment at the hands of the Soviet occupiers.
Many of those who stayed were shortly removed through formal or
informal de-Nazification proceedings; in many factories, we are
told, the workers, "under Communist leadership," spontaneously
drove the "Fascists" out without bothering to wait for formal au-
thorization.[3] Subsequently, engineers and scientists were "lured"

---

[1] Quoted in Klaus Marschke, "Drei Begegnungen," *Sonntag* (January 13, 1963), p. 6.
[2] Stefan Doernberg, *Die Geburt eines neuen Deutschlands* (Berlin: Rütten &
Loening, 1959), p. 280.
[3] *Ibid.*, pp. 278, 281; Walter Ulbricht, *Zur Geschichte der neuesten Zeit* (Berlin:
Dietz Verlag, 1955), I, 159–160, 249–250, 260–275. For a Western account, which

to the West by their former employers and others through the promise of better living conditions.[4] We have no exact figures, but clearly the flight and purging of members of the economic and technical intelligentsia and the expropriation by the Soviet Union of the services of others,[5] together with the high rate of German war casualties, left East Germany with a critical shortage of trained technical personnel and with an acute gap in the age brackets from which such a deficit might most easily be filled.

The problem of recruiting the needed technicians was conditioned, like much else in East Germany's first years, by two not fully compatible sets of interests. On the one hand, the Soviet Union was anxious to utilize the East German economy for the rebuilding of its own; the flow of ample "reparations" from East German industrial production could only be assured when those industrial plants which had not been crated and shipped to Russia were restored to operation and adequately staffed.[6] On the other hand, both Soviet occupiers and German Communists shared an interest in laying the economic and ideological groundwork for a new socialist order.[7] Moreover, the relief of the immediate emer-

---

among other things minimizes the frequency of the spontaneous workers' actions, see J. P. Nettl, *The Eastern Zone and Soviet Policy in Germany* (London: Cambridge University Press, 1951), pp. 127–128, 149ff.

[4] Ulbricht, *op. cit.*, p. 270, fn. 1.

[5] Nettl, *op. cit.*, pp. 218–219.

[6] Exacting reparations from their zone seems to have been the Soviet occupiers' overriding concern until just prior to the first Two-Year Plan (1949–1950). Max Gustav Lange, Ernst Richert, and Otto Stammer, "Das Problem der 'Neuen Intelligenz' in der Sowjetischen Besatzungszone," in *Veritas, Iustitia, Libertas* (Berlin: Colloquium Verlag, 1954), p. 227. Available figures suggest that the value of reparations from current production (34.7 billion marks) greatly exceeded that of the dismantled plants (5 billion marks). The first estimate is from the official East German reparations office, the second from an unofficial Western source. Bundesministerium für gesamtdeutsche Fragen, *SBZ von A bis Z* (Bonn: Deutscher Bundes-Verlag, 1966), pp. 400–401. Dismantling, involving as it did plants vital for reconstruction and coming entirely in the years 1945–1948, seems, however, to have been deeply resented by many SED functionaries. See Wolfgang Leonhard, *Child of the Revolution* (Chicago: Regnery, 1958), pp. 433–434, 461.

[7] Many analysts, among them Ernst Richert, argue that the Soviet Union originally envisaged a reunited Germany, and therefore sought to "bolshevize" its occupation zone primarily with a view to creating a strong Communist power position in the reunified state. This suggests an important long-term divergence between their interests and those of the German Communists, quite apart from the reparations problem. In Richert's view, only in 1953, or possibly as late as 1955, did the Russians finally commit themselves to a separate "Soviet Germany." *Das zweite Deutschland* (Gütersloh: Sigbert Mohn Verlag, 1964), pp. 52–53, 61.

gency demanded that the measures taken be quick and quickly effective.

The response to these often conflicting imperatives was a mixture of conscious policy and improvisation. Both have left their mark on the character of the DDR intelligentsia, its relationship to the political structure, and its place in DDR society. The status and material rewards granted the intelligentsia in those years, for example, and the distrust they kindled among older functionaries and rank-and-file workers, both set precedents for later relationships. The ambivalent mix of early policy between the pragmatic satisfaction of pressing economic needs and the doctrinaire insistence on rigid ideological fidelity and party control of all possible loci of power was also to persist, albeit with a gradual shift of the balance of the two.

The conscious segment of policy was formulated in so far as possible on the basis of Soviet precedents and Stalin's ideological dicta. In the DDR, Reinhard Bendix wrote in 1956, "the 'Soviet experience' is officially propounded as the model to be emulated in all aspects of social, economic, and intellectual life. In the field of industrial organizations, specifically, most of the institutional arrangements and, indeed, many of the written materials employed are direct translations from official Russian texts." [8] There was, however, no avoiding the need to adapt the Soviet example to the exigencies of a somewhat chaotic reality. It is not difficult to find parallels between the treatment of the Russian "bourgeois" intelligentsia under the New Economic Policy, the rise of a class of professionally untutored "Red directors," and Stalin's later efforts to educate a corps of young Communist managers, and the policies followed by the SED in the first postwar years.[9] The process, however, came to be very considerably telescoped in time.

In accord with its general policy of seizing the "commanding heights" of the East German economy and society, the SED put reliable "anti-fascists" in charge of the newly nationalized factories

[8] Bendix, *Work and Authority in Industry* (New York: Harper Torchbooks, 1963), p. 351. See also Max Gustav Lange, "Ausbildung und Erziehung der kommunistischen Partei- und Gewerkschaftsfunktionäre in der Sowjetischen Besatzungszone Deutschlands," unpublished manuscript [Berlin? 1957?], pp. v–vi.

[9] See Jeremy R. Azrael, *Managerial Power and Soviet Politics* (Cambridge: Harvard University Press, 1966). Chaps. 3 and 4.

and placed experienced Communist functionaries at the head of the leading economic organs and ministries. While few if any of the latter had technical backgrounds, some, like Heinrich Rau, Fritz Selbmann, and Bruno Leuschner, were successfully to make the transition to economic specialization and to become defenders of a perspective emphasizing the values of economic rationality and productivity. We have less evidence of a parallel development among the factory directors. While many of the political "trustees" originally charged with taking over nationalized enterprises seem to have done badly and were replaced by more qualified individuals,[10] the post of factory manager continued for some years to be a preserve of politically loyal but technically unprepared cadres;[11] even at the end of the 1950s many such "political" managers remained, much to the distress of the planners.[12]

On the other hand, remaining members of the old "bourgeois" intelligentsia were recruited for secondary positions in the economic structure and indeed by 1950 were being accorded special favors and privileges not enjoyed by other sectors of the population. The position of technical director, for example, was generally filled by an experienced member of the old intelligentsia, as were lower positions when such personnel were available. Despite the massive purge of educational personnel generally, university professors in the exact sciences—even those openly critical of the regime—were also permitted, indeed encouraged, to retain their posts.[13]

[10] Lange *et al., op. cit.,* p. 227.

[11] In 1947 21.7 percent of the factory directors were supposedly former workers, 30.7 percent former white-collar employees, 23.6 percent small retail businessmen, 17.8 percent engineers, and only 6.2 percent managers. It is possible that the terms "small businessman" and "engineer" conceal additional personnel with managerial experience. That this number remains small, however, seems confirmed by the report that in Saxony in 1948 80.6 percent of the factory directors had only an elementary school education while but 2.6 percent had university training. Doernberg, *op. cit.,* pp. 400–401. Proposals to put the factories in the hands of the members of the old intelligentsia were explicitly rejected as dangerous to "democratic development." *Ibid.,* p. 402.

[12] A study of 293 East German industrial plants in 1959 indicated that 30.9 percent were led by well-trained members of the old intelligentsia, 16.6 percent by "self-made men" who had risen through the ranks on the basis of their own ability, 7 percent by young graduates, and 38 percent by "pure party functionaries" without any technical training. The background of 7 percent could not be determined. See Georg von Wrangel, "Das staatliche Industriemanagement in der Sowjetunion und in der SBZ," *Deutsche Studien,* II (August 1964), 177.

[13] See Ulbricht's remarks cited in Marianne Müller and Egon Erwin Müller,

Despite the intense efforts of the regime to "win" the old intelligentsia "for socialism," thousands of technical posts had to be filled on a stopgap basis. In the words of the DDR's first premier, Otto Grotewohl, the "best, most active, most faithful, and most class-conscious segments of the working class" were employed in such positions in the economy and state administration,[14] and evidently talented white collar employees often received similar opportunities.[15] Lacking any prior training (though some acquired it later), these young recruits were forced to learn the required skills on the job. That they could be absorbed with relative success may be attributed in part to the rigid centralization of the East German economy and the strict subordination inherent in the principle of "one-man management" adopted from the Soviet Union in administration as well as in the economy proper.[16]

The utilization of members of the old intelligentsia and the recruitment of ill-trained but loyal cadres to temporarily fill technical positions were the two short-term prongs of a three-pronged policy; over the long run, following the injunction of Stalin, the East German Communists meant to create their own "new socialist intelligentsia." The new intelligentsia was to be drawn largely from the working and peasant classes and was to emerge from a greatly expanded and reformed educational system. Both relatively conventional technical personnel (engineers and technical directors) and new categories peculiar to a highly centralized planned economy (planning officials and "head bookkeepers") were to be trained in massive numbers.[17] Formally, the campaign to build a "new intelligentsia" began with full propaganda accompaniment in 1948 and has continued ever since, with some diminution in recent years.[18] Since that date coincides with the announcement of the first Two-Year Plan, it may be regarded usefully as the turning

---

". . . *stürmt die Festung Wissenschaft!*" (Berlin: Colloquium Verlag, 1953), pp. 216, 222. One consequence of this policy has been to make the universities one of the leading preserves of former Nazis in the DDR. See the biographies in *SBZ-Biographie* (Bonn and Berlin: Bundesministerium für gesamtdeutsche Fragen, 1964).

[14] Quoted in Kurt Lungwitz, *Über die Klassenstruktur in der Deutschen Demokratischen Republik* (Berlin: Verlag die Wirtschaft, 1962), p. 32.

[15] Lange *et al.*, *op. cit.*, p. 226.   [16] *Ibid.*   [17] *Ibid.*, pp. 227–228.

[18] *Ibid.*, pp. 192–193; Ulbricht called for the creation of such an intelligentsia at the First State Political Conference of the SED in July 1948. Richard Herber and Herbert Jung, *Wissenschaftliche Leitung und Entwicklung der Kader* ([Berlin]: Staatsverlag der Deutschen Demokratischen Republik, [1964]), p. 62.

point between postwar improvisation and the conscious implementation of a permanent policy and plan.

We shall turn to the measures creating the new intelligentsia in
the next chapter; first, let us examine more closely the situation
of the stopgap appointees and the old intelligentsia. About the first
there are few generalizations to be made. "Tens of thousands" of
workers and peasants, a 1953 Central Committee declaration recalled, had been placed in leading positions after the war; "many
of them have already become specialists in their fields, leaders of a
new type, closely bound to the masses and enjoying their confi-
dence." To be sure, they still needed to improve "continually"
their technical and political knowledge.[19] The number of these,
like those unmentioned many who must have failed in their assignments and returned to the workbench can only be conjectured.
A refugee study from 1958 to 1959 indicates that 40.3 percent of
the higher technical managers questioned ($N = 528$) had completed no more than elementary school; the same was true of 50
percent of the lower managers and engineers ($N = 137$), 38 percent of the sales managers ($N = 161$), 49 percent of the administrative managers ($N = 70$), and 79 percent of the "political
managers" ($N = 86$)—a figure presumably including the factory
directors.[20] Of all the managers and engineers under forty questioned in a similar 1957 investigation, roughly half had begun their
careers as skilled (*gelernte*) workers, though only a tiny handful as
unskilled workers. Those over forty came predominantly from the
middle and upper classes although here also a substantial minority
—perhaps one-third—had been skilled workers.[21]

A perhaps untypical example of a successful working class recruit of this sort was Fritz Schenk, who rose to be personal adviser

[19] "Die Bedeutung der Intelligenz beim Aufbau des Sozialismus," Central Committee declaration, *Neues Deutschland* (May 24, 1953), p. 3 (hereafter *Neues Deutschland* will be abbreviated *ND*).

[20] Karl Valentin Müller, *Die Manager in der Sowjetzone* (Köln and Opladen: Westdeutscher Verlag, 1962), p. 51. The figures cited are from a questionnaire given by
Müller to refugees. Like all his findings they are to be used with considerable caution (see my Preface). The more selective and intensively interviewed Infratest
refugees were much better educated but still not as well as their Western counterparts. Fifteen of this group of eighty had begun their occupational careers as workers
or peasants, six as white-collar employees, six in other nonintelligentsia jobs. *Die
Intelligenzschicht in der Sowjetzone Deutschlands* (München: Infratest GmbH & Co.,
November 1960), mimeographed, I, 55–56 (hereafter cited as *Intelligenzschicht*).

[21] Müller, *op. cit.*, p. 45.

(*Referent*) to Bruno Leuschner, head of the State Planning Commission.[22] The son of an SED functionary, Schenk was chosen at the age of nineteen to be trained in all aspects of the printing industry, where he had just completed an apprenticeship in typesetting, and was sent on to engineering school in Leipzig. Within a year, however, and without being permitted to finish his training or even to enter the engineering college, he was moved into a leading administrative position in the plant. To his protest that he preferred to remain in technical work, he was told: "Here [in planning and administration] are the best opportunities for a party member. We can put bourgeois and nonparty elements in the technical positions." [23] After brief schooling in a party factory academy, he became assistant to the plant director in the branch factory at Niedersedlitz; a year later he was suddenly elevated to the staff of the State Planning Commission. Despite his brief experience and haphazard training, the cadre director of the commission assured him: "Your background is in our view exemplary; you have systematically risen in your own field of work. That is an exception. The Central Committee proposes many comrades to us whom we can't use because they've had nothing but a few quick whiffs of experience wherever they've been." [24] At the end of May 1952, at the age of twenty-two, Schenk found himself a personal assistant, the "right hand," to the commission's chairman, Bruno Leuschner, one of the most powerful men in the DDR.[25]

While Schenk, by his own accounting, had early attracted internal party criticism through his neglect of political duties, his rapid advancement seems to have been made possible by his party membership as well as by the position of his father. Although members of the old intelligentsia—those trained prior to 1945 and lacking any political ties to the new regime—came to be courted assiduously by the SED, they were largely confined to positions without great political or administrative significance. Thus, what Müller calls a *Zweigeleisigkeit* (approximately, "dual tracks") of leader-

---

[22] Fritz Schenk, *Im Vorzimmer der Diktatur* (Köln: Kiepenheuer & Witsch, 1962), pp. 11–110. Schenk defected to the West in 1957.
[23] *Ibid.*, p. 43.   [24] *Ibid.*, p. 66.
[25] Schenk relates the similarly spectacular rise of a friend, Willi Heinrich, by a slightly different route. Beginning as a trained typesetter, Heinrich was made borough mayor of a section of Dresden by the Russians, then moved on to the staff of the SED Central Committee, and finally was placed in charge of the organizational-instructional division of the Planning Commission. *Ibid.*, pp. 63–64.

ship elites emerged in the early years of the DDR's economic bureaucracy: The upper decision-making echelons of the hierarchy
as well as those lower positions with social and political functions
were manned by a group of largely working class origins, limited
education and, often, talent, and little if any technical experience,
but with a party emblem as their source of authority; while the
lower, technical echelons included old men with substantial training and experience, generally of middle class origins with an orientation centered on their jobs and a relative indifference to politics.[26]

The latter group, the "old intelligentsia," has been viewed am-
bivalently by the SED, as witness a 1953 Central Committee pronouncement: While demanding "comradely cooperation of the
progressive workers and the leading functionaries of the Party and
the state apparatus with the old intelligentsia" and its support "by
all the population," the Committee promised a "decisive and uncompromising struggle against those representatives of the intelligentsia . . . who with criminal intent, ignoring their social duties,
establish contacts with Western imperialist agents and attempt to
carry on espionage, sabotage, and diversion in the German Democratic Republic." [27] Judging from the frequent complaints published in the party press,[28] it is clear that lower party officials were
frequently guilty of treating the old intelligentsia as the class
enemy and of demanding they master the dogmas of Marxism-
Leninism; workers sometimes bitterly complained of the special
emoluments granted valued technicians in order to keep them
from departing for the West.

Official policy, however, was to woo the old intelligentsia for
nonsensitive but vital posts largely on its own terms. It was hoped,
of course, that the old intelligentsia would eventually become loyal
supporters of the DDR, by virtue of working alongside the working class and through "comradely persuasion" by colleagues from
the party. The party men, however, were told to make no demands; "patience" and "tact" were required in all cases. Respect

[26] See Müller, *op. cit.*, p. 35. A 1959 study, however, indicated that by that year
30.9 percent of the factory directors belonged to the old intelligentsia. See above,
fn. 12.

[27] "Die Bedeutung," p. 3.

[28] See, for example, *ibid.; ND* (June 7, 1953), p. 1.

and tolerance were even due those preferring to ignore "social questions" in favor of concentration on their work, as well as those who expressed honest "reservations" about the new order.[29] It is clear that this solicitous treatment, not enjoyed by most groups in the DDR, was motivated by the urgent need of the DDR for the services of the old intelligentsia. So were the generous material benefits accorded them.

Later I shall discuss in more detail the rewards provided to members of the technical intelligentsia; here I shall note that they usually owed their introduction to the need to purchase the loyalty of the "bourgeois" engineers, managers, and scientists. Thus, "individual contracts" (*Einzelverträge*) offered to the higher echelons of the technical and scientific intelligentsia guaranteed salaries as high as 15,000 marks per month, the provision of "suitable" housing, long vacations, generous bonuses and premiums, and a college education for the children.[30] (The last might otherwise have been denied them because of the favoritism then shown worker and peasant offspring.) Of particular relevance to the old intelligentsia were also the supplementary old age pensions introduced first in 1950 and guaranteeing technical personnel 60 and in some cases 80 percent of their average monthly income in their last year of work.[31] In the harsh postwar days of severe shortages and strict rationing (which did not end entirely until 1958), the technical intelligentsia received special ration cards, extra coal, and access to well-stocked shops where only they could buy.[32] During a major party campaign on their behalf in May and early June 1953, Ulbricht went so far as to publicly scold plants which had refused to provide special concerts and tennis courts for their intelligentsia

[29] "Die Bedeutung," p. 3; *ND* (May 23, 1953), p. 4; *ibid.* (June 16, 1953), p. 1; Herrnstadt speech, *ibid.* (June 26, 1953), p. 3; Kurt Hager, "Freie Bahn für die sozialistische Wissenschaft," concluding statement at Third SED Universities Conference, *ibid.* (March 6, 1958), p. 4; Müller and Müller, ". . . *stürmt die Festung Wissenschaft!*" pp. 216, 222.

[30] Alfred Leutwein [Siegfried Mampel], *Die 'Technische Intelligenz' in der sowjetischen Besatzungszone* (Bonn: Bundesministerium für gesamtdeutsche Fragen, 1953), pp. 9, 12–13.

[31] *Ibid.*, pp. 10–12.

[32] *Ibid.*, p. 22; Schenk, *op. cit.*, p. 133; Georges Castellan, *DDR: Allemagne de l'Est* (Paris: Editions du Seuil, 1955), p. 240. The special cards were abandoned in 1953 in favor of the shops, perhaps, as Castellan suggests, because of worker protests against the former.

and promised to see that delays in providing them with scarce wares were eliminated.[33]

The justification of this favoritism toward "bourgeois intellectuals," especially during a period when it could only be at the cost of the "ruling" working class, was frankly utilitarian. Rudolf Herrnstadt,[34] speaking to a plant meeting shortly after the revolt of June 17, 1953, was asked by a worker why he received only 400 marks per month when an engineer might receive 2,000 marks plus premiums. "In the 2,000 marks which you pay the engineer today," Herrnstadt answered, "is included not only the money that he gets for his work, but also the money you pay to win time for the development of your own children and your children's children, for the maintenance and strengthening of [your] power, for the preservation of peace." That unqualified and incompetent technicians also occasionally benefitted was part of the necessary "historical charges the working class must pay in erecting its rule." [35]

The implication of this sort of reasoning that the day might come when the old intelligentsia could be thrown on the scrap heap, once the regime's own cadres had been created in sufficient numbers, was denied by Herrnstadt, as it has been by later DDR spokesmen.[36] Today, in fact, the regime boasts that "great portions" of the old intelligentsia have been won to "our way." [37] That is doubtless true; probably the more typical case, however, is that of the man quoted in the epigraph at the beginning of this chapter. Basically nonideological, having worked for I. G. Farben in the Hitler period as loyally as he now serves the socialist state, he gets his satisfaction primarily from his job (which even refugee data indicates is a common pattern in the DDR) and lives a comfortable existence, even by Western standards. The number of the old intelligentsia is, of course, gradually diminishing; despite regime assurances, some of those remaining do feel insecure in the

[33] *ND* (May 30, 1953), p. 4.
[34] Herrnstadt, editor of *Neues Deutschland,* was shortly purged in the aftermath of the June 17, 1953, uprising. His statement here seems an authentic expression of regime policy, however.
[35] *ND* (June 26, 1953), p. 3.
[36] *Ibid.;* Hans Reinhold, "Über die führende Rolle der Arbeiterklasse auf geistigem Gebiet," in *Sozialismus und Intelligenz* (Berlin: Dietz Verlag, 1960), pp. 107–108.
[37] Walter Ulbricht, "Die nationale Mission der Deutschen Demokratischen Republik und das geistige Schaffen in unserem Staat," speech at Ninth Plenum of SED Central Committee, *ND* (April 28, 1965), p. 7.

face of the rising university-trained cadres. Having contributed in no small measure to what economic success the DDR enjoyed in its first two decades, they have become a shrinking minority, left by the regime in relative peace to finish out their careers.

Have they left a legacy to the younger generation, in terms of outlook and ideology? Doubtless; the mechanisms by which such influence was exerted is expressed in the testimony of a refugee, circa 1958: "The young people come into a VEB as technical intelligentsia, perhaps to a drawing board. At work to the right and left are standing, for the most part, the old intelligentsia. The young intelligentsia now attempts to imitate the habits and ways of the old intelligentsia. Now naturally that also brings with it the political inactivity of these young people." [38] For the young specialists trained under the auspices of the Communist regime, then, members of the old intelligentsia are a source of counter-socialization. They induct the new graduates into the ways in which the practice of the DDR economy deviates from the drawing board model, and can furnish sometimes invidious comparisons to the capitalist past. As the numbers of the old intelligentsia dwindle, however, and as the generational gap between those remaining and the new recruits widens, their influence necessarily also diminishes.

[38] *Intelligenzschicht,* III, 37.

2

EDUCATING THE NEW INTELLIGENTSIA

[The factory director, age thirty-six, is one of those men] who always comes to work wearing a tie, but in the course of the morning regularly tears it impatiently from his collar and stuffs it into his coat pocket. And this . . . man . . . not only directs the fortunes of the only new zinc smelting works in the DDR, but also those of an entire complex employing 6,000 persons in four foundries and three mining works, including 250 engineers with university and *Fachschule* educations!

[Like his parents, he would have remained a ceramics worker] if it had not been decided in the DDR twelve years ago to construct socialism and if the rapid education of new middle and higher industrial cadres had not become more and more a question of survival. His party thus took him away from the kiln and sent him as a plant assistant into a foundry.

For him, that day was the beginning of a turbulent, almost bone-crushingly hard ten-year-long hurdles race through every imaginable course of technical, economic, and political instruction, through short periods of practical experience in every possible job, and through extensive smelting and mining studies.

The personnel files of the majority of his closest co-workers are similar.

Sonntag, May 6, 1962[1]

IN *Problems of Leninism* Stalin laid down the principle that "no ruling class has ever survived without its own technicians" and insisted that the working class was no exception to this rule. Thus, one of the most important tasks of Soviet power was to develop a highly trained technical intelligentsia from its own ranks.[2] While

---

[1] Jean Villain, "Freiberger Guckkasten," *Sonntag* (May 6, 1962), p. 4.
[2] Quoted in Alfred Leutwein [Siegfried Mampel], *Die 'Technische Intelligenz' in der sowjetischen Besatzungszone* (Bonn: Bundesministerium für gesamtdeutsche Fragen, 1953), p. 6.

quotations from Stalin are no longer favored in the DDR, its leaders' pronouncements and policies have closely followed his dictum. The production of adequate numbers of loyal and well-schooled technical specialists has been regarded as one of the central tasks of party and society,[3] and the educational system has been shaped as the principal instrument for achieving that end.

The members of the "new intelligentsia" are expected to be prototypes of new socialist man: free of bourgeois values, at home in the collective, firmly bound to the masses and unquestioningly loyal to the "party of the working class." [4] In general, this means that the new intelligentsia must be recruited from the younger segments of the population, those socialized largely if not entirely under the present regime.[5] It also implies a preference for a working class background, a requirement temporarily abandoned in the mid-1960s but then resurrected under Honecker. It is hoped that the technicians will thereby be relatively innocent of bourgeois influences and, in the case of workers and their offspring, doubly loyal to the regime for providing them an opportunity which capitalism would not have. The young intelligentsia is also expected to be highly qualified technically, capable of manning the machinery of the technical revolution through which the ideologists promise the Soviet bloc will overtake capitalism and enter a new phase of history.

THE ECONOMIZATION OF EDUCATION

The system of education intended to produce this intelligentsia must thus be viewed from two not entirely separable perspectives: as a program of technical or professional training and as an instrument of political socialization. On the technical side it is not unjust to speak of a thoroughgoing "economization" of DDR schools and

---

[3] See, for example, Richard Herber and Herbert Jung, *Wissenschaftliche Leitung und Entwicklung der Kader* ([Berlin]: Staatsverlag der DDR, [1964]), p. 13.

[4] For a description of the "socialist leadership personality" along these lines, see *ibid.*, pp. 34–36.

[5] However, one writer suggests that those members of the old intelligentsia who have "overcome . . . the mentality of the past" may also be regarded as part of the new intelligentsia. Erich Dahm, "Für ein enges Kampfbündnis der Arbeiterklasse mit der wissenschaftlich-technischen Intelligenz beim sozialistischen Aufbau der Deutschen Demokratischen Republik," in *Sozialismus und Intelligenz* (Berlin: Dietz Verlag, 1960), pp. 26–27.

universities. The ruling party has consciously shaped the structure and content of East German education to fit the needs and goals set forth for the economy. Thus, the number, assortment, and distribution of school and university graduates is determined by the state economic plan,[6] and the character of both teaching curricula and research is shaped in accordance with the specific needs of East German industry.[7] According to Ernst Richert's calculations, some 60 to 70 percent of the time of twelve- to sixteen-year-olds in the DDR's basic ten-class schools is occupied with scientific, mathematical, technical, and economic subjects.[8] Most of the available places in universities and advanced technical schools (*Fachschulen*) are also in technical and economic disciplines, and under the sweeping university reform begun in 1966 a concentration of academic energies and financial resources on fields closely relevant to the "critical tasks" (*Schwerpunktaufgaben*) of the economy was formally decreed. Those explicitly listed include mathematics, physics, chemistry, biology, electronics, data processing, engineering and automation technique, building construction, and cybernetics and operations research.[9] On both the high school and university levels vocational training in neighboring factories or corresponding establishments is included in the student's program. Generally the student is expected to sign a contract with his future place of work at least a year before graduation; his practical training, if feasible, will take place there.[10]

Economization extends as well to the organization of the university, which is to follow as closely as practicable the management principles of the DDR's "Economic System of Socialism." The affairs of the university are to be administered on a rationalized, cost accounting basis; the structure of authority in each "section"

[6] See "Jugendgesetz" (May 4, 1964), para. 18(4), in *Gesetzblatt*, I, 75, cited in Forschungsbeirat für Fragen der Wiedervereinigung Deutschlands, *Vierter Tätigkeitsbericht, 1961–1965* (Bonn: Bundesministerium für gesamtdeutsche Fragen, 1965), p. 79.

[7] See "Die Weiterführung der 3. Hochschulreform und die Entwicklung des Hochschulwesens bis 1975." Beschluss des Staatsrates der Deutschen Demokratischen Republik vom 3. April 1969, *Forum*, No. 7 (1969), reprinted in *Deutschland Archiv*, II (May 1969), 509–528.

[8] Richert, *Das zweite Deutschland* (Gütersloh: Sigbert Mohn Verlag, 1964), pp. 216–217. See also the table of subject matter distribution in school years six through ten in Jean Edward Smith, *Germany Beyond the Wall* (Boston: Little, Brown, 1969), p. 166.

[9] "Die Weiterführung," p. 526.   [10] "Jugendgesetz"—see fn. 6 above.

(roughly, department) is to follow the hallowed Soviet industrial principle of "one-man management," joined to "collective consultation." The universities and their sections are further expected to sign formal contracts with individual enterprises and the umbrella firms (*Vereingung Volkseigener Betriebe, VVB,* Union of Publicly Owned Factories)[11] over them, as well as with local government organs and research institutes, for the integration of research, training, and production.[12]

The weight given to technical disciplines and the high degree of specialization of East German colleges and universities have been frequently remarked upon; it has been suggested that political as well as economic purposes lie behind them. Taken together with the emphasis on technical subjects in the lower schools, this type of training allows the student little contact with the humanistic subjects—language and literature, history, the classics—traditionally emphasized in Germany. "Thought training," Richert remarks,

> is largely developed through the calculations of numerical inter-
> dependences and their application . . . [The young people], in the
> view of astute observers, always think about history, their political
> surroundings, and their fellow men in stereotypes, and are satisfied
> with the thin scaffolding that historical materialism provides them
> while their genuine and lively interest is increasingly given to the
> broad, concrete realm of technical and economic subjects.[13]

Thus the emergence of the wide-ranging and critical intelligence that might be provided by a more liberal education, even in the sciences themselves, is inhibited.[14] The degree of specialization

---

[11] The VVBs each include all the factories in a single branch of the economy; there are now over 100 of them.

[12] "Die Weiterführung," pp. 522–523, 526; Wolfgang Buchow, "Aktuelle Aspekte und Tendenzen der Hochschulreform in der DDR," *Deutschland Archiv,* I (June 1968), 251–253; Ernst-Joachim Giessmann, "Unser Ziel: Pionierleistungen in Forschung und Lehre," speech before Staatsrat, *Sozialistische Demokratie* (October 11, 1968), Beilage, reprinted in *Deutschland Archiv,* II (April 1969), 427.

[13] Richert, *Das zweite Deutschland,* pp. 216–217; see also his *"Sozialistische Universität"* (Berlin: Colloquium Verlag, 1967), pp. 219–220.

[14] A comment of André Gorz, directed at advanced capitalism, is of interest in considering DDR education: "Out of fear of creating men who by virtue of the too 'rich' development of their abilities would refuse to submit to the discipline of a too-narrow task and to the industrial hierarchy, the effort has been made to stunt them from the beginning: they were designed to be competent but limited, active but docile, intelligent but ignorant of anything outside of their function, incapable of having a horizon beyond that of their task. In short, they were designed to be specialists. Anything in their education or even in their environment that could

within technical courses of study has proven to have its disadvantages for the system, however. The responsibilities now delegated to lower economic functionaries, while still limited, require a degree of initiative and imagination not previously considered desirable, and the rapid modernization of production techniques quickly renders much specialized training obsolete. "We do not need the subaltern bureaucratic type of man," Ulbricht has said; rather the new leaders of the DDR economy must be distinguished by their "enthusiasm for responsibility, creativity, and boldness," as well as by their "business competence (*geschäftliche Sachlichkeit*), sober calculation, and iron work discipline." [15] Accordingly, the recent university reform seeks to maximize the "flexibility" of its graduates by reducing the emphasis on teaching detailed information in favor of providing a broad foundation of basic theory and methodological skills and instilling work habits that will enable the student to adapt readily to changes in technology. Practice in the creative, adaptive use of knowledge is encouraged by a shift toward more participatory class formats: seminars, colloquia, and "problem courses." In the past several years, explicit training in "socialist economic leadership" has been made part of the course of study in those fields whose graduates are expected to assume leading economic positions; here, especially, flexibility and imagination are necessary to accommodate the frequent changes of role such cadres normally undergo.[16]

In marked distinction to earlier practice, courses of study devoted explicitly to preparing students for leadership roles in the economy now exist on every level of DDR higher education. In common with the other Soviet bloc nations, the DDR has looked with great interest to management theory and training in the West and has somewhat self-consciously developed the discipline of "socialist economic leadership." [17] The first institution devoted spe-

---

allow them to find outside their work the self-accomplishment denied them in their work has been eliminated." *Strategy for Labor* (Boston: Beacon Press, 1967), p. 107.

[15] Walter Ulbricht, *Die Durchführung der ökonomischen Politik im Planjahr 1964*, speech at Fifth Plenum of SED Central Committee (Berlin: Dietz Verlag, 1964), pp. 31–32; see also Richert, "*Sozialistiche Universität*," pp. 234–235.

[16] See Karl-Marx-Universität, Leipzig, *Studienführer, 1969–1970* (Leipzig, 1969), pp. 100ff.; "Die Weiterführung," p. 519.

[17] See Walter Ulbricht, "Die nationale Mission der Deutschen Demokratischen Republik und das geistige Schaffen in unserem Staat," speech at Ninth Plenum of SED Central Committee, *Neues Deutschland* (hereafter cited as *ND*) (April 28, 1965),

cifically to preparing economic leaders was the *Hochschule für Ökonomie* in Karlshorst, created initially in 1950 for staffing the state planning commission and its lower level counterparts. In most universities and *Fachschulen*, the course of study especially oriented to the preparation of industrial leaders has been that in *Ingenieur-Ökonomie*. As the name implies, training in economics is supplemented by a detailed technical grounding in the field in which the student is expected to assume a management position.[18] In most technical fields, courses in the psychological, organizational, and pedagogical elements of leadership are now part of the obligatory curriculum; similar training is available to those already at work through factory and night courses at different levels.[19] At the Karl Marx University in Leipzig a section for "Marxist-Leninist Organization Science" offers programs for future economic functionaries with emphasis on data processing, statistics, and cost accounting.[20] Crowning the structure of management training in the DDR is the "Central Institute for Socialist Economic Leadership," which was opened in 1965. It is charged with the advanced training of leading managerial cadres; in its first course seventeen VVB directors and three deputy ministers were participants.[21]

In general, the recent DDR educational reforms should not be mistaken for a move toward intellectual openness. East German university curricula are less narrowly specialized than before, and individual study is encouraged, but the student's regimen remains

---

p. 7; on the Soviet Union and other East European countries see Michael Gamarnikow, "The End of the Party Hack?" *East Europe* (November 1965), p. 8.

[18] See *Das Studium an den Universitäten, Hoch- und Fachschulen der Deutschen Demokratischen Republik*, hrsgg. von Staatssekretariat für das Hoch- und Fachschulwesen (Berlin: Staatsverlag der DDR, 1965), Section B/IVa/1, pp. 1–2.

[19] See Herber and Jung, *Wissenschaftliche*, pp. 253–255; Alfred Neumann, *Der Volkswirtschaftsplan 1965 in der Industrie*, speech at Seventh Plenum of SED Central Committee, December 1964 (Berlin: Dietz Verlag, 1964), p. 8; Joachim Siebenbrodt, "Arbeitspsychologische Grundlagen," *Die Wirtschaft* (August 19, 1963), p. 24.

[20] *Studienführer, 1969–1970*, pp. 144–145. The term "organization science" has already fallen out of favor because it allegedly subordinates "leadership" to "organization." See Kurt Hager, *Die entwickelte sozialistische Gesellschaft* (Berlin: Dietz Verlag, 1971), p. 41.

[21] Herber and Jung, *op. cit.*, p. 253; Peter Christian Ludz, "East Germany: The Old and the New," *East Europe* (April 1966), 26; "Zentralinstitut für Weiterbildung von Wirtschaftsführern erhielt Promotionsrecht," *SBZ-Archiv*, XVII No. 11 (1966), 163; Ludz, "Bildungsstätte für zentrale Führungskräfte, *SBZ-Archiv*, XVII, No. 15 (1966), 230–232.

highly structured and demanding. He still has virtually no opportunity for intellectual exploration outside his own field and is given little time for reflection on what he has been taught. It would be an error to expect that the technical broadening of DDR education, the introduction of sociological and psychological elements in leadership training, and the official praise of creativity and adaptability will in themselves prove a new source of ferment.

THE EXPLOSION OF NUMBERS

At the same time, the quantitative record of the expansion of DDR education is impressive. There were only 17.2 university students for every 10,000 DDR residents in 1951, but by 1955 that number had jumped to 41.7 and by 1971 to 89.3 (the comparable figure for the Federal Republic was 69.7 in 1970).[22] The number of students in *Fachschulen* grew from around 19 per 10,000 in 1951 to a high of 82.6 in 1961; it then declined to 65.3 in 1964, only to rise again to 102.3 in 1971.[23] Over 70 percent of the *Fachschule* students in 1971 were engaged in engineering and technical studies or economics; another 8 percent were studying toward degrees in agriculture or forestry. The bulk of the students at universities and *Hochschulen* are also in scientific, technical, or economic fields; if those preparing to become teachers of such subjects in the upper grades of the schools are included, their proportion among the total number of students reaches 69.4 percent. Another 4.1 percent are studying agriculture or forestry. This represents a considerable shift in educational priorities. Using a slightly different statistical base, a DDR writer points out that the proportion of students in

[22] *Statistisches Jahrbuch der Deutschen Demokratischen Republik 1970* (Berlin: Staatsverlag der DDR, 1970), p. 386 (hereafter cited as *Statistisches Jahrbuch*); *ibid.* 1972, pp. 393–395; *Statistisches Taschenbuch der Deutschen Demokratischen Republik 1972* (Berlin: Staatsverlag der DDR, 1972), p. 144 (hereafter cited as *Statistisches Taschenbuch*). Figures for the Federal Republic are calculated from *Statistisches Jahrbuch für die Bundesrepublik Deutschland 1972* (Stuttgart: W. Kohlhammer Verlag, 1972), pp. 25, 78. Comparability is affected by the facts that, on the one hand, DDR figures include over one-fourth night and correspondence students, and, on the other hand, students in the Federal Republic normally spend more semesters in the university.

[23] *Statistisches Jahrbuch 1970*, p. 381; *ibid.* 1972, pp. 390–391; *Statistisches Taschenbuch 1972*, p. 144. The figure for the Federal Republic was 44.4 in 1970; see *Statistisches Jahrbuch für die Bundesrepublik Deutschland 1972*, p. 71.

TABLE 2.1. University and *Fachschule* Students in the DDR 1951–1971

Year	University total	Students per 10,000 population	*Fachschule* total	Students per 10,000 population
1951	31,512	17.2		
1955	74,742	41.7		
1961	112,929	65.9	141,500	82.6
1965	108,791	63.8	111,800	65.7
1966	106,422	62.3	119,300	69.9
1967	106,534	62.4	124,100	72.6
1968	110,581	64.7	140,600	82.3
1969	122,790	71.9	151,000	88.4
1970	138,541	81.2	164,571	96.5
1971[a]	152,315	89.3	174,360	102.3

[a] "Preliminary" figures.

Sources: *Statistisches Jahrbuch der Deutschen Demokratischen Republik 1970* (Berlin: Staatsverlag der DDR, 1970), pp. 381, 386; *Statistisches Taschenbuch der Deutschen Demokratischen Republik 1972* (Berlin: Staatsverlag der DDR, 1972), p. 144.

natural science and technical subjects in 1954 numbered only 37.5 percent.[24]

The lower schools have also been expanded and transformed to match the needs of the economy and to feed the universities and technical schools. Under the "unified socialist educational system" all East German youths are obliged to complete the "ten-class general polytechnical *Oberschule*," which as its name implies, combines a general education, stressing science and mathematics, with specific training for a vocation, including on-the-job experience in a factory or other workplace.[25] A student completing the ten-class school is eligible for admittance to the engineering and technical *Fachschulen*. Admission to the universities and *Hochschulen* requires an additional two years of "polytechnical" study leading to the *Abitur*; alternatives are the completion of the *Fachschule* or, in "exceptional cases," passage of a special examination.[26]

Among the institutions of advanced education, the *Fachschulen*

[24] W. Walter, "Studienwünsche, Zulassungen, Perspektiven," *Forum,* No. 8 (1963), p. 23.

[25] In 1967, four hours per week for the last three years. Smith, *Germany Beyond the Wall,* p. 166.

[26] "Gesetz über das einheitliche sozialistische Bildungssystem" in *Unser Bildungssystem—wichtiger Schritt auf dem Wege zur gebildeten Nation* ([Berlin]: Kanzlei des Staatsrates der DDR, 1965), pp. 83–133.

TABLE 2.2. *Fachschule* Students According to Field of Study, 1971

Field of study	Total	Percentage
1. Technical sciences (engineering)	68,922	39.5
2. Agricultural sciences and forestry	13,264	7.6
3. Medical and pharmaceutical technology	1,747	1.0
4. Economic sciences (incl. industrial and engineering economics)	55,444	31.8
5. Teaching	30,237	17.3
6. Other	4,746	2.7
	174,360	99.9
Economic and technical subjects combined (1, 3, 4)	125,290	71.9

Source: Statistisches Jahrbuch der Deutschen Demokratischen Republik 1972 (Berlin: Staatsverlag der DDR, 1972), pp. 390–391. The figures are described as "preliminary."

are charged with educating the middle and lower ranks of the technical intelligentsia. As noted, requirements for admission are lower than those of the universities and *Hochschulen,* and the usual *Fachschule* course of study lasts three years rather than the four now designated as normal at the former.[27] As Table 2.2 reveals, nearly 40 percent of the *Fachschule* students in 1971 were preparing to become engineers, and another 15 percent were studying industrial or "engineering" economics; 25 percent more were in agriculture or other economics and accounting courses of study. In an effort to upgrade the quality of engineering education, the DDR in 1969 created some ten new engineering *Hochschulen,* in part out of earlier *Fachschulen,* and by 1971 over 40 percent of all engineering students were enrolled in programs leading to a university diploma.[28] The universities and *Hochschulen* already train most of the mathematicians and natural scientists.

A high proportion of *Fachschule* students are enrolled in either correspondence or night courses, the percentages in 1969 being 39.1 and 23.7, respectively, a total of 62.8. In the universities, 26.0 percent are correspondence, but only 0.8 percent evening stu-

---

[27] See *Das Studium, op. cit., passim.*
[28] Ralf Rytlewski, "Hochschulen und Studenten in der DDR," *Deutschland Archiv,* V (July 1972), 735; Giessmann, "Unser Ziel," *op. cit.,* p. 426. The new *Hochschulen* were created from engineering schools which continue to function simultaneously as *Fachschulen.*

TABLE 2.3. University and *Hochschule* Students According
to Field of Study, 1971

Field of study		Total	Percentage
1. Mathematics and natural sciences		14,337	9.4
incl. mathematics	4,208		
physics	3,024		
chemistry	4,975		
2. Technical sciences (engineering)		52,548	34.5
incl. mechanical engineering	19,742		
electrical engineering	17,116		
civil engineering	6,467		
3. Medicine and pharmacy		9,683	6.4
4. Agriculture and forestry		6,317	4.1
5. Economics[a]		23,239	15.3
6. Philosophy, history, law, society sciences		6,289	4.1
incl. law	4,624		
7. Cultural sciences, sports		2,352	1.5
8. Theology		469	.3
9. Literature, linguistics, journalism		1,694	1.1
10. Art		2,353	1.5
11. Teaching (technical and scientific subjects)		15,534	10.2
incl. 10-class schools	13,739		
vocational schools, *Fachschulen*	1,795		
12. Teaching (other fields)		17,500	11.4
Grand total		152,315	99.8
Total technical, sciences, economics w/o teachers (1, 2, 5)		90,124	59.2
Same incl. teachers (1, 2, 5, 11)		105,658	69.4
Same plus agriculture and forestry (1, 2, 4, 5, 11)		111,975	73.5

[a] While no breakdown is available for 1971, in 1969 two-thirds of the economics students were said to be studying industrial and engineering economics, one-fourth political economy, and just over one-tenth economic cybernetics and organization sciences.

Source: *Statistisches Jahrbuch der Deutschen Demokratischen Republik 1972* (Berlin: Staatsverlag der DDR, 1972), pp. 393–395. The figures are described as "preliminary."

dents.[29] In both cases the completion of a given course of study by correspondence takes about two years longer than by direct, full-time attendance. The large number of students thus trained while continuing in their jobs permits the DDR to minimize any further reduction in its already insufficient working force and provides the

[29] Calculated from *Statistisches Jahrbuch 1972*, pp. 385, 392.

unity between education and "practice" which the regime finds so desirable. It also permits the tapping of the most talented workers who for one reason or another were not chosen for advanced education earlier in their careers; the largest group here at present are the offspring of bourgeois families who were earlier discriminated against in admissions policies.

Factories in the DDR are strongly and repeatedly encouraged to "delegate" their best workers to a course of advanced study. Many of the larger ones also provide their own extensive schooling facilities. In the "factory academy" of the model VEB (*Volkseigener Betrieb,* publicly owned factory) electrical apparatus plant in Berlin-Treptow, for example, a skilled worker in 1963 could become a *Meister* (foreman) in two years of night study, a "technician"—the next step—in three, and an engineer in five.[30] The continuing campaign to urge workers and the lower intelligentsia to "qualify themselves" for higher positions is accompanied by advanced training in "socialist leadership" and in new technical and economic innovations, which all higher intelligentsia and plant functionaries are now expected periodically to undergo.[31] Once again, education is closely integrated with "practice," the dangers the regime sees in "abstract" university learning are circumvented, and the intelligentsia—it is hoped—develop additional ties of loyalty and community to their place of work.[32]

The vast expansion of the supply of engineers, economists, and scientists has not always been met with a corresponding ability of DDR industry to absorb them. In mid-1963 Ulbricht angrily called attention to a finding by the State Economic Council (*Volkswirtschaftsrat*) that only 30 percent of the coming year's graduates in chemistry, physics, and mathematics could expect to be placed. The comrades in industry, he acidly remarked, "obviously have not understood what is at stake in the economic competition be-

---

[30] "Die Qualifizierung der Werktätigen: Betriebsakademien berichten," *Einheit,* XVIII (May 1963), 136.

[31] See Weidemann, "Was hemmt die Erwachsenenbildung?" *Die Wirtschaft* (May 27, 1963), p. 15, which cites a Lichtenberg VEB where 50 percent of the employees participated in a "regular" program of *Qualifizierung* in 1962. In 1970, 697,534 workers are reported to have taken part in such schooling, the majority, however, on the subintelligentsia level or in limited special areas. *Statistisches Jahrbuch 1972,* pp. 382–383 (including delegations to *Fachschulen* and universities). See also "Die Weiterführung," pp. 519–521.

[32] See Richert, *Das zweite Deutschland,* pp. 305–306, on this point.

tween capitalism and socialism." [33] The regime has often insisted that a genuine shortage of scientific and technical cadres exists and that "ideological" failings and conservatism among industrial officials are responsible for the difficulties in placing graduates. It has been argued that in the utilization of university and *Hochschule*-trained personnel, the DDR lags seriously behind the Soviet Union and some of the capitalist nations; that, in the chemical industry, for example, the DDR employed only 14.5 graduates per 1,000 total personnel in the early 1960s, the USSR 42.[34] The SED Central Committee committed itself in 1968 to equaling the "world's highest" proportion of graduates to workers "by 1975 or 1976." While this policy was to be implemented in part by upgrading *Fachschulen* to *Hochschulen* and pressing *Fachschule* graduates to complete *Hochschule* degrees at night or by correspondence, it also meant a new substantial expansion of scientific and technical advanced education, following some years of virtual stagnation after the erection of the Berlin Wall.[35] Without doubt the growing number of graduates will create additional placement problems; the resultant competition and insecurity among the technical intelligentsia may be expected to stimulate performance and possibly serve as a means of social control. But the additional numbers and the rise in educational level of the technical intelligentsia can hardly help but further expand its influence on the style and character of East German society.

The Question of Class Character

The classical Stalinist conception of the new intelligentsia insists that it belong, in some sense, to the proletariat, for in this question of class identity the very power of the working class is believed to be at stake. For many years the DDR has sought through a variety

[33] Walter Ulbricht, "Das neue ökonomische System der Planung und Leitung der Volkswirtschaft in der Praxis," speech at Economic Conference of the SED Central Committee and the DDR Council of Ministers, June 24, 1963, *Die Wirtschaft* (June 28, 1963), p. 19.

[34] Herber and Jung, *Wissenschaftliche*, pp. 115–119; also see Ulbricht, "Das neue ökonomische System."

[35] "Die Weiterführung," pp. 527–528. DDR statistics indicate that it has moved from last to fifth among the seven COMECON countries in university students per 10,000 population since 1968. *Statistisches Jahrbuch 1970*, Anhang, p. 18; *ibid.* 1972, Anhang, p. 25.

of administrative measures to assure that its technical intelligentsia be proletarian both in actual composition and in outlook. The DDR press celebrates extravagantly the working class backgrounds of prominent managers and technicians; overall, it is claimed that 75 percent of the managers in the socialist sector of the economy are of working class origins.[36] Western visitors have also noted the high proportion of those of such origins in the more prominent technical positions in DDR industry.[37] For many years scions of the working class were to be found most often in "political" positions in the factory—as directors of labor, party secretaries, cadre directors, and overall plant managers—rather than in the more purely "technical" positions, which were frequently occupied by "bourgeois" managers, often from the old intelligentsia.[38] The trend, however, has been to an increasing working class predominance in the more technical positions as well.

The most notorious device for assuring the "proletarianization" of the technical intelligentsia was the requirement imposed until 1963 that 60 percent of *Oberschule* and university students be of working class or peasant origin. The intent of the 60 percent requirement was, of course, to insure that the new intelligentsia be loyal to the regime and devoted to the goals of socialism.[39] Together with the ideological assurance of the virtue of the working class and a—doubtless often justified—distrust of the influences at work on children from bourgeois families, the regime calculated that those who would otherwise have remained workers all their lives might be especially grateful for the opportunities given them as well as resistant toward any capitalist restoration. The 60 percent quota was by itself a crude and wasteful device to this end but was not left alone. In 1949 the so-called "Workers' and Peasants' Faculties" were initiated to facilitate the admission of members of these classes to the universities. They offered two-to-three-year courses for experienced workers under thirty years of age, "delegated" by their factories, collectives, military units, or mass

[36] Hager, *Die entwickelte,* p. 17; see also the quotation at the head of this chapter; and Herber and Jung, *op. cit.,* p. 62.

[37] See, for example, Hans Apel, *Ohne Begleiter* (Köln: Verlag Wissenschaft und Politik, 1965), pp. 41, 160; Smith, *op. cit.,* pp. 99–100.

[38] See the figures in Karl Valentin Müller, *Die Manager in der Sowjetzone* (Köln and Opladen: Westdeutscher Verlag, 1962), pp. 38, 52, 54–55.

[39] See, for example, Günter Mittag, "Die Aufgaben der Parteiorganisationen in den Vereinigungen Volkseigener Betriebe," *Einheit,* XIII (August 1958), 1143.

organizations, and prepared the students for admission to the *Hochschulen*.[40] In practice, the graduates of the Workers' and Peasants' Faculties proved to be of dubious competence,[41] and in 1963 they were dissolved. However, worker and peasant offspring were guaranteed more generous scholarships than those from other class backgrounds until 1968,[42] and, as we have seen, a number of programs continued to encourage the delegation of talented workers to study or their enrollment in night and correspondence courses.

While admissions regulations continued to require an "appropriate proportion" (*erforderlichen Anteil*) of proletarian and peasant students, emphasis was now shifted to the criterion of performance: "Above all, those young people are to be favored who are particularly gifted for certain fields and are capable of extraordinary achievements." [43] Under the new provisions the proportion of working class[44] and peasant offspring dropped sharply, from 58.2

[40] Max Gustav Lange, Ernst Richert, and Otto Stammer, "Das Problem der 'neuen Intelligenz' in der Sowjetischen Besatzungszone," in *Veritas, Iustitia, Libertas* (Berlin: Colloquium Verlag, 1954), pp. 217–218; *Universitäten und Hochschulen in der Sowjetzone* ([Bonn]: Bundesministerium für gesamtdeutsche Fragen, 1964), pp. 45–48.

[41] See, for example, Fritz Schenk, *Im Vorzimmer der Diktatur* (Köln: Kiepenheuer & Witsch, 1962), p. 26.

[42] Thomas Ammer, "Neue Stipendienordnung in der DDR," *Deutschland Archiv*, III (January 1970), 98.

[43] The quote is from the "Jugendgesetz"—see fn. 6 above—quoted in *Das Studium*, *op. cit.*, Section Z/I/1, p. 1; and also Section A/I/a, p. 1; Section A/I/3, p. 1.

[44] A crucial question in evaluating these statistics is the definition of "worker." Earlier, only those who were manual workers on January 1, 1942, were included, presumably in order to screen out former members of the bourgeoisie who were forced because of war guilt or other reasons to turn to manual trades after the war. Lange *et al.*, *op. cit.*, p. 212. A 1958 directive, however, defined as members of the working class those who had been active as workers at least five years in industry, agriculture, commerce, or crafts, or who were once workers and presently performed functions in the party, the mass organizations, or the military. *SBZ von A bis Z* (Bonn: Deutscher Bundes-Verlag, 1966), p. 27. The figures in Table 2.4 obviously separate out most peasants and artisans, but it is doubtful whether party functionaries are included in the category "intelligentsia," though for some purposes they are considered just that. For a discussion of the many unresolved problems of fitting a "Marxist" classification to Communist social structure, see Kurt Lungwitz, *Über die Klassenstruktur in der Deutschen Demokratischen Republik* (Berlin: Verlag die Wirtschaft, 1962), *passim*. Müller (*op. cit.*, p. 100) suggests that at least in the 1950s the party was extremely flexible in assigning students to the category of "worker" for purposes of admission to advanced education or for scholarships and thereby diminished in some measure the impact of the 60 percent rule. In general, it seems evident that considerable incentive existed—both among officials trying to fill such a quota and among parents anxious to win advantages for their children—to stretch the definition to cover what must have been a large number of borderline cases.

percent in the *Hochschulen* and 70.5 percent in the *Fachschulen* in 1958 [45] to 36.6 and 48.4 percent, respectively in 1967 (calculated from Table 2.4).[46] The proportion coming from white collar or intelligentsia backgrounds increased correspondingly; in 1967 these two groups together constituted a majority in the *Hochschulen*. The bulk of those whose parents belong to the intelligentsia, however, were part-time students, strongly suggesting that many who were formerly denied an advanced education because of their "bourgeois" origins were taking advantage of the liberalized admissions rules while continuing their jobs. If this is so, the proportion of students from the intelligentsia might have been expected to diminish again, at least in the short run. But like their Soviet counterparts the members of the new intelligentsia are deeply concerned to assure their own children a university education,[47] and in the absence of strict countermeasures the future class composition of students might come to reflect the tendencies to intelligentsia self-perpetuation already evident in the USSR.[48] The apparent strong preference of intelligentsia children for the *Hochschulen* over the *Fachschulen* should also be noted as a potential index of class distinctions in DDR education.[49] The restoration of favoritism toward working class children under Honecker evidently sought to halt such tendencies; it is still too early to assess its success.

The inconsistent application of measures favoring the admission

[45] Herber and Jung, *Wissenschaftliche*, p. 67.

[46] Figures on the class composition of students were dropped from the *Statistisches Jahrbuch* after the 1968 edition.

[47] Smith, *Germany Beyond the Wall*, pp. 171–172, reports this to have been a universal preoccupation of the technicians and managers he interviewed.

[48] See, for example, a survey of secondary school graduates in Novosibirsk revealing that 82 percent of secondary school graduates with parents from the intelligentsia went on to advanced study, as opposed to 61 percent of industrial and only 10 percent of agricultural workers. V. N. Shubkin, "Youth Enters Life," in *Voprosy filosofii* (May 1965), pp. 57–70, transl. in *Current Digest of the Soviet Press*, XVII (30), (August 18, 1965), 6. "By 1958, some 60 to 70 percent of the students in Moscow's institutions of higher education were children of 'officials' and 'members of the intelligentsia.'" Jeremy R. Azrael, *Managerial Power and Soviet Politics* (Cambridge: Harvard University Press, 1966), p. 250, fn. 14. See also his article, "Soviet Union," in James S. Coleman, ed., *Education and Political Development* (Princeton: Princeton University Press, 1965), pp. 250–254.

[49] Some of the students were assigned to class categories according to their past or present jobs rather than their parents' occupations, and *Fachschule* students are more likely to have had some work experience. Thus, to some extent, the difference may be a statistical artifact.

TABLE 2.4. Students in *Fachschulen* and *Hochschulen* by Social Origin,[a] 1967
(in percentages except for N)

	Workers	Employees[b]	Cooperative members[c]	Intelligentsia	Independent earners[d]	Others	N
Hochschulen							
Full-time study	38.2	23.5	7.8	20.4	7.1	3.0	74,705
Correspondence and night study	11.9	30.8	1.8	53.8	1.4	0.4	27,387
Other forms of study							3,549
							893
All students	30.6	25.6	6.0	30.1	5.6	2.2	106,534
Fachschulen							
Full-time study	52.0	20.5	11.7	8.9	4.9	2.0	54,700
Correspondence and night study	31.0	61.2	5.1	1.9	0.3	0.5	43,800
							24,700
All students	40.4	43.1	8.0	5.0	2.3	1.2	123,200

[a] Social origin apparently determined by employment of parents or by previous and present employment of students.
[b] Employees = *Angestellte*, that is, white collar workers.
[c] Cooperative members are largely peasants from collectives, plus members of artisans' cooperatives.
[d] Independent earners include small private businessmen, independent artisans.
Source: Statistisches Jahrbuch der Deutschen Demokratischen Republik 1968 (Berlin: Staatsverlag der DDR, 1968), pp. 465, 470, 473.

of worker and peasant children reflects at least in part the suspicion that class origin by itself often does not produce the desired proletarian outlook and loyalty; recurrent complaints that technicians with working-class beginnings display a cool disregard for their former comrades bear witness to this fact.[50] A different type of effort to foster identification with the working class and the nobility of manual labor was undertaken in partial imitation of the Khrushchev reforms in the Soviet Union: the requirement that each student complete a year of practical work experience (or, alternatively, military service) before being admitted to the university or *Fachschule*.[51] The possibly romantic assumption that close contact with workers and the process of labor will increase the respect of the rising intelligentsia for labor and thwart the development of class barriers finds reflection in other DDR policies as well, notably the polytechnical school curriculum and "socialist community work" in the factories (see chap. 4). The "practical year," however, served merely to increase the work of the factories and interrupt the educational process. Like its Soviet forerunner, it has been abandoned.

POLITICAL SOCIALIZATION IN THE UNIVERSITY

In admissions policies and practical work experience, then, the attempt to proletarianize DDR education has competed with the desire to recruit the most gifted students wherever they are found and to train them so that they are able to serve DDR industry in the most productive way possible. The present revival of a measure of discrimination favoring working class admissions to higher education, while a victory of dogma over pragmatism, is apt to be brief and ineffectual. The distinction between a working class and bourgeois background did have significant implications for regime loyalty at the beginning of the 1950s, but the subtleties of contemporary DDR class structure and the habituation of members of all groups to relatively open mobility channels have made any

[50] Ulrich Abraham, "Die Bedeutung des neuen Charakters der Arbeit im Sozialismus für das Bündnis zwischen Arbeiterklasse und technischer Intelligenz," in *Sozialismus und Intelligenz* (Berlin: Dietz Verlag, 1960), pp. 153–154.
[51] See Richert, *"Sozialistische Universität,"* pp. 178–180; on the Soviet Union, Azrael, "Soviet Union," pp. 259–261; also Azrael's "Bringing Up the New Soviet Man," *Problems of Communism* (May–June 1968), pp. 23–31.

such assumptions now doubtful. The myth of the proletarian character of DDR society remains honored in rhetoric, but the ideologists have come in practice to rely less on class composition than on suffusing the life of the student with Marxism-Leninism as they understand it.[52]

Students and faculty in the *Hochschulen* have in the past so resisted the strenuous efforts of the SED to politicize them according to its own lights that Honecker was driven to concede in 1958 that "in most faculties bourgeois ideology still predominates (*vorherrscht*)." [53] The impact of Robert Havemann's 1964 lecture series in East Berlin's Humboldt University, calling for open discussion of scientific and political issues, and the large-scale attacks on "skepticism" in the *Hochschulen* in the crackdown on intellectuals in late 1965 indicate that East German higher education remains one of the less certain pillars of the regime. Yet the SED has spared few efforts in attempting to turn the *Hochshulen* into effective instruments for schooling the new intelligentsia ideologically.

Admissions criteria, for example, continue to be geared in part to political standards. The recommendations of a candidate's factory or other institution and of the mass organizations (Free German Youth [*Freie Deutsche Jugend*, FDJ], trade union) to which he belongs are to be considered along with his record of scholarship in the admissions proceedings; selection depends upon, among other things, "active participation [*Einsatz*] in the building of socialism in the DDR and readiness to defend its accomplishments" and "good study and work discipline combined with the effort to continually broaden one's knowledge and abilities in the interest of socialist development." Of the six members of each admissions commission, one represents the leadership of the university FDJ, one the trade union, and a third is often the Prorector for Study Matters, a political appointee. Three of the four members of the Appeals Commission for admissions are similarly political rather than academic officials. For the *Fachschulen,* three of the five members of the Admissions Commission and three of the four on the

[52] See Arthur M. Hanhardt, Jr., "Political Socialization in the German Democratic Republic," paper delivered at 1970 meeting of the American Political Science Association.

[53] "Aus dem Bericht des Politbüros an das 35. Plenum des Zentralkomitees der SED," *ND* (February 2, 1958), p. 4.

Appeals Commission are political.[54] Because of the large number of openings in technical and scientific disciplines and the special aptitudes they require, however, the effectiveness of this political sieve is doubtful, except perhaps for aspiring economists. In general, it is said, the commissions accept the recommendations of the faculty member evaluating the candidate's aptitude examination.[55]

Once admitted, the student is expected to follow a demanding regimen which combines formal studies with work experience and societal duties, each of which is expected to contribute to his political education. At the Karl Marx University in Leipzig the official schedule includes:

40 weeks for classes, practical work experience, excursions, guided and controlled independent study (42 weeks after the first two years)

2 weeks paramilitary education (1st and 2nd years)

3 weeks participation in "Leipzig Student Summer" (FDJ brigades in critical sectors of industry, agriculture, and building construction, activity in Pioneer Camps, etc.)

4 weeks university holidays

3 weeks free of classes (Christmas, Easter, Pentecost)[56]

This may be contrasted to the highly permissive schedules of West German universities with their five months of vacation each year.

In the universities, all students are required to complete what are called "basic studies in the society sciences" (*gesellschaftswissenschaftliches Grundstudium*). Typically these will include, during the first three years of the student's course of study, classes in "Dialectical and Historical Materialism," "The Political Economy of Capitalism and Socialism," "Scientific Socialism," and "The History of the German Working Class Movement," [57] although there is some variation in this pattern according to faculty. The principles of Marxism-Leninism are regarded as the "foundation for the theoretical and practical solution for the development problems

---

[54] *Das Studium, op. cit.*, Section A/I/2, p. 1; Section A/I/3, pp. 1–4. The regulations cited here were modified in some details in July 1971 but appear unchanged in general character.

[55] Richert, *"Sozialistische Universität,"* pp. 229–231.

[56] *Studienführer, 1969–1970*, p. 104.

[57] The example is drawn from Martin Luther Universität, Wittenberg, *Personal- und Vorlesungsverzeichnis* (Fall semester 1965–1966), p. 15.

of our socialist society" [58] and therefore as the "basis of all special-ized study." [59] While once demanding 20 percent or more of the student's time,[60] the proportion allotted to the "basic studies" has dropped to about 10 percent, and some of the examination requirements have been eliminated.[61]

The reduction in emphasis on the *Grundstudium* is doubtless to be attributed in part to the growing technological demands on the curriculum, but the proximate cause was their distinct unpop-ularity, expressed most dramatically in 1956 by student demonstra-tions demanding (among other things) their abolition.[62] In July 1961 a leading DDR education expert, Dr. Heinrich Deiters, re-portedly proposed precisely that, only to be quickly put to rights by the veteran SED functionary Franz Dahlem.[63] But even Ul-bricht was moved to complain that the "society scientists" suffered from dogmatism and a lack of imagination and produced more hypocrisy than dedication among their students.[64] The patent so-lution party officials have always proposed to these infirmities has been to make ideological teachings more relevant to the student's own field of interest, a suggestion which has found echoes among other academics as well.[65] Under the 1969 guidelines for university reform, it is stressed that the study of Marxism-Leninism must be systematically joined to its "creative appropriation and applica-tion" in political struggle; while the hours of formal "Gewi" study are not to be expanded, the entire educational process is expected to be "permeated" by socialist ideology.[66]

The view of a medical student is probably typical: "We all

[58] "Die Weiterführung," p. 515.

[59] Marianne Müller and Egon Erwin Müller, *". . . stürmt die Festung Wissen-schaft!"* (Berlin: Colloquium Verlag, 1953), p. 241.

[60] In "Ingenieurökonomie" in 1955 such subjects required 54 of 236 weekly hours required for graduation. Lange, "Ausbildung und Erziehung," unpublished ms., [Berlin? 1957?], chart following p. 226.

[61] Gustav Leissner, *Verwaltung und öffentlicher Dienst in der sowjetischen Besat-zungszone Deutschlands* (Stuttgart & Köln: W. Kohlhammer Verlag, 1961), pp. 307–308; *SBZ von A bis Z*, pp. 169–170; *Universitäten und Hochschulen*, pp. 64–65.

[62] Richert, "Sozialistische Universität," pp. 130ff.

[63] Frank Hiob, *Aspekte der Wissenschaftspolitik in der SBZ* (Bonn: Bundesminis-terium für gesamtdeutsche Fragen, 1962), pp. 5–6.

[64] *Ibid.*, p. 9. More recently, in the same vein, see Hannes Hörnig, "Hauptaufgabe: Wirksamkeit," *Forum*, No. 11 (1970), p. 14.

[65] Richert, "Sozialistische Universität," p. 133; see also Kurt Hager, "Die Intelli-genz und der V. Parteitag," *Einheit*, XIII (August 1958), 1130.

[66] "Die Weiterführung," p. 515.

sleep in the Marxism-Leninism lectures; that we already know thoroughly." [67] There are complaints that those who express deviating views in the obligatory "discussions" are liable to be subjected to "unpleasantries" so that in general these remain sterile and tiresome elaborations of official doctrine.[68] Nevertheless, the very subject matter of the *Gesellschaftswissenschaften* brings students into contact with political, social, and ideological problem areas they might not otherwise be likely to examine. Exposition of the formal doctrines of Marxism-Leninism and the attempt to apply them to the DDR's contemporary situation inevitably must highlight some of the radical inconsistencies between the two.[69] In that sense, the repeated demands for greater "relevance" are unlikely to be satisfied. Given also the stolid unimaginativeness of many teachers in this field, the *Grundstudium* may produce more skepticism and criticism among DDR students than genuine indoctrination.[70]

The principal device for assuring both academic and political discipline in the universities is the so-called "seminar group," consisting of twenty to thirty students of the same year and field of specialization. The group is under the leadership of an FDJ functionary although generally a member of the faculty is also assigned to it. Each group is to function as a "collective," remaining together for the full course of study of its members. In it, poor academic performance or indolence in studying is subjected to general discussion, criticism, and self-criticism; the group is expected to "help" the wayward student overcome academic difficulties as well as political errors. Students are not absolutely required to belong to the FDJ, but most do, and that organization is explicitly regarded as the organ of student representation and charged with the task of political leadership.[71]

[67] Hans Apel, *Ohne Begleiter*, p. 78; Hanhardt, "Political Socialization," p. 34.

[68] Hiob, *op. cit.*, p. 10; see also "Test in der Mensa academica: Studenteninterviews," *Sonntag* (March 1, 1964), pp. 4–5.

[69] Leissner, *op. cit.*, p. 308, makes a similar point.

[70] Hanhardt concludes that civics instruction in the polytechnical high schools has likewise "not been very effective as an instrument of socialization." See *op. cit.*, pp. 34–37, and the East German studies cited there.

[71] See "Gesetz über das einheitliche sozialistische Bildungssystem," *op. cit.*, p. 123; Martin Luther Universität, Halle-Wittenberg, *Vorlesungsverzeichnis*, p. 14; Lange, *Wissenschaft im totalitären Staat* (Stuttgart & Düsseldorf: Ring Verlag, 1955), p. 270; Lange *et al.*, "Das Problem," pp. 221–222; Müller and Müller, ". . . *stürmt*

That this device has been far from a fully effective means of political control is in part due to the almost universal character of FDJ membership. Many view membership with impatience and even disdain—it is time-consuming and "boring" [72]—but few refuse to join; hence, the loyalty and dedication of many FDJ members and even functionaries is not what the SED would wish. In February 1966 the FDJ's publication for students and young intelligentsia, *Forum,* complained of the

> unmilitant standpoint of many FDJ members and FDJ functionaries, [their] silence toward the spreading of imperialist ideology—especially by Western radio and television, [their] tolerance of student loafing [*Studienbummelei*], [their] reluctance to unconditionally embrace the policies of the SED and the DDR, to defend them unwaveringly, and to help put them into effect, [their] lack of readiness to participate actively in the military defense of our socialist homeland and to acquire basic military knowledge.

The efforts of FDJ leaders at the university in Halle to make the organization "attractive" by departing from the time-honored modes of SED agitprop was branded as the "abandonment of principles" and "spontaneity." [73]

Richert notes the unpopularity of the organization among students, revealed even in its own opinion surveys, and argues that since 1963 its influence in the universities has "sharply declined." [74] The FDJ has sought to revive its standing by emphasizing its involvement in scientific and economic modernization through series of competitions and other programs and has tried to identify with the "revolutionary" DDR university reforms, presenting itself as the instrument of meaningful student participation in university leadership. The results have apparently been disappointing to the organization's functionaries. [75]

---

die Festung Wissenschaft!" pp. 328–329. On the philosophy underlying Communist study collectives in general, see Azrael, "Soviet Union," pp. 243–247.

[72] Letter from Ehrenfried Rohde, physics graduate, *Forum,* No. 10 (1963), p. 9: "Many of my friends and colleagues perhaps are of the opinion: 'what does the FDJ matter to us, we're glad when we can get out of it "respectably" when we graduate from the university or *Fachschule.*' This phenomenon is widespread among the *Hochschule* graduates when they begin their work in industry."

[73] Wolfgang Herger and Hans Kleinschmidt, "Der 20. Jahrestag der SED und die FDJ an den Universitäten, Hoch- und Fachschulen," *Forum,* No. 3 (1966), reprinted in part in *SBZ-Archiv,* XVII, No. 5 (1966), 80.

[74] Richert, *"Sozialistische Universität,"* pp. 168, 215–217, 236.

[75] See Horst Helas, "Die Rolle der Freien Deutschen Jugend an der Karl Marx

Complaints are raised of students "who claim for themselves the 'right' to criticize and cast doubt upon everything," are guilty of "petty bourgeois skepticism," or, most interestingly, derive a "subjectivist-neutralist" position from the model of the natural sciences.[76] Students are also accused of arrogance toward workers and peasants and of falsely speaking of the "leadership role" of an "intelligentsia elite." [77]

Skepticism and outright opposition from students is nothing new in the DDR, as a long series of conflicts and arrests, particularly in the first decade of its existence, testifies. While students played no significant role in the uprising of June 17, 1953, the Hungarian Revolution and the events of October 1956 in Poland provoked a wave of demands and protests in Berlin, Leipzig, Halle, Rostock, Jena, and, not least, at the *Technische Hochschule* in Dresden, which the regime felt obliged to counter by mustering armed factory "battle groups" in the capital.[78] While technical and scientific students were not absent from the protests, their strongest adherents seem to have come rather from "bourgeois" faculties, for example, medicine, veterinary medicine, and agriculture.[79]

The years have undoubtedly increased the proportion of students who have made their peace with the system, as they have among the rest of the DDR's population; even prior to the construction of the Berlin Wall, it is estimated that 70 percent of DDR students remained politically essentially apathetic but accommodated themselves comfortably to the requirements of the system.[80] Nevertheless, the persistent complaints of "skepticism," "pes-

Universität," in *Studienführer, 1969-1970*, pp. 167-170; Peter Brokmeier, "Die FDJ und ihre neuen Aufgaben," *Deutschland Archiv*, III (February 1970), 135-142; Frank Grätz, "Hochschulreform in der DDR," *Deutschland Archiv*, IV (March 1971), 246-249.

[76] Herger and Kleinschmidt, *op. cit.*, p. 80. For similar complaints about "pessimism" as a "modern form of opportunism" among the students see Wolfgang Richter, "Meine Ansicht: Diskussion langweilig," *Sonntag*, No. 13 (1964), p. 8.

[77] Herger and Kleinschmidt, *op. cit.*, p. 80; Richter, *op cit.*, p. 8.

[78] Martin Jänicke, *Der dritte Weg* (Köln: Neuer Deutscher Verlag, 1964), pp. 148-154.

[79] Richert, *"Sozialistische Universität,"* pp. 132ff.

[80] *Ibid.*, pp. 247-248. Based on interviews with faculty refugees. In a journey through the DDR in 1964, a sympathetic American journalist found that over one-half of the twenty students he interviewed expressed "open opposition" to the regime and only one-fourth supported it; no other group he interviewed showed anything like such a degree of opposition. Hans Apel, *Ohne Begleiter*, pp. 98-99.

simism," "passivity," and "resignation" show that the SED has still to convert the universities into entirely reliable training grounds for a new, reliable "socialist" intelligentsia.[81]

This highly unsatisfactory state of affairs, from the regime's point of view, is generally laid at the door of "bourgeois" faculty members. Following the war, the number of Communist professors was quite small, and the universities had to be staffed largely from the old bourgeois intelligentsia. The politically more sensitive fields—history, economics, philosophy, pedagogy, etc.— were quickly brought under SED control, but other fields, the scientific and technical disciplines among them, remained preserves of an older generation of academics. At a 1958 *Hochschule* conference individual professors were singled out for their "anti-Marxist" teachings;[82] Kurt Hager, the SED secretary responsible for education, complained of the "many nonparty academics who still orient themselves toward the West," and proclaimed an "offensive of Marxism-Leninism in our universities." [83] But even party members—including the DDR's two most notorious academic heretics, the economist Fritz Behrens and the physicist Robert Havemann—have contributed to university dissent.[84] In 1961, for example, members joined nonmembers in Leipzig, Dresden, and elsewhere in the wave of protests following the erection of the Berlin Wall; some of the former were removed from the party in consequence.[85]

The party stresses the "high responsibility"' of the university scholar and his importance as a role model for his students.[86] The training of a new generation of professors, whose education in-

---

[81] See examples cited in text above; also Thomas Hager, "Die Stichpunkte," *Forum*, No. 13 (1970), p. 10; also the charges of "offenses against socialist morality" and "ideological diversion" in DDR universities cited by Kai Hermann, "Stalins Rückkehr nach Ostberlin," *Die Zeit* (N. Am. edition), (December 14, 1965), p. 3; *idem.*, "Zwischen Sex und Siebenjahrplan," *Die Zeit* (N. Am. edition), (December 21, 1965), p. 3.

[82] Annemarie Podrabski, "Marxistische Agrarökonomie lehren," *ND* (March 4, 1958), p. 5; Prof. Dr. Werlie, "Arbeiten wir zusammen für den Sozialismus," *ND* (March 3, 1958), p. 5.

[83] Kurt Hager, "Freie Bahn," *ND* (March 6, 1958), p. 6.

[84] On Behrens and Havemann, see below, Chaps. 6 and 9.

[85] Jänicke, *op. cit.*, pp. 209ff.

[86] "Die Weiterführung," p. 510; Kurt Hager, "Partei und Wissenschaft," *Einheit*, XXI (April 1966), 447.

cludes advanced studies in Marxism-Leninism, and the reorganization of the universities to reduce the traditional power and isolation of the German *Ordinarius* are among the corrective measures that have been undertaken. Older faculty are being replaced by young cadres who often combine industrial, government, or party positions with academic ones.[87]

In general, however, it seems clear that politicalization in the universities and *Hochschulen* of the DDR has been a two-edged sword. The influences to which the students are exposed are by no means exclusively those cultivated by the regime. The socialist verities drilled into pupils in the lower schools are met with considerably more skepticism and even contradiction when expounded in *gesellschaftswissenschaftliche* lectures at the universities. The evidence indicates that the universities, in fact, have been principal foci of political skepticism and revisionism and, on occasion, even outright opposition. For most of the young scientific and technical intelligentsia of the DDR, their university years are still those most likely to bring them into contact with such forms of political nonconformity.

The enormous expansion of technical and scientific education in the DDR and its close gearing to economic development is revealing of the commitments of the regime and of how they are meant to shape the new intelligentsia and the role it is expected to play. There are subtle socialization effects in the technical side of DDR education: East German youth grow up in a world where technological values are emphasized, where the approved role models are of scientists, engineers, and managers, and where the language of productivity and efficiency dominate sectors of life quite apart from the economy.

The efforts devoted to conscious ideological socialization—intensified in the past few years—should occasion no surprise. If nothing else, they reveal the inherited and quite genuine doctrinal faith of the older generation of party leaders and the perceived self-interest of the ideological and organizational apparatus, as

[87] On the training of the *wissenschaftlicher Nachwuchs* in the DDR, see Lange, *Wissenschaft,* pp. 272–273; *Universitäten und Hochschulen,* pp. 60–62; *SBZ von A bis Z,* pp. 38–39.

well as a continuing insecurity of power and uncertainty of legitimacy.

There is a persistent tension between technical and traditional ideological values in DDR educational policy, as there is in other sectors of East German life. In part, the strengthening of regime legitimacy depends upon achieving a high level of congruence between socialization patterns in the school and the attitudes and activities most valued in the outside world. Both the skills and the attitudes of the technical graduates must be appropriate to the needs of a technologically oriented society; their education must simultaneously encourage them to identify their own professional goals with the DDR's success. The resulting competing pulls on educational policy may be seen in the choice of top educational functionaries; a technical expert, Ernst-Joachim Giessman, was appointed State Secretary (and later Minister) for University and *Fachshule* affairs in 1962, only to be replaced by a former history teacher and professor of education at the end of the decade.[88] In the competition for curricular time, the technical disciplines have won some modest victories. But I have suggested that in part the reduction in formal ideological training represents an acknowledgment of its low yield and an inclination to rely instead on the organization of study, the use of extracurricular organizations, and the "permeation" of all fields by a Marxist-Leninist perspective.

The DDR, it should now be clear, has devoted its best energies to the schooling system. Especially in the first postwar years and on the subuniversity level, the purge of unreliable elements and their replacement by party cadres was most thoroughgoing in the pedagogical sphere; subsequently, repeated and sweeping educational reforms have been undertaken—the universities, for example, are now on their third; and an extraordinary proportion of the DDR's financial resources have been invested in expanding and improving education. The products of this intense effort, the technical intelligentsia, are not, as we shall see, in every respect the new socialist men that were contemplated. Conscious socialization has been supplemented by an unintended, informal political learning which reveals inconsistencies between theory and practice, teaches modes of accommodation, and reveals openings for

[88] See Richert, *"Sozialistische Universität,"* p. 211.

change.[89] The DDR's educational system has indeed produced a new intelligentsia, one which serves its creators well in many respects, but still not quite the intelligentsia they intended.

[89] On alternative sources to official socializing agencies in the Soviet Union, see the stimulating essay by Frederic J. Fleron, Jr., and Rita Mae Kelly, "Personality, Behavior, and Communist Ideology," *Soviet Studies*, XXI (January 1970), 297–313, esp. 305.

3

STRATUM IDENTITY AND CONSCIOUSNESS

> We may not be able to achieve it soon, but we must at all costs achieve a situation in which specialists—as a separate social stratum, which will persist until we have reached the highest stage of development of Communist society—can enjoy better conditions of life under socialism than they enjoyed under capitalism insofar as concerns their material and legal status, comradely collaboration with the workers and peasants, and in the mental plane, i.e., finding satisfaction in their work, realizing that it is socially useful and independent of the sordid interests of the capitalist class.
>
> V. I. LENIN[1]

> The intelligentsia has never been a class, and never can be a class—it was and remains a stratum, which recruits its members from among all classes of society. In the old days the intelligentsia recruited its members from the ranks of the nobility, of the bourgeoisie, partly from the ranks of the peasantry, and only to a very inconsiderable extent from the ranks of the workers. In our day, under the Soviets, the intelligentsia recruits its members mainly from the ranks of the workers and peasants. But no matter where it may recruit its members, and what character it may bear, the intelligentsia is, nevertheless, a stratum and not a class.
>
> J. STALIN[2]

To ASSESS fairly the role of the technical intelligentsia in the East German political system, we must explore the degree to which it can be said to form a unified "class" with similar charac-

---

[1] V. I. Lenin, "The Role and Functions of the Trade Unions Under the New Economic Policy" (1922), in *Selected Works* (New York: International Publishers, 1967), III, 660.

[2] J. Stalin, *Problems of Leninism* (Moscow: Foreign Languages Publishing House, 1953), pp. 702–703.

teristics, common attitudes and aspirations, and a consciousness of its own identity. In the introduction I included six groups within the technical intelligentsia: the chief governmental planners and economists; bureaucrats with important economic, technical, or scientific responsibilities; industrial managers; physical scientists and mathematicians; engineers; and educators and journalists in scientific, technical, and economic fields. This corresponds roughly with the East German usage of the term although sometimes the technical intelligentsia is further distinguished from the "academic intelligentsia" (*wissenschaftliche Intelligenz*) and occasionally the "agricultural intelligentsia," the "intelligentsia in the state administration," and that in the "democratic parties and mass organizations." [3] In the broader sense, these groups all include members of the technical intelligentsia, though by no means *only* members of it. Such borderline groups as medical personnel, agronomists, and biological scientists are excluded from the definition.

DDR census figures do not normally distinguish members of the intelligentsia from the broad category of "workers and employees." However, in 1971, 738,000 DDR citizens (11.9 percent of the total) who were employed in the "socialist economy" had completed a university or *Fachschule* education.[4] Their number had more than doubled in ten years, suggesting a disproportionately youthful group. The figures on fields of study cited in the preceding chapter suggest that at least two-thirds, or some 500,000, belong to the technical intelligentsia.

In Communist theory, the intelligentsia do not constitute a "class"—which must be based upon a distinctive relationship to the means of production—but rather an "intermediary stratum" (*Zwischenschicht*), distinguished by its orientation toward mental rather than physical labor. "The special role of the intelligentsia," says a DDR writer, "finds its expression in certain occupations and activities requiring high qualifications which as a rule presuppose a university, *Fachschule,* or other specialized education." The intelligentsia does not enjoy the unity of a class, coming as it does from a variety of classes and other strata, and will disappear in the

[3] Kurt Lungwitz, *Über die Klassenstruktur in der Deutschen Demokratischen Republik* (Berlin: Verlag die Wirtschaft, 1962), p. 127.
[4] *Statistisches Taschenbuch der Deutschen Demokratischen Republik 1972* (Berlin: Staatsverlag der DDR, 1972) , p. 39.

ultimate Communist society where the divergence between "hand" and "brain" work will be overcome.[5]

There are good reasons to identify the technical intelligentsia as a stratum but not as a class, though not, in every respect, the official one. We must begin with the somewhat ironic fact that whatever identity this group may have has been lent to it by the regime itself. It has been singled out repeatedly in official statements and party propaganda as an indispensable element in the building of socialism; books and well-publicized conferences have been devoted to it; professional organizations and social clubs have been created for its members; and special honors and generous emoluments have been granted it. A man's status situation, or stratum, in Max Weber's formulation, is made up of those components of his life "determined by a specific, positive or negative, social estimation of honor." [6] The East German regime, it is clear, has spared little effort to assure that the technical intelligentsia's place of honor be a high one.

Yet the SED clearly wants to limit the extent to which the technical intelligentsia regards itself as a distinctive stratum. The repeated efforts to span the division between workers and intelligentsia illustrate this: the campaign to encourage "socialist cooperative work" in the factories, the attempt to bring working class "innovators" and foremen into the intelligentsia's *Kammer der Technik* (KDT, Chamber of Technology), and the recurrent emphasis on the gradual merging of intellectual and manual labor.[7] More important, the party has no intention of allowing the technical intelligentsia to become a political class in any sense; the ideology, which insists that political conflict ends with the consolidation of the proletarian revolution, will not permit it. The two great classes of socialist society, the workers and peasants, are

[5] Lungwitz, *op. cit.*, pp. 113, 125, 127. The distinction between intellectual and physical work as part of the societal division of labor is attributed to Engels; Lenin is quoted to the effect that the intelligentsia must remain a special stratum until the attainment of the highest stage of Communism; and Stalin is the uncited source of the concept of the intelligentsia as an "intermediary stratum" (see epigraphs at the beginning of this chapter). See also Siegfried Grundmann, "Intelligenz und Arbeiterklasse in unserer Zeit," *Technische Gemeinschaft* (May 1969), pp. 5–6; "Intelligenz," in *Wörterbuch der Marxistisch-Leninistischen Soziologie* (Berlin: Dietz Verlag, 1969), pp. 225–227.

[6] Hans H. Gerth and C. Wright Mills, eds., *From Max Weber* (New York: Oxford University Press, 1958), pp. 186–187.

[7] See Lungwitz, *op. cit.*, pp. 121–124.

described as "nonantagonistic"; the intelligentsia created by these classes serves them and has no political life of its own.[8]

Contemporary DDR discussions of class structure hold that the differences between the intelligentsia and the working class are progressively diminishing. This shift is attributed in part to the development of parallel "scientific-technical" and socialist revolutions, which broaden the intellectual and creative dimensions of the workers' tasks while fundamentally changing the place of the specialist in the productive process. It is also said to reflect declining income differentials and, in the rhetoric of the late Ulbricht period, was credited to the "growing political-ideological and moral unity of the socialist human community."[9] In 1967 Honecker himself stated that the "majority of our intelligentsia" belonged to the working class, and one writer subsequently went so far as to argue that to speak of a separate intelligentsia "social stratum" was no longer proper.[10] After Ulbricht's removal, however, the persistence of class differences was stressed anew; party spokesmen asserted that the distance between intelligentsia and workers, based on the objective role of each in the "societal organization of work," remained substantial and ought not to be minimized.[11]

Both these interpretations of the intelligentsia's class position were meant to refute Western and "counterrevolutionary" suggestions that the intelligentsia might take over a "leadership role" in Communist societies.[12] Under Honecker, however, the sharpened class distinction has served the larger purpose of qualifying the prestige extended to the intelligentsia during the economic reform period in favor of a reassertion of the ideological preeminence of the working class. The importance of the intelligentsia,

[8] See *ibid.*, p. 159. The thesis that interest conflict on group lines is natural and legitimate in socialist societies, put forward by the Czechs in their Action Program and elsewhere, has received some discussion in the DDR. See esp. Uwe-Jens Heuer, *Demokratie und Recht im neuen ökonomischen System der Planung und Leitung der Volkswirtschaft* (Berlin: Staatsverlag der DDR, 1965).

[9] "Intelligenz," in *Wörterbuch*, p. 226; see also Werner Lamberz, "Die führende Rolle der Arbeiterklasse in der DDR," *Forum*, No. 7 (1970), p. 9.

[10] *Neues Deutschland* (hereafter cited as *ND*) (April 21, 1967), p. 3, cited in Grundmann, *op. cit.*, p. 3.

[11] Kurt Hager, *Die entwickelte sozialistische Gesellschaft* (Berlin: Dietz Verlag, 1971), pp. 19–20.

[12] See Grundmann, *op. cit.*, pp. 4–6. The author specifically cites the Czech philosopher Ivan Svitak in this connection.

although it is by no means to be "diminished," is argued to be entirely dependent on its alliance with the working class, which is, after all, the "chief force of production." [13]

The numerous articles dealing with the relationship between the intelligentsia and the working class bear witness to the continuing unresolved state of East German class theory.[14] The need to grant enough prestige to the technical intelligentsia to attract qualified personnel and to maintain performance-based authority competes with the conviction that the party's own legitimacy depends on upholding the myth of working class rule. DDR class theory also suffers the disability of having to serve simultaneously as an ideological weapon and as a conceptual instrument that East German sociologists must use in dealing with their complex and developing social system. Whatever the ambiguities of the official theory, however, the reality is one of a rather sharply delimited stratum, whose social position is a matter of persistent concern to the SED leadership.

REWARDS

One useful indicator of the place the regime envisages for members of the technical intelligentsia in East German society is the system of rewards established for them. In any society the material and nonmaterial compensations granted members of a group will variously reflect the prestige they enjoy or that a ruling elite wishes to accord them, the value that is placed on their services, their relative scarcity, their influence within the political or social system, or a combination of these. In the DDR the technical intelligentsia has been treated with noteworthy generosity relative to other groups although substantial differentiations are made among different subgroups within it. The initial impetus to this policy was provided without much doubt by the factor of scarcity and the fear that valuable personnel might leave for the West,[15] together with the ever-present example of Stalinist Russia. That an

---

[13] Hager, *op. cit.*, pp. 21–23.
[14] See the excellent discussion in Hans-Werner Prahl, "Konfusion in der Klassentheorie," *Deutschland Archiv*, III (August 1970), 888–892.
[15] "Die Bedeutung der Intelligenz beim Aufbau des Sozialismus," *ND* (May 24, 1953), p. 3.

attractive schedule of rewards continues to be maintained even after the numbers of technical intelligentsia have become ample and all exits to the West have been closed reflects in some degree the prestige and influence they have come to enjoy. The technicians are now in a position to defend for themselves what was originally granted them by the party on rather transparent grounds of expediency.

This is not to say that the incomes of the DDR's technical intelligentsia approach anything like affluence. The basic structure of salaries was apparently fixed in 1952, when the ratio of the average engineer's income to that of the "qualified" worker was advanced from 1.75:1 to 2.6:1.[16] The income schedule for "scientists, engineers, and technicians" of that time ranged from a low of 400 to 460 marks per month for those in the lowest of five income groups (presumably based on training, experience, and the like) in the fishing industry, to 1,910 to 2,190 marks per month for those in the highest income group in several categories of underground mining.[17] In an East Berlin construction firm in 1955 managerial salaries ranged from 490 marks (cadre instructor, planning statistician) to 1,800 marks (director, technical director); this range was apparently typical for that period.[18] More recent figures are difficult to obtain, but Frank Grätz, a DDR sociologist now in the West, reports that in 1970 the average gross monthly income of an engineer or economist holding a university degree was 1,330 marks, that of a factory director in a plant with 1,500 employees 1,800 marks, and that of a general director in a large industrial *Kombinat* 3,500 marks. The average income of *all* DDR workers and

[16] "Naturally you have to realize the following: In many cases the party naturally grants the intelligentsia advantages to a degree that the lower SED cadres don't comprehend: including material, personal-material advantages that take on a quantity that even from our point of view exceed any reasonable measure but which are granted because the party leadership has an insane fear that this or that really good, qualified, respected man might leave. Naturally these are all things that a lower party functionary, who works near this man and doesn't see him work with his hands, but only muse at his desk, can't understand." Refugee interview, *Die Intelligenzschicht in der Sowjetzone Deutschlands* (München: Infratest GmbH & Co., November 1960), mimeographed, III, 155 (hereafter cited as *Intelligenzschicht*).

[17] Werner Bosch, *Die Sozialstruktur in West- und Mitteldeutschland* (Bonn: Bundesministerium für gesamtdeutsche Fragen, 1958), pp. 213–214. This schedule apparently did not include the salaries of persons occupying managerial positions, nor did it include those with *Einzelverträge* ("individual contracts").

[18] *Ibid.*, pp. 212–213.

employees in that year was about 750 marks.[19] Reports of visitors on individual cases confirm the impression of a steady increase across the board over the years, maintaining the considerable disparity between top managerial salaries and the wages of ordinary workers.[20] As a whole, incomes in the DDR rose an average of 30 percent from 1960 to 1969.[21]

Most members of the technical intelligentsia in the past had some limited opportunity to supplement their incomes through bonuses based on the fulfillment or overfulfillment of production norms in their place of work.[22] "Loyalty premiums" were also paid to the higher categories of the technical intelligentsia who remained in the same plant for two or five uninterrupted years; they receive a supplement of 5 or 8 percent, respectively, of their yearly salary.[23] The amount of the technician's bonuses relative to his total income remained, under these regulations, rather insubstantial. But with the introduction of the New Economic System, from 10 to 20 percent of the *base* salaries of leading economic and technical personnel were made "dependent upon performance," that is, upon the achievement of various indices of production. The higher the income level and responsibilities of the official concerned, the higher proportion of his salary was to be determined by such indices.[24] Since the functionaries in question often had little personal impact on the fulfillment of the indices and since the new policy apparently made possible only a drop, not an increase, in their income, they greeted it with little enthusiasm.

[19] Grätz, "Wirtschaftsführer in Ost und West," *Deutschland Archiv*, IV (October 1971), 1035–1036.

[20] See, for example, Hans Apel, *Ohne Begleiter* (Köln: Verlag Wissenschaft und Politik, 1965), pp. 9–21, 35, 151, 160, 176; Jean Edward Smith, *Germany Beyond the Wall* (Boston: Little, Brown, 1969), pp. 98–99.

[21] *Bericht der Bundesregierung und Materialien zur Lage der Nation 1971* (Bonn: Bundesministerium für innerdeutsche Beziehungen, 1971), p. 131.

[22] In 1951 the quarterly premium for fulfillment of the plan ranged from 5 to 20 percent of the monthly income of some technicians although others received only the premiums of 2 to 5 percent per 1 percent of overfulfillment. See Alfred Leutwein [Siegfried Mampel], *Die 'Technische Intelligenz' in der sowjetischen Besatzungszone* (Bonn: Bundesministerium für gesamtdeutsche Fragen, 1953), pp. 15–17, 51–54.

[23] *Ibid.*, p. 17; see also *Tribüne* (July 16, 1965), p. 6. As the *Tribüne* article concedes, the purpose of this payment is to counter the rapid turnover of personnel frequent in DDR factories.

[24] Forschungsbeirat für Fragen der Wiedervereinigung Deutschlands, *Vierter Tätigkeitsbericht, 1961–1965* (Bonn: Bundesministerium für gesamtdeutsche Fragen, 1965), p. 61. See also *Bericht der Bundesregierung, op. cit.*, pp. 128–129.

The highest salaries go to those with "individual contracts" (*Einzelverträge*).[25] These were introduced in 1950 for those technical specialists most valued and needed by the DDR: "highly qualified scientists, technicians, and engineers," who might receive up to 4,000 marks per month, and "particularly distinguished specialists in the DDR who have served the German people with special merit in the areas of science and technology," who earned up to 15,000 marks per month. Under such agreements, for example, in 1964 the director of the important iron works *Kombinat* at Eisenhüttenstadt received 2,800 marks per month with the chance to earn up to 500 marks more in tax-free premiums; the director of the equally important oil processing plant at Schwedt/ Oder received 3,000 marks plus "some supplements." [26] Both of these belonged to the younger party intelligentsia. By contrast, the nuclear physicist Heinz Barwich, a member of the older intelligentsia and director of the Central Institute for Nuclear Physics until his flight in 1964, received 8,000 marks per month and had 250,000 marks in his bank account; he had a villa in Dresden, an apartment in Berlin, an official car with chauffeur, and a large Russian automobile of his own.[27] The former general director of the Buna Chemical Works, Johannes Nelles, reportedly received over 10,000 marks a month.[28] Only a few such "star salaries" still exist, according to DDR sources, and they are being phased out,[29] but the more moderate ones persist.

The *Einzelverträge* specify not only the amount of income but such things as working conditions, the period of notice, the payment of premiums, the length of vacations, the provision of suitable living accommodations, sickness benefits, supplementary retirement benefits, and guarantees of a higher education for the technician's children. These benefits are in general considerably more generous than those provided the population at large, but

---

[25] See Leutwein, *op. cit.*, pp. 9–21.

[26] As reported to me by a Western journalist who visited both plants.

[27] *Die Zeit* (N. Am. edition), (November 2, 1965), p. 18; the luxury in which the physicist, Baron Manfred von Ardenne, lives in a Dresden villa is described by Welles Hangen, *The Muted Revolution* (New York: Knopf, 1966), pp. 136–137. It was reported to Smith that "at least eight professors" in Dresden made over 15,000 marks per month in 1967 (*op. cit.*, p. 55).

[28] Grätz, *op. cit.*, p. 1035.   [29] Interview.

most of them have been extended to the bulk of the technical intelligentsia whose terms of work are regulated through *Kollek-
tivverträge*.[30] In the early years of the DDR the technical intelligentsia received special food rationing cards entitling them to
receive provisions above and beyond the regular allocation. These
"Intelligentsia cards" were exceedingly unpopular with the workers and were abolished in 1953 and replaced by special stores
where only the intelligentsia could shop. Generous supplementary
old age pensions, already mentioned, were tailored particularly to
the interests of the older bourgeois intelligentsia, and "technical
cabinets" were established for the exchange of scientific and technical information and the provision of technical literature, domestic, "socialist," and, later, Western.[31] *Intelligenz* clubs were also
established for more social purposes, and so-called "luxury clubs"
were opened for the narrow elite holding the most lucrative
Einzelverträge. The clubs seemed to have aroused considerable resentment as well as being the subject of much rumor and speculation; one of the most notorious is the "Dresdner Klub," headed
until recently by the distinguished physicist Manfred von Ardenne,
in a refurbished palace overlooking that city.[32] An outside ob-
server, however, might be inclined to describe its accommodations
as comfortable rather than elegant.

"Comfortable" might also best characterize the economic status
of the DDR's technical intelligentsia as a whole, by the standards
of the ordinary wage earner. The technicians do less well in comparison with their counterparts in the Federal Republic, especially
in higher managerial positions.[33] Except perhaps for the few remaining "star" *Einzelverträge*, no technician's or manager's salary seems grossly disproportionate to other DDR incomes, and

[30] "Collective contracts," made between the management of a plant and its trade
union.
[31] See Leutwein, *op. cit.*, pp. 23–24; Max Gustav Lange, Ernst Richert, and Otto
Stammer, "Das Problem der 'Neuen Intelligenz' in der Sowjetischen Besatzungszone"
in *Veritas, Iustitia, Libertas* (Berlin: Colloquium Verlag, 1954), p. 230
[32] *Intelligenzschicht*, III, 164; Smith, *Germany Beyond the Wall*, pp. 54–55.
[33] Grätz, "Wirtschaftsführer," pp. 1035–1036. Werner Bosch, after a careful study of
incomes in the DDR in the mid-1950s, concluded that many members of the
technical intelligentsia were better paid than their Western counterparts, leaving
purchasing power out of account; that no longer appears to be true. See his *Die
Sozialstruktur*, pp. 93–94.

young graduates beginning their work are still only modestly compensated. "When people whisper about high incomes in the DDR, they are usually talking about artists, doctors, and artisans." [34]

The rewards offered the technical intelligentsia are not, of course, entirely monetary or even material. The regime has been somewhat self-consciously concerned to lend members of the intelligentsia the prestige they enjoy in the West;[35] one device to this end is the granting of honorary titles and accompanying medals (often with cash bonuses). For example: Honored (*Verdiente*) Inventor, Honored Technician of the People, Distinguished Scientist of the People, Activist, Honored Activist, Honorary Chief Engineer, and recipient of the "Banner of Labor." [36] The limited evidence we have leaves it unclear whether such official marks of prestige are matched by the unofficial esteem of the DDR population. Refugees interviewed in a West German reception camp (prior to 1961) ranked the occupations of technical director and electrical engineer just below the traditionally highest status ones of doctor and university professor.[37] A 1956 study of working class refugees revealed that fifty of the sixty-nine interviewed regarded the intelligentsia with considerable resentment as an *"Oberschicht"* (upper stratum) consciously promoted by the regime and separated rather sharply from themselves;[38] this may be viewed as a negative acknowledgement of status. Grätz, however, remarks on the "relatively limited respect" enjoyed by economic functionaries, owing variously to their narrow decision-making prerogatives, the tendency of the population to regard them as bureaucratic or political functionaries, and the insufficient education of some of them. Prestige is lower, he suggests, among those trained in economics

[34] Grätz, *op cit.*, p. 1034.

[35] "I think it is a matter of rewarding effective performance in a much higher degree with—shall we say—marks of prestige than has previously been the case. Performance must receive greater social recognition." "Was heisst ökonomisch denken? Aufzeichnungen eines Gespräches mit Klaus Korn," *Forum*, No. 22 (1963), p. 3.

[36] Leutwein, *Die 'Technische Intelligenz,'* pp. 21–22; *Technische Gemeinschaft* (December–January 1969–1970), p. 41; *ibid.* (February 1970), pp. 2–3.

[37] Karl Valentin Müller, *Die Manager in der Sowjetzone* (Köln & Opladen: Westdeutscher Verlag, 1962). Asked how they thought the DDR population in general would rank the director and engineer, the refugees placed them fourth and fifth, the position of army major intervening in third place (pp. 92–93).

[38] Viggo Graf Blücher, *Industriearbeiterschaft in der Sowjetzone* (Stuttgart: Ferdinand Ende Verlag, 1959), p. 27.

than in engineering or science; indeed, the former sometimes feel a conscious sense of inferiority to the latter. However, he agrees that the reforms of the New Economic System and the accompanying effort to popularize leading economic figures did improve their prestige until both the reforms and the popularization were curtailed.[39]

THE SOURCES OF CONSCIOUSNESS

The material and nonmaterial rewards given the technical intelligentsia, then, tend to single it out as a distinctive stratum of DDR society. The question remains whether this stratum enjoys a coherence and sense of its own identity sufficient to allow us to view it as a self-conscious actor in East German politics. West German writers have expressed skepticism on this point. Otto Stammer and Ludwig Auerbach, for example, both stress the "unhomogeneous composition" of the intelligentsia, which prevents it from demonstrating any "firm social profile." [40] The authors of the Infratest study agree that the great variety of occupations and sociological groupings encompassed by the intelligentsia prevent it from being a "social unity"; at best, its members are distinguished only by "their vague feeling of belonging in fact to the intelligentsia, to a group privileged by the regime." [41] While these conclusions all refer to the intelligentsia as a whole, they apply almost equally well to the technical intelligentsia.

The present level of "class consciousness"—one of the criteria of class discussed in the introduction—and thus of group solidarity among the entire technical intelligentsia is consequently held to be minimal. "For the intelligentsia as a whole," the Infratest study concludes, "an understanding of its own social position and reflection over it leading to identical or similar social views, to a common social ideology characteristic of [it], cannot be estab-

---

[39] Grätz, *op. cit.*, pp. 1032–1034. Grätz's remarks are based on his own dissertation prepared in Halle in 1968: "Zur gesellschaftliche Stellung und sozialen Situation der Ökonomen in der DDR."

[40] Otto Stammer, "Sozialstruktur und System der Werthaltungen der Sowjetischen Besatzungszone Deutschlands," *Schmollers Jahrbuch für Gesetzgebung, Verwaltung und Volkswirtschaft*, LXXVI, No. 1 (1956), 93; Ludwig Auerbach, "Menschen in der Sowjetischen Besatzungszone," *Werkhefte*, XVI (January 1962), 41.

[41] *Intelligenzschicht*, III, 200.

lished." [42] One might add that this degree of consciousness is not
to be found among intelligentsia groups in the West either and is
rare among other broad groups as well. On the other hand, a recent study of Soviet elites through the content analysis of specialist
journals claims its data provides evidence for the emergence of
such group consciousness among economic, military, and legal specialists, and the literary intelligentsia.[43] While I have no such
concrete data, a close examination of the elements conditioning
the DDR technical intelligentsia's sense of itself should serve to
illuminate its role in East German society.

Potential consciousness depends on such matters as: (1) the sim-
ilarity of social background, (2) the absence of generational differences, (3) common educational experiences, (4) similarities in
styles of life, (5) similarities in the relationship to work, (6) similarities in the relationship to authority, (7) possibilities for communication, and (8) possibilities for organization. I shall examine
each of these in turn, giving particular stress to those areas where
change is taking place or is likely to take place.

(1) Divergences in the class origins of members of the technical
intelligentsia tend to produce differences in political predisposi-
tions. I have already noted that there is a rough, though by no
means complete, coincidence between the "old" and the "bourgeois" intelligentsia, an identification reinforced by being stressed
in DDR propanganda. Müller shows a strong relationship, on the
one hand, between age and previous occupational status among
managers and, on the other hand, between the type of managerial
position concerned and these two variables; that is, the more predominantly technical the position, the more likely it is to be occupied by an older man with a bourgeois background.[44] His figures, based as they are on refugees or on secondhand reports by
refugees, are not necessarily accurate in an absolute sense but
probably do reflect group differences reliably. If so, they suggest
not only important divisions along class, age, and occupational
lines among DDR managers and technicians but also that these

[42] *Ibid.*, p. 199.
[43] Milton C. Lodge, *Soviet Elite Attitudes Since Stalin* (Columbus, Ohio: Merrill,
1969), esp. pp. 33–44, 94–98.
[44] Müller, *op. cit.*, pp. 22–23, 34, 45.

divisions tend to reinforce one another. They further suggest, however, a trend toward the dominance of younger managers of predominantly working class backgrounds across the board. As noted above, the regime has claimed—without making clear the basis of its categorization—that 75 percent of the "managers in the socialist economy" are of working class origins.[45] A study of 1963 figures broken down by faculties from East Berlin's Humboldt University indicates that workers and their offspring were slightly overrepresented among those going into mathematics and the natural sciences in comparison with other fields and greatly overrepresented among those in the "economic sciences." [46] In so far as these figures can be projected to the DDR as a whole, they indeed indicate that "bourgeois" children are a minority, although a substantial one, of those entering the technical intelligentsia. The large numbers of intelligentsia children in these figures (necessarily mostly children of the older and, hence, bourgeois, intelligentsia) points, moreover, to an impressive degree of self-perpetuation.

The importance of differing class backgrounds in dividing the technical intelligentsia within itself should not be overstressed. There are those of humble origins, as I have already remarked, who feel a special loyalty to the regime because they doubt they would have been able to rise out of their class in a capitalist system;[47] but others have come to accept their training as a matter of right. The class division becomes more pronounced when it accompanies (2) a generational gap; members of the old intelligentsia may be politically mistrusted and treated to such expletives as "AEG-Hasen" (roughly, "General Electric stooges") by fanatical younger elements.[48] More often, members of the older generation fear that their jobs are threatened by younger men with more im-

---

[45] Hager, *Die entwickelte*, p. 17.

[46] Humboldt Universität zu Berlin, *Jahrbuch, 1963* (Berlin: Humboldt Universität, 1964), pp. 577–578, 592–601. The greatest proportion of intelligentsia children in 1963 were in the medical faculty (excepting the tiny theological faculty), the smallest proportion in the law faculty.

[47] See Auerbach's distinction of five groups within the new intelligentsia on this basis, *op. cit.* (March 1962), 128–129.

[48] Erich Dahm, "Für ein enges Kampfbündis der Arbeiterklasse mit der wissenschaftlich-technischen Intelligenz beim sozialstschen Aufbau der Deutschen Demokratischen Republik," in *Sozialismus und Intelligenz* (Berlin: Dietz Verlag, 1960), p. 42.

peccable class and political credentials and/or better and more up-to-date training.[49] Curiously, some of the older party members in the intelligentsia join in the complaints over the "arrogance" of the young, who allegedly are ungrateful for the "accomplishments of socialism" that "fall in their laps" and instead place unreasonable demands upon it.[50] For their part, the young technicians, who are often in some oversupply anyway, are impatient at seeing the road upward blocked by the older intelligentsia, particularly when the propaganda for the "Economic System of Socialism" urges innovations from them. The Infratest refugees reported a much higher degree of acceptance of the regime's political demands among the younger than the old intelligentsia, and 30 percent described the relationship between the two groups in their place of work as "strained." [51] My own interviews also confirmed the existence of these tensions.[52] Again, however, the passage of time is reducing the importance of the generational division.

(3) It is a commonplace that common educational experiences may help to produce a sense of identity and solidarity among social groups; the impact of the French system of elite administrative schools on the castelike outlook of higher civil servants has frequently been noted, and students of Soviet politics have noted the importance of "old school ties" for managers in that country.[53] The present members of the DDR's technical intelligentsia have had a wide variety of educational experiences. Some were trained under "bourgeois" auspices before 1945; some in the transitional

[49] See Walter Ulbricht, "Das neue ökonomische System der Planung und Leitung der Volkswirtschaft in der Praxis," speech at June 1963 Economic Conference, *Die Wirtschaft* (June 28, 1963), p. 20; Günter Mittag, "Die Aufgaben der Parteiorganisationen in den Vereinigungen Volkseigener Betriebe," *Einheit*, XIII (August 1958), 1142.

[50] "Wunschtraum eines Ingenieurs," *Sonntag* (June 24, 1962), p. 4.

[51] *Intelligenzschicht*, I, 154–155; III, 35, 40.

[52] One man, the most dissatisfied of those with whom I talked, alleged that the party had tried to make his "temporary" replacement (while he was ill) into a permanent one, thus jeopardizing his pension, which depends on his income in his last year. He complained about the "arrogance" and the poor education of many young technicians who, to his mind, were placed too quickly in responsible positions.

[53] See, for example, F. F. Ridley, "French Technocracy and Comparative Government," *Political Studies*, IV (February 1966), 34–52; Anthony Sampson, *The New Europeans* (London: Hodder & Stoughton, 1968), pp. 329–347; John A. Armstrong, "Sources of Administrative Behavior: Some Soviet and Western European Comparisons," *American Political Science Review*, LIX (September 1965), 650.

period, 1945–1951, before many of the more drastic changes in education were introduced; and even those trained since have experienced a variety of reforms—the *Arbeiter-und-Bauern* faculties, the work experience requirements, and the reduction in formal Marxism-Leninism classes, for example. Even as presently constituted, the DDR educational system offers varied routes to technical intelligentsia positions: the universities versus the *Fachschulen;* full-time direct study versus part-time, night, and correspondence study; the factory academies; and so on. There are also important differences in the extent to which each educational institution and branch of it is under effective SED political control. On the other hand, the highly centralized character of the East German regime permits it to impose uniform admissions requirements, schedules, curricula, and study materials, and the permissive element in DDR education—for teachers as well as students—remains low. It is particularly important to note that basically similar educational programs serve to prepare engineers, managers, functionaries in the economic bureaucracies, and party technical experts. This is training cither in engineering or in economics or both. The variations within the first two courses of training are many, but relatively minor; the differences between them are significant, largely in that the latter is regarded as a "society science" and is hence much more politicized (and less prestigious) than the former. The gap, however, is narrowed by the introduction of numerous economics courses in engineering programs, and vice versa. The training of scientists, of course, diverges substantially from both. Finally, training in these fields is so widespread and open as to preclude much of an elite mentality. Possibly individual institutions—like the *Hochschule für Ökonomie,* which trains planners, or the Central Institute for Socialist Economic Management—might one day take on an elitist character, but there is no evidence of it to date. The number of leading economic functionaries trained in the party's Institutes of Marxism-Leninism and of Society Sciences is still too small to constitute a distinct political-economic elite but bears watching.

(4) The relatively high incomes and special privileges of the technical intelligentsia, we have seen, set them apart from other elements of DDR society. But the gap within the technical intelli-

gentsia between young technicians, who hardly earn more than skilled workers, and those with generous *Einzelverträge* is so large as to make any assertions of group solidarity based on a common life style dubious. (5) Another indicator of group unity might be the degree of interchangeability of technical roles. If it is easy and in practice common to move from, say, engineering jobs to managerial ones, from managerial posts to ones in the economic ministries or State Planning Commission, from university teaching to research positions in industry, or from technically oriented jobs in the party bureaucracy to such jobs in the state bureaucracy, then one might expect to find a greater community of outlook and class-consciousness among the technical intelligentsia than would otherwise be the case.

Such interchangeability, I would assert, has been high, at least in the past. That is in part due to the fact that most members of the DDR technical intelligentsia are ranged within essentially the same state economic bureaucracy, and even those in outside institutions (notably the party and the educational system) are tied closely to it; note the party membership of leading state functionaries and managers, the official recommendations that cadres gain experience in both party and state apparatuses,[54] the close ties between many party plant secretaries and plant management, the frequency with which individuals hold joint positions in the economic apparatus and on university faculties,[55] and the cooperation between factories and colleges in arranging the students' "practical experience," in placing graduates, and in coordinating research with production. There is not the (by no means complete) discontinuity between the government, the universities, and business that generally exists in the West. The improvisational character of recruitment to the technical intelligentsia in the first postwar years in East Germany no doubt also contributed to the expectation of frequent shifting between these roles, as did the longer tradition of all-sidedness among Communist functionaries in the prewar years.

---

[54] "Grundsätze über die planmässige Entwicklung, Ausbildung, Erziehung und Verteilung der Kader. . . ," decision of Central Committee Secretariat, February 17, 1965, *Neuer Weg*, XX, No. 6 (1965), 341.

[55] See *SBZ-Biographie* (Bonn and Berlin: Bundesministerium für gesamtdeutsche Fragen, 1965), *passim*.

Among the higher echelons of the technological elite, inter-changeability remains high.[56] Take, for example, the case of the former Central Committee candidate Wolfgang Schirmer, who un-til 1962 was plant manager of the VEB Leuna "Walter Ulbricht," then became assistant director of the DDR Research Council, as-sistant director of the Academy of Science's Institute of Physical Chemistry, and chairman of the Standing Commission for the Chemical Industry in COMECON. Concurrently, he has taught chemistry at the technical *Hochschule* in Leuna-Merseburg and, since 1963, at East Berlin's Humboldt University.[57] Even on the middle levels of the technical intelligentsia, such a variety of activ-ities is not infrequent, as the inspirational biographies appearing from time to time in *Forum* and elsewhere make clear.[58] The great range of positions listed in the DDR universities' guide as open to the graduates of each course of study described is further evi-dence,[59] as are the present educational reforms emphasizing basic knowledge and adaptability in place of narrow expertise. Never-theless, the increasing sophistication of the DDR economy and the economic reforms have brought with them pressures for increased specialization, and the long-term trend may be away from the easy exchange of roles, at least on the lower levels of the economic system.

(6) A further criterion for the existence of a "class" may be adapted from Dahrendorf: In some sense its members stand in a

[56] See also below, Chap. 7; but cf. Peter Christian Ludz, *Parteielite im Wandel* (Köln and Opladen: Westdeutscher Verlag, 1968), pp. 222–223.

[57] *SBZ-Biographie*, 1965, pp. 304–305.

[58] For instance: "Prof. Dr. [Gerd] Friedrich: 35 years old. 1947–1950 studies in the Economics Faculty of Humboldt University. Then *Assistent* at the *Hochschule für Ökonomie*. Since 1951 director of the Institute for Industrial Economics there (with interruptions). 1955 completed graduate work . . . 1957/1958 . . . scientific assistant to the Vice Chairman for Machine Building of the State Planning Commission. 1958–1960 Prorector for research matters of the *Hochschule für Ökonomie*. 1959 three months work in Guinea, advising on the working out of the Republic of Guinea's Three-Year Plan. Scientific publications: with Prof. Dr. Rudolph, *Outline of Economic Planning*, 1959, *Tasks and Work Style of the VVB*. Additional publica-tions mainly on problems of leadership in industry; since 1960 turning to mathe-matical problems in the economy. Worked in the leadership of the experimental VVBs in preparation for the Economic Conference. Research work in BGW, here direction of a Circle for Functionaries on matrix calculation and linear optimizing." It is particularly significant that this biography preceded an article by Dr. Friedrich entitled "Narrow-Gauge Economists Not Wanted." *Forum*, No. 17 (1963), p. 3.

[59] *Das Studium an der Universitäten, Hoch- und Fachschulen der Deutschen Demo-kratischen Republik* (Berlin: Staatsverlag der DDR, 1965), *passim*.

common relationship to authority.[60] It will be evident from the materials later presented that there is no homogeneity among the DDR's technical intelligentsia on this score. Not only do some technicians participate importantly in the decision-making process and thus belong to the "rulers" (see Chapters 7 and 8) while others clearly enough belong to the "ruled," but the views of DDR authority held by different members of the technical intelligentsia diverge sharply. We will discuss the political attitudes of the scientists and technicians in detail below, for now it is enough to know that they run the gamut from implacable opposition to fawning support. The gap between the old and new intelligentsia is particularly large on this point. As the former die out, however, there is some evidence of a set of outlooks developing among the intelligentsia which combine a common pragmatic style and vocabulary with differing degrees and kinds of political commitment. I shall return to this matter shortly.

(7, 8) For a social group to attain sufficient cohesion to be regarded as a class, there must be adequate means of communication among its members to permit the diffusion and acceptance of common values and vocabularies. For it to act in common in the social and political arena, an effective network of communications must be supplemented by the means of organization. One of the most familiar characteristics of a government with "totalitarian" aspirations is, however, its attempt to monopolize communications and organization in order to keep isolated and ineffective any potential rivals for power.[61] The SED, as we know, has not been laggard in this regard: The press is a party press, all formal organizations except the churches are party and state organizations, and unofficial rivals are not permitted. It is true that with the relative relaxation of terror, party control of publications and organizations becomes more difficult to maintain with all strictness, and the regime's own creations may be subtly turned against it. Thus, for some years the literary magazine *Sinn und Form,* under the editorship of Peter Huchel, promoted an "ideological coexistence" anathema to

[60] See Ralf Dahrendorf, *Class and Class Conflict in Industrial Society* (Stanford: Stanford University Press, 1959), pp. 136, 173, and *passim.*

[61] See, for example, Carl J. Friedrich and Zbigniew Brzezinski, *Totalitarian Dictatorship and Autocracy* (Cambridge: Harvard University Press, 1956), Chaps. 1 and 11. For the DDR see Ernst Richert *et al., Agitation und Propaganda* (Berlin: Vahlen, 1958).

the regime, and magazines like *Forum* and *Sonntag* brought out occasional articles with a distinctly revisionistic flavor. In 1956 and 1957, the journal *Wirtschaftswissenschaft* published articles on the economy subsequently deemed revisionist.[62] Dissidence has arisen on occasion in both the FDJ and the FDGB (*Freier Deutscher Gewerkschaftsbund*, Free German Trade Union Federation), and it seems clear that the social and professional gatherings of the *Kammer der Technik* and the *Intelligenzklubs* provide opportunities for other than official communications among the technicians. Yet, by and large, the regime succeeds in sponsoring extensive professional and technical communications while isolating the technical intelligentsia socially and politically. The finding of the Infratest researchers that the individual's political and social "vision" rarely goes beyond his own work situation still seems justified.[63] The "ideological climate" prevailing there is his relevant reference point; his free time is too limited and his information too scanty to permit much coordination of views and feelings of unity with his counterparts in other plants, much less other sections of the country. The limited knowledge displayed by the members of the intelligentsia of prominent revisionists—such as Fritz Behrens, Robert Havemann, and Ernst Bloch—provides striking testimony to this isolation.[64]

The evidence, then, is mixed. The DDR's technical intelligentsia appears to be more homogeneous than comparable Western groups in terms of its education and the organization of its work, probably less homogeneous in its social composition and political views, and certainly less able to communicate and organize for political or social purposes. The net degree of group unity, much less conscious solidarity, among the technicians is thus too limited to justify the use of the term "class." Yet a kind of identity, and one with political relevance, arises from the fact that the technical

---

[62] See the discussion of the Behrens affair below in Chap. 9.

[63] *Intelligenzschicht*, I, 176.

[64] Only 15 to 25 percent of the Infratest refugees knew the names of Fritz Behrens, Arne Benary, Kurt Vieweg, and Ernst Bloch, most of them in the individual's field of specialization; the best known were Wolfgang Harich, the philosophy instructor, and Alfred Kantorowicz, the writer, who had been given special publicity because of the former's trial and the latter's flight to the West. *Intelligenzschicht*, III, 103. Ernst Richert reports similar findings among refugee students in *"Sozialistische Universität"* (Berlin: Colloquium Verlag, 1967), p. 250; I found comparable ignorance concerning Robert Havemann among engineers I talked to in East Berlin.

intelligentsia shares a particular outlook or orientation toward their jobs and roles in society. The single English word which best, though hardly fully, describes this outlook is "pragmatism." Perhaps a still better word is the German *Sachlichkeit,* which conveys a sober objectivity and an orientation to the most direct and businesslike achievement of material goals. It is a quality significant in that it departs clearly from the more specifically ideological orientation of the older Communist elite.

DIMENSIONS OF PRAGMATISM

Western visitors to the DDR show remarkable agreement in describing the "new men" occupying the top managerial posts of the East German economy.[65] They are young, talented, and, although most are members of the SED, scrupulous in avoiding the tortured phrases of "party Chinese," or *Kaderwelsch,* as an East German word play has it. They speak the language of the technical revolution, of cybernetics, data processing, and sophisticated uses of mathematics; they talk realistically about the needs and shortcomings of their industries and are willing to listen to and acknowledge the correctness of many criticisms of past policies; they are energetic workers, willing to take initiative and exhibit a kind of daring that the timid bureaucrats who often preceded them would not have. This practical spirit appears to pervade the technical intelligentsia as a whole: The authors of the Infratest study describe the attitudes of their subjects as "pragmatic" and "reality-bound." Insofar as these men rejected Communism, it was on "practical" not "ideological" grounds; their assessments of the virtues and disadvantages of the system of state ownership stressed its consequences for economic efficiency as much or more than abstract ethical considerations.[66]

The party and regime view this spirit with some disquiet. While the precepts of the "Economic System of Socialism" stress the need for rationalization and realism in the economic process, there is a

---

[65] Marion Gräfin Dönhoff, Rudolf Walter Leonhardt, and Theo Sommer, *Reise in ein fernes Land* (Hamburg: Die Zeit Bücher, 1964), pp. 33ff., 115, and *passim;* Hans Apel, *Ohne Begleiter, passim;* Smith, *Germany Beyond the Wall,* pp. 63, 99–100; Hangen, *The Muted Revolution,* pp. 84–90, 98–100; interviews.
[66] *Intelligenzschicht,* III, 77, 91–94, 100, 191.

deep fear of what is termed "practicism." Herber and Jung, in the leading DDR textbook on cadre building, repeatedly return to the denunciation of this cardinal sin of economic leadership.[67] They view it as an excessive emphasis on fulfilling day-to-day production goals at the expense of a broader concern with overall societal development and the "perspectives" of economic modernization. When Korn and Weigelt similarly denounce those "practical people" for whom "mere functioning is more important than creative change," they doubtless have hold of a genuine problem among some sectors of the intelligentsia.[68] But there is little doubt that the vigorous attacks on "practicism" are inspired by the fear that attention to ideological principles and, hence, adherence to them will suffer. For if the pragmatism of the technical intelligentsia admits of any short summary statement, it would have to be described as a preoccupation with economic results, even at the expense of political and ideological considerations. Fred Oelssner, before being purged and in the process, ironically, of denouncing Fritz Behrens, once wrote that "the Plan is not an icon, which one can only pray to, but an instrument of our economic policy." [69] The fear of the party is that the "practicists" will come to view Marxism-Leninism as a meaningless icon without relevance to economic policy.

The consequences of the pragmatic spirit are several. One is a great impatience with oppressive bureaucratic requirements and with petty regulation from above by administrators of doubtful technical competence. Since the struggle against "bureaucratism" is one of the recurring themes of the ideology, complaints about it from members of the technical intelligentsia frequently find their way into the party press,[70] and economic functionaries are praised for eliminating superfluous paperwork and jobs.[71] The Infratest intelligentsia complained about the lack of technical qualifications ("catastrophic") on the part of middle and lower ad-

---

[67] Richard Herber and Herbert Jung, *Wissenschaftliche Leitung und Entwicklung der Kader* ([Berlin]: Staatsverlag der DDR, [1964]), pp. 87, 103, 154, 183, 191.

[68] Klaus Korn and Werner Weigelt, "Was 100 000 Ingenieure leisten könnten," *Forum*, No. 7 (1963), pp. 3–4.

[69] Fred Oelssner, "Staat und Ökonomie in der Übergangsperiode," *Wirtschaftswissenschaft*, V (April–May 1957), 327.

[70] See, for example, Korn and Weigelt, *op. cit.*, p. 5.

[71] See "Dr. Karl-Heinz Klein," *Die Wirtschaft* (October 28, 1963), p. 21.

ministrative personnel with whom they had to deal and felt these
were "ideologically overzealous" and followed all directives from
above "to the letter" and without flexibility.[72] A pro-regime economics student complained to Hans Apel that "many of our best
specialists were virtually forced to flight when incapable functionaries were put over them." [73] The antibureaucratic animus on a
higher level is well illustrated by Schenk's account of Bruno
Leuschner's method of handling a large backlog of "urgent" communications to the State Planning Commission:

> Leuschner took every item in hand, glanced over it, and ripped most
> of them in half. Then he gave the pieces to the secretary and said:
> "Just look again to make sure there are no classified documents in
> between, otherwise rip them up some more and put them in the
> paper shredder." . . . Of the approximately one hundred letter
> files I had put before him on the table, he kept at most ten that he
> found worthy of an answer.[74]

As this example suggests, a second characteristic of technocratic
pragmatism is a willingness to go outside channels and, if necessary, to break the rules and even the law in order to accomplish
economic ends. Sometimes, of course, such behavior is unavoidable if the plan is to be fulfilled.[75] Korn and Weigelt complain
that many young engineers quickly learn to accept the maxim,
"You don't usually get anywhere on a straight road. You get to
your goal only by many tortuous detours." [76] On the other hand,
Sonntag quotes with evident approval SED member Dr. Blume's
account of how he put together a vital apparatus for the Leuna
plant:

> That too we could only do half-legally. Here we got something on
> the black market, there we overlooked an inventory number. Sub-
> stantively, we were doubtless right, but taken literally we were guilty

[72] *Intelligenzschicht*, III, 138–142. Forty-six percent of the interviewees regarded
the work of the lower administrators as "poor, inadequate," twice as many as had
positive judgments.

[73] Hans Apel, *op. cit.*, p. 174.

[74] Fritz Schenk, *Im Vorzimmer der Diktatur* (Köln: Kiepenheuer & Witsch, 1962),
pp. 126–127.

[75] See Joachim Schultz, *Der Funktionär in der Einheitspartei* (Stuttgart and Düsseldorf: Ring Verlag, 1956), p. 162; on the same phenomenon in the USSR see Joseph
Berliner, *Factory and Manager in the USSR* (Cambridge: Harvard University Press,
1957), esp. Chaps. 6–11.

[76] Korn and Weigelt, *op. cit.*, p. 5.

of some transgressions. . . . One way or the other, what kind of socialists would we be if we had permitted the new equipment in Schwedt to produce only 1.3 liters of gasoline when we know it can produce two liters? [77]

A third element of the technical intelligentsia's pragmatism is its urging that ideology not be made dogma and that it be granted maximum flexibility in carrying out its tasks. One expression of this is an impatience with too much political interference in the work schedule, a matter which will be discussed at greater length below. Complaints are often leveled that economic functionaries who are SED members have a tendency to withdraw into their professional concerns and ignore their party responsibilities.[78] Günter Mittag, the SED secretary responsible for industry, has himself attacked the loss of production time due to "avoidable" meetings, mostly of the party and mass organizations, and pointed out that most "societal activities" should take place outside of working hours.[79] A related phenomenon is the attempt of factory functionaries to "capture" the plant's party organization in order to keep it from making trouble or, at least, to persuade the party secretary that his own interests require that he ally himself with them rather than maintain a hostile, controlling posture;[80] he becomes part of Berliner's "family circle" arrangements.[81]

While these elements of pragmatism or *Sachlichkeit* are shared in greater or lesser degree by the large majority of the technical intelligentsia, they are reflective of three quite distinct postures toward politics (excluding, for the moment, the oppositional posture, for whose advocates pragmatism might serve as a means of escape from political pressures). The first, which is also familiar to the West, is essentially that of the apolitical, the *Nurfachmänner* (the "professionals only"). "Not a few," complains Korn, "conceal

---

[77] Klaus Marschke, "Drei Begegnungen," *Sonntag* (January 13, 1963), p. 7. Schenk reports that high bureaucrats in the economic ministries sometimes clandestinely supplied the Planning Commission with technical arguments against their own minister's "political" decisions (*op. cit.*, p. 219).

[78] See, for example, Dahm, "Für ein enges Kampfbündis," *op. cit.*, pp. 40–41; also Schultz, *op. cit.*, p. 47; Ernst Richert, "Ulbricht and After," *Survey* (October 1966), pp. 156–157.

[79] Günter Mittag, discussion speech at 1963 Economic Conference, *Die Wirtschaft* (June 28, 1963), p. 28.

[80] See Schultz, *op. cit.*, pp. 159–160, and below, Chap. 4.

[81] Berliner, *op. cit.*, Chap. 15.

behind a loud 'on to practice' a silent 'away from theory.' . . .
How else can we interpret it when students of industrial economics
suggest that the study of Marx's *Capital* is no longer needed, and
certainly no special seminar on *Capital* is necessary? . . . So many
[students] confuse the university with a vocational training
school." [82] For the apolitical, the pragmatic outlook permits them
to immerse themselves in what they care about, their work, and to
ignore politics. Indeed, some argue that their work itself, in the
absence of any ideological understanding or interest, is a contribution to the building of socialism. [83]

The second group is equally disinterested in Marxism-Leninism
but has developed a more self-consciously technocratic view of the
world. They see the imperatives of the "second industrial revolution" as essentially the same, East or West, and the problems of
the DDR's industry and science as basically not different from
those under capitalism. [84] Thus, they are particularly willing to
follow Western examples and believe themselves capable of an
"objective" view of society not influenced by the class conflict or
the East-West struggle—in crass contradiction, of course, to the
Marxist view. [85] It would be thoroughly misleading to suggest that
"technocracy" is a well-articulated ideology in the DDR or that it
has a cohesive body of followers, but its principles seem clearly to
influence many members of the technical intelligentsia, even some
on the highest levels of power.

The predominant posture, however, of technical specialists
within the DDR's political elite, as well as many technicians on
lower levels, is the philosophy which found its incorporation in the
reforms of the New Economic System. Economic pragmatism is
viewed as a means to the success of socialism in the DDR. Such
men are loyal Communists but feel that the DDR's viability can

[82] Klaus Korn, "Was geziemt dem Bürokraten? Und was dem Wissenschaftler?"
Forum, No. 2 (1963), p. 2.
[83] Siegfried Schiemann, "Parteilichkeit und Wissenschaftlichkeit," in *Sozialismus
und Intelligenz,* p. 83.
[84] See, for example, Ulrich Abraham, "Die Bedeutung des neuen Charakters der
Arbeit im Sozialismus für das Bündis zwischen Arbeiterklasse und technischer Intelligenz," in *Sozialismus und Intelligenz,* p. 152. Jeremy R. Azrael identifies a similar
group in the Soviet Union but dismisses its political significance. *Managerial Power
and Soviet Politics* (Cambridge: Harvard University Press, 1966), pp. 154–157, 170–
171.
[85] See Dahm, *op. cit.,* p. 31.

only be maintained through a more flexible interpretation of the ideological verities governing economic policy and through a realistic acceptance of "economic facts." [86] As Theo Sommer puts it: "If the young managers, the socialist concern bosses, have one ambition above all others, then it is this: to contribute to making socialism function. They do not want to overthrow the system but perfect it, not to destroy its foundations but eliminate its inadequacies." [87]

What is significant is that men with these three quite different underlying rationales have found a common ground in the pragmatic outlook I have described. The critical question then becomes the extent to which this common outlook sufficiently bridges their differences to make some sort of common influence on policy possible. Self-conscious, unified action does not take place; those who, like a few university students in the FDJ, can be accused of even discussing the " 'leadership role' of an intelligentsia elite" [88] are the exception. The existence, however, of a common pragmatic, *sachlich* orientation does suggest that influence may be exerted in less conscious and unified ways, further, that the outlook of the technical intelligentsia at large may affect the behavior of its elite representatives. To investigate these problems, we must examine the political aspects of the technical intelligentsia's work situation and then its more overt political behavior.

[86] See, for example, Oelssner, "Staat und Ökonomie," pp. 326–327. Schenk (*Im Vorzimmer*, p. 114) remarks at one point that "Leuschner would like a liberalization of the system—which however must be initiated from Moscow in his view—in order to extend the influence of the SED to all of Germany."

[87] Dönhoff *et al., Reise,* p. 115.

[88] Wolfgang Herger and Hans Kleinschmidt, "Der 20. Jahrestag der SED und die FDJ an den Universitäten, Hoch- und Fachschulen," *Forum,* No. 3 (1966), reprinted in part in *SBZ-Archiv,* XVII, No. 5 (1966), 80.

4

INTELLIGENTSIA AND PARTY
IN THE WORKPLACE

I am not a member of the SED, but for seventeen years—since
I've been in this position—the relationship between the party
leadership and the plant managers, between the party leadership and myself, has grown steadily closer. We discuss all questions of fundamental importance, either the party secretary and
I, or in regular meetings every two weeks in which the party and
all other organizations and the managerial staff participate. I'm
no advocate of numerous, and especially not of long, meetings,
but here we talk about the basic issues. The district [Kreis]
party secretary is always aware of everything that happens in the
plant. However, the party does not interfere directly with the
leadership structure, the basic order of the plant, or the daily
routine. It steps in only insofar as special circumstances require
it or as is necessary for party activities. But we have no arbitrary
interference and never have. The party leadership knows that
the managers are fully responsible for the plant's work. And conversely the manager knows that in our state the party plays the
leading role.

JOHANNES NELLES, manager of VEB Chemical Works, Buna[1]

T HE POLITICAL role of the technical intelligentsia cannot be
entirely understood unless we examine the degree to which
political interventions color the atmosphere and conditions of its

---

[1] Johannes Nelles, "Zu einigen Fragen der Leitung eines sozialistischen Grossbetriebes," *Einheit*, XVII (September 1962), 36. In spite of Nelles' disclaimer of party
membership, it should be noted that he is a member of the Academy of Sciences,
vice chairman of the DDR's Research Council, a DDR representative to a COMECON
commission, and holds several state medals. *SBZ-Biographie* (Bonn and Berlin: Bundesministerium für gesamtdeutsche Fragen, 1964), p. 251.

work. Moreover, work relationships in individual factories and laboratories may adumbrate those on higher levels; officials who rise from either one of these to leading positions of responsibility in the state or party receive much of their political socialization here. If, for example, we can discover the existence of fundamental conflicts between different groupings on the shop or plant level, we might expect to find them reflected in some form on higher levels as well. My special concern will be with the relations between party and economic functionaries in the industrial enterprises. Just as the line between the functions of leading governmental officials and those of the party leadership is ill-defined and often shifting, the prerogatives of the factory director and the party secretary are not specified unambiguously, and the relationship between the two is subject to constant adjustment.[2]

ONE-MAN MANAGEMENT AND PARTY CONTROL

The ideological basis of the organization of authority in East German factories and administrative agencies is the Leninist principle of "one-man management."[3] Standing in sharp contrast to the principle of "collective leadership" which is supposed to govern the party,[4] "one-man management" is intended to serve the interests of economic efficiency and permit responsibility to be clearly fixed for success or failure. In the DDR the slogan has been variously invoked: against the efforts of over-ambitious party groups to take over management tasks themselves, against making two functionaries equally responsible for the same area of work, and in

[2] Otto Stammer sees the "social structure" of the DDR factory as the "basic framework" (*Kerngerüst*) for class relationships in the industrial sector of the entire society. "Sozialstruktur und System der Werthaltungen der Sowjetischen Besatzungszone Deutschlands," *Schmollers Jahrbuch für Gesetzgebung, Verwaltung und Volkswirtschaft*, LXXVI, No. 1 (1956), 74.

[3] *Politische Ökonomie des Sozialismus und ihre Anwendung in der DDR* (Berlin: Dietz Verlag, 1969), pp. 715–716. See also Reinhard Bendix, *Work and Authority in Industry* (New York: Harper Torchbooks, 1963), pp. 362ff.; Jerry F. Hough, *The Soviet Prefects* (Cambridge: Harvard University Press, 1969), pp. 80–86. Hough argues that in the Soviet Union the concept "has a much more limited meaning than the usual English translation would indicate" (p. 81).

[4] "Plant management as a collective leadership organ contradicts socialist leadership principles." S. Böhm, "Gibt es eine Werkleitung," summarized in *Die Wirtschaft* (June 10, 1963), p. 18.

justifying the broad authority granted the VVB directors under the New Economic System.[5]

Against the principle of "one-man management," however, must be placed the SED's pervasive powers of control in the interests of the "working masses" and the larger society and the proliferating devices intended to give the worker some sort of participatory role on the job. In practice, the manager's authority is subject to very real, if ill-defined, limitations. Perhaps most fundamentally, his prerogatives tend to lag behind his responsibility.[6] The priority assigned by the state plan to his industry for investment, the assignment of personnel, and material allocation; his dependence on the performance of other economic organs for supplies, sales, and so on; and the tendency of superior organs to issue detailed and inflexible directives all place limits on his freedom of action, which were only fleetingly mitigated by the New Economic System.[7] He is subject to a variety of controls within the plant itself, not only from its party unit but also from its trade union, his chief bookkeeper,[8] and the Workers' and Peasants' Inspectorate, the Soviet-inspired successor to the State Control Commission. The Inspectorate is both a party and a state instrumentality and includes within its ranks a strong "popular" element—workers, peasants, technicians, etc.—and representatives of the mass organizations, along with professional inspectors.[9] It was introduced in 1963

[5] See Erich Apel and Günter Mittag, *Wissenschaftliche Führungstätigkeit: Neue Rolle der VVB* (Berlin: Dietz Verlag, 1964), pp. 22–27.

[6] Two DDR authors report interviews with university and *Fachschule* graduates that revealed that some were reluctant to accept managerial positions on the grounds, among others, that "there was no congruence between the responsibility of the director and his powers." Rainer Falke and Hans Modrow, *Auswahl und Entwicklung von Führungskadern* (Berlin: Staatsverlag der DDR, 1967), p. 116. Bendix wrote in 1956 that "the principle that the responsibility of every executive official should exceed his authority" seemed to be a general one in the East German political system (*op. cit.*, pp. 353–354).

[7] See Günter Mittag, "Wir brauchen jetzt ein durchdachtes System der ökonomischen Leitung," *Die Wirtschaft* (January 28, 1963), p. 7.

[8] Under the NES the control function of the chief bookkeeper atrophied, and in some instances the position was abolished altogether. In 1970 the Politburo ordered its restoration as a control instrument. Günter Mittag, *Die Durchführung des Volkswirtschaftsplanes im Jahre 1970*, speech at Thirteenth Plenum of SED Central Committee (Berlin: Dietz Verlag, 1970), pp. 54–56.

[9] "Beschluss des ZK der SED und des Ministerrates der DDR über die Bildung der Arbeiter- und Bauerninspektion der Deutschen Demokratischen Republik," *Die Wirtschaft* (May 20, 1963), pp. 3–4. See also Peter Christian Ludz, *Parteielite im*

more or less simultaneously with the New Economic System and was perhaps intended as a check on it. The obligation to hold "production meetings" with the workers (generally under the aegis of the FDGB), seeking their advice before making any major decision and giving them a taste of participation in plant management, supplemented in 1963 and after by the creation of standing "production committees," provide additional limitations.[10]

One-man management, it is repeatedly insisted, may not be permitted to degenerate into *Managertum,* that is, autocratic leadership eschewing close consultation with the factory "collective," as represented by the party and the union. "In the socialist factory there is no directing stratum of managers standing opposite the directed mass of workers. Plant management and the plant collective work for the same goal. They have objectively common interests." [11] Any contradiction between managerial independence and party control is thereby verbally ruled out. In practice, official propaganda tends to emphasize first one, then the other, in what Bendix has described as "a kind of organizational simulation of the business cycle," [12] permitting the regime to exert pressures on whichever area appears under the conditions of the moment to require them.

The ostensible task of the basic party unit (*Grundorganisation*) and its secretary is to assist the manager in fulfilling his economic duties by mobilizing the work force for greater productivity; but also to exercise vigilance against mismanagement, to guard the interests of the larger society, and to make sure that central party directives are fully implemented.[13] Under NES the party was ex-

Wandel (Köln and Opladen: Westdeutscher Verlag, 1968), pp. 128–136. Cf. Paul Cocks, "The Rationalization of Party Control," in Chalmers Johnson, ed., *Change in Communist Systems* (Stanford: Stanford University Press, 1970), pp. 165–178.

[10] See Karl-Ernst Reuter, "VVB kontra Managertum," *Neues Deutschland* (hereafter cited as *ND*) (March 7, 1958), p. 3; Ludz, *op. cit.,* pp. 136–141.

[11] Rosemarie Pechman and Wolfgang Pechman, "Wie die Leitung—so die Leistung," *Forum,* No. 12 (1963), p. 16; *Einheit,* XXII, No. 6 (1967), 659ff., as cited in Eckart Förtsch, *Die SED* (Stuttgart: W. Kohlhammer Verlag, 1969), p. 65.

[12] Reinhard Bendix, "The Cultural and Political Setting of Economic Rationality in Western and Eastern Europe," in Gregory Grossman, ed., *Value and Plan* (Berkeley and Los Angeles: University of California Press, 1960), pp. 245–261; also Bendix's *Work and Authority,* pp. 380–381.

[13] See *Statut der Sozialistischen Einheitspartei Deutschlands* (Berlin: Dietz Verlag, 1968), paras. 57, 63. Bendix, *Work and Authority,* pp. 364–366; also Ernst Richert, *Macht ohne Mandat* (Köln and Opladen: Westdeutscher Verlag, 1963), pp. 49–50; Förtsch, *op. cit.,* pp. 45–46.

pected to be the "motor" behind the implementation of the new reforms and the promotion of technical and economic progress.[14] Ulbricht further instructed each party organization to set forth *"how and with what means* the highest scientific-technical level, the further increase of work productivity, the raising of quality and the lowering of costs can be attained in the plant or institute." [15] Should management resist the party's recommendations, however, the responsible party secretary was put in a quandary: Should he risk violating the one-man management principle when the alternative might be to share the blame for any plant losses or perhaps to be replaced for a failure of "vigilance"?

Herber and Jung distinguish the responsibilities of management, which is principally concerned with the direction of work, from those of the party secretary in this way: "A party secretary must have much more of an overview of political and economic relationships and be able to explain them to people in order to develop their socialist consciousness. . . . In this process he cannot confine himself to generalized agitation but must explain political and economic problems in the closest association with . . . concrete tasks in the relevant area of work." [16] This by no means implies, in theory, that each should remain exclusively in his own narrowly defined sphere, the manager confining himself to technical leadership and the secretary to political agitation. That is condemned as *Ressortwesen,* a practice which ignores the overall responsibility of the manager for the "socialist education" of those under him and the secretary's responsibility for production; the principle declaring the unity of ideology and economics may not be thus neglected.[17] Indeed, the party secretary has the right to take part in management meetings and to inspect the plant files while the plant director may participate in meetings of the party leadership.[18]

Given the somewhat unilluminating set of principles governing

[14] Richard Herber and Herbert Jung, *Wissenschaftliche Leitung und Entwicklung der Kader* ([Berlin]: Staatsverlag der Deutschen Demokratischen Republik, [1964]), p. 80.

[15] Cited in *ibid.,* p. 69; his italics.

[16] Herber and Jung, *ibid.,* pp. 237–238.

[17] Richard Herber, "Zur Leitung der Parteiarbeit nach dem Produktionsprinzip," *Einheit,* XVIII (May 1963), 14.

[18] Hartmut Zimmerman, "Wandlungen der Leitungsstruktur des VEB in soziologischer Sicht," *Deutschland Archiv,* Sonderheft, III (October 1970), 108.

them, it is not surprising that in practice party-management relationships in the factories and other workplaces vary greatly. Numerous items in the official press provide evidence of conflicts
arising between the two, most notably the repeated injunctions
against party attempts to "take over" management functions. At a
Central Committee plenum in December 1964, Ulbricht reported
that there were "still tendencies for party organs and party functionaries . . . to take over state functions themselves" and warned
that in spite of the heightened importance of fulfilling economic
goals such encroachments could not be permitted.[19] Thirteen years
earlier the same complaint was already being made; the Politburo
felt obliged to tell party organs that they were not authorized "for
example, to countersign production directives." [20] In a 1962 case,
"impatient" party officials at Schwarze Pumpe had to be stopped
from assuming jobs they thought were being done inadequately by
economic functionaries and were instructed that their job was
rather to "educate" them "to do justice to their duties." [21] Party
pressures short of the outright usurpation of functions is often,
however, urged in the official press. In a discussion in the brown
coal industry it emerged that for some work directors "the control
of the party and the necessity of working together with the unions
was burdensome. In the BKW 'Friendship' in the Cottbus district
the party organization only succeeded in getting some comrade
economic functionaries to go into production to discuss the overcoming of existing difficulties with the miners by [imposing] direct
party assignments [on them]." [22] In 1958 Günter Mittag cited with
approval the refusal of a factory party group to support their manager's protest against the size of his plan quotas. "Together with
the planning activist group (*Aktiv*) of the factory, they considered
how production could be increased and made cheaper. . . . The

[19] Walter Ulbricht, *Antwort auf aktuelle politische und ökonomische Fragen* (Berlin: Dietz Verlag, 1964), pp. 20, 35; see also Kurt Hager, *Bericht des Politbüros an
die 7. Tagung des Zentralkomitees der SED* (Berlin: Dietz Verlag, 1964), p. 24, who
also complains of party units taking over trade union functions; Herber and Jung,
op. cit., pp. 76, 82–83, 96.

[20] Cited in Joachim Schultz, *Der Funktionär in der Einheitspartei* (Stuttgart and
Düsseldorf: Ring Verlag, 1956), p. 163, also p. 168.

[21] Rolf Franke, "Die Partei orientiert den Wettbewerb in 'Schwarze Pumpe' auf
Planerfüllung und Vorverlegung wichtiger Investtermine," *Die Wirtschaft* (January
10, 1963), p. 3.

[22] Reuter, "VVB kontra Managertum," *op. cit.*, p. 3.

. . . production workers, brigade members, and foremen in attendance spoke unanimously in favor of the high[er] targets . . . so that the manager had to correct his behavior." [23]

Probably a more common situation than open conflict between party and management is close cooperation, or even collusion, between them. The party secretary shares an interest with the managerial staff in maintaining a high level of output, for that is the most readily available measure of his performance. In addition to this affinity of interest, genuine personal sympathies may grow up between the plant manager and the secretary, particularly when the former is himself a more than nominal party member and the latter has been given some technical training. Often, as indicated by the epigraph heading this chapter, they consult closely and regularly together on principal matters of factory policy, and astute managers are fully aware of the usefulness of having the party organization work for and not against them. The regime views such collaboration with considerable disquiet, for it effectively undermines the party's control function.[24] Thus, it is not uncommon to read complaints about party and management officials making decisions in closed meetings excluding the mass of factory workers and functionaries or that the party has not maintained its vigilance and "tolerated" production failures.[25] It is probable, however, that the level of collusion is much higher in successful than unsuccessful enterprises since in the latter case close association with management loses its utility for the party functionary's career.

In other cases conflicts occur which cut across the lines of both party and managerial organization. Thus, young technicians may join a party organization in pressing demands on "conservative" senior managers,[26] or groups of party activists may find themselves

[23] Günter Mittag, "Die Aufgaben der Parteiorganisationen in den Vereinigungen Volkseigener Betriebe," *Einheit*, XIII (August 1958), 1140–1141.

[24] See Schultz, *op. cit.*, pp. 159–160, and the examples cited there. The classic exposition of these "family circle" relationships in Soviet industry is Joseph S. Berliner, *Factory and Manager in the USSR* (Cambridge: Harvard University Press, 1957).

[25] Albert Schnelzki, "Eng mit den Angehörigen der Intelligenz verbunden," *Neuer Weg*, XVIII, No. 1 (1963), 8; Reinicke, "Sozialistische Gemeinschaftsarbeit," *Die Wirtschaft* (May 6, 1963), p. 12; Walter Ulbricht, "Die nationale Mission der Deutschen Demokratischen Republik und das geistige Schaffen in unserem Staat," speech at 9th Plenum of SED Central Committee, *ND* (April 28, 1965), p. 6.

[26] See interview with party secretary Rüdiger, "Engere Zusammenarbeit der Parteiorganisationen mit der Kammer der Technik," *Die Wirtschaft* (May 6, 1963), p. 9.

opposed to the plant's party leadership. This was the case, for example, in a Magdeburg factory, where local newspapers supported a divisional (*Abteilung*) party organization in an attack on the technical director, backed for his part, evidently, by the central party leaders and the plant manager.[27]

The sociological characteristics of managers and party functionaries suggest some important differences between them. Müller's pre-Wall refugee study indicated that "technical" managers, including plant directors, technical directors, and production directors, were older, better educated, and more frequently of "bourgeois" origins than "political" managers, including party secretaries.[28] Even in 1969 only 31 percent of all officials of SED basic (including plant) units had completed a university or *Fachschule* education.[29] The age and education gap is compounded by a status gap: The available evidence strongly suggests that plant managers enjoy much greater prestige than party secretaries, who are almost entirely unpaid, part-time functionaries.[30]

The result is doubtless in some cases to facilitate the manager's keeping his party secretary subordinate and submissive; where the party secretary does interfere, however, the success of his intervention is dependent upon the support he receives from higher party organs. Such support is by no means assured, but the secretary's special access to information on the attitudes and grievances of employees provides him with an important weapon in such disputes.

One index of the significance of such differences, apart from reports of open conflict, is the testimony of the Infratest refugees on the building of informal groups in their places of work. A machine building engineer told his interviewer that "my colleagues held together, each according to whether they inclined toward the management group or the party leadership. Those supporting the managers were also members of the party. But there were no loud,

[27] Irene Thalberg, "Der Irrtum des Direktors," *Magdeburger Volksstimme* (April 15, 1964), p. 3.
[28] Karl Valentin Müller, *Die Manager in der Sowjetzone* (Köln and Opladen: Westdeutscher Verlag, 1962), pp. 22–23, 34, 45, 51, 53.
[29] "Qualifizierung der SED-Bezirksfunktionäre," *Deutschland Archiv*, III (January 1970), 106–107; see also Förtsch, *Die SED*, pp. 107–108.
[30] Hough, *The Soviet Prefects*, pp. 94–96, stresses a similar inequality of the manager-party secretary relationship in the Soviet Union.

vigorous arguments; it was more a secret solidarity." [31] In other cases groups divided along the lines of party members and non-members (31 percent of all cases). Where the members of the SED were a minority but had considerable power, they often held together; in other cases, the young intelligentsia, fresh from the *Hochschulen,* formed a distinguishable group. Other groups formed along essentially nonpolitical lines: between different divisions or institutes (29 percent) or between subordinates and superiors (29 percent). Altogether about two-thirds of the respondents reported on frictions between groups in their place of work, about half of them along (though not even then always exclusively) political lines.[32] More than half stressed that membership in the SED per se made little difference: "In so far as their professional knowledge didn't have any gaps they were treated as equal colleagues." [33] To be sure, there was a tendency to regard party members as a group as less capable professionally than non-members.[34] In other cases, the entire managerial group, whatever their political status, stood in solidarity against superior organs (for example, the VVB) or unreasonable regime demands.[35]

The Infratest data is from 1958 to 1959, long before the reforms of the New Economic System, and it seems plausible that a similar study today would reveal a further political blurring of group divisions. The broadened range of authority granted individual enterprises under NES was accompanied by a parallel expansion of the powers of the basic party units; yet there was no apparent increase in the level of manager-party conflict.[36] The reorganization of the SED on the "production principle," the growing num-

---

[31] *Die Intelligenzschicht in der Sowjetzone Deutschlands* (München: Infratest GmbH & Co., November 1960), mimeographed, I, 152 (hereafter cited as *Intelligenzschicht*).

[32] *Ibid.,* 152, 156–159.   [33] *Ibid.,* III, 156.

[34] *Ibid.,* I, 106, 115, 156. Müller (*op. cit.,* p. 71) found a very high negative correlation between evaluations of the competence of members of the technical intelligentsia by their colleagues, and evaluations of their political fervor. Infratest (*Intelligenzschicht,* I, 115) found a similar relationship between the evaluation of political engagement and professional competence of superiors. Among the activists, eighteen were rated favorably and twenty-two unfavorably; among the politically inactive, the numbers were thirty and three.

[35] *Intelligenzschicht,* I, 148–150. Altogether, 26 percent reported a "pronounced solidarity." Of the conflicts reported by the rest, 39 percent were said to be political, 40 percent personal, 35 percent professional, 34 percent financial, and 18 percent organizational; some were obviously more than one of these.

[36] Ludz, *Parteielite,* p. 69; Förtsch, *op. cit.,* p. 73.

ber of party functionaries provided a specialized technical education, and, above all, the concentration of party work itself on technological rationalization and development militated against any
classic confrontation between party "dogmatists" and managerial
"realists." The frequent subsequent criticism that party meetings
were often turned into mere "production discussions" [37] indeed
suggests an undesired degree of harmony; how much the post-NES
retrenchment will dissipate this spirit remains to be seen. If the
party secretary and the plant manager can in some sense be said
to be prototypes, they are prototypes of cooperation as well as conflict, of training and political commitments that may be similar
as often as they are divergent.

POLITICAL INCURSIONS AT THE WORKPLACE

Beyond the dimension of personal and group conflict, there is the
question of the extent to which political requirements interfere
with the normal conduct of work and, thereby, help create a common set of perceived interests which can provide a motivation for
the technical intelligentsia to try to influence political decisions
themselves. The economic functionary is at least nominally expected to be a political and ideological leader as well: "He is no
administrator of objects, he also cannot be only a technician, he is
leader of a collective of human beings . . . their educator and
guardian (*Betreuer*)." [38] The manager is not to leave ideological
duties to his party secretary, any more than the secretary is justified in ignoring the factory's economic development. However,
practice may not match theory here; frequent official complaints
suggest that many managers do in practice ignore their agitational
obligations.[39]

[37] Horst Dohlus, "Die Erhöhung der Kampfkraft unserer marxistisch-leninistischen
Partei," *Einheit*, XXVI, No. 1 (1971), 12; "Mitgliederversammlung—inhaltsreich und
erzieherisch," *Neuer Weg*, XXVI, No. 2 (1971), 52.

[38] Gerhard Fritsch, "Der junge Leiter," *Forum*, No. 8 (1963), p. 1. See also Chap.
5 below.

[39] A DDR study shows plant directors rated "social-moral posture" only sixth
among the necessary qualities of a manager; subordinate managers ranked it eighth.
Falke and Modrow remark that this finding demonstrates the persistence among part
of this group of a "false conception of a division of labor between the plant director,
his collective, and the party leadership" (*Auswahl*, pp. 64–66).

It is apparently not as easy to avoid the numerous meetings with party officials, union representatives, activists, innovators, brigades, research groups, and sometimes the entire work force; their frequency has inspired the term "Sitzungswesen" to describe the situation of the manager who spends more time "sitting" at such affairs than performing his substantive duties. "The day's schedule in the plant," says a chief technologist, "consists . . . to a large extent of meetings and discussions. I have little chance to visit the workshops which is supposed to be my main job." [40] The technical intelligentsia similarly regard with distaste the numerous forms and reports required of them by various superior and controlling authorities, for those too keep them away from other work; more generally they object to overly detailed and bureaucratic direction from above.[41] "Many comrades active in the economy," said Mittag at the outset of the New Economic System, "talk about having their activities prescribed up to the last detail by their respective superior organs, about having too little authority to decide questions on their own responsibility." [42] Although "bureaucratism" remained one of the principal verbal targets of NES, it resisted most of the efforts to tame it. When the reform program was gradually liquidated at the end of the decade, new paperwork requirements and demands for detailed bureaucratic supervision again proliferated.[43]

The expanding number of mechanisms intended to permit workers some forms of participation in management, planning, research and technical innovation is sometimes another source of

[40] "Wunschtraum eines Ingenieurs," *Sonntag* (June 24, 1962), p. 5.

[41] See the objections discussed in Walter Ulbricht, "Probleme des Perspektivplanes bis 1970," speech at Eleventh Central Committee Plenum, *ND* (December 18, 1965), reprinted in part in *SBZ-Archiv*, XVII, No. 3 (1966), 47. It is worth noting, however, that the majority of the Infratest refugee intelligentsia, interviewed some years before the introduction of NES, described their own prerogatives as "normal," "fully sufficient," or "average." Moreover, the technical-economic respondents reported that objections could be filed against directives from above with some hope of success; criticism, if confined to technical and professional questions, was not only permitted but was an expected part of operations. Several added that it was, nevertheless, important to know the "rules of the game" and not to criticize decisions once they were finally made. *Intelligenzschicht*, I, 137–140, 164–169.

[42] Mittag, "Wir brauchen," p. 6; see also Nelles, "Zu einigen Fragen," p. 36.

[43] See, for example, Heinz-Werner Hübner, "Wie erreichen wir eine höhere Stabilität des Volkswirtschaftsplanes 1971?" *Die Wirtschaft* (January 27, 1971), pp. 4–5.

friction for the technical intelligentsia although it may also provide channels for younger technicians to influence senior management. To begin with, the difficulty of establishing relationships of mutual trust and respect between workers and intelligentsia has troubled the SED since the establishment of the DDR. For the workers' part, the most acute grievance has been the special treatment and generous pay provided the technical intelligentsia in a putative workers' state. In 1953 Rudolf Herrnstadt defended these privileges in a post-uprising factory discussion against a "declared hostility toward the intelligentsia" on the part of his listeners.[44] In 1956 the Infratest study of refugee workers revealed that 45 percent took a "critical position" toward the intelligentsia and regarded them as overpaid while 28 percent expressed still more intense feelings of "strong aggression" (N = 69).[45] There is some reason to believe that relations have since improved, but even in 1965 a DDR sociologist found that 80 percent of the workers surveyed in a Berlin plant (N = 114) regarded the existing form of payment as "unjust," in part because the "technologists and scientists" were responsible for waste, whose costs were deducted from the workers', but not their own, paychecks.[46]

In official publications the intelligentsia often finds itself accused of an "arrogance" toward the workers "handed down from the past," a refusal to recognize the "decisive role of the popular masses" in the DDR, and a tendency to inhibit the "initiative, the creativity, and the application of the rich work experiences and capabilities" of the proletariat.[47] "Even some technologists coming from the working class," it is charged, "close themselves off from the workers, give excessive emphasis to their [own] work, and display a certain tendency to minimize the performance of the workers." [48] Of the seventy-one Infratest workers responding, fifty-two

[44] *ND* (June 26, 1953), p. 3.
[45] Viggo Graf Blücher, *Industriearbeiterschaft in der Sowjetzone* (Stuttgart: Ferdinand Enke Verlag, 1959), p. 27.
[46] Peter Armélin, "Zur Problematik des Betriebsklimas—Ergebnisse einer industriesoziologischen Untersuchung," *Wirtschaftswissenschaft*, XIII (February 1965), 246.
[47] Erich Dahm, "Für ein enges Kampfbündnis der Arbeiterklasse mit der wissenschaftlich-technischen Intelligenz beim sozialistischen Aufbau der Deutschen Demokratischen Republik," in *Sozialismus und Intelligenz* (Berlin: Dietz Verlag, 1960), p. 32.
[48] Ulrich Abraham, "Die Bedeutung des neuen Charakters der Arbeit im Sozialismus für das Bündis zwischen Arbeiterklasse und technischer Intelligenz," in *Sozialismus und Intelligenz*, p. 153.

agreed: "The ones who rise up don't look at the workers any more."[49]

Worker participation in DDR factories has been given growing ideological emphasis in the past several years as the realization of socialist democracy in the most fundamental social arena, the workplace. The principle of one-man management is supplemented (though not, it is insisted, weakened) by the requirement imposed on the director for "collective consultation" with plant personnel.[50] This obligation has been institutionalized in several forms. *Produktionsberatungen,* modeled after the Soviet Union's permanent productivity councils, were introduced under FDGB auspices in 1958 with the purpose of permitting worker discussion of changes in the work processes, planning, and the like. According to the Infratest intellectuals, truly open discussion in them was rare and their success limited.[51] Beginning in 1963 they were replaced in large factories by "Production Committees," headed by the party secretary and ostensibly including representatives of the workers, technicians, managers, and mass organizations. The committees were frankly conceived as control as well as advisory bodies, and the director was "obliged to examine [their] recommendations or standpoints, to take account of them in [his] decisions, and report differing opinions to higher organs for resolution."[52] They appear to have provided younger members of the plant intelligentsia a significant opportunity for criticism and consultation in the making of management policy, but efforts by committees to extend their powers to the issuance of directives were sharply rejected as an encroachment on the director's prerogatives.[53] In 1972 the committees were (apparently) dissolved in favor of an

[49] Blücher, *op. cit.,* pp. 25–26. See also Irmhild Rudolph and Erhard Stölting, "Soziale Beziehungen im VEB im Spiegel betriebssoziologischer Forschung in der DDR," *Deutschland Archiv,* Sonderheft, III (October 1970), 115–116.

[50] *Politische Ökonomie,* p. 715.

[51] Werner Scholz, "Die Bedeutung des Gesetzes über die Vervollkommnung und Vereinfachung der Arbeit des Staatsapparates für die Entwicklung und Festigung sozialistischer Beziehungen zwischen der Arbeiterklasse und der Intelligenz," in *Sozialismus und Intelligenz,* p. 206; *A bis Z* (Bonn: Deutscher Bundes-Verlag, 1969), p. 497; *Intelligenzschicht,* I, 163–164; Hartmut Zimmermann, "Der FDGB als Massenorganisation und seine Aufgaben bei der Erfüllung der betrieblichen Wirtschaftspläne," in Peter Christian Ludz, ed., *Studien und Materialien zur Soziologie der DDR* (Köln and Opladen: Westdeutscher Verlag, 1964), pp. 137, 144, fn. 73; Rudolf Becker, "Die sozialökonomische Funktion der Produktionsberatungen," in *ibid.,* pp. 169–186.

[52] *Politische Ökonomie,* pp. 718–719; *A bis Z,* p. 498; Ludz, *Parteielite,* pp. 136–141.

[53] Zimmermann, "Wandlungen," pp. 106–107.

expanded emphasis on similar control and consultation activities by the trade unions.[54]

Several forms of worker participation are included under the intensively propagated ideal of "socialist cooperative work" (*sozialistische Gemeinschaftsarbeit*). Most of them are expected to bring together production workers and technical intelligentsia and thus facilitate the gradual merging of physical and mental labor promised by the ideology. They include scientific research cooperatives, "innovator" (*Neuerer*) collectives, and "brigades of socialist labor." *Sozialistische Gemeinschaftsarbeit* is regarded as the "most effective form of societal work in socialism" and is expected to support the development of the "socialist collective spirit" and the socialist personality.[55]

The primary purpose of the research cooperatives is to promote the joint development of scientific and technological improvements applicable to production in the plant. At the same time, they are to help the intelligentsia acquire an understanding of the leading role of the working class and its party and to achieve a "new relationship to physical work"; workers, for their part, are to be qualified for new jobs emerging from the rationalization and modernization of industry. In some cases, however, the technical intelligentsia resists this form of cooperation ("in the last analysis, individual research is really more effective than cooperative work"[56]) or sees it as being no different from capitalist "teamwork."[57] More frequently, the participation of ordinary production workers is seen as a burden; they do not have sufficient technical knowledge, it is suggested, to be of any use.[58] In one chemical

---

[54] See, for example, Herbert Warnke, "Gewerkschaften—im Arbeiterleben verwurzelt," *Einheit*, XXVII, No. 7 (1972), 862.

[55] *Wörterbuch der Marxistisch-Leninistischen Soziologie* (Berlin: Dietz Verlag, 1969), pp. 138–139; *Politische Ökonomie*, pp. 720–721; Kurt Lungwitz, *Über die Klassenstruktur in der Deutschen Demokratischen Republik* (Berlin: Verlag Die Wirtschaft, 1962), pp. 121–124; Horst Taubert, "Die sozialistische Gemeinschaftsarbeit als eine höhere Stufe des Bündnisses zwischen Arbeiterklasse und technischer Intelligenz," in *Sozialismus und Intelligenz*, pp. 159–186.

[56] Harald Wessel and Manfred Vorwerg, "Die Führungskraft im Kollektiv," *Forum*, No. 6 (1963), p. 4.

[57] Taubert, *op. cit.*, pp. 173–174.

[58] *Ibid.*, p. 178. After criticizing this view, however, Taubert adds that "it is not a matter—as many party organizations have interpreted it—of securing a numerical majority of workers in the cooperatives" (*Ibid.*, p. 180). See also Rudi Weidig, "Soziologische Probleme der Leitung der sozialistischen Gemeinschaftsarbeit in Industriebetrieben," *Wirtschaftswissenschaft*, XVI (July 1968), 1069–1084, reprinted in

plant, a 1963 article complained, only a single worker was active in *six* cooperative work groups.[59] Elsewhere, the workers are relegated to a secondary role: "The scientists concern themselves, so to speak, with how the plant will be completely automated in the future, and the workers discuss how the culture room in this plant will look." [60] Sociological research in the DDR suggests that the cooperatives have been more successful in dealing with concrete organizational and technical problems than as devices of political socialization or expressions of participatory democracy.[61]

The *Neuerer* movement is intended to encourage workers to devise improvements in their work processes and, equally important, to create a group of socialist models for their fellows to emulate. There is some evidence that economic functionaries and engineers dislike the movement, feeling that it produces conflicts and extra paperwork, and that the economic costs of the "innovations" often exceed their benefits.[62] The regime, however, claims that utilized *Neuerer* proposals now save the economy some 2 billion marks annually,[63] quite apart from the strengthening of morale and identification with official economic goals.

Additional burdens imposed on management in the name of socialist democracy are the obligatory annual discussions of the economic plan[64] and the monthly report on the state of plant operations which managers are required to present to their employees or their representatives. This *Rechenschaftsablegung*—literally, the rendering of an accounting—may in practice be transformed by the manager into an exhortation to his underlings for better

Peter Christian Ludz, ed., *Soziologie und Marxismus in der Deutschen Demokratischen Republik* (Neuwied and Berlin: Luchterhand, 1972), II, 174–175.

[59] Reinicke, "Sozialistische," *op. cit.*, p. 12.

[60] Paul Liehmann, "Arbeiterklasse und Intelligenz," in *Der Staat sind wir* (Berlin: Dietz Verlag, 1960), p. 102.

[61] Rudolph and Stölting, "Soziale Beziehungen," pp. 117–118; Weidig, *op. cit.*, p. 184.

[62] See, for example, Erich Zimmermann, "Neuerer und sozialistische Rationalisierung," *Die Wirtschaft* (February 4, 1963), pp. 10–11; also Hartmut Zimmermann, "Der FDGB," p. 135.

[63] *Statistisches Jahrbuch der Deutschen Demokratischen Republik 1970* (Berlin: Staatsverlag der DDR, 1970), p. 71.

[64] The discussion of the plan takes place in a number of organs: the production committees and lower level production advisory councils, brigades, trade union groups, etc. *Politische Ökonomie*, p. 715. See also Becker, "Die sozialökonomische Funktion," *op. cit.*; Richert, *Macht ohne Mandat*, pp. 123–124.

performance.[65] In general, it can be said that none of the DDR's devices of workplace participation provide ordinary employees a role in management decisions approaching that afforded by the Yugoslav workers' councils. Their role, rather, remains advisory and somewhat ritualistic, apart from the socialization, control, and mobilization functions they may serve. From the managers' point of view they may make some contribution to plant morale, but otherwise are time-consuming and a potential source of pressures and conflict.

In similar ways, the various requirements in DDR education for "practical experience" in industry may be felt to interfere with the work process. While the technical intelligentsia largely support the principle of polytechnical instruction, they often view the weekly "day in production" of high school students as an irritating disruption of normal factory routine.[66] In some cases, the students are disposed of by being assigned to routine jobs as supplementary labor; female students in a Teltow factory, for example, filed and bored disks for a year; "they learned nothing about the meaning and value of their work." [67] Other periodic party campaigns, for example on behalf of increases in work productivity,[68] may also be negatively received. An earlier source of dispute was the attempt to introduce Soviet methods arbitrarily even into factories where more advanced techniques were already in use.[69]

[65] Werner Bönisch, "Rechenschaftslegung in Torgelow," *Die Wirtschaft* (June 9, 1971), p. 12.

[66] Ernst Richert, *"Sozialistische Universität"* (Berlin: Colloquium Verlag, 1967), p. 205; *Intelligenzschicht*, III, 181–182; Arthur M. Hanhardt, Jr., "Political Socialization in the German Democratic Republic II," paper delivered at 1972 meeting of the American Political Science Association, p. 31.

[67] S. Neumann, "Ist der Nachwuchs ein Stiefkind?" *Die Wirtschaft* (April 29, 1963), p. 24; also see Herber and Jung, *Wissenschaftliche*, p. 167.

[68] Ulbricht mentions the resistance of economic functionaries to such a campaign in his speech before the 1963 Economic Conference, "Das neue ökonomische System der Planung und Leitung der Volkswirtschaft in der Praxis," *Die Wirtschaft* (June 28, 1963), p. 13.

[69] See, for example, Fritz Schenk, *Im Vorzimmer der Diktatur* (Köln: Kiepenheuer & Witsch, 1962), pp. 49ff.; also Schultz, *Der Funktionär*, pp. 160–161. The most severe form of political interference, of course, is that familiar to us from the Stalin era in the USSR: the arrest or use of other severe sanctions against managers for "economic sabotage," which often was an act no more malicious than failing to fulfill the quota. A surprising 44 percent of the economic and technical intelligentsia (N = 24) among the Infratest refugees reported being subjected to "sharp" sanctions: party or administrative trials, the threat of arrest, and so on. Another 17 percent

PLACEMENT, TURNOVER, AND PLANT EGOISM

It remains to discuss briefly several other sources of dissatisfaction for the technical intelligentsia with possible political overtones. One recurring difficulty has been with the placement of the young intelligentsia after their graduation from the university or *Fachschule*. In spite of attempts at placement planning, it often happens that the young technicians and the factories choose each other somewhat arbitrarily. In consequence, an official spokesman complains, "there are factories where the young engineers are sitting on top of one another, although there is no place for them there while in others (for example, locally directed industry) there is an acute shortage of engineers." [70] Some graduates are given positions in a factory before it can be determined what the most appropriate place for them really is; others are "handed around" for years without receiving a regular post corresponding to their training and abilities. DDR studies indicate that as many as half of all new graduates feel their jobs are inferior to the level of their training, and that many of their tasks ought to be performed by auxiliary help. Still others are given important responsibilities and fail at them because they are left to themselves, without help from more experienced people. [71] We are already familiar with the additional

---

reported "minor" sanctions—demotion, salary cuts, *Bewährung* (probationary service), etc. *Intelligenzschicht*, II, 37, 44. The small size of the sample and the fact that several had become refugees precisely in order to escape these sanctions doubtless artificially inflates these figures. In the first years of the DDR, however, it was not uncommon for heavy fines to be imposed for violations of the plan; a 1945 Soviet Military Administration decree threatened prison sentences of up to fifteen years and even death for particularly severe cases. Alfred Leutwein [Siegfried Mampel], *Die "Technische Intelligenz" in der sowjetischen Besatzungszone* (Bonn: Bundesministerium für gesamtdeutsche Fragen, 1953), pp. 29–32, 55. Bendix cites a case in which officials "responsible" for a mining disaster were sentenced for from four to twelve years at hard labor even though the regime's "unremitting pressure" for higher production and its negligence in investigation deserved at least equal blame. *Work and Authority*, pp. 374–375. DDR law continues to provide severe penalties for "crimes against socialist property and against the economy" although it seeks to distinguish minor "mistakes" (*Verfehlungen*) from criminal acts. *A bis Z*, pp. 735–736. The fear of "economic sabotage" and the need for scapegoats for economic failure were, however, characteristic of a period when the regime was considerably less secure than it is today, and no similar cases of recent years have come to my attention.

[70] Klaus Korn and Werner Weigelt, "Was 100 000 Ingenieure leisten könnten," *Forum*, No. 7 (1963), p. 4.

[71] Herbert F. Wolf, "Zu einigen soziologischen Problemen der Vorbereitung von Ingenieurstudenten auf die Leitungstätigkeit im Betrieb," *Jugendforschung*, No. 15

complaint that young technicians may be intentionally kept down because their superiors fear for their own jobs.[72] Such situations can clearly lead to professional disillusionment and perhaps to political dissatisfaction.

A related problem is the high rate of turnover among the technical intelligentsia (as well as among other groups, including industrial workers). DDR law forbids one VEB from bidding for the services of staff members of another; more generally, "societal interest" is a legal justification for preventing individuals from switching their jobs. Nevertheless, loopholes can easily be found in practice, and *Fluktuation,* as it is called, between jobs thrives in the DDR. This phenomenon is of great concern to the regime, which complains that functionaries barely have time to become acquainted with the particular problems and needs of one plant before moving on to another.[73] Accordingly, it has busied itself with sociological studies of the problem and offers "loyalty premiums" of 5 and 8 percent to those technicians, managers, and scientists who remain on the same job for two or five years.[74] The causes of high turnover are probably less widespread job dissatisfaction, though surely for some it is a method of escaping political and other work pressures, than such factors as the rapid development of new jobs in the DDR, the considerable wage differentials between different industries, and shortages of qualified personnel in some areas (although, to repeat, many categories of younger intelligentsia are in oversupply). Aside from what dissatisfactions are either reflected or produced by high turnover, it should be noted that it in part offsets the isolation of the intelligentsia by

---

(1970), pp. 31–39; Gerhard Schellenberger, "Soziologische Untersuchung der Einsatzbedingungen von Hoch- und Fachschulabsolventen," *Wirtschaftswissenschaft,* XVI (September 1968), 1477–1493, reprinted in Ludz, ed., *Soziologie und Marxismus,* II, 136–140. For similar problems in the Soviet Union see Albert Parry, *The New Class Divided* (New York: Macmillan, 1966), p. 253.

[72] Ulbricht, "Das neue ökonomische System," p. 20. Regime spokesmen commonly appeal for the "bolder" advancement of the young cadres: see Herber and Jung, *op. cit.,* pp. 204ff.; Günter Mittag, "Für ein festes Bündnis mit der Intelligenz," *Neuer Weg,* XIV, No. 19 (1959), 1253–1254.

[73] Falke and Modrow, *Auswahl,* pp. 38–111. Herbert F. Wolf, *op. cit.,* p. 33; Nelles, "Zu einigen Fragen," pp. 29–30; Herber and Jung, *Wissenschaftliche,* p. 215; Müller, *Die Manager,* p. 55; interview. The same problem has troubled the Soviet leadership. See David Granick, *The Red Executive* (Garden City, N.Y.: Anchor Books, 1961), pp. 112–115.

[74] *Tribüne* (July 16, 1965), p. 6.

bringing them into contact with different colleagues and work situations in the DDR.

Turnover among managerial personnel may also reflect the heavy work burden imposed on them. DDR studies estimate the average work week of the factory director to be between sixty and seventy hours.[75] As much as two-thirds of the time of top managers may be occupied by meetings and diverse unscheduled "intrusions" by external agencies and other plant functionaries.[76] In addition to their professional responsibilities and the paper work these require, the managers are expected by the regime to devote a good deal of time to cadre work and also to assume "voluntary" political and "societal" positions—in the party or FDGB, the *Kammer der Technik*, factory academies, the Society for Soviet-German Friendship, and so on. The seven top managers of a VEB investigated by an East German researcher occupied an average of four such positions and spent an average of over seven hours per week on the duties they required.[77] The result is what one manager calls a "hectic busyness" with long hours of overtime and little opportunity to reflect on anything but the immediate problems of the job.[78] In consequence, long-term "perspectives," so dear to the regime, are neglected; on the other hand, there is also little time to indulge in political reflection.

In the light of all this, the surprising fact that most of the DDR intelligentsia still regard the general atmosphere of their place of work as "good" should be stressed. Visitors to DDR factories often remark on the "collegial tone" among the intelligentsia and even between intelligentsia and workers.[79] There are, of course, many

[75] Hartmut Zimmermann, "Wandlungen," p. 109; Günter Reimann, "Unmittelbare Zusammenhänge zwischen der Gestaltung des Arbeitsprozesses und der freien Zeit bei leitenden Mitarbeitern, dargestellt am Beispiel eines Volkseigenen Betriebes," in *Fragen der marxistischen Soziologie III* (Berlin: Humboldt Universität, 1968), 155–187, reprinted in Ludz, ed., *Soziologie und Marxismus*, II, 97–98.

[76] Reimann, *op. cit.*, pp. 95–97.

[77] *Ibid.*, p. 103. Two-thirds of the Infratest intelligentsia held an average of three such positions; those in the economic and technical intelligentsia also performed extracurricular research and development work. *Intelligenzschicht*, I, 67–68. Many of the respondents, nevertheless, spoke favorably of their extra activities which brought them both prestige and, sometimes, additional pay.

[78] Hermann Danz, "Was soll der Werkleiter tun?" *ND* (November 25, 1962), p. 4; also interview; "Wunschtraum," p. 5; Herber and Jung, *op. cit.*, p. 154. "The number of personnel who separate from their jobs for reasons of health between the ages of forty and fifty is relatively high" (Falke and Modrow, *op. cit.*, p. 33).

[79] Hans Apel, *Ohne Begleiter*, pp. 151, 163.

exceptions; an engineer interviewed in *Sonntag* remarked that
when the plan was not fulfilled, relations in his plant tended to
degenerate into a "war of all against all." [80] Engineers whom I interviewed described both "open drawer" and "closed drawer" situations, with the mark of mutual trust in the plant being the
willingness or unwillingness of engineers to leave their own projects in unlocked desks, open to the scrutiny of their colleagues or
rivals. Eighty-five percent of the Infratest refugee intelligentsia
viewed their work positively; they judged favorably their relations
to their co-workers and to their superiors, the quality of the work
performed, and their incomes. On the other hand, they judged
negatively their personal chances for advancement and their job
security—often on political grounds.[81] Yet the authors of the Infratest report conclude that for the majority, their work was not
"politically deformed." [82]

From the point of view of the regime, however, relations and
conditions within a given factory may be optimal, but it may still
be working at cross-purposes to the state and the plan. This is the
offense of "plant egoism," the attempt to satisfy the interests and
goals of the individual economic unit without regard to the
broader interests of the society.[83] This is hardly an unnatural tendency, but it is significant for our purposes in that the regime regards it as an apolitical or even antipolitical posture; the man who
as a plant manager follows "egoistic" policies might also single-
mindedly pursue his branch's special interests as a high functionary
in, say, the planning commission. To that extent the existence of
"factory egoism" betrays a failure to create the desired class of Red
experts who can balance political and professional interests. Plant
and, in particular, VVB egoism came under sharp attack at the
11th Central Committee Plenum in December 1965 by Ulbricht,
who blamed it for producing "disproportionalities" in economic
development. He noted that many VVBs employed "various tricks"
to get additional investment funds from the state, such as devoting
their resources to secondary projects in the expectation that the

---

[80] "Wunschtraum," *op. cit.*, p. 5.   [81] *Intelligenzschicht*, III, 26–27.
[82] *Ibid.*, I, 84, 99.
[83] "The self-responsibility of the plant has nothing in common with plant egoistic
thinking." Hans Winterfeld, "Einheitliche politisch-ideologische Arbeit im Kombinat," *Neuer Weg*, XXVI, No. 1 (1971), 26.

state would bail them out on the more vital ones.[84] Other supposed manifestations of plant egoism include attempts to get a lower plan in order to secure higher premiums,[85] the reluctance to delegate valued workers to university study,[86] efforts by plants to keep experienced technicians and scientists from taking jobs in the VVBs and higher administrative bodies,[87] hoarding materials to guard against slack days,[88] attempts to influence price revisions in the plant's or branch's own interest,[89] and resisting the terms of contracts with the VVB director which are supposed to regulate the factory's choice of projects, scale of production, supply, etc.[90] Perhaps the most persistent "egoism" charges, however, revolve around the inclination of managers to devote themselves to the immediate tasks of fulfilling production quotas rather than long-run development and modernization; it is often overlooked that in many cases this economic "conservatism" is inspired by the regime's own planning system.[91]

SCIENTIFIC RESEARCH: THE PRIORITY OF PRODUCTION

Up to this point this chapter has been concerned with conditions of work for the technical intelligentsia principally in the factories and VVBs. Many of the observations made here apply with equal force to other places of work—research institutes, economic administrative agencies, such as the planning commissions and ministries, and even the universities. But the special problems of the research scientists deserve some additional attention. In general, scientists, in comparison to factory-based personnel, appear to have enjoyed

---

[84] Ulbricht, "Probleme," reprinted in part in *SBZ-Archiv*, XVII, Nos. 1–2 (1966), 30. In 1963, he complained in similar terms about the tendency of "some managers" to reach limitlessly into the "state pot" for investment financing; "how [these funds] get into the pot concerns them little" ("Das neue ökonomische System," p. 8).

[85] Ulbricht, quoted in Hans-Dieter Schulz, "Die Hoffnung heisst 'Nöspl,'" *Die Zeit* (April 30, 1965), p. 36.

[86] Mittag, "Die Aufgaben," p. 1143.

[87] Ulbricht, "Das neue ökonomische System," p. 17.

[88] Richert, *Macht ohne Mandat*, p. 125.

[89] Alfred Neumann, *Der Volkswirtschaftsplan 1965 in der Industrie*, speech at Seventh Plenum of SED Central Committee (Berlin: Dietz Verlag, 1964), p. 18.

[90] Wolfgang Lungershausen, discussion contribution to 1963 Economic Conference, *Die Wirtschaft* (June 28, 1963), p. 24.

[91] See Apel and Mittag, *Wissenschaftliche Führungstätigkeit*, pp. 110–111, 114; Hager, *Bericht*, p. 12. On similar "technical conservatism" in the USSR, see Wolfgang Leonhard, *The Kremlin Since Stalin* (New York: Praeger, 1962), p. 343.

equal or greater freedom from political intervention. In recent years, however, the growing insistence of the regime that science be integrated more closely with the critical sectors of the economy and thus made to serve demonstrably useful ends has been productive of some frictions.

"Every scientific project," the president of the *Kammer der Technik* has insisted, "has one criterion. What benefits does it provide for the strengthening of our DDR?" [92] To this end and to overcome the serious Balkanization of DDR science, the development of so-called "Major Research Centers" was undertaken by the regime; in the course of 1970 some 28 percent of scientific university and *Fachschule* graduates were expected to be active in them.[93] The centers were apparently intended to be a scientific counterpart to the industrial VVBs. In them the responsibility of the scientist was to "extend from the scientific research to its transference into production to its productive use." [94] The centers, however, were not referred to at or after the Eighth Party Congress following the removal of Ulbricht, and their present status is uncertain.

There seems little question that basic research in the DDR has suffered from the long emphasis on the rapid application of scientific work to production, in spite of regime protestations to the contrary. The extent of financial dependence of research on contractual arrangements (*Vertragsforschung*) with economic enterprises and other state agencies and the payment of premiums to scientists based on the speed of introduction and the usefulness of their work in production have furthered this tendency. After the Eight Congress, university officials called for more "balanced" attention to basic research and argued that their institutions should resist demands of their economic "partners" to carry out "any sort

[92] Horst Peschel, "Der Beitrag der Kammer der Technik zur weiteren allseitigen Stärkung der Deutschen Demokratischen Republik," *Technische Gemeinschaft* (April 1970), p. 14. For similar, earlier sentiments see Walter Ulbricht, *Dem VI. Parteitag entgegen,* speech at second plenary meeting of DDR Research Council (Berlin: Dietz Verlag, 1962), pp. 108, 115; "Gesetz über das einheitliche sozialistische Bildungssystem," in *Unser Bildungssystem—wichtiger Schritt auf dem Wege zur gebildeten Nation* ([Berlin]: Kanzlei des Staatsrates der DDR, 1965), p. 122; Kurt Hager, "Partei und Wissenschaft," *Einheit,* XXI, No. 4 (1966), 439–450.

[93] Günther Prey, "Schlüsselproblem für Pionier- und Spitzenleistungen—Sozialistische Wissenschaftsorganisation," *Technische Gemeinschaft* (April 1970), pp. 26–27.

[94] Günter Schneider and Gerhard Krause, ". . . die man an ihre lebendige Arbeit erkennt," *Forum,* No. 13 (1970), p. 6.

of applied research in any desired quantity." [95] Nevertheless, since future economic growth in the DDR, with its shortages of labor and natural resources, is apt to depend heavily on technological innovation, the pressures for quickly utilizable science will likely continue, even if at a serious long-run cost.[96]

This account should make it evident that the DDR's technical intelligentsia works in an atmosphere profoundly conditioned by the political and ideological purposes of the regime. Yet it should be emphasized that the younger generation of East German technicians has never known things to be any different; the party, with its functions of basic policy making, personnel selection, and control is as accustomed a part of their professional environment as are stockholder and union pressures in the West. The institutions of worker participation, however burdensome to the technicians, are also hardly to be imagined away in a state claiming to be "socialist." These are the givens within which the technical intelligentsia is accustomed to act.

Nevertheless, it remains significant that the party, superior government organs, and factory institutions of participation do intervene more frequently and in greater detail in the work process than is customary in the West. Perhaps the most persistent and deeply felt complaint of the DDR's technical intelligentsia is that against "bureaucratism"—excessive paper work, meetings, and petty regulation from above. The New Economic System reforms promised a reduction of bureaucratism and a corresponding expansion of the prerogatives of economic specialists and managers. This was perhaps the element of NES that they welcomed with the greatest enthusiasm, and it is hard to imagine anything but deep resentment now that these expectations have been disappointed and the reforms suppressed.[97]

[95] Karl-Heinz Wirzberger, "Grundlagenforschung an der Universität schafft Bildungsvorlauf," *Das Hochschulwesen,* XIX (October 1971), 305–306.

[96] See Peter Christian Ludz, *The German Democratic Republic from the Sixties to the Seventies* ([Cambridge]: Harvard University Center for International Affairs, 1970), pp. 16–17.

[97] The suicide in 1971 of Arne Benary, the young economist who joined Fritz Behrens in his "revisionist" reform proposals of 1956 and then was sent into industry for "probationary service," has been attributed to his disappointment over the liquidation of the NES reforms. Christian Gerber, "Arne Benary," *Deutschland Archiv,* IV (November 1971), 1125–1126.

Common grievances enhance the perception of common interests, and undoubtedly the many forms of political intervention in the work process in the DDR contribute to the formation of the distinctive political attitudes and style I attributed to the technical intelligentsia in the preceding chapter. Those technicians and managers who move into positions of greater political importance are likely to use their influence as a conscious means of rectifying such professional dissatisfactions. Precisely because they must acquire a measure of political sophistication and group consciousness to perform their jobs successfully, they may indeed come to seek out political influence and thus gradually be drawn into an upward career path leading to the technical-political strategic elite.

Yet while the grievances of the technical intelligentsia at the workplace are numerous, they are not so acute as to inspire its members to radical opposition. By and large the problems are seen as limited and correctible and amenable to incremental strategies; there is no evidence that the great majority of the technical intelligentsia feel deep dissatisfaction with the conditions of their work. Above all, it must be repeated that the workplace is not an arena of dichotomous conflict between "party" and "managers." The intervention of the party, so far as one can judge from the outside, has become a thoroughly institutionalized and integrated component of East German industrial life; the specifics of its role may well change over time, but its continued presence is taken for granted.

5

PRINCIPLES AND MEANS
OF POLITICALIZATION

One day the blow-up came.

I was ordered to Walter Rehnert, the Party Secretary, who immediately put me under the gun.

"Today I read the report on your technical education and have the impression that you've developed well. The party leadership is interested in receiving similar reports on your societal work."

Why should I have lied?

I replied:

"I can't write such a report."

"Why not?"

"Because so far I've hardly attended any meetings."

"And you say that so baldly? As if you hadn't ever gone to the movies or hadn't once been in a theater?"

"I didn't do that either. Up to now I've had so many professional things to do I couldn't find a free minute for anything else."

"That's not possible. You have to have time for life. The party is our life. A comrade who doesn't participate in party work is dead, he doesn't exist."

FRITZ SCHENK[1]

COMMUNIST THEORY insists that "partyness" (*Parteilichkeit*) and scientificness constitute a "dialectical unity," that science can only have its true unfolding in a society governed according to the principles of Marxism-Leninism.[2] Hence, scientists and technicians who regard politics as being outside of their "objective" concerns err; even narrow specialists need a knowledge of

[1] Fritz Schenk, *Im Vorzimmer der Diktatur* (Köln: Kiepenheuer & Witsch, 1962), pp. 30–31.

[2] See Siegfried Schiemann, "Parteilichkeit und Wissenschaftlichkeit," in *Sozialismus und Intelligenz* (Berlin: Dietz Verlag, 1960), pp. 55–87; Horst Kramer, "Wissenschaft und Partei," in *Deutsche Zeitschrift für Philosophie*, XIV, No. 4 (1966), 434–449.

Marxist-Leninist principles in order to "better recognize the laws of social development and to be able to work . . . correspondingly in their own areas of specialization and thus consciously contribute to the effecting of objective laws." [3] Where members of the technical intelligentsia lead collectives of men, their political knowledge is particularly important; as state employees they are entrusted with a societal duty toward those they lead.[4] "It is not enough for them to adopt a positive attitude toward our state. If they are to fulfill their tasks adequately, they must possess deep insight into the nature and the development of our society and our state." [5]

Thus, the new intelligentsia is regarded as an appropriate and important object of politicalization in the principles of the ideology and in loyalty to the existing leadership and its policies. Yet, observers report with unusual unanimity—and many official and semi-official sources provide confirmation—that the technical intelligentsia in practice are subjected to substantially fewer indoctrination pressures than most other social groups and certainly fewer than any other elite group. The Infratest study of intellectuals produced many fewer reports of heavy ideological pressures among the economic-technical and scientific intelligentsia than among teachers and administrators; while those technicians and economists in the higher and more critical economic organs were subject to "strong" party influence, those in ordinary factories experienced "little." [6] Müller reports a "striking tolerance . . . toward the widely spread political indifference" of technical officials.[7] Regime spokesmen alternate between cautions

[3] Richard Herber and Herbert Jung, *Wissenschaftliche Leitung und Entwicklung der Kader* ([Berlin]: Staatsverlag der DDR, [1964]), p. 150. Ulbricht is quoted by the authors in support of the same principle.

[4] See *ibid.*, pp. 150–151; Rainer Falke and Hans Modrow, *Auswahl und Entwicklung von Führungskadern* (Berlin: Staatsverlag der DDR, 1967), pp. 64–67.

[5] Werner Scholz, "Die Bedeutung des Gesetzes über die Vervollkommnung und Vereinfachung der Arbeit des Staatsapparates für die Entwicklung und Festigung sozialistischer Beziehungen zwischen der Arbeiterklasse und der Intelligenz," in *Sozialismus und Intelligenz*, p. 192.

[6] *Die Intelligenzschicht in der Sowjetzone Deutschlands* (München: Infratest GmbH & Co., November 1960), mimeographed, I, 193–195 (hereafter cited as *Intelligenzschicht*). "In production proper," the authors conclude elsewhere, "the quality of personnel is not sacrificed for ideological faithfulness" (*ibid.*, p. 111).

[7] Karl Valentin Müller, *Die Manager in der Sowjetzone* (Köln and Opladen: Westdeutscher Verlag, 1962), p. 8.

against "overenthusiastic" agitation directed toward scientific and technical personnel [8] and complaints about their unconcern over politics and society.[9]

Politicalization pressures among the technical intelligentsia vary in response to several factors. Perhaps the most important of these is the vigor and dogmatism of the relevant party unit and its secretary and the kind of relationship built up between the party and the officials concerned—problems we explored in the previous chapter. More regularized differences in indoctrination levels may be observed between the old and new intelligentsia, between "pure" technical and political-technical jobs, and between lower- and higher-level positions. Of course, the political expectations to which members of the party are subject are greater than those placed on nonmembers.

Political conversion of members of the older technical intelligentsia is seen as an unpromising enterprise which may undermine their economic performance; it is the younger and presumably more malleable generation whose indoctrination is viewed as critical for the DDR's future. The utilitarianism of this approach has been frankly expressed by Kurt Hager:

> There are scientists, engineers, doctors, and other members of the old intelligentsia who are only specialists and wish to work in a spirit of professionalism without concerning themselves with new socio-political problems. The party of the working class and the worker and peasant state value and encourage the activity of the specialists and demand of them only that they work competently with us. But in the education of the young intelligentsia we must seek to make of every specialist a convinced supporter of socialism; for on the degree of his insight into societal relationships will depend in large measure his future position in life and the fruitfulness of his work.[10]

The distinction between old and new intelligentsia has not always

[8] Ulbricht in *Neues Deutschland* (hereafter cited as *ND*) (June 14, 1958); cited in Hans Reinhold, "Über die führende Rolle der Arbeiterklasse auf geistigem Gebiet," in *Sozialismus und Intelligenz*, pp. 106–107.

[9] Rudolf Bahroi, "Geistige Reserven, oder Was hemmt die Produktivität der jungen Naturwissenschaftler an unseren Hochschulen und Universitäten?" *Forum*, No. 18 (1963), p. 27.

[10] Kurt Hager, "Die Intelligenz und der V. Parteitag," *Einheit*, XIII (August 1958), 1126.

been observed in practice, as complaints over attempts to force training in Marxism-Leninism on the former make clear.[11] Generally, however, Ulbricht's injunction to demand "no conditions" of the older intelligentsia in political matters has been followed.[12]

The further distinction between those engaged solely in technical activities and those who combine technical and "political" (usually leadership) functions is reflected in the Infratest finding that while economic functionaries were often subject to explicitly political pressures sufficient to force their flight to the West, refugees in purely technical fields interviewed were more likely to have left for occupational reasons;[13] it also lends confirmation to Müller's *Zweigeleisigkeit* notion.[14] Since the direction of others is defined as a "political" task, it is not surprising that as the scope of authority of the economic functionary increases, so do the ideological expectations and hence the political demands upon him. The Sixth Party Congress's program demanded of leading economic cadres that they possess a "thorough knowledge of Marxism-Leninism, firm solidarity with the working class, love of people, and those traits of character which are necessary to build and lead a stable collective of employees."[15] Schenk observes that it was possible on the factory level to "entrench" oneself in technical expertise, but on the higher levels of economic administration, "only doctrine ruled."[16]

On all levels, however, spokesmen of the regime periodically emphasize that political indoctrination must be patient and tactful, stressing persuasion and eschewing force; the frequency of this injunction and the attacks on "sectarianism" that often accompany it are an indicator that such subtlety does not always obtain. "We seek to win all those for our way who are to be won," Hager said in an otherwise uncompromising speech at the 1958 universities conference; "and that, comrades, can be achieved only through

[11] See "Die Bedeutung der Intelligenz beim Aufbau des Sozialismus," *ND* (May 24, 1953), p. 4.

[12] Cited in *Intelligenzschicht*, III, 24.

[13] *Intelligenzschicht*, III, 17–19; also see Schenk, *Im Vorzimmer*, p. 43, where the distinction is between planning and purely technical positions. For a similar distinction, see *Svobodene Slovo* (Prague), March 21, 1965, quoted in Michael Gamarnikow, "The End of the Party Hack?" *East Europe* (November 1965), p. 7.

[14] See pp. 29–30.

[15] In Ulbricht, *Das Programm des Sozialismus und die geschichtliche Aufgabe der Sozialistischen Einheitspartei Deutschlands* (Berlin: Dietz Verlag, 1963), p. 343.

[16] Schenk, *op. cit.*, p. 103.

steady, patient, persistent daily work with these scholars, through discussion and the open conflict of views." [17] Ulbricht, in the "New Course" period of 1953, went so far as to assure scientists and scholars that "of course" it was permissible to defend scientific opinions not based on Marxism-Leninism: "[Ulbricht said that] every preconceived characterization of scholars is harmful. To be sure it would also do little harm for them thoroughly to study the society sciences. But force and pressure in this matter were always harmful." [18] Abuses on the part of lower functionaries of these calls to patience (owing in part to the regime's alternating calls to militance) continue, as a 1963 article makes clear: "However sharp the principled criticism of wrong or even ideologically hostile scientific ideas, it may never be imputed to the criticized that he himself is an enemy or that his intentions with us are not honest." [19] The ideal remains not "tutelage" but open and frank discussion in which the independent judgments of the intelligentsia are freely expressed.[20] But to reconcile such an ideal with the existence of an authoritative doctrine which it is believed must finally triumph demands a profound faith in the ability of "correct" ideas to drive out incorrect ones by the force of their own logic. Lower-ranking party agitators evidently often become too impatient or frustrated to maintain such faith.

THE MEANS OF POLITICALIZATION

Nevertheless, in the majority of cases politicalization of the technical intelligentsia on the job seems to be characterized by relative

[17] Kurt Hager, "Freie Bahn für die sozialistische Wissenschaft," *ND* (March 6, 1958), p. 6.

[18] *ND* (May 30, 1953), p. 4.

[19] G. Handel, "Über die Meinungsstreit in der Wissenschaft," *Forum*, No. 3 (1963), p. 9.

[20] "The intelligentsia must be given more opportunity than in the past to put forward their ideas and objections. We must enter upon a truly open conflict of opinion. In the past there were often signs of tutelage in discussions and conversations with the intelligentsia, and that awoke in many the impression that we wanted to deny them the capability of making independent judgments. It is not a matter of regimenting the members of the intelligentsia or taking their own thinking away from them. On the contrary, we want to have their personal responsibility and stimulate their initiative. . . . The discussions of comrade Walter Ulbricht with members of the intelligentsia are model examples of a candid and open exchange over basic question of our policies and ideology." Schiemann, "Parteilichkeit," *op. cit.*, p. 53.

laxity. The focus of the effort to produce a faithful corps of technical specialists is upon what might be termed "prepoliticalization"—the selection and education of the technological elite (discussed in Chapter 2). Growing research in the West has increased our awareness of the significance of childhood experiences in the formation of political convictions;[21] the East German regime, while ignoring no potential avenues for indoctrination, has effectively placed its major reliance upon the eventual dominance of a generation socialized politically solely under its own auspices. The integration of ideology with basic school subjects, the later introduction of specialized instruction in Marxism-Leninism, and the emphasis under the rubric of "polytechnical education" on practical experience in the factory (which, in Ulbricht's view, "secures an intense influence of the working class on the building of consciousness among the young")[22] are intended to insure the success of this purpose. The participation of the FDJ and the official trade union in selecting university and *Fachschule* students is meant—not fully successfully, as we have seen—to bar the way to the new elite for those of uncertain loyalties. The range of indoctrination techniques within higher education itself is supposed to reinforce and give some sophistication to earlier socialization. Finally, the control of the party over the placement of graduates in industry, the universities, and government[23] and, more particularly, its control over promotion through the "nomenclature" system administered by its cadre divisions[24] provide a filter intended to exclude those who give insufficient evidence of doctrinal purity.

In fact, the success of "prepoliticalization" has not been unqualified; the filter has been too gross to catch all the unconvinced and the underpersuaded. Thus, even were it not for the continued

[21] See, for example, Richard Dawson and Kenneth Prewitt, *Political Socialization* (Boston: Little, Brown, 1969), and the works cited therein; Arthur M. Hanhardt, Jr., "Political Socialization in the German Democratic Republic," paper delivered at 1970 meeting of the American Political Science Association.

[22] Ulbricht, *Das Programm*, p. 193.

[23] This process, called *Berufslenkung*, is primarily intended to match the number of graduates with the planned needs of the different sectors of the economy, but also offers opportunities for excluding the potentially disloyal from key industries and choosing the more dedicated for the equivalent of junior executive positions.

[24] See Joachim Schultz, *Der Funktionär in der Einheitspartei* (Stuttgart and Düsseldorf: Ring Verlag, 1956); Eckart Förtsch, *Die SED* (Stuttgart: W. Kohlhammer Verlag, 1969), pp. 76–83.

presence of many who were socialized under earlier German regimes, politicalization efforts in the factories and laboratories themselves would continue. Here the party and its mass organizations are expected to take the leading role. Party membership itself—and the responsibilities it entails—is increasingly a requisite of advancement as one moves up in the economic or bureaucratic structure. Administrative agencies sometimes demand not only party membership but the successful completion of studies in a party school;[25] in the factories it is quite possible for second-line managerial personnel to remain outside of the party, but most higher officials are members. Müller provides us with comparative figures on the salaries of members and nonmembers in the late 1950s; the latter were virtually excluded from the highest salary group (over 2,000 marks), but it seemed to make little difference whether membership was judged to be nominal or "from conviction." [26] Among particularly able or particularly scarce managers even refusal to join the SED has not been an insuperable barrier. Smith cites the example of a seventy-three-year-old construction engineer who despite his political passivity received a "handsome" individual contract and membership in the exclusive Dresdner Klub.[27] Among distinguished scientists, nonmembership has indeed been rather common: Of the 130 members of the East German Academy of Sciences in 1960, only thirty-two were party members.[28] It must be recalled, however, that most such men belong to the old intelligentsia; for the new managerial cadres, party membership is a necessary (but, one should again stress, not a *sufficient*) condition for advancement beyond the lower-middle management level.

The "mass organizations"—in particular the trade union federation (FDGB) and the Free German Youth—are utilized for the political and ideological enlightenment and control of those out-

---

[25] Schultz, *op. cit.*, p. 142.   [26] Müller, *Die Manager*, pp. 115–117.
[27] Jean Edward Smith, *Germany Beyond the Wall* (Boston: Little, Brown, 1969), pp. 53–54.
[28] Excluding membership in West. Arthur M. Hanhardt, Jr., "Die ordentlichen Mitglieder der Deutschen Akademie der Wissenschaften zu Berlin (1945–1961)," in Peter Christian Ludz, ed., *Studien und Materialien zur Soziologie der DDR* (Köln and Opladen: Westdeutscher Verlag, 1964), p. 252. The academy, however, has since been reorganized with the intent of making it a "socialist research academy." Thomas Ammer, "Reform der Deutschen Akademie der Wissenschaften zu Berlin," *Deutschland Archiv*, III (May 1970), 546–551.

side the party.[29] Membership in the FDGB is almost universal both
for workers and members of the technical intelligentsia, owing
largely to the fringe benefits accompanying it: The FDGB is virtually the only agency through which inexpensive holiday trips
may be booked.[30] Even academics are organized through the "science union," the *Gewerkschaft Wissenschaft*. Like other Soviet
bloc unions, the FDGB has in principle been a representative of
the state and party meant to spur production and enlist support
for official policy. Under Honecker, the organization has been
upgraded, labeled the "interest representative" of its members,
and told to display "a certain measure of obstinacy" on their behalf; the official rhetoric leaves little doubt, however, that mobilization remains its primary mission.[31] The FDJ apparently has
no great importance at the factory level, though it does organize
within its ranks some of the younger technicians; there have
been complaints that graduates of the universities and *Fachschulen* frequently use the opportunity to drop out of the FDJ "respectably" as soon as they take their first job.[32]

The closest thing to a professional association for the technical
intelligentsia is provided by the *Kammer der Technik,* which
was organized by the FDGB in 1946 to replace earlier technical
and scientific associations, all of which were outlawed. With the
banning in particular of all-German associations and a prohibition
on most travel to international conferences,[33] the *Kammer* has
become especially important as a window to broad professional
developments for its members. It now has some 174,000 members, with "sections" in about 2,100 factories, as well as in universities, *Fachschulen,* and institutes; it is also organized in specialized committees (*Fachverbände*) and study groups on a national
and regional basis. It is supposed to include "innovators" as well
as engineers, economists, and scientists, perhaps to help inhibit

[29] As frankly admitted by Günter Mittag, "Die Aufgaben der Parteiorganisationen
in den Vereinigungen Volkseigener Betriebe," *Einheit,* XIII (August 1958), 1141.
[30] See *SBZ von A bis Z* (Bonn: Deutscher Bundes-Verlag, 1966), p. 138.
[31] Erich Honecker, *Bericht des Zentralkomitees an den VIII. Parteitag der SED*
(Berlin: Dietz Verlag, 1971), pp. 58–60. See also Hartmut Zimmermann, "Der FDGB
als Massenorganisation und seine Aufgaben bei der Erfüllung der betrieblichen
Wirtschaftspläne," in Ludz, ed., *Studien und Materialien,* pp. 115–144.
[32] Ehrenfried Rohde, letter in *Forum,* No. 10 (1963), p. 9.
[33] See Ernst Richert, *"Sozialistische Universität"* (Berlin: Colloquium Verlag, 1967),
p. 201.

the development of any technocratic class identification, but in practice the former do not join. The *Kammer* is not a mass political organization in the sense that the FDGB and FDJ are but rather operates in the area where politics and professional concerns overlap: the improvement of planning and production techniques, the promotion of the "innovator" program and "socialist *Gemeinschaftsarbeit*," the recruitment of young people and women into the technical intelligentsia, education in the problems and organization of planning and research, and the organization of factory courses. These purposes are accomplished through a great number of lectures, courses, conferences, trips, colloquia, forums, and the like.[34] The technicians value the opportunities the KDT gives them for professional exchange, the many technical journals it publishes, and the libraries of foreign technical literature it provides, and do not regard it as particularly "political." Yet it is, like the other mass organizations, subject to the direction of the party,[35] and its statute pays homage to the "unity of political-ideological and professional activity." It is perhaps fair to see the KDT's political function as primarily that of promoting acceptance and implementation of government technical and economic policies, not of producing a more generalized acceptance of regime ideals and norms. In many ways the *Klubs der Intelligenz*, formed in cities and regions under the aegis of the national *Kulturbund*, perform similar functions; they are supposed to be centers of intellectual exchange for both the cultural and technical intelligentsia and are somewhat more oriented to social diversion than the KDT.[36]

[34] See statistics on the number of such events and the number of participants in *Statistisches Jahrbuch der Deutschen Demokratischen Republik 1970* (Berlin: Staatsverlag der DDR, 1970), pp. 498–499.

[35] See the complaint of a Berlin party functionary that the regional *Kammer* is giving too little attention to the New Economic System and thus needs more vigorous direction. "Büro für Industrie und Bauwesen Berlin organisiert Parteiarbeit nach dem Produktionsprinzip" (interview with Rudi Rübbel), *Die Wirtschaft* (August 19, 1963).

[36] This paragraph is based on the "Statut der Kammer der Technik," *Technische Gemeinschaft*, No. 4 (1970), pp. 55–59; "5. Kongress der Kammer der Technik," *ibid.*, pp. 2–5; *Statistisches Jahrbuch 1970*, pp. 498–499; Günter Mittag, "Für ein festes Bündnis mit der Intelligenz," *Neuer Weg*, XIV No. 19 (1959), 1255; *Die Wirtschaft* (October 28, 1963), pp. 32–35; *A bis Z* (Bonn: Deutscher Bundes-Verlag, 1969), pp. 324, 333; *SBZ von 1945 bis 1954* (Bonn and Berlin: Bundesministerium für gesamtdeutsche Fragen, 1961), pp. 27, 35, 151; *Intelligenzschicht* III, 165; interviews.

In general the burden of politicalization efforts in the work-places of the technical intelligentsia is concentrated on implementing the specific economic and technical requirements of the regime rather than on producing abstract support of the government and ideology. Periodic recruitment campaigns seek to enlist the most admired technicians as SED members, thus associating job success with the honor of belonging to the party. Members are expected to engage in personal agitation among their colleagues on an informal basis and to organize party courses, seminars, and study circles. These appear to deal principally with explaining and "selling" technological and organizational innovations, although there are also study groups in Marxism-Leninism and the like. The plant newspaper, published in some 650 of the larger factories of the DDR by each one's party organization, is similarly focused on such relatively subtle "production propaganda" and popular science and technology.[37] Important campaigns of the party and new programs of the regime, whether of an ideological, organizational, social or economic character, are discussed in assemblies of the party, the union, or the plant as a whole. These may range from political campaigns against the United States' Vietnam policy through discussions of the youth and family codes to forums on elements of the "Economic System of Socialism." The most important of these is probably the annual discussion of the plan, which gives the plant's work force a taste of participation in its formulation and application to their own spheres of work, and is an additional instrument spurring them on to more efficient performance and to acceptance of current technical and organizational policy.[38]

A final avenue of politicalization on the plant level leads through the system of cadre selection, a highly developed set of mechanisms for determining the suitability of individuals for promotion to positions of greater technical and political responsibility. The cadre division of each plant, laboratory, or other appropriate unit or subunit maintains a "development file" for all of its leading personnel, containing records of each individual's

[37] See Günter Mittag, "Parteilehrjahr für die Lösung unserer ökonomischen Aufgaben nutzen," *Die Wirtschaft* (October 28, 1963), p. 6; *SBZ von A bis Z*, 1966, p. 78.
[38] See Ernst Richert, *Macht ohne Mandat* (Köln and Opladen: Westdeutscher Verlag, 1963), pp. 123–124.

past work, personal attributes, and political history, including his participation in advanced schooling, his involvement in "social" and political activities, his "moral" behavior, and his political attitudes.[39] The leading functionary of a particular unit (for example, the plant director), together with the cadre division, is expected to evaluate his subordinates regularly on the basis of observed performance, particularly in the independent, creative, and responsible completion of assigned tasks or "problems," work in collective undertakings (for example, "socialist community work," KDT projects, professional conferences, directing FDJ programs), and personal conversations (*Kadergespräche*).[40] The party organization is responsible for the political development of the cadres and exercises its customary supervisory role over all cadre work.[41] The most general criterion for promotion is outstanding performance in "carrying out party decisions";[42] this suggests a mix of tested professional capability with interpersonal leadership and administrative skills and with political activism and loyalty. The official literature complains of a lack of uniformity, and sometimes of due attentiveness, in cadre development practices;[43] it is evident that the idiosyncratic standards of the particular manager continue to play an important part in cadre selection and that these usually stress professional qualities above political ones. Nevertheless, the political component in the process of cadre selection, together with the pervasive attention given to the process as a whole, exerts strong pressures on the ambitious technician toward political conformity.

[39] See Falke and Modrow, *Auswahl*, pp. 126–127; *SBZ von A bis Z*, 1966, p. 233.

[40] "Grundsätze über die planmässige Entwicklung, Ausbildung, Erziehung und Verteilung der Kader . . . ," decision of Central Committee Secretariat, February 17, 1965, *Neuer Weg*, XX, No. 6 (1965), 339; Falke and Modrow, *op. cit.*, pp. 117–134.

[41] "Grundsätze," *op. cit.*, p. 342. In past years, specific political themes have been specified as subjects for *Kadergespräche*, for example, in 1954 the employee's behavior during the June 17 uprising of the previous year and his "understanding" of the background of the "provocations" of that date. Gustav Leissner, *Verwaltung und öffentlicher Dienst in der sowjetischen Besatzungszone Deutschlands* (Stuttgart and Köln: W. Kohlhammer Verlag, 1961), p. 296.

[42] "Grundsätze," *op. cit.*, pp. 339, 341.

[43] Falke and Modrow, *op. cit.*, pp. 105–112.

FLUCTUATIONS IN PRESSURE

It would be erroneous to leave the impression that the style and intensity of efforts to politicize the technical intelligentsia have been always consistent and unchanging. The alternating waves of "hard" and "soft" policies toward groups within the population characteristic of Communist rule have found their reflection in the degree of toleration shown political nonconformity among the intelligentsia. If any principle can be discerned in these fluctuations, it is one of rival insecurities: the fear of the loss of the indispensable services of the intelligentsia against the fear of the corrosive effects of political diversity. Thus, during the purge of party membership lists in 1951, intellectuals were treated with special solicitude—none were formally expelled and only half the average were stricken from the party rolls[44]—but the emphasis on "sharpening the class struggle" in party propaganda in 1952 and early 1953 led to at least a verbal intensification of the demand that the technicians be thoroughly indoctrinated. Hermann Axen, then the Central Committee's Secretary for Agitation, gave expression to the uncompromising spirit of this period: "The great task of educating the technical and scientific cadres can be mastered only in unison with the heightening of political vigilance, the strengthening of the ideological struggle, the broad development of self-criticism and criticism from below, the removal of incapable people from their functions, the elimination of enemy and demoralizing elements." [45] Scarcely a month later, however, as part of the liberalizing "new course" initiated on Soviet demand and formally announced June 11, Ulbricht called for the establishment of a "relationship of mutual trust" between the regime and the intelligentsia. An article in *Neues Deutschland* on May 24 became the basis of discussion for an "Intelligentsia Conference" held on June 27; here "sectarian" treatment of the bourgeois intellectuals was condemned and the right to the expression of non-Marxist opinions affirmed.[46]

[44] Schultz, *Der Funktionär*, p. 141.

[45] Hermann Axen, "Der Beschluss der II. Parteikonferenz und die Aufgaben auf dem Gebiet der Kaderpolitik," *ND* (April 30, 1953), p. 4.

[46] *Op. cit.*, "Die Bedeutung, " *ND* (May 24, 1953), pp. 3–4; *ND* (May 28, 1953), p. 1; *ND* (May 30, 1953), p. 4; Martin Jänicke, *Der dritte Weg* (Köln: Neuer Deutscher Verlag, 1964), pp. 24–29.

A major attempt to intensify pressure against academic intellectuals in particular followed the period of relative thaw of 1956–1957, the expression of student protests in conjunction with the Hungarian Revolution and the Polish October, the open expression of "revisionist" ideas by leading academic figures (see below), and the Harich affair. This reaction reached its zenith with the 1958 *Hochschule* conference, at which the "socialist transformation" of the universities was announced: SED and FDJ secretaries were to be included in leading university organs, including faculty councils, new measures combining "practice" and military experience with study were announced, and ideological deviations were roundly denounced. The new course, Kurt Hager charged in the conference's major address, had produced "ideological stagnation"; on most faculties, "bourgeois ideology" in fact predominated. "We are gathering our forces for the attack, for the offensive of Marxism-Leninism in the universities!" He complained of the "customary separation" of professional training from political and ideological training; a "socialist" orientation had to become part of every academic field. "We expect of a DDR scholar that he make himself conversant with the laws of socialist development and the ideas of socialism in order to be in a position to actively support the workers' and peasants' state in its great endeavors." [47] The upshot of these pronouncements, together with those of other conferences for other groups of intellectuals,[48] was an unprecedented flight of the intelligentsia to the West, at a time when overall refugee figures were steadily declining. Of the 752 university teachers going West between 1954 and 1961, over two-thirds left between 1957 and early 1959.[49]

Shortly, however, the pendulum swung back once more; indeed attacks on "sectarianism" in the treatment of the intelligentsia

---

[47] Kurt Hager, "Freie Bahn," p. 6; Hager, "Der Kampf für die sozialistische Hochschule," *ND* (March 1, 1958), p. 4. See also Ernst Richert, "*Sozialistische Universität*," pp. 180–185; *Intelligenzschicht*, II, 28.

[48] The *Kulturbund*, which includes members of the technical as well as the cultural intelligentsia, was another focal point of the struggle against "bourgeois ideology" in 1957–1958. Heinz Gambke, "Zu einigen Problemen der Bündnispolitik der SED mit der Intelligenz in der Periode des Sieges der sozialistischen Produktionsverhältnisse (1956–1961)," *Beiträge zur Geschichte der deutschen Arbeiterbewegung*, VIII, No. 1 (1966), 23–42.

[49] Richert, "*Sozialistische Universität*," p. 199.

never really ceased.[50] But following the serious social upheaval in the wake of the collectivization drive of spring 1960, the regime became especially solicitous of key groups, including the technical specialists.[51] At a Central Committee meeting in December, Herbert Warnke criticized "unjustified interference in the scientific or pedagogical work of the intelligentsia," and Ulbricht assured the intellectuals that there should no "longer" be grounds for their leaving the DDR: They "are being allowed time to become conversant with the new problems of social development in Germany." [52]

The erection of the Berlin Wall in 1961 considerably revised the problem of political indoctrination of the technical intelligentsia. On the one hand, the closing of the possibility of escape to the West eliminated the most obvious motive for generous treatment of politically dubious but technically invaluable personnel; as has earlier been suggested, the Wall indeed left something of a surplus of technical and scientific specialists for the DDR to choose among. On the other hand, the long-term general effect of the Wall was to relax substantially political pressures among all sectors of the population. If in the first months the SED employed intense propaganda and even terror techniques to suppress protests against the Wall and to make unmistakable the totality of the break with the West, it soon came to realize that, with the closing of the DDR's boundaries, continuous and intense political vigilance was not only no longer necessary but indeed counterproductive. The Wall gave the SED a feeling of security it had never before enjoyed; it had the *time* to work its revolution with the circumspection and at the pace that would most readily bring the population with it. It could afford to allow its citizens freedom to complain and even freedom to be apolitical; it knew its ultimate control had become unchallengeable.

Moreover, the erection of the Wall provided a solution—however unsatisfactory in some respects—to the "class" struggle with the capitalist West and thereby permitted the already evi-

[50] See, for example, Mittag, "Für ein festes Bündnis," p. 1255.
[51] Richert, *Macht ohne Mandat*, p. 57.
[52] *SBZ von 1959 bis 1960* (Bonn and Berlin: Bundesministerium für gesamtdeutsche Fragen, 1964), pp. 300–301. In the same vein see Günther Wyschofsky and Karl-Heinz Schäfer, *Die Zusammenarbeit mit der Intelligenz: Erfahrungen aus der chemischen Industrie* (Berlin: Dietz Verlag, 1961).

dent trend toward the "economization" of East German politics to be accelerated. Since at least 1956, the goals of economic development and economic growth had come to be an increasingly important emphasis of DDR policy; with it came a growing willingness to adopt economically rational means to achieve them and thus to discard or deemphasize Cold War or formal ideological criteria in many instances of decision making.[53] The economic sphere, however, could not simply be cut loose from political demands; rather, politics and ideology themselves were redefined so as to become coextensive, though imperfectly so, with the promotion of economic development. The hoary Marxist-Leninist principle of the unity of politics and economics,[54] earlier invoked against those demanding some autonomy for economic institutions,[55] was now turned to giving an economic content to politics. It was necessary, Herber and Jung wrote, to place economic tasks "at the center" of political activity;[56] at the present, said Apel and Mittag, the solution of economic problems was the "principal question of politics." [57] "The new," Ulbricht said, "consists of binding economic and political-ideological tasks still more closely together." [58] Such unity was to be obtained in part by providing party functionaries with technical educations and, conversely, improving the "political" education of economic functionaries.[59] While the latter concern did not signal any substantial change in previous practice and was largely rhetorical, the former, while itself an old ideal, was implemented on a broad scale for the first time.

[53] See below, Chap. 9.

[54] Lenin's statement that politics is "the most concentrated expression of economics, its generalization and completion" is frequently quoted by DDR writers. See Richard Herber, "Zur Leitung der Parteiarbeit nach dem Produktionsprinzip," *Einheit*, XVIII (May 1963), 3–4.

[55] See, for example, Reinhold, "Über die führende Rolle," pp. 199–200.

[56] Herber and Jung, *Wissenschaftliche*, pp. 105–106.

[57] Erich Apel and Günter Mittag, *Wissenschaftliche Führungstätigkeit: Neue Rolle der VVB* (Berlin: Dietz Verlag, 1964), pp. 108–109; see also the discussion in Uwe-Jens Heuer, *Demokratie und Recht im neuen ökonomischen System der Planung und Leitung der Volkswirtschaft* (Berlin: Staatsverlag der Deutschen Demokratischen Republik, 1965), pp. 151–159.

[58] Walter Ulbricht, "Das neue ökonomische System der Planung und Leitung der Volkswirtschaft in der Praxis," speech at Economic Conference of June 24, 1963. *Die Wirtschaft* (June 28, 1963), pp. 1–21.

[59] See, for example, Herber and Jung, *op. cit.*, pp. 98–101.

The new wedding of politics and economics meant several things in terms of the politicalization of the economic and technical specialists. The engineer, manager, or scientist had to prove his loyalty to party and regime less through the mastering of the unwieldy syllables of "party Chinese" and the repetition of slogans denouncing the hyenas of imperialism than through a verbal adherence to the regime's current economic dogmas. Since the dogmas increasingly were those of innovation, rationalization, cybernation, managerial independence, and the like, he was likely to find his political education undemanding and even congenial. Moreover, the party secretary supervising his plant, division, or laboratory was less likely to be an obdurate Stalinist with no understanding of economic and scientific problems than a man with at least sufficient technical background to understand and sympathize with the plant's problems and to be reluctant to make unreasonable "political" demands that might upset its operation. Even where the party functionaries and the technicians came to speak in the common vocabulary of the "economic revolution," however, conflicts between them often merely shifted ground rather than disappeared. It is perfectly clear that the presumed new competence of the *apparatchiki* in economic matters invited new kinds of doctrinal demands that they would have been reluctant and even unable to embark upon earlier. Nevertheless, for a technician to be politicized after 1962 meant something quite different from and, by and large, more congenial than— and also more ambiguous than—what it had meant earlier. And it had become considerably easier for an economic functionary with little real interest in or concern for politics nevertheless to appear to satisfy the official requirements of political and ideological consciousness.

This is not to say that the traditional modes of political indoctrination ceased or that older themes of the Cold War and the class struggle were abandoned. After the first wave of economic reforms and especially following the Czech "spring," the fear that ideology had been too greatly subordinated to economic policy found its expression in a renewed and even strident demand for recognition of the leading role of the party, Marxist-Leninist training, and devotion to the Soviet Union on the part of the technical intelligentsia.[60] With Erich Honecker's assumption of the SED's leadership in 1971, these themes were reiterated and linked to an attack on the "positivistic" use of a systems vocabulary and the uncritical invocation of the "scientific-technical revolution," as well as to an emphasis on the incompleteness of the technical intelligentsia's integration into the working class.[61] The regime denied from the first that it intended any "political devaluation" of the intelligentsia and continued to stress its importance to the development of socialism.[62] But the intelligentsia campaign mirrored the fear of party leaders that the economic reforms had left a certain ideological slackness as their legacy. Legitimacy considerations thus dictated a renewed emphasis on working class preeminence but also that it be qualified by a simultaneous reaffirmation of the technical intelligentsia's worth. On balance, the ideological curriculum directed at the technicians still mixed the values of productivity and efficiency with those of the class struggle, thus inevitably compromising the purity and force of the latter.

[60] See, for example, Erich Honecker's remarks at the 6th ZK plenum in 1968, cited in Ilse Spittmann, "Die 6. Tagung des Zentralkomitees," *Deutschland Archiv*, I (July 1968), 413; Günter Mittag, *Die Durchführung des Volkswirtschaftsplanes im Jahre 1970* (Berlin: Dietz Verlag, 1970), pp. 58–63.

[61] See Kurt Hager, *Die entwickelte sozialistische Gesellschaft* (Berlin: Dietz Verlag, 1971), pp. 12, 25–27; Erich Honecker, *Fragen von Wissenschaft und Politik in der sozialistischen Gesellschaft* (Berlin: Dietz Verlag, 1972), p. 13.

[62] Hager, *op. cit.*, p. 21; Werner Lamberz, "Partei und Massen," *Einheit*, XXVII, No. 7 (1972), 849.

6

POLITICAL ATTITUDES AND POLITICAL BEHAVIOR

> Power is not air and not a word on paper. Power—that is the factories, mills, fields, laboratories, institutes, etc. He who cannot control them—and develop them, since the world doesn't stand still—loses his power. But the factories, agriculture, the state can't be maintained without engineers, chemists, agronomists, doctors, etc., that is, without the intelligentsia.
>
> RUDOLF HERRNSTADT, speaking to workers' meeting on June 26, 1953[1]

> You say: "I can't carry the banner, I've got a book in my hand."
>
> Chemist interviewed by Infratest[2]

I N ITS ideal-typical form, the Marxist-Leninist state is the totally politicized state. Passivity toward the system is not permitted; the regime spares no effort to inculcate its ideals in all sectors of the population and to make all activities serve its goals. Total mobilization of this sort is difficult if not impossible to achieve in the real world, and I will try to show that the DDR has significant gaps in its fabric of political controls. But its failures in politicizing its population in the desired manner have not resulted from want of effort. I have already examined the extent of ideological schooling, the use of mass organizations, and various forms of political intervention in the workplace in some detail. In this chapter I will explore what evidence is available concerning the

---

[1] *Neues Deutschland* (hereafter cited as *ND*) (June 23, 1953), p. 3.

[2] *Die Intelligenzschicht in der Sowjetzone Deutschlands* (München: Infratest GmbH & Co., November 1960), mimeographed, I, 109 (hereafter cited as *Intelligenzschicht*).

actual political attitudes and behavior of the technical intelligentsia and devote special attention to the problem of dissent.

As we have seen, the technical intelligentsia, like other groups in the DDR, works in an atmosphere conditioned by the goals of the regime and by the organization of political power. It is politicized in two important senses: first, through overt propaganda and agitation and, second, through having to cope with the political environment as it affects its work. It is characteristic of DDR technicians, especially in leading managerial and bureaucratic positions, that in order to accomplish their jobs they must have a reasonably sophisticated understanding of the operation of the political system. A manager needs to know the meaning for himself of subtle shifts of ideological emphasis; he needs to know which laws may be circumvented and which not, which superior or parallel organs can safely be ignored and which must be cultivated, where the system will bend and where it will not.[3] Being politicized in this sense is an indispensable requirement for professional success. For such an individual there can be no separation of the economic from the political. There can, however, be an attempt to depoliticize one's own workplace by neutralizing party control, ignoring indoctrination campaigns, and so on. But to do that itself demands a good understanding of what the political parameters are.

To express it another way, all technicians are politicized, but there are a variety of *responses* available to politicalization.[4] One is simply to conform to the demands and expectations of the regime—not always a simple task since the demands can be contradictory and ambiguous. A second is to utilize one's political training and experience for purposes of modifying or even opposing the existing political order. The regime, I am suggesting, by making the technical intelligentsia politically conscious and by giving it, less willingly, an understanding of the system's power relationships, has furnished some of the tools by which it can

[3] On a high level of power, Bruno Leuschner exhibited something of a mastery of such knowledge and technique. See Fritz Schenk, *Im Vorzimmer der Diktatur* (Köln: Kiepenheuer & Witsch, 1962), pp. 249–255 and *passim*.

[4] Cf. Schenk's classification of functionaries in the state bureaucracy into *Mitläufer* ("fellow travelers"—loyal older Communists and former Socialists), "opponents of the system" (mostly from a Marxist standpoint), "Stalinists," and "careerists" (*ibid.*, pp. 82–89).

act for political change. None of these tools is easy to wield in normal circumstances, however, and in the absence of deep and widely spread dissatisfactions, their use will be limited and only modestly effective.

The third posture is that of opportunistic accommodation, elements of which, it should be noted, are likely to appear in the first two responses as well. The opportunistic accommodator conforms to regime norms for his role so far as is necessary to serve his own, private purposes. I do not mean to give a pejorative cast to this position. Accommodation is necessary for survival in one's job; even those who wish to change the system must appear to obey its demands. By "opportunism" I simply mean to suggest that the technician accommodates for personal ends, not, as in the first response, because he believes what he is taught, not, as in the second, because he wishes to reform the system. The ends sought need by no means be despicable; the most common one is simply that of being left alone to pursue professional interests. This is the response of those who remain essentially apathetic politically. No more than their fellows can they avoid politics entirely, but they use what they know about it precisely in order to guard their private spheres and to keep their arenas of work as free as possible from extraprofessional incursions. Naturally, the lower the position, and the fewer the leadership responsibilities of the individual in question, the more successful this response is liable to be.

POLITICAL ATTITUDES: THE AVAILABLE DATA

This section will discuss what evidence we have concerning the political attitudes of the technical intelligentsia. The difficulty, however, in arriving at any accurate estimation of the proportions of the intelligentsia to be found in particular camps is made clear by the problem of "accommodation." Almost all accommodate outwardly, whatever their internal motivations. Degrees of accommodation can be distinguished in some cases, and refugee data throws some light on these problems. But estimating even rough numerical proportions of those to whom one attitude or another can be attributed is not possible.

Müller provides us with the broadest set of statistical data on the political attitudes of the technical intelligentsia prior to the construction of the Wall, but it is of uncertain reliability. (See Table 6.1). His figures are based upon the reports of refugees and visitors to West Berlin on their co-workers and superiors in the East. Thus, they have the advantage of not referring to the refugees themselves—obviously a highly skewed sample—but they also have the pitfalls one might expect from secondhand reports. Overall, they indicate a surprisingly high degree of support for the system: Only 4.2 percent were classified as "opponents" and 32.6 percent as politically indifferent or aloof in the last of three surveys. But these figures by and large reflect only the outward posture of the managers; given their exposed positions, it seems quite plausible that many concealed their real views from all except a few intimates. The figures, then, tell us nothing about the distribution of actual political support and opposition among the technicians; they do make it clear that few were willing to risk being openly known as opponents of the regime while almost one-third either did not find it necessary to or were unable to conceal a posture of political indifference. Because of the immense size of the sample it seems safe to assume that the differences between categories of managers were meaningful, even though the absolute figures may not have been. Over half of the technical directors, divisional technical directors, production directors, chief bookkeepers, and justiciaries were regarded as either indifferent or, in the case of 5 to 7 percent of each group, oppositional. Labor directors, cadre directors, and party secretaries, on the other hand, were considered to be "radical Communists" or loyal and active party followers in 85 to 90 percent of all cases. Among the plant managers themselves 55 percent were assigned to these first two categories, and only 20 percent were seen as "indifferent" and a bare 2 percent as oppositional. It is not unlikely that the tendency in recent years to replace untrained party functionaries in this post with young, appropriately educated and experienced cadres would affect comparable current figures. The sharp divergences between the three groups in most cases parallel the differences in age, training, and social background discussed earlier. Yet given the evidence of the preceding chapters, it is clear that what differences remain do not generally produce sharp animosities in the workplace, in part be-

Table 6.1. Political Views of DDR Managers According to Reports of Refugees and Visitors
(in percentages except for N)

	1 Radical Communist	2 Loyal, active	3 Fellow traveler	4 Indiff., aloof	5 Opponent	6 Unknown	N
Total, all managers[a]	26.2	22.8	12.3	32.6	4.2	1.9	3349
Selected categories							
Factory managers, all	27	38	13	20	2	—	266
SED members	30	41	10	17	1	1	240
Party secretaries[b]	57	33	4	4	1	1	230
("Technical" managers)							
Technical directors	9	12	19	54	6	—	283
SED members	17	22	18	41	2	—	143
Chief bookkeepers	6	20	12	54	5	3	130
SED members	11	35	11	33	4	6	72
Production directors	9	22	10	50	6	3	144
SED members	15	35	11	35	1	3	86
Divisional tech. dir.	13	13	14	51	7	2	764
SED members	25	26	13	31	2	2	374
("Political" managers)							
Labor directors[b]	45	38	7	8	—	2	209
Cadres directors[b]	59	30	5	6	—	—	251

[a] Müller's total includes a variety of functionaries not listed here, including sales officials, justiciaries, dispatchers, and union and police officials.

[b] All or virtually all members of these groups are SED members; hence there is no separate listing.

Source: Based on Karl Valentin Müller, *Die Manager in der Sowjetzone* (Köln and Opladen: Westdeutscher Verlag, 1962), p. 81. The data is from a refugee survey taken by the Untersuchungsausschuss Freiheitlicher Juristen, West Berlin, ca. 1960.

cause they are bridged by a common pragmatic style, in part because of the "expertization" of plant managers and party functionaries in the past several years.

The Infratest study of intelligentsia refugees revealed, of course, hostility to the DDR regime but by no means a corresponding enthusiasm for Western or capitalist ideals—a testimony to the impact of political socialization on even the most resistant subjects. Some 13 percent subscribed to what the investigators defined as a "Communistic" political-ideological position, 20 percent to a mixture of Communist and Western ideas, and another 17 percent were "indifferent" or fundamentally "opportunist"; two-thirds of those giving a clear response favored a "dualistic" economic order rather than a pure or modified Communist or capitalist system.[5] Perhaps the most significant finding, however, was of a strong tendency to accommodation in the preflight *behavior* of interviewees. These results, based on "a very thorough investigation of the history of the flight" of the refugee intelligentsia, showed that only 10 percent were willing to risk open opposition before leaving, a fact which also underscores the limitations of Müller's data. Curiously, all the open opposition was found among the "pedagogical-scientific" and "technical-economic" intelligentsia, perhaps because all but the teachers were subject to less thoroughgoing political controls than other groups. But the great majority (88 percent) "accommodated" themselves to their political surroundings, the bulk of them (63 percent) "extensively" with only "occasional" inner reservations.[6] Why then did they flee? Half of the respondents, in the judgment of their interviewers, fled primarily for political (44 percent) or religious-ethical (6 percent) reasons, 28 percent primarily for professional reasons, and 20 percent for personal, family, or material reasons.[7] The majority of cases, moreover, of the po-

---

[5] *Intelligenzschicht*, III, 45, 90.   [6] *Ibid.*, II, 107; III, 45.

[7] *Ibid.*, II, 8. The refugees themselves attributed their departures more often to political (56 percent) and religious-ethical (11 percent) factors and less often to professional (18 percent) and personal, family, or material (13 percent) ones. It is to be noted that "political" refugees received special assistance from the West German government, and, hence, individuals had a particular interest in seeking to establish themselves as such. Most flights involved several different elements; thus, political grounds figured in 84 percent (94 percent in their own estimation) of the cases, professional in 60 percent, personal and family in 49 percent, religious and ethical in

litical grounds became so only through the interpretation of the regime; a mistake by the refugee, for example, was viewed as an act of political opposition. In 60 percent of all cases the grounds were "conditioned by the situation" and not "subjective" (28 percent); that is, refugees were moved to flee, and in some cases forced to, because of specific incidents in their work or elsewhere; this was true in 85 percent of the cases where political, religious, and ethical grounds predominated.[8]

This suggests that the westward flow of refugees from the intelligentsia was not a measure of political opposition per se; it was, perhaps, a measure of the frequent political incompatibility between the demands of the regime and the work and lives of the technical intelligentsia. Between 1954 and 1961 18,872 "engineers and technicians" fled the DDR; 770 university teachers left, and between 1952 and 1961 14,825 university students.[9] The somewhat haphazard categorization of refugees by the West German government and the uncertainty over the total number belonging to the DDR's technical intelligentsia make exact estimates impossible, but what Lange, Richert, and Stammer observed in 1954 appeared to remain true until the building of the Wall, that the proportion of the intelligentsia among the refugees lay "in no case above average, rather a little under it."[10] Looked at from another perspective, however, the refugee stream was substantial enough to cost the DDR between 10 and 20 percent of her technicians by 1961.

Both the Müller and Infratest studies agree that the old intelligentsia was viewed by their respondents as less compliant toward the Communist regime than the younger. In Müller's figures those described as "radical Communist" ranged from 39 percent of those under thirty to 12 percent of those over sixty; those described as "indifferent" from 21 percent of the youngest to 56

36 percent, and material in 19 percent. *Ibid.,* II, 11. Other Infratest studies indicate that political grounds played a much larger role among the intelligentsia than among workers interviewed and a somewhat larger role than among white collar workers. *Ibid.,* II, 24.

[8] *Ibid.,* II, 60, 81–82.

[9] *SBZ von A bis Z* (Bonn: Deutscher Bundes-Verlag, 1966), p. 146.

[10] Max Gustav Lange, Ernst Richert, and Otto Stammer, "Das Problem der 'Neuen Intelligenz' in der Sowjetischen Besatzungszone," in *Veritas, Iustitia, Libertas* (Berlin: Colloquium Verlag, 1954), p. 246.

percent of the oldest group.[11] Time, in other words, appeared to be clearly on the side of the regime; not only had education and propaganda begun to do their work upon those who had come to maturity since the war, but they affected the middle age brackets as well. Infratest notes that in one of every six of their refugee intellectuals, certain Marxist-Leninist premises had "taken root" in place of earlier Western values, "unreflectedly." [12] One can only assume that over ten years later, among the DDR intelligentsia as a whole, the percentage is far higher.[13]

There can be no question but that the building of the Wall fundamentally redefined the spectrum of viable political alternatives for all DDR citizens. Opponents of the regime no longer retained the safety valve option of a flight to the West when pressures on them became too severe; their choice was essentially reduced to "inner emigration" or some form of accommodation. Those oriented primarily to professional success learned that they would be able to achieve it only within the institutions of the DDR; the temptations of West German capitalism had ceased to be real. Regime supporters, for their part, lost their principal alibi for the DDR's economic difficulties and were forced at least to consider the abandonment of uncritical apologetics, in favor of the advocacy of reforms that might make socialism "work."

Virtually all observers of the DDR agree that visible support (some might say, acquiescence) of or toward the regime expanded dramatically among most groups after 1961. With rare exceptions, serious internal dissent and criticism in the DDR today begins with the assumption that the fundamental socialist order, however defined, will remain intact. Unlike the Infratest intelligentsia and Müller's managers, the critical technical intelligentsia

[11] Müller, *op. cit.*, p. 77. Of the Infratest refugees 55 percent felt that the old intelligentsia as a whole "rejected" the ideological-political claims of the regime and only 3 percent that it agreed with them; the corresponding figures for the young intelligentsia were 28 percent and 33 percent, respectively. Moreover, both the older and younger respondents agreed with the evaluation. *Intelligenzschicht*, III, 35, 40. It is worth noting that no such differences appeared among the refugees *themselves*; see *ibid.*, II, 104.

[12] *Ibid.*, III, 51.

[13] On this point we have the perhaps dubious testimony of Hans Apel, *Ohne Begleiter* (Köln: Verlag Wissenschaft und Politik, 1965), *passim*, the bulk of whose technical interviewees were favorable to the regime, excepting the students. Moreover, among a small group (15 percent) he classes as "Arrivierten," who support the regime largely because of their own personal success, all but one were "scientists or practitioners" in technical fields. *Ibid.*, pp. 47–48.

of the early 1970s is effectively limited to a constricted sort of Communist "reformism" that could plausibly modify the existing system only through its cumulative effects, if at all.

Especially since 1961, given the bent to accommodation and the repressive character of the regime, political expression among the technical intelligentsia has taken on clearly oppositional or revisionistic form only in isolated circumstances. Almost all published expression (with exceptions to be noted below) is at least ostensibly in accord with regime policy. Cautious dissent from proposals is possible in officially sponsored discussions, as are attacks on organs and individuals not superior to oneself for being in "violation" of the intent of the party; the sophisticated reader may occasionally uncover "coded" expressions of more fundamental dissatisfactions in such guises. Openly negative sentiments are more likely to emerge in plant discussions and the like; they may find their way into the public prints by virtue of an attack upon them. Among the intelligentsia several themes which particularly upset party loyalists are revealed by their recurrence in the official literature.

Thus, there are often complaints that the intelligentsia "underestimates the danger issuing from [West] German militarism and imperialism," that it does not understand the reasons for the construction of the Wall or other restrictions on East-West travel, or that it is otherwise unsympathetic to the party's hard line vis-à-vis the Federal Republic.[14] A related charge is that many technicians orient themselves uncritically toward the West (*Westdrall*), using its radio and television broadcasts as sources of information and viewing its technological and economic achievements as examples for their own plants and laboratories, to the neglect of the officially commended model, the Soviet Union.[15] It is frequently said that the intelligentsia fails to understand the

[14] See, for example, Rudolf Bahroi, "Geistige Reserven, oder Was hemmt die Produktivität der jungen Naturwissenschaftler an unseren Hochschulen und Universitäten?" *Forum*, No. 18 (1963), p. 26; Erich Dahm, "Für ein enges Kampfbündis der Arbeiterklasse mit der wissenschaftlich-technischen Intelligenz beim sozialistischen Aufbau der Deutschen Demokratischen Republik," in *Sozialismus und Intelligenz* (Berlin: Dietz Verlag, 1960), p. 19; "Wunschtraum eines Ingenieurs," *Sonntag* (June 24, 1962), p. 5.

[15] Günther Wyschofsky and Karl-Heinz Schäfer, *Die Zusammenarbeit mit der Intelligenz: Erfahrungen aus der chemischen Industrie* (Berlin: Dietz Verlag, 1961), pp. 11, 45; Günter Mittag, "Meisterung der Ökonomie ist für uns Klassenkampf," *ND* (October 27, 1968), p. 4.

"leading role of the working class," or of its party, with regard to such matters as *Gemeinschaftsarbeit* or "criticism from below." [16] Another theme is intelligentsia impatience with supply problems, poor organization, or discipline, which are sometimes taken to be inherent weaknesses of socialism.[17] The problem of reconciling Christianity and Marxism and the specific efforts to impose the secular ceremony of "youth dedication" (*Jugendweihe*) in place of confirmation occasionally arises,[18] and the intelligentsia, seizing upon the phraseology of de-Stalinization, sometimes accuses party ideologists of "dogmatism." "I would like us finally to understand that very often a dogma is opposed and in reality socialism is meant," a regime writer lamented.[19] Perhaps the most frequent complaint is that the intelligentsia fails to study Marxism-Leninism seriously and tries to separate professional concerns from political and ideological ones.[20]

Indeed, the most common reaction to politicalization among the technical intelligentsia is to seek refuge in one's professional work. In the words of one engineer: "I want to have nothing to do with politics; politics is for the politicians. We need specialists in the factory, then we can fulfill the plan. I'm a specialist and want to do my work; the rest doesn't interest me." [21] Such a "flight into the individualistic," as Ulbricht has called it, is sometimes justified by the "bourgeois" reasoning that one has done his duty when he has performed his work well.[22] And in fact the

[16] See, for example, Horst Taubert, "Die sozialistische Gemeinschaftsarbeit als eine höhere Stufe des Bündnisses zwischen Arbeiterklasse und technischer Intelligenz," in *Sozialismus und Intelligenz,* p. 178.

[17] See, for example, Erwin Stüber, "Das humanistische Wesen der Wissenschaft und seine Verwirklichung in der Deutschen Demokratischen Republik," in *ibid.,* p. 131.

[18] See, for example, Kurt Hager, "Freie Bahn für die sozialistische Wissenschaft," *ND* (March 6, 1958), p. 4; *Intelligenzschicht,* I, 191.

[19] [Günter] Heidorn, "Der dialektische Materialismus verlangt Konsequenz," *ND* (March 4, 1965), p. 5. See also Förtsch's citation of the recurring references to "misinterpretations" of the CPSU 20th Congress. Eckart Förtsch, *Die SED* (Stuttgart: W. Kohlhammer Verlag, 1969), p. 101.

[20] See *ibid.;* also, Hager, "Freie Bahn," p. 4; Richard Herber and Herbert Jung, *Wissenschaftliche Leitung und Entwicklung der Kader* ([Berlin]: Staatsverlag der DDR, [1964]), pp. 100–101; Günter Mittag, *Die Durchführung des Volkswirtschaftsplanes im Jahre 1970* (Berlin: Dietz Verlag, 1970), pp. 59–62.

[21] Quoted disapprovingly by Siegfried Schiemann, "Parteilichkeit und Wissenschaftlichkeit," in *Sozialismus und Intelligenz,* p. 57. See also *Intelligenzschicht,* I, 45, 101.

[22] *ND* (July 7, 1958), cited in *SBZ von 1957 bis 1958* (Bonn and Berlin: Bundesministerium für gesamtdeutsche Fragen, 1960), pp. 256–257.

apolitical posture of many technicians probably reflects in part the German expert's traditional self-image of political neutrality.[23] But more is also involved; the Soviet Union has also been plagued by apolitical attitudes among the professionals.[24]

Many see a conflict between the demands of science and those of the ideology—between *Wissenschaftlichkeit* and *Parteilichkeit*.[25] They believe that scientific method allows them—indeed, obliges them—to seek a form of truth above classes and not admitting of subjection to official dogma. This is condemned by the party as "objectivism," or, alternatively, "subjectivism-neutralism"; it has even appeared in so unlikely a place as an FDJ group of physics students in Leipzig, who allegedly sought to use modern quantum theory to prove that "one could be objective but not *parteilich*." [26] Most, however, do not justify their apoliticalness with such elaborate reasoning; they simply prefer to devote themselves to their work and to escape the time-consuming and, to them, dull requirements of political activism.[27] Even in the State Planning Commission, Schenk testifies, the chairman Bruno Leuschner and his co-workers heartily disliked party meetings and for some time managed to maintain a "politische Windstille" (political dead calm) in his Secretariat.[28]

The Party managed in this case to get the wind circulating again by imposing a Secretariat reorganization.[29] In general the SED and its leaders react sharply to political apathy.

Not remaining aloof from political questions, but insight into political relationships, the support of progressive social forces gives professional work its goal. . . . In the Marxist ideology . . . partyness and scientificness constitute a dialectical unity, both of whose poles condition and influence one another. The working class is the

[23] This point is made by Melvin Croan in his "East German Revisionism: The Spectre and the Reality," in Leopold Labedz, ed., *Revisionism: Essays on the History of Marxist Ideas* (New York: Praeger, 1962), p. 241.

[24] See Albert Parry, *The New Class Divided* (New York: Macmillan, 1966), pp. 142–147, for numerous examples.

[25] Schiemann, *op. cit.*, p. 56.

[26] Wolfgang Herger and Hans Kleinschmidt, "Der 20. Jahrestag der SED und die FDJ an den Universitäten, Hoch- und Fachschulen," *Forum*, No. 3 (1966), reprinted in part in *SBZ-Archiv*, XVII, No. 5 (1966), 80. See also Mittag, *Die Durchführung*, p. 62.

[27] See the remarks on "pragmatism" in Chap. 3.

[28] Schenk, *Im Vorzimmer*, p. 276.   [29] *Ibid.*, p. 277.

first class in history whose class interests require the discovery of objective truth in all areas of the natural and society sciences.[30]

Another version of this argument holds that technicians and scientists ought to study dialectical materialism simply because it is itself scientific, comparable with the great comprehensive theories in the natural sciences.[31]

The desire of the regime to end apoliticalness among the technical intelligentsia may be more verbal than substantive. In practice it has been willing to permit the old intelligentsia its apathy and has tolerated political indifference even among the young more readily than in other social groups. The technicians have functioned reliably and well for the regime; insofar as their apathy is genuine, the power of those presently ruling is rid of at least one potential challenge.[32] The regime worries, however, for two reasons: It is like other governments with totalistic aspirations frightened of a vacuum where its power is uncertain or ambiguous; it needs the constant reassurance of overt support. Second, it is not sure the apathy is genuine. If the Infratest data can be extended even in small measure to the DDR's present generation of technicians, apathy is sometimes a sign of genuine political indifference, but at other times it is a cloak for views departing from those of the regime. This group's misgivings about the present order of things are not sufficient to provoke it to open opposition, but should a serious challenge to the regime arise from another source, especially from within the elite, the "apathetic" might suddenly become its supporters.

Because of the resemblance of their outward postures, the "apathetic" shade rather imperceptibly into the "loyal"; even the latter often maintain a pragmatic style and are not very enthusiastic about Communist political ritual. They are numerous; even in 1960 one of the authors in *Sozialismus und Intelligenz* concluded that the technical intelligentsia "belongs to the most progressive

[30] Schiemann, *op. cit.*, pp. 58, 63. He later adds that although the *findings* of the natural sciences, unlike those of the society sciences, are "class-indifferent," the classes *use* them in their political struggles (p. 76).

[31] Kurt Hager, "Die Intelligenz und der V. Parteitag," *Einheit*, XIII (August 1958), 1134–1137.

[32] So argue Lange *et al.*, "Das Problem," p. 235; and, in more general reference to Russia and Eastern Europe, Günter Bartsch, "Die Kommunisten und das Generationsproblem," *Osteuropa*, XIV (May 1964), 333.

sectors" of the intelligentsia as a whole.[33] One index of loyalty is membership in the party. At the end of 1966 representatives of the (entire) intelligentsia constituted 12.3 percent of the total SED membership,[34] almost twice their proportion of the work force. These 218,000 members were about one-third of the total working intelligentsia. In the Soviet Union the figures are comparable[35] although in that country total party membership is only about half that in the DDR proportionate to population. Unsurprisingly, the higher the position and the more "political" its orientation, the greater the likelihood of party membership. Ninety percent of Müller's plant managers—and virtually all of the labor directors and cadre directors—were party members, but only 50 percent of the technical directors and 60 percent of the production directors were members.[36] On the higher levels membership is almost universal; only among scientists, including the most distinguished, do membership proportions appear to be comparatively low.

The significance of party membership as an index of political loyalty is, however, limited. Müller's figures indicate that a manager's political views usually depended more upon his position than upon his party membership; thus 41 percent of the technical directors belonging to the SED were reported to be "indifferent" to politics, as compared with 54 percent of all technical directors, and with 8 percent of all labor directors. In each case membership made a substantial but not a determining difference. Reports are frequent of party members who assert in private that "das ist alles Quatsch" [37] while many others, in notable contradiction to the party statute, are simply inactive politically or prefer (like nonmembers) to withdraw into their occupational concerns.[38] Some resist membership because of the obligations and burdens they

[33] Dahm, "Für ein enges Kampfbündis," *op. cit.*, p. 29.

[34] *ND* (April 17, 1967), p. 12, as reported in Peter Christian Ludz, *Parteielite im Wandel* (Köln and Opladen: Westdeutscher Verlag, 1968), p. 146. It is probable that this official figure is low since some present intelligentsia may be classified as workers on the basis of their occupation at the time of joining the party. On this problem see Hans-Werner Prahl, "Von der Arbeiterpartei zum Grosssystem," *Deutschland Archiv*, IV (June 1971), 624.

[35] Zbigniew Brzezinski and Samuel P. Huntington, *Political Power: USA/USSR* (New York: Viking Press, 1964), p. 100.

[36] Müller, *Die Manager*, p. 67; see also Table 6.1.

[37] Approximately, "It's a lot of baloney" (interview).

[38] See Förtsch, *Die SED*, p. 100, and citations there.

believe to be attached to it, even though in numerous cases they are at least as loyal as those who join.[39] The technical intelligentsia who do join do so for a variety of reasons, ambition and professional necessity being at least as important as conviction, with rank opportunism not uncommon.[40] There are apparently also exceptional cases in which individuals unsympathetic to the regime nevertheless join the party in the hope of influencing it from within.[41]

The problem the party recruiters face in building a disciplined and devoted Leninist cadre party is very nearly insoluble. Legitimacy concerns dictate the enrollment of a large and reasonably representative membership; for the DDR citizen, membership is an all but indispensable requisite to attaining influence and high status positions in the society in which he has no alternative but to live.[42] However intensive the SED's efforts at self-purification, it seems unavoidable that membership will continue to be no more than a highly diluted measure of ideological fervor.[43]

"CONSULTATION" WITH THE INTELLIGENTSIA

It is appropriate to ask here whether any channels are open to overtly loyal rank-and-file technicians, whether party members

[39] *Ibid.*, p. 74, lists some of the reasons frequently given for the declining of party membership.

[40] "I asked Eckstein and Kaufmann why they had joined the party. 'To get ahead, naturally, like most other people our age. There are a few "two-hundred percenters," but not many. We know one another fairly well. There are some of our colleagues with whom we could not be having such a conversation, but not many.'" Jean Edward Smith, *Germany Beyond the Wall* (Boston: Little, Brown, 1969), p. 44. See also Jeremy R. Azrael, "The Internal Dynamics of the CPSU, 1917–1967," in Samuel P. Huntington and Clement H. Moore, eds., *Authoritarian Politics in Modern Society* (New York: Basic Books, 1970), p. 279.

[41] Interview. See also Schenk's account of a man self-consciously so motivated, Willi Heinrich. Schenk concludes that Heinrich's subsequent flight to the West, and his own later one, show the "fruitlessness" of such efforts. *Im Vorzimmer*, pp. 65, 85, 102–104.

[42] In 1966 over 10 percent of the DDR's population belonged to the SED, a proportion double that of the Soviet Union and greater than that of any other East bloc state except Czechoslovakia. Förtsch, *op. cit.*, p. 66. For an excellent discussion of the tension in the SED's view of itself between "mass" and "cadre" orientations, see *ibid.*, pp. 18–33.

[43] In 1970, after a hiatus of several years, the SED called in its membership books, the customary beginning of a purge. But only .5 percent of its members were refused new ones. See Erich Honecker, "Bericht über den Umtausch der Parteidoku-

or not, for influencing the policies of the regime. The SED has made a highly visible display of engaging in "consultation" with members of the technical intelligentsia in advance of important economic decisions in recent years, a sign of the importance it attributes to winning the support of this constituency. One device to this end is the calling of "economic conferences," either for the entire economy or for branches of it. Some 3,500 participants were called to such a conference in October 1961, after the construction of the Wall, in order to discuss problems in the implementation of two current campaigns: the *Produktionsaufgebot* ("produce more in the same time for the same money") and *Aktion Störfreimachung* (intended to free the DDR economy from dependence on West Germany), and to explain the new division of the State Planning Commission into two parts.[44] If this affair was largely declamatory, later conferences—one in December 1962 for economists and "economic practitioners" to discuss possible economic reforms, including Liberman-style proposals,[45] and a broader, major gathering in June 1963—seemed to invite direct participation by technicians in preparing the way for the New Economic System. In the latter conference, which preceded by a month the issuance of the "directives" officially formulating the NES, 950 "distinguished representatives of the party, state apparatus, and economy, leading scholars (*Wissenschaftler*), general directors of the VVBs, plant managers and party secretaries in the leading branches of the economy, as well as representatives of the unions, the FDJ, the KDT and other mass organizations" took part.[46] They were provided with copies of the first draft of the directives and told by Walter Ulbricht: "We place great value on the participants in our meeting setting forth their experiences and making their proposals. Since it is a matter of such extraordinarily complicated questions, we ask all participants to express their opinion openly in order that after the discussion at this conference the

---

mente," *ND* (December 14, 1970), reprinted in *Deutschland Archiv*, IV (January 1971), 101–103.

[44] See Fritz Schenk, "Konzil der Wirtschaftsbürokraten," *SBZ-Archiv*, XII, No. 21 (1961), 329–332; Ludz, *Parteielite*, pp. 103–113.

[45] See Ernst Richert, *Macht ohne Mandat* (Köln and Opladen: Westdeutscher Verlag, 1963), p. 50.

[46] *Die Wirtschaft* (June 28, 1963), p. 2; see also Ludz, *Parteielite*, pp. 113–114.

decisions made can be implemented everywhere in unified fashion." He assured his audience that their proposals would be "taken into consideration" in writing the final version.[47]

The discussions of the plan, both yearly and the longer-term "perspective," afford the technical intelligentsia further limited opportunity to participate in policy making. The 1964–1970 perspective plan underwent a particularly thorough discussion. Preliminary programs were worked out for the "leading branches" of the economy in 1962 with the help of "a great number of scientists and practitioners"; the program for electronics, for example, enlisted the help of some 300 from the state organs, factories, universities, and institutes. It was then to go to the "districts, counties (*Kreisen*), cities, and villages" to be worked out in detail.[48] The plan was still unfinished, however, in September 1964, when a new phase of discussion was initiated in a meeting of a Perspective Plan Commission, attended by a cast roughly approximating that listed above for the 1963 Economic Conference. The meeting consisted of a *Referat* by Ulbricht, discussion by commission members and guests, and closing remarks by Erich Apel, head of the Planning Commission. It "assigned" to the Planning Commission the working out of the final directives and "orientation figures" ("considering" its own instructions) for submission to state and economic organs. The plan was then to be discussed and its details worked out in factory discussions between October 1964 and February 1965, before being returned to the Planning Commission to be put in final form.[49] The variety if not the length of consultations is similar for the yearly plans, whose discussion is one of the major agitational efforts of the party. Ernst Richert observes, however, that in the past several years the plans have emerged from such discussions and submission to a variety of lower organs with no important changes; he argues that with the use of input-output analysis (*Verflechtungs-*

[47] Walter Ulbricht, "Das neue ökonomische System der Planung und Leitung der Volkswirtschaft in der Praxis," speech at Economic Conference of June 24, 1963, *Die Wirtschaft* (June 28, 1963), pp. 1, 3.

[48] Walter Ulbricht, *Das Programm des Sozialismus und die geschichtliche Aufgabe der Sozialistischen Einheitspartei Deutschlands,* speech at Sixth SED Congress (Berlin: Dietz Verlag, 1963), p. 62.

[49] *ND* (September 11, 1964), pp. 1, 3. The plan did not in fact emerge in final form until early 1967, probably because of reasons having to do with Apel's suicide and the Soviet trade pact.

bilanzierung) of the interrelationships between different sectors of the economy, major changes in any one of them are discouraged.[50] More generally, in all such discussions the line between the genuine solicitation of advice and their use as a mobilization or cheerleading device is a nearly invisible one. Letters to editors, conferences, discussions, and contributions to professional journals can have a limited influence; following the example of the Soviet Union, the DDR regime uses these devices as conscious instruments of rule.[51] The most influential of the technical specialists, however, apart from members of the top elite, are officials in key state organs and various scientific advisory councils whose expertise is constantly required by political and state leaders; these will be discussed below.

THE RECORD OF DISSENT

What of those who dissent from the policies of the SED and seek to express their dissent? The known record of resistance and revisionism in the DDR[52] includes only limited participation by members of the technical intelligentsia. As we have seen, technicians joined the flow of escapees to the West in substantial but probably less than average numbers. In the uprising of 1953 they joined workers' strikes and protests in isolated instances— for exmple, in the Köpenick radio plant and the Zeiss works in

[50] See Richert, *op. cit.*, pp. 122–124.

[51] See Wolfgang Leonhard, *The Kremlin Since Stalin* (New York: Praeger, 1962), on the use of discussions in the Soviet Union, pp. 237ff., 274–275, 294–296; also Joel J. Schwartz and William R. Keech, "Group Influence and the Policy Process in the Soviet Union," *American Political Science Review*, LXII (September 1968), 840–851.

[52] For a useful survey of the problem, see Martin Jänicke, *Der dritte Weg* (Köln: Neuer Deutscher Verlag, 1964). Peter Christian Ludz's harsh criticism of Jänicke ("Ein Mythos vom dritten Weg," *SBZ-Archiv*, XVI, No. 8 (1965), 119–123) errs in not treating it as a modest survey but rather subjecting it to the standards to be expected only from a more definitive work of analysis.

There is, of course, a vast difference between anti-Communist "resistance" and "revisionism"; in practice, however, the distinction is not always easy to make. Resistance, engaging in the art of the possible, may cloak itself as revisionism; on the other hand, the regime often escalates revisionism into "enemy activity" in its own reports or, as in the quote in the text directed at a Dresden student group, treats the two as identical. In other cases, especially in the last few years, limited dissent in specific subject areas has been permitted and even encouraged. See the intelligent distinctions and discussion in H. Gordon Skilling, "Background to the Study of Opposition in Communist Eastern Europe," *Government and Opposition*, III (Summer 1968), 297–301.

Jena[53]—but resentment of the intelligentsia's generous pay and privileges by the workers helped to prevent this alliance from being more universal. Students in technical and scientific subjects joined the protests of their fellows in the ferment accompanying the Hungarian revolution in 1956, particularly at Berlin, Leipzig, Halle, and Jena. At the Technical *Hochschule* in Dresden students protested in May against restrictions on travel to the West, observed a moment of silence in November after the smashing of the Hungarian revolt, then signed petitions against the punishment of the instigators, and in May 1957 once again protested travel restrictions; an oppositional "National Communist Student Group" also came to light.[54] After the building of the Wall, a "revisionist" and "enemy" (*staatsfeindliche*) group at Dresden was expelled from the party, as were several professors; one chemist openly compared the DDR to a "fascist concentration camp." [55]

The chemical industry in the Halle region was the center of the best example we have of coherent acts of opposition by members of the technical intelligentsia on the plant level. "A part of these leading cadres were proponents of openly antiparty tendencies . . . in the fall months of 1956, and the young intelligentsia maturing in these plants very often allowed themselves to be influenced by them." [56] In the Leuna plant "Walter Ulbricht," the production director, Dr. Sundhoff, was accused of writing an oppositional platform, attacking the policies of the central economic apparatus for ineptness and neglect of the chemical industry in favor of unprofitable economic monuments like "Schwarze Pumpe." [57] Opposition among the workers—going

---

[53] Jänicke, *op. cit.*, pp. 53, 233, fn. 177. See also Stefan Brant [Klaus Harpprecht], *Der Aufstand* (Stuttgart: Steingrüben Verlag, 1954).

[54] Jänicke, *op. cit.*, pp. 150–155. Cf. also Ernst Richert, *"Sozialistische Universität"* (Berlin: Colloquium Verlag, 1967), pp. 132–142, who argues that the main elements in the unrest were "bourgeois" students in such fields as medicine, veterinary medicine, and agriculture.

[55] Jänicke, *op. cit.*, p. 210.

[56] Fritz Selbmann, at the 32nd Central Committee Plenum, *ND* (July 17, 1957), cited in Jänicke, *op. cit.*, p. 97.

[57] The Schwarze Pumpe project was an ambitious attempt to implement a process for converting East German brown coal into coke, thus making it usable for steel production. A monument to Stalinist economics, it was beset by technical difficulties and is only now being completed in considerably revised form. Ironically, in the

so far as "Mordhetze" ("incitement to murder") against "leading comrades"—apparently was not in phase with that of the intelligentsia and many old Communists in the party organization; it turned to an angry passivity in 1957 while expressions of dissent among the latter groups continued. "Social-Democratism," the failure to believe in the SED's German policy or its prospects of success in "building socialism," and even the charge that the old I. G. Farben management had done a better job than the party in providing social benefits, were attributed to the intelligentsia and party members. Only a purge of the plant leadership and a reassertion of control by the central party leadership slowly brought things back to order in the following months.[58]

CASES OF REVISIONISM

Especially in the earlier years of the DDR, generalized references to "enemy agents," "spies," and "wreckers" among the technical intelligentsia decorated the literature.[59] In more recent years the regime has tended to see a more serious threat stemming from "revisionist" thinking within these circles. Such thinking has come primarily from academic economists and scientists, not from the "practitioners" of the factory or state economic organs. Much of it emerged in the "thaw" period of 1956 and evidently was not usually regarded by its authors themselves as "revisionistic." [60] "Since I have been in the working class movement, I have stood on the left wing and have regarded revisionism and the revisionists as my opponents and my enemies," Fritz Behrens protested in his initial self-criticism.[61]

1960s the development of the chemical industry became the focal point of DDR investment.

[58] Jänicke, *op. cit.*, pp. 97–98.

[59] See, for example, "Die Bedeutung der Intelligenz beim Aufbau des Sozialismus," Central Committee statement, *ND* (May 24, 1953), p. 3; Hermann Axen, "Der Beschluss der II. Parteikonferenz und die Aufgaben auf dem Gebiet der Kaderpolitik," *ND* (April 30, 1953), p. 4.

[60] See Croan, "East German Revisionism," p. 251, who suggests that men like Fritz Behrens, Arne Benary, and Kurt Vieweg were loyal supporters of the regime who took literally the party's call for the "conflict of scientific opinion" in a period when the denunciation of Stalinism had blurred the boundaries of orthodoxy.

[61] Fritz Behrens, "Meine Konzeption war revisionistisch," *ND* (March 4, 1958), p. 5.

A persistent theme of revisionist criticism has been the weaknesses of the economic system and the need for its reform. One of the earliest critics, Bruno Warnke, was answered in the vocabulary of the Stalin era a few months after the Russian dictator's death. Warnke, an economist of the *Hochschule für Planökonomie*, the training academy for DDR planners, was accused of "spreading Trotskyist conceptions, embracing objectivism, denying the role of the great Stalin as a scientist, and falsifying Stalinist teachings. . . ." He was expelled from the SED but rehabilitated three years later.[62] More cautiously, the economist Heinz Freyer in 1953 used quotations from the Marxist "classics" to argue for worker control of the factories; his views were attacked sharply by *Neues Deutschland*.[63] By 1956 the entire Institute of Economic Sciences, a branch of the Academy of Sciences very close to leading figures in the regime, had become a center of "revisionist" economic thought.[64] Behrens and Arne Benary proposed a decentralization of the economy with increased worker participation along the lines of the Yugoslav workers' councils, the use of profitability criteria, and, following from these, the beginning of the "withering away of the state." Günther Kohlmey, head of the institute, sympathized on many points and added the proposal that the banks should serve as self-regulating devices of economic control through their lending powers; the finance expert Herbert Wolf and Benary seconded Kohlmey's views, as evidently did in part Grete Kuckoff, who was subsequently removed as president of the DDR's *Deutsche Notenbank*. Kurt Vieweg, of the Agricultural Sciences Academy, proposed the dissolution of unprofitable collective farms, a position which came to find its adherents within the regime, including Fred Oelssner, who also taught at (and later became the head of) the Institute of Economic Sciences.[65] At Halle, two professors of agriculture were accused of "consciously" teaching "un- or anti-

[62] Jänicke, *op. cit.*, p. 26.   [63] *Ibid.*, p. 62.
[64] "The discussions of the personality cult and its consequences which took place in this Institute after the 20th Party Congress of the CPSU revealed more or less strong ideological waverings in a number of the staff, which also found their impact in the goals and content of scientific work." Karl Kampfert, "Gegen das Aufkommen revisionistischer Auffassungen in der Wirtschaftswissenschaft," in *Zur ökonomischen Theorie und Politik in der Übergangsperiode, Wirtschaftswissenschaft*, V (3. Sonderheft, 1957), 11.
[65] See Jänicke, *Der dritte Weg*, pp. 104–112; Richert, "Sozialistische Universität," pp. 159–164; and below, Chap. 9.

Marxist" doctrines—presumably on the same subject—and thereby arousing "skepticism" toward party policies.[66]

During the period of the New Economic System reforms, when a number of the economic proposals of Behrens and other critics were adopted without acknowledgement, a small literature of what Ludz calls "institutionalized revisionism" began to appear. In a strict sense, institutionalized revisionism is not revisionism at all but rather a set of ideological trial balloons permitted by the regime as a basis for discussion and possible future authoritative adoption.[67] Neither of the two most prominent exponents Ludz discusses are, strictly speaking, members of the technical intelligentsia; George Klaus is a philosopher who has written extensively on cybernetics while Uwe-Jens Heuer is a legal theorist. Both, however, have sought to explore the relationship between the economic system and the character and organization of society as a whole.

Heuer is of particular interest to us here. In his 1965 book *Demokratie und Recht* he analyzes the economy of the DDR as a cybernetic system and focuses upon the necessity of permitting the "self-organization" of its subsystems, defined as their ability to change not only their behavior but their very structure in response to signals from the environment. Accordingly, he argues for a broad measure of decentralization, granting factories and VVBs a degree of decisional autonomy inscribed in and protected by law.[68] He presents such a reform as a large and meaningful step toward "socialist democracy," which he explicitly treats as a goal superior to that of democratic centralism. Democratic relations in the factory and the "opportunity to decide oneself questions concerning one's own sphere of work" are ends in themselves and are critical for overcoming boredom and developing "free individuality" (Marx) among men. He recommends the "highest possible measure of co-determination (*Mitentscheidung*) of individuals and groups." [69]

---

[66] Annemarie Podrabski, "Marxistische Agrarökonomie lehren," discussion at Universities Conference, *ND* (March 4, 1958), p. 5.

[67] Ludz, *Parteielite*, pp. 52–54, 294ff.; see also Skilling, "Background," pp. 308–310.

[68] Uwe-Jens Heuer, *Demokratie und Recht im neuen ökonomischen System der Planung und Leitung der Volkswirtschaft* (Berlin: Staatsverlag der DDR, 1965), pp. 98–114, 162–181, and *passim*.

[69] *Ibid.*, pp. 168–173; *ibid.*, "Gesellschaft und Demokratie," *Staat und Recht*, XVI, No. 6 (1967), 918.

Heuer's work was immediately criticized, but the attacks took on particularly virulent tones after the Czech crisis of 1968, understandably so, since Heuer's discussion of conflict in socialist societies and espousal of worker co-determination were very much in the spirit of the Czech reforms. Heuer was not, however, purged but deprived of teaching responsibilities at Humboldt University and transferred to a research position at the Central Institute for Socialist Economic Management.[70] In the same period Behrens was again sharply attacked—for using a 1967 West German colloquium on Marx to praise a trend he saw in socialist countries toward the reduction of state control of the economy and a transition to "delegated group property" and "self-administration" in the factories; he specifically cited Yugoslavia, Czechoslovakia, and Hungary.[71] Günther Kohlmey also came in for renewed criticism for slighting the role of the party in his writings and using concepts allegedly borrowed from West German economists in his writings.[72]

The second important stream of revisionist thinking among the technical intellectuals went beyond economic policy to the roots of Marxist ideology itself. It sought to confront the core concept of dialectical materialism, as interpreted by the party ideologists, with the discoveries and the outlook of modern science. In its simplest form it demanded freedom for scientists from ideological restrictions on their work and the development of free discussion of issues where science and ideology meet, or clash. Kurt Mothes, a distinguished botanist often honored by the regime, expressed these views in a 1958 exchange with Ulbricht in attacking the "scholasticism" party dogma imposed on scientific research:

> Progress in science consists of putting the past in question. But when such opinions are incessantly presented to us as that Mendel's

[70] See Rudolf Schwarzenbach, "Zentrale staatliche Leitung und Eigenverantwortung im Gesellschaftssystem der DDR," *Deutschland Archiv,* II (February 1969), 143–144, and articles cited there; Peter Christian Ludz, *The German Democratic Republic from the Sixties to the Seventies* ([Cambridge]: Harvard University Center for International Affairs, 1970), p. 59.

[71] Fritz Behrens, "Kritik der politischen Ökonomie und ökonomische Theorie des Sozialismus," in Walter Euchner and Alfred Schmidt, eds., *Kritik der politischen Ökonomie heute: 100 Jahre 'Kapital'* (Frankfurt: Europäische Verlagsanstalt, 1968), pp. 296–298; Schwarzenbach, *op. cit.,* pp. 144–146.

[72] Mittag, "Meisterung," p. 4.

laws are false, that the universe is infinite, because Engels said so, and when the physicists say the world is finite, that is false—to that it can only be said that we scientists can only exist by questioning everything. We question not only the story of creation but also Engel's thesis that the world is infinite. We need professors who have the courage to go their own way. I often ask myself whether with this situation in our universities today men like Karl Marx and Engels would be allowed to speak.[73]

It is noteworthy that Mothes coupled these remarks with more concrete objections to stripping objectionable individuals of their academic degrees and to admissions policies in the universities, and referred to the "outer and inner unrest" which kept scientists from their work.[74]

A more philosophical discussion of the role of dialectical materialism in science was carried on in the pages of *Sonntag* and *Neues Deutschland* in the last half of 1956.[75] Three of the sharpest critics of the received Stalinist doctrine were professors at East Berlin's Humboldt University. Two were philosophers of science: Friedrich Herneck (docent for dialectical materialism) and Martin Strauss (professor of theoretical physics). Herneck argued that the dialectical method had not visibly influenced the great scientific discoveries of the past century; dialectical materialism could only be an instrument of research if it were a product of research. This positivist view Herneck reinforced by stressing the influence of Comteian positivism on Marx and Engels; for his pains he was removed from the party and lost his teaching job. Strauss went so far as to challenge Lenin's theses in *Materialism and Empiriocriticism* and attacked the party view as "legends" sponsored by "dogmatists and dilettantes" who without any knowledge of modern physics sought to make definitive philo-

---

[73] Quoted in *SBZ von 1957 bis 1958*, p. 220.

[74] See *ibid.*, pp. 220–221; *Intelligenzschicht*, I, 191; *SBZ-Archiv*, XVI (December 1965), 373.

[75] Although they are tangential to our subject, it should be noted that the ideas of Georg Lukacs and Ernst Bloch lurked in the background of much of the discussion of dialectical materialism, and particularly its deterministic aspect, in this period. Several of Bloch's students were among the leading philosophical "revisionists" (Richard Lorenz, Gerhard Zwerenz, Günter Zehm). The work of the economic historian Jürgen Kuczynski, who cast doubt on the revolutionary character of the working class and thereby on the premises of historical materialism, should also be mentioned. See Richert, "*Sozialistische Universität*," pp. 143–159.

sophical pronouncements on it;[76] he subsequently fled to the Federal Republic.[77]

The third critic was the distinguished physicist Robert Havemann, himself once a Stalinist who had been fired as head of a West Berlin institute in 1950 and had become director of Humboldt University's Institute for Physical Chemistry. Havemann, who later averred that he was deeply shaken by the revelations of the Twentieth CPSU (Communist Party of the Soviet Union) Congress,[78] used Heraclites' words—"conflict is the father of all things"—as the theme for an article in *Neues Deutschland* attacking "dogmatism" and the tyranny of the Marxist philosophers over science. Although he granted that all scientific knowledge was dialectical and materialistic, the scientist did not need to know or recognize this; and the doctrine of the "primacy of philosophy over the individual sciences" inhibted discovery and produced Lysenkos. "The history of every science provides eloquent testimony of how in the final reckoning space is created for new knowledge only through tireless discussion, through the conflict of opinion and counteropinion carried through to the end." [79] This doctrine, reminiscent of John Stuart Mill, was not well received, particularly in the campaign against revisionism following the 1957–1958 purges of leading party officials; in 1956, a professor of the "society sciences" told Havemann, "we couldn't discuss, but had to slug the enemy in the puss!" (*den Gegner in die Fresse schlagen*).[80] Havemann was accused of "arrogance" and "bourgeois individualism" but not punished, probably because of his reputation and possibly because of protection by influential friends.[81]

"Havemannism" erupted again in September 1962 when the physicist, in an address at Leipzig, returned to his 1956 themes:

[76] Jänicke, *Der dritte Weg*, pp. 124–126.

[77] Richert, *op. cit.*, p. 154.

[78] Robert Havemann, "'Ja, ich hatte unrecht,'" *Die Zeit* (May 7, 1965), p. 2.

[79] Robert Havemann, "Meinungsstreit fördert die Wissenschaften," *ND* (July 8, 1956), Beilage, p. 3.

[80] Robert Naumann, "Hand in Hand mit der Arbeiterklasse," *ND* (March 4, 1958), p. 5.

[81] Jänicke suggests that his name was needed for the then-current anti-atom campaign (*op. cit.*, p. 126); Ulbricht and Apel have been named as his highly placed friends. Marion Gräfin Dönhoff, Rudolf Walter Leonhardt, and Theo Sommer, *Reise in ein fernes Land* (Hamburg: Die Zeit Bücher, 1964), p. 126; *Frankfurter Allgemeine Zeitung* (December 20, 1965), p. 5.

"Science does not have the task of confirming the principles of philosophy, nor is philosophy the intellectual and ideological watchman over the errors and confusions of science." Dialectical materialism was not a "catechism" spelling out "immutable, eternal, and binding" laws and assertions; it was a *"Weltanschauung,* a basic intellectual position, a way of thinking," which developed with scientific discoveries and could not be a tribunal for judging them.[82] In December discussions on these themes took place at Humboldt, where one philosopher criticized another for defending "mechanical materialism" and "discredit[ing] Marxist philosophy in the eyes of the natural scientists." [83]

The next October Havemann began his now-famous lecture course at Humboldt, in which he sought to reformulate the concept of dialectical materialism in order to save its relevance for science. Again he returned to his earlier themes, stressing the need for freedom of opinion and attacking the philosophers. But he expanded on these to give them more clearly political meanings, in the case of the former calling for freedom of speech for all citizens and the unrestricted supplying of information which alone could make that freedom meaningful; "every limitation" on information and its exchange hindered social development.[84] In speaking of the second theme he added:

> I must say, I am far from questioning the connection between political relationships and philosophical dogmatism. . . . However, political relationships are not only the cause of philosophical dogmatism, but philosophical dogmatism also contributes its obedient bit to the development of the political relationships. The philosophers who overcome this dogmatism will also contribute to changing the political relationships.[85]

Additionally, he unburdened himself of attacks on capital pun-

---

[82] Reprinted in Robert Havemann, *Dialektik ohne Dogma? Naturwissenschaft und Weltanschauung* (Hamburg: Rowohlt Verlag, 1964), pp. 19–20.

[83] Hubert Laitko and Reinart Bellman, "Dogmatismus ist kein Schwarzer Peter" and "Echter Meinungsstreit und eine Fehlende Antwort," both in *Forum,* No. 1 (1963), p. 4. The philosopher, a Dr. Stehr, was also criticized for citing certain philosophical theses of Werner Heisenberg: "This uncritical identification with the controversial philosophical interpretations of bourgeois scientists, masquerading as anti-dogmatic, is in fact dogmatic because it inhibits the creative and rounded development of an independent Marxist standpoint" (*ibid.*).

[84] Havemann, *Dialektik,* pp. 51–52.

[85] *Ibid.,* p. 72.

ishment in "socialist" countries, the belief that the capitalist
world, too, was going through a "process of transformation," observations on socialist morality, and the view that "to change the
world is no undertaking with a guarantee of certainty, but [one]
with an uncertain outcome." [86] He concluded with a call for overcoming the legacy of the Stalinist past, which would require, to
be sure, "changes of personnel," but above all a turn toward
democracy; "socialism without democracy is not to be realized." [87]

Some 1,250 students registered for Havemann's course. Mimeographed copies of the lectures were distributed to all these and,
reportedly, circulated widely in the DDR; the published version,
brought out in the West in a pocket-sized paperback edition,
doubtless also found its way into the DDR in considerable quantity. Havemann, interviewed on the subject in March by a Hamburg newspaper, admitted having "intended" the "vigorous" reaction the lectures produced: "What has been possible for a long
time in the other lands of the socialist camp ought to be possible
in the DDR too." [88] The interview was the final straw; Havemann was stripped of his SED membership and his lecture post,
and it was suggested that he "intended to continue his university
work in West Germany." [89] He did not but rather continued his
research work in photochemistry with the German Academy of
Sciences. The East Berlin Akademie-Verlag brought out the
book *Wissenschaft contra Spekulation* to "refute the ungrounded
attacks of Robert Havemann on dialectical materialism," a measure of the SED's concern over the impact of his ideas.[90] Havemann published additional articles in the West: a reply to an
attack on his Stalinist past by *Forum*, which had refused to print
it,[91] a speech read in his absence at a conference on Christianity
and Marxism in Salzburg, which he was not allowed to attend.[92]
Finally, in December 1965, he gave an interview to the West
German *Der Spiegel* proposing that a parliamentary opposition
be allowed in the DDR, asking whether workers ought not to

[86] *Ibid.*, pp. 157–158, 150, 140ff., 126.   [87] *Ibid.*, p. 155.
[88] Interview reprinted in *SBZ-Archiv*, XV, No. 6 (1964), 95–96.
[89] New York *Times* (March 13, 1964), p. 15.
[90] K. H. [Kai Hermann], "Grosse Offensive gegen Havemann," *Die Zeit* (January
29, 1965), p. 5.
[91] Havemann, " 'Ja, ich hatte unrecht,' " *op. cit.*, p. 2.
[92] Excerpts in *Die Welt* (May 8, 1965), p. 5.

have the right to strike, and calling it a "distortion" that there should be fewer rights and freedoms under socialism than in a bourgeois society.[93] He was promptly fired from his research position[94] and expelled from the Academy of Sciences, the last in violation of its statutes, since the mandatory two-thirds vote was not obtained.[95] He has since lived in enforced retirement in East Berlin, writing his memoirs and additional articles for Western publication. In 1968 he attracted some attention with his praise of the Czech reform experiments; later that year his two sons were arrested for demonstrating against the invasion of that country.[96]

The Havemann case is noteworthy in illustrating the difficulties of communication confronting the oppositional intellectual. Richert points out that none of the "podium rebels" of 1956–1957 succeeded in becoming anything like an "intellectual event" in his own university, much less in the community or the DDR at large. This he attributes in large measure to the rigidity of the East German university system which, contrary to German tradition, makes it nearly impossible for a student in one faculty to attend a lecture in another.[97] Havemann, to be sure, drew over 1,000 students and did become something of an event, but in spite of the concern of the party, his inability to publish his lectures or later statements in the East greatly circumscribed his influence. The SED has similarly barred the publication of other East European reform documents.[98] I have already cited the Infratest finding that the then-recent "revisionist" activities of Benary, Behrens, Vieweg, and Bloch were known only to from 15 to 25 percent of the interviewees; equally few knew of revisionist activities in other East European countries, and virtually none knew what had actually been proposed. Many were uninterested in such matters, viewing them as internal affairs of the party.[99] I found similar ignorance over Havemann.

There have been further difficulties in communication between

---

[93] *Frankfurter Allgemeine Zeitung* (December 18, 1965), p. 3.

[94] *Ibid.* (December 27, 1965), p. 4. He allegedly had not been fired before because the Soviets had a special interest in the results of the project.

[95] See "Scherbengericht über Havemann," *Die Zeit* (N. Am. edition) (March 22, 1966), p. 3.

[96] See Heinz Lippmann, "The Limits of Reform Communism," *Problems of Communism* (May–June 1970), p. 18.

[97] Richert, *"Sozialistische Universität,"* p. 148.

[98] See Lippmann, *op. cit.,* p. 21.   [99] *Intelligenzschicht,* III, 103–105.

the oppositional forces themselves. It has frequently been remarked that in the DDR, unlike Hungary and Poland, workers' and intellectuals' revolts were never brought together; in 1953 the intelligentsia stood aside, in 1956 the working class.[100] Moreover, there has been only limited affinity between the proposals of rebels in the cultural intelligentsia and those in the scientific and technical intelligentsia, and less personal communication. The main thrust of opposition in the latter case has come from university professors; these are particularly isolated in their positions by German university structure, but also, one might suggest, by temperament.[101]

A further problem is that of communication between the intellectual critics and those within the top elite itself; with exceptions, it has been slight.[102] On all levels there is a range of distinctions between routine dissatisfactions, reformism, revisionism, and full-scale opposition; from without it is not always easy to tell which is which. Differences in the intensity and purposes of dissent make the forming of alliances difficult. Nevertheless, it is not impossible for diverse intellectual criticism and dissent to become joined to a broader range of discontents and to provide an ideological inspiration for reforming action: That is demonstrated by the Czechoslovak case. There, however, one must look to special circumstances: the severe failures of the Czech economy, the nationalistic strivings of Slovakia for greater autonomy, the relatively open intellectual atmosphere that was permitted in the last years of Novotny's rule, and the greater relative size and openness of the Czech party, which made it more accessible to reformist elements. To date, none of these has obtained in the DDR, and the SED has retained its ability and determination to constrict dissent.

It should also be repeated that dissent and revisionism among the technical intelligentsia are exceptional; accommodation, though with pragmatic and nonideological overtones, remains the rule. As a group, the cultural intelligentsia undoubtedly harbors

[100] Günter Grass's *Die Plebejer proben den Aufstand* (Neuwied and Berlin: Luchterhand, 1966), dramatizes the division in 1953.

[101] The recent restructuring of DDR universities and the close links established between them and industry have undoubtedly reduced this isolation, however.

[102] Havemann's friendship with Erich Apel (see below, Chap. 8) is one exception; the important advisory role of the Institute of Economic Sciences in the mid-1950s, mentioned above, is another.

more critics and dissenters than the technicians. It has often been suggested that the scientific method and spirit are fundamentally inconsistent with a dogmatic ideology, such as that pre-eminent in the DDR, or a rigid bureaucratic setting, such as the DDR imposes.[103] The widespread inclination of the DDR technical intelligentsia to view the professional and the political as distinct spheres and to withdraw as much as possible into the former reflects in part a perception, conscious or unconscious, of the tension between the two. Only infrequently does it issue in open political dissent or the advocacy of revisionist doctrines. That is why, its rhetoric to the contrary, the SED has often permitted "productive activity [to] purchase a man freedom from socio-political mobilization, whether he be a nominal member of the SED or not." [104]

Furthermore, such revisionism as there is may ultimately prove of positive use to the regime. "The history of domination," Ludz remarks, "has demonstrated that the powerful and their accomplices have consistently learned from their critics." [105] The ideas of Behrens and Benary were in some part incorporated into the New Economic System; even in combating "Havemannism," the party felt obliged, for balance, to reject "dogmatism" in science. Undoubtedly, it is of significance that most of the prominent economic and scientific "revisionists" have been permitted to continue their intellectual work in the Academy of Sciences and elsewhere, though their publications have often been restricted and some have been kept from teaching.[106] However small their impact when first presented, the ideas planted by the revisionist never certainly die but are there for both old leaders and oncoming ones to utilize when it becomes expedient to do so.

[103] Ralf Dahrendorf, for example, draws an analogy between the method of empirical science and the "constitution of liberty." "Empirical sciences can thrive only in a liberal political context, unless they violate their own rules of the game." *Society and Democracy in Germany* (Garden City, N.Y.: Anchor Books, 1967), p. 150 and *passim*. Similarly, Don K. Price remarks that "the pursuit of science itself is a nonhierarchical affair"; insofar as scientists have influenced bureaucratic development in the West, they have "introduced into the stodgy and responsible channels of bureaucracy the amiable disorder of a university faculty meeting." "The Scientific Establishment," in Robert Gilpin and Christopher Wright, eds., *Scientists and National Policy Making* (New York: Columbia University Press, 1964), p. 37.

[104] Ernst Richert, "Ulbricht and After," *Survey* (October 1966), p. 156.

[105] Ludz, *Parteielite*, p. 294.

[106] Richert, "Sozialistische Universität," p. 199.

PART II

The Technical Intelligentsia as a Strategic Elite

7

RECRUITMENT INTO THE ELITE

> Top functionaries have moved from one apparatus to another
> with astonishing frequency. These elites are in great measure
> interchangeable with one another, quite in contrast to the ap-
> paratus of repression or the diplomatic service. The subject
> matter has primacy here, not the question of whether one belongs
> to the "party" or the "government." The party and state ap-
> paratuses are—certainly since the mid-1950s—no longer in com-
> petition.
>
> ERNST RICHERT[1]

THOSE MEMBERS of the technical intelligentsia "whose judgments, decisions, and actions have important and determi-
nable consequences for many members of society" [2] may be said to
belong to the "strategic elite" of DDR technicians. Suzanne Keller
has argued that advanced industrial societies bring the proliferation of expert strategic elites performing the specialized functions
such societies require. In her view such elites are relatively au-
tonomous yet interdependent, are recruited largely on the basis of
achievement criteria, and are the guardians of community and
moral consensus in society. In contemporary societies they typically include political, military, economic, scientific, moral, and
cultural elites, performing the Parsonian functions of goal attainment, adaptation, integration, and pattern maintenance.[3]

The concept of elite has customarily carried with it a good deal
of ideological and conceptual baggage, and Keller's formulation is
no exception. Her assertion that the very plurality and interde-

[1] Ernst Richert, *Die DDR-Elite* (Hamburg: Rowohlt Verlag, 1968), pp. 109–110.
[2] Suzanne Keller, *Beyond the Ruling Class* (New York: Random House, 1963), p.
20.
[3] *Ibid.*, pp. 57–58, 66ff.

pendence of strategic elites implies limits on the arbitrary exercise of power[4] is of special interest to this study, and I shall return to it in a later chapter. For now let me remark that in addition to Keller and other writers on Western societies,[5] specialists on Communist systems have also noted the emergence of plural elite structures with the advance of economic modernization.[6] Milton Lodge, for example, has examined the Soviet *apparatchiki* and four additional "specialist elites": the military, economic administrators, the literary intelligentsia, and legal professionals. Much in the spirit of Keller, he suggests that since Stalin's death they have acquired increasing autonomy and self-consciousness, thus mitigating the monolithicity (and presumably the oppressiveness) of the Soviet system.[7]

I adopt the term "strategic elite" only with some modification of Keller's usage. First, there is the matter of definition, with its consequences for the delimitation of the group I will examine in this and the following three chapters. Keller's definition, quoted above, avoids some pitfalls: The conception which sees elites as the guardians of values and standards in society,[8] that which includes all groups of high status,[9] and that which limits itself to strictly "political" elites based on the power to make "severely sanctioned

[4] *Ibid.*, pp. 57, 273–274; see also the comments of Peter Bachrach, *The Theory of Democratic Elitism* (Boston: Little, Brown, 1967), pp. 62–64.

[5] For example, Raymond Aron, "Social Structure and the Ruling Class," *British Journal of Sociology*, I (March–June 1950), 1–16, 126–143; Karl Mannheim, *Man and Society in an Age of Reconstruction* (London: Routledge & Kegan Paul, 1940), pp. 82ff.

[6] See, for example, H. Gordon Skilling, "Interest Groups and Communist Politics," *World Politics*, XVIII (April 1966), 435–451; H. Gordon Skilling and Franklyn Griffiths, eds., *Interest Groups in Soviet Politics* (Princeton: Princeton University Press, 1971); Vernon Aspaturian, "Social Structure and Political Power in the Soviet System," in H. Albinski and L. Pettit, eds., *European Political Processes* (Boston: Allyn and Bacon, 1968), pp. 150–176. Cf. also the intelligent critique of Andrew C. Janos, "Group Politics in Communist Society," in Samuel P. Huntington and Clement H. Moore, eds., *Authoritarian Politics in Modern Society* (New York: Basic Books, 1970), pp. 437–450.

[7] Milton C. Lodge, *Soviet Elite Attitudes Since Stalin* (Columbus, Ohio: Merrill, 1969), pp. 1, 114–115, and *passim*. Lodge's use of content analysis techniques to establish this growing differentiation of elites is inventive but not free of serious problems of method and interpretation.

[8] Mannheim, *op. cit.*, pp. 82–85; Philip Selznick, "Institutional Vulnerability in Mass Society," *American Journal of Sociology*, LVI (January 1951), 320–323; William Kornhauser, *The Politics of Mass Society* (Glencoe, Ill.: Free Press, 1959), p. 51.

[9] T. B. Bottomore, *Elites and Society* (Harmondsworth: Penguin Books, 1964), p. 14.

choices" [10] are all unsatisfactory for our purposes. But Keller's formulation remains necessarily imprecise, offering little guidance for the rigorous identification of an elite in a concrete instance. In the present case we shall examine a group of men designated "elite" by virtue of their positions, with a few additional figures selected through an intuitive assessment of their significance.[11] The positions are those on the party Politburo, Secretariat, and Central Committee, and at the head of government ministries, the Planning Commission, and other central government offices.

A more important issue is that of distinguishing between strategic elites, particularly the economic and political elites, and establishing the relationship between them. Keller, in my view, errs in treating all strategic elites as essentially equal and in insisting that no individual may belong to more than one at the same time.[12] In Western as in Eastern industrial societies, the political elite is distinguished by the at least nominal power to dictate the conditions of existence of all other elites; this is a necessary consequence of the greater generality of its functions and of their claimed authoritative character. In that sense the political elite may be viewed as a kind of master elite. Because of the very importance of its role, however, the political elite is apt to be more "open" than other elites: A greater diversity of background and education is acceptable for entrance into it, and "circulation" in and out of it is likely to be more rapid. Thus, it is frequently more easily penetrable and controllable by members of other elites—for example, economic, legal, military—than are the others, which usually have strong incentives for penetrating it, and which themselves are often protected by more specialized and rigid entrance standards. This is not to assert that in modern societies the po-

[10] Harold D. Lasswell, Daniel Lerner, and C. Easton Rothwell, *The Comparative Study of Elites* (Stanford: Stanford University Press, 1952), pp. 6–13; see also Lasswell and Abraham Kaplan, *Power and Society* (New Haven: Yale University Press, 1950), pp. 201–204.

[11] Richard L. Merritt, *Systematic Approaches to Comparative Politics* (Chicago: Rand McNally, 1970), discusses these and other approaches to the identification of elites, pp. 113–118; cf. also Frederic J. Fleron, Jr., "Note on the Explication of the Concept 'Elite' in the Study of Soviet Politics," *Canadian Slavic Studies*, II (Spring 1968), 111–115. It is necessary to note that the selection of the positions is ultimately intuitive as well although there appears to be a scholarly consensus on their importance.

[12] Keller, *op. cit.*, p. 57.

litical elite is apt to lack an identity separate from that of other elites, even when it is controlled by them. The political elite is set apart by its distinctive functions and usually by a set of professional values and "folkways" quite its own. The political elite always occupies a special position in relation to other strategic elites, whether it is truly a master elite or instead the mere cat's-paw of one or more of the others.[13]

In principle, this asymmetrical relationship between the political and other elites might also be said to obtain in Communist societies. But in such societies matters are complicated by the very pervasiveness of politics, so much so that Ralf Dahrendorf has spoken of the "gradual fusion of elites" from all sectors of DDR society with the party leadership and the subordination of those incapable of fusion.[14] Leading positions in the specialized elites (economic, military) are regarded simultaneously as leading political positions, and positions within the party elite proper tend to be functionally specialized, with their incumbents maintaining often intimate links to their counterparts outside the high party organs. Yet to speak only of the fusion of elites perpetuates the misleading image of a totalitarian monolith and ignores the growing divergencies of interest and outlook remarked by observers such as Lodge and, for the DDR, Peter Ludz.

What appears best to describe the elite structure of the contemporary Soviet Union and DDR is the superimposition of an overarching political elite, united by party membership and a nominally common ideology, on a series of more specialized elites, some of whose members belong to the political elite and some of whom do not. One of these specialized elites, the men of the party organization, or *apparatchiki,* has traditionally regarded itself as the core of the political elite and the guardian of its values, but, as we shall see, this self-image no longer fully reflects reality. Instead the *apparatchiki* share political dominance with members of other specialized elites: economic functionaries, military and police officials, educators, ideological and propaganda specialists. These in turn are the objects of ambivalent pressures: from their specialist con-

---

[13] As it is in the classic Marxian view, as well as in such works as C. Wright Mills, *The Power Élite* (New York: Oxford University Press, 1957).

[14] Ralf Dahrendorf, *Society and Democracy in Germany* (Garden City, N.Y.: Anchor Books, 1967), p. 405.

stituencies, on the one hand, and from their own attachment to the political elite and close association with the *apparatchiki,* on the other.

Our principal focus of interest in this and the subsequent chapters will be those members of the economic-technical-scientific elite who are simultaneously members of the political elite; this is the strategic elite of our concern. It should now be clear why we have given as much attention as we have to the socialization and political and work attitudes of the stratum of technical intelligentsia as a whole. The attitudes and behavior of members of the strategic elite of technicians can be understood only if we understand the stratum from which they emerged and to which in some sense they continue to feel affinities and loyalties.

At the same time it is evident that members of the strategic elite constitute no simple, representative cross-section of the technical intelligentsia as a whole. It is the task of this chapter to bridge the discussions of stratum and elite by exploring the principles and conditions of recruitment from the first into the second and to suggest some of the consequences of the selection process for the latter's behavior.

RECRUITMENT MECHANISMS

Recruitment into the politically significant echelon of the technical elite is organized and carried out through the cadre divisions of the party, with responsibilities for individuals and positions assigned according to the "nomenclature" system.[15] Most of the positions I am concerned with, including those of ministers and state secretaries, belong to the nomenclature of the SED Central Committee, that is to say, the Secretariat. While the cadre and party organs divisions of the central apparatus bear primary responsibility for cadre work,[16] it is likely that the entire Secretariat deals with major appointments.[17] Potential young recruits for lead-

[15] See also above, Chap. 5; Jerry F. Hough, *The Soviet Prefects* (Cambridge: Harvard University Press, 1969), Chap. 7.

[16] For many years this area of party work was under the supervision of Erich Honecker; following his elevation to SED First Secretary, the young functionary and new "member" of the Secretariat Horst Dohlus appears to have taken over many of these functions.

[17] The SED party statute names the "selection of party workers" (cadres) as one of the two basic functions of the Secretariat. *Statut der Sozialistischen Einheitspartei*

ing positions are to be singled out early, according to an authoritative Secretariat decision of 1965; "their path of development is to be individually determined" by the relevant state organ or division of the party apparatus, with the latter in any case "controlling" the work of the former. Thus, while a prominent technician in the early stages of his career may be within the formal purview of a regional or lower-ranking cadre unit, the Secretariat division has the ability and authority to follow his progress and if desired intervene. The young cadres are to be placed under the personal tutelage of an experienced leader or scientist, who is expected to bestow his accumulated wisdom, experience, and work habits on his charge and supervise him in the independent performance of responsible tasks.[18]

The 1965 Secretariat document specifies the criteria for advancement only in broad terms: The cadres must have proven themselves through "outstanding successes" in carrying out party decisions; they must, if they are to be considered for top-level functions, be highly educated and have already demonstrated in practice their leadership capacities. A university or *Fachschule* education, "solid knowledge" of Marxism-Leninism, and specialized training appropriate to their contemplated responsibilities are named as requirements for all higher cadres.[19] As a whole, the cadres document is remarkable in the extent to which it emphasizes achievement criteria in contrast to the rather perfunctory attention given overt political requirements. Later pronouncements have sought to correct this imbalance.[20] The recruitment ideal frequently enunciated by Ulbricht has, however, persisted: "Red experts" are demanded, combining in equal measure technical expertise and devotion to Marxism-Leninism.[21]

Deutschlands (Berlin: Dietz Verlag, 1968), para. 41. See also *A bis Z* (Bonn: Deutscher Bundes-Verlag, 1969), p. 450; Richert, *Die DDR-Elite*, p. 41.

[18] "Grundsätze über die planmässige Entwicklung, Ausbildung, Erziehung, und Verteilung der Kader . . . ," decision of Central Committee Secretariat, *Neuer Weg*, XX, No. 6 (1965), pp. 341–342. See also Eckart Förtsch, *Die SED* (Stuttgart: W. Kohlhammer Verlag, 1969), pp. 76–83.

[19] "Grundsätze," *op. cit.*, p. 341.

[20] "It is . . . not simply a matter of greater professional skill, greater specialized knowledge. What we need are 'socialist experts' who know their jobs and have a clear political standpoint and responsible attitude toward our society." Heinz Edlich and Lothar Hummel, "Alle Talente fördern, alle Fähigkeiten entwickeln," *Einheit*, XXVI, No. 1 (1971), 46–47.

[21] See, for example, Ulbricht, "Das neue ökonomische System der Planung und

The principles actually used are of course likely to depart from those formally specified; in some measure they may be inferred from the examination of the biographies and career patterns of leading economic functionaries which follows. Preliminary to their discussion, it will be useful to list briefly some of the criteria which might govern selection:

1. Qualities of personality
2. Personal "connections"
3. Age
4. Education
5. Professional abilities
6. Leadership and personal interaction skills
7. Political loyalty, as demonstrated by
   a. fact of party membership
   b. length of party membership
8. Political activism
9. Experience in regular part-time or full-time political roles
10. Self-selection

Popular commentaries often purport to discover in Soviet and East European leadership changes the development of personal followings, sometimes based on regional or ethnic biases. The SED statute itself sternly admonishes against selecting cadres "on the basis of relationships of kinship or friendship or personal loyalty. . . ." [22] Yet there is no persuasive evidence that these elements play an unusually large part in the DDR, particularly in the technical and economic sphere.[23] Youth and advanced specialized education are both frankly advanced as desirable criteria for elite recruitment, and the evidence presented below suggests they

---

Leitung der Volkswirtschaft in der Praxis," *Die Wirtschaft* (June 28, 1963), pp. 5–6; Ulbricht, *Probleme des Perspektivplanes bis 1970*, speech at Eleventh Central Committee Plenum (Berlin: Dietz Verlag, 1966), p. 97.

[22] *Statut, op. cit.*, para. 2k.

[23] It seems undoubted that especially after the 1957–1958 purges personal loyalty to Ulbricht was a requisite for selection to the Politburo or Secretariat, and several new party appointees to the Politburo or regional First Secretary positions appear to have close career ties to Honecker. Here, however, we are primarily concerned with initial recruitment into the elite, that is, at its lower echelons. Richert, *op. cit.*, provides some discussion and speculation on interpersonal relationships among the top SED leaders. Perhaps the most visible personal ties are the position of Honecker's wife Margot as education minister and of her brother Manfred Feist as a central committee section head. See Karl Wilhelm Fricke, "Honeckers Mannschaft," *Deutschland Archiv*, IV (September 1971), 961–967.

indeed have been, although least of all for the top party organs, the Politburo and Secretariat.

The particular mix between "objective" standards of talent and achievement (items 5 and 6 above), on the one hand, and political tests (7 through 9), on the other, that is demanded of elite candidates is a critical variable in determining its character. The cadre selection principles already cited commend a roughly equal balance between the two. While the evidence shows unambiguously that achievement criteria, as measured, for example, by level of education, have grown steadily in importance over the years, that does not necessarily imply a corresponding relaxation of political standards. The examination of the recruitment paths of the technical strategic elite—the degree to which their prior work experience and socialization has taken place in more or less highly politicized spheres—reveals no single consistent pattern. Many of the present leaders have divided their time between differentially politicized sectors; indeed, that is a conscious principle of DDR cadre policy. "A proven method," states the 1965 cadre decision, "is an astutely planned exchange and rotation of leadership cadres from socialist enterprises and the state apparatus into the party apparatus and vice versa." [24]

Membership in the party from an early age appears to be an all but ironclad requirement for advancement into the technical strategic elite. Highly visible political activism, much less experience in part- or full-time political roles (for example, party organizational work, functions in the trade unions or FDJ), does not appear to be. While many leading technical functionaries have such experience, as our figures will show, for men with highly valued professional capabilities, long party membership by itself seems to be regarded as an adequate earnest of political loyalty.

Nothing very precise can be said concerning the significance of either positive or negative self-selection in the recruitment process. Jeremy Azrael, in his study of the Soviet managerial classes, argues that the "liberals" and "technocrats" among them are inclined to avoid party membership and to retreat into specialized careers outside of politics while those who strive upwards toward elite

[24] "Grundsätze," *op. cit.*, p. 341.

positions tend to be conventional and loyal if not zealous adherents of the existing order.[25] In the DDR the initial and possibly critical choice of whether to decline the possibility of political eminence comes at an early age. It is the choice of whether to turn down candidacy to SED membership or, what is often the same thing, to drop out of the FDJ as early as is "opportune." [26] Yet the political learning process that inclines a technician to liberal or technocratic views may not have its most forceful impact until after he has committed himself to membership.[27]

CAREER PATTERNS

I have made a listing of fifty-one of the leading economic and technical functionaries of the DDR and have sought to generalize their recruitment and career patterns and put them in tabular form (see Table 7.1). They have been selected largely according to their positions, as follows:

1. All members of the Council of Ministers with economic, technical and scientific responsibilities or backgrounds, as of August 1970. (Biographical data is available on 23 of 25 possible.)
2. All members and candidate members of the SED Politburo or Secretariat with such responsibilities or backgrounds (8 of 8).
3. Those heads of the divisions of the Central Committee apparatus with such responsibilities who are simultaneously members or candidates of the Central Committee itself (3 of 3).
4. Heads of State Secretariats, Committees, Offices, and Administrations with such responsibilities (11 of 15).
5. State Secretaries in the Planning Commission and the Council for Agricultural Production and the Food Industry (1 of 2).
6. The Rectors or Directors of the institutes and academies responsible for training leading economic functionaries (*Hochschule für Ökonomie,* Central Institute for Socialist Economic Leadership, Academy for Organization Sciences, Institute of Society Sciences) (4 of 4).

[25] Jeremy R. Azrael, *Managerial Power and Soviet Politics* (Cambridge: Harvard University Press, 1966), pp. 154–167.

[26] Richert, *op. cit.,* pp. 41–42

[27] That is to say, during his university education or, even more, in the first years of his confrontation with the "realities" of his job. See above, Chaps. 2 and 4.

7. The chairman of the DDR Research Council (1 of 1).
8. The chairman of the *Kammer der Technik* (1 of 1).[28]

Five additional figures have been selected on an ad hoc basis: two former ministers who are presently deputy chairmen of the State Planning Commission (Helmut Lilie, Hugo Meiser), the Minister for University and *Fachschule* Affairs (Ernst-Joachim Giessmann) replaced in 1970 by a nontechnician, the distinguished and often dissident economic theorist Fritz Behrens, and the veteran party economic functionary Margarete Wittkowski (now president of the State Bank).[29] A few names have had to be eliminated because of insufficient biographical information.[30]

The population selected thus includes a high proportion from the government side, particularly members of the Council of Ministers (23). This appears justified by the present division of labor in economic decision making in the DDR. While the fundamental economic policy decisions continue to be laid down by the SED Politburo, secondary decisions and important operational questions have become the province of the council, which is now largely an economic body performing some of the functions that once belonged to the Planning Commission or National Economic Council.[31] Given the high interchangeability between government and party roles that we shall observe in a moment, the distinction between the two spheres is in any case diminishing in importance.

An examination of Table 7.1 immediately reveals several important data. The DDR's technical strategic elite is predominantly middle-aged, averaging 47 in 1970 (standard deviation = 7.7), with the median 44 and a range from 38 to 68. Since most entered their present positions between 1963 and 1967, a slight ageing

---

[28] All but the last have been identified from the list of leading government, party, and mass organization officials published in *Deutschland Archiv*, III (October 1970), 1056–1068.

[29] The total listed here is greater than fifty-one because of some overlapping of functions, particularly between the SED Politburo and high governmental offices.

[30] For example, the new Minister for University and *Fachschule* Affairs Hans-Joachim Böhme; the new Minister for Material Economy Erich Haase; and Ulbricht's personal economic adviser Wolfgang Berger.

[31] See *Politische Ökonomie des Sozialismus und ihre Anwendung in der DDR* (Berlin: Dietz Verlag, 1969), pp. 363–365; Peter Christian Ludz, *Parteielite im Wandel* (Köln and Opladen: Westdeutscher Verlag, 1968), p. 236; Ernst Richert, "Trend zur Entsachlichung in der SED-Führung?" *Deutschland Archiv*, II (May 1969), 487.

trend has already set in. Not unexpectedly, all but 4 are SED members.[32] Despite their relative youth, 30 had joined the party by 1949; 6 more had joined by 1953; 1 in 1955; and the date of membership for the remaining ten is unknown. All or most thus became party members as very young men—the median age is 21 for those whose date of joining we know—and have belonged to it a minimum of fifteen years. Three-fifths have served on the Central Committee or held some other major, part-time party position (most usually as *Volkskammer* delegate), though only 13 have ever held a nontechnical party job as their primary position.[33] Twenty-one (including 9 of the 13) have previously held economic or technical positions within the party apparatus (for example, as directors of the functional divisions of the Central Committee, economic secretaries in regional party organizations, etc.). Only 10 of the party members remain, then, whom we do not know to have occupied important party posts of one sort or another. The interweaving of party and nonparty roles is thus apparent, but their significance varies with the party position in question. Those in party economic-technical roles are probably subject to many of the same pressures and motivations as nonparty technicians; and it is to be doubted whether honorific selection to the Central Committee or *Volkskammer* has an important socialization effect on those chosen, though of course it is a mark of past loyalty. One might expect the 25 percent who have occupied full-time, nontechnical party offices to be most sympathetic with something like an *apparatchik* outlook. Such an inference, however, would require confirmation from other, presently unavailable, data.

At least 43 members of the technical elite have had some advanced education. Twenty have earned a doctor's degree, and another 13 a university diploma. As Table 7.2 shows, 13 of the former and 8 of the latter are in economics, including engineering economics. As I noted in Chapter 2, the course of study in eco-

---

[32] Hans Reichelt is a functionary of the DBD, a "satellite" party; I have no information on the party affiliation of Helmut Koziolek, head of the Institute for Socialist Economic Leadership, or Horst Peschel, president of the KDT, though it seems probable that at least the former is an SED member. Max Steenbeck, the sixty-six-year-old physicist who is chairman of the State Research Council, belongs to no party.

[33] It should be stressed that here as elsewhere in this section the figures given are minimum ones since some of the biographical information is incomplete.

TABLE 7.1. Careers of Leading DDR Economic Functionaries

	(1)	(2)	(3)	(4)	(5)	(6)	(7)	(8)	(9)	(10)	(11)
			Past experience (principal ec.-tech. jobs)							Other major party functions	
			State (ec.-tech. only)								
Name	Present function	Party	Min-istry	SPC, etc.	Re-gional or other	Acad.	Indus.	Year of birth	Party member	Prim.	Auxil.
Behrens, Fritz	Acad.			p		x		1909	1932		
Bernicke, Hubertus	Inst. dir.		s, o	p		x		1919	SED		
Böchmann, Manfred[a]	S. S.	r						?	SED		
Böhm, Siegfried	Min.	c						1928	1948	x	cc, o
Donda, Arno	Off. dir.		o					1930	1955		
Ewald, Georg[b]	Ch. AFC				r			1926	1946	x	pb, o
Fichtner, Kurt[b]	Min.		o, m	p, v	r		VEB	1916	1946		
Georgi, Rudi	Min.						VEB, VVB	1927	1946		cc
Giessmann, Ernst-Joachim	Min.		o, s		r	x	VEB	1919	1946		o
Görbing, Rolf[a]	Off. dir.							1930	SED		
Grüneberg, Gerhard	CC Sec.	t	m					1921	1946	x	pb, o
Halbritter, Walter[b]	Min.	c	o, s	p				1927	1946	x	pb, o
Hemmerling, Joachim	Off. dir.				o	x		1926	SED		o
Hörnig, Hannes	CC funct.	c						1921	1945		cc
Jarowinsky, Werner[b]	CC Sec.		o, s			x		1927	1945	x	pb, o
Junker, Wolfgang	Min.		s				VEB	1929	1951		cc
Kiesler, Bruno	Agr. funct.	o						1925	1946	x	o
Kleiber, Günter[b]	S. S.	r	s			x		1931	1949	x	pb, o
Koch, Helmut	S. S.		o, s		r			1922	SED		
Koziolek, Helmut	Inst. dir.			p		x		1927	?		

Name	Office										
Krack, Erhard	Min.	o		v	r			1930	1951	x	cc, o
Kramer, Erwin	Min.	c	s				o	1902	1929		
Kuhrig, Heinz	V. ch. AFC	c				x		1929	1947		0
Lange, Alfred	Rector	c				x		1927	SED		
Lilie, Helmut	V. Ch. SPC		m		o	x	o, VEB	1923	1945		cc, o
Matthes, Heinz	Min.	r			r			1927	1947		
Meiser, Hugo	V. Ch. SPC		m	p	r			1921	SED		
Mittag, Günter[b]	CC Sec.	c, t		v				1926	1946		pb, o
Müller, Margarete	PB-Cand.				r		LPG	1931	1951		cc, o
Neumann, Alfred[b]	Min.		m	v		x		1909	1929	x	pb, o
Peschel, Horst	Pres. KDT				r	x		1909	?		cc
Pöschel, Hermann	CC funct.	c			o			1919	1945		cc, o
Prey, Günter	Min.		s				Komb	1930	1953		cc, o
Rauchfuss, Wolfgang[b]	Min.		o, s	l	o			1931	1951	x	0
Reichelt, Hans	H.G.O.		s, m					1925	DBD-49		cc, o
Reinhold, Otto	Inst. dir.	o				x		1925	1950	x	cc, o
Rochlitzer, Johann[a]	Off. dir.				o			1904	SED		
Schürer, Gerhard[b]	Ch. SPC	o, c	s	p	r			1921	1948		cc, o
Seemann, Hans-Joachim	Off. dir.			l		x		ca. 1928	SED		
Sieber, Günther	Min.	o		p	o			1930	1946		0
Siebold, Klaus	Min.	c		p, v			VEB	1930	1948	x	
Singhuber, Kurt	Min.					x	VEB	1932	SED		
Sölle, Horst	Min.	c	s					1925	1945	x	cc
Steenbeck, Max	Ch. Res. Cncl.					x		1904	none		
Steger, Otfried	Min.		s	v			VEB, VVB	1926	1945		cc
Weiss, Gerhard[b]	Min.				r			1919	1948		cc, o
Weiz, Herbert[b]	Min.		s, o	p	r		VEB	1924	1945		cc, o
Wittik, Hans	Min.	o	o, s	v	r			1923	1947		cc
Wittkowski, Margarete	Bank pres.		m	p	o			1910	1932		cc, o
Wyschofsky, Günter	Min.	c		p			VEB	1929	1945		cc, o
Zimmermann, Gerhard	Min.	r					VEB, VVB	1927	1946		cc

TABLE 7.1. (continued)

a Only limited information available.

b "Top elite."

Key:

Col. 1: Acad. = academic = university, research institute positions.

Inst. dir. = institute or academy director.

S.S. = state secretary.

Min. = minister, member of Council of Ministers.

Off. dir. = director of state office, committee, or administration.

Ch. = chairman; V = vice.

CC Sec. = Central Committee secretary.

Funct. = functionary.

AFC = Agriculture and Foodstuffs Council.

SPC = State Planning Commission.

PB-Cand. = Politburo candidate.

KDT = *Kammer der Technik* = Chamber of Technology.

H.G.O. = high government official not otherwise classifiable.

Res. Cncl. = research council.

Col. 2: (previous economic and technical positions within the party)

r = regional party functionary.

c = functionary in Central Committee apparatus.

t = top leadership position.

o = other.

Col. 3: (positions in economic-technical ministries)

s = state secretary, deputy minister.

o = other.

m = minister.

Col. 4: (positions in State Planning Commission, *Volkswirtschaftsrat, Landwirtschaftsrat*)

p = Planning Commission.

v = VWR = People's Economic Council.

l = LWR = Agricultural Council.

Col. 5: (regional economic-technical functionaries and other)

r = regional.

o = other.

Col. 6: Those holding academic positions.

Col. 7: (industrial or agricultural positions)

VEB = *Volkseigene Betriebe* = factories.

VVB = *Vereinigung volkseigener Betriebe*.

o = other.

LPG = collective farm.

Komb. = *Kombinat*.

Col. 9: Date of entrance into KPD up to 1945; into SED from 1946 on.

SED = member but date of entrance unknown.

DBD = Demokratische Bauernpartei Deutschlands (Democratic Farmers' Party of Germany).

Cols. 10 and 11: (other major party and mass organization functionaries)

Prim. = primary functions.

Auxil. = auxiliary functions.

cc = Central Committee member.

o = other.

pb = Politburo.

Sources: SBZ-Biographie, 1965; *SBZ von A bis Z*, 1966; *SBZ-Archiv*, XVIII, Nos. 11–12, 14 (1967), 184–195, 218; Ludz, *Parteielite im Wandel, passim*; files of Institut für Politische Wissenschaft, Berlin; *Die Volkskammer der Deutschen Demokratischen Republik*, 5. Wahlperiode (Berlin: Staatsverlag der DDR, 1967); *A-Z*, 1969; *Deutschland Archiv*, III (October 1970), 1056–1068; *Technische Gemeinschaft* (March 1970), p. 42.

TABLE 7.2. Education of the Technical Elite[a]

Field of study	Doctorate	University diplomas	Other advanced study
Economics	13	8	0
Engineering	3	3	6
Natural sciences	3	1	0
"Society sciences"	0	2	0
Agriculture	1	1	0
Unknown	0	0	2
Total	20	15	8

[a] Figures given are for the highest level of education attained by individual members of the group.

nomics is substantially more politicized, and the student body more predominantly proletarian in origin, than in either engineering or the natural sciences. While I have no precise figures, a number of these degrees were earned not in universities but in party institutes; in addition, several members of the elite have studied at professional or party schools in the Soviet Union. It is only a slight exaggeration to conclude that the technical strategic elite is primarily an elite of economists, with engineers and scientists coming in a relatively poor second and poorer third, respectively.

It is apparent from both Tables 7.1 and 7.3 that there is no single dominant career pattern which brought the DDR's technical leaders to their present positions. All but a few have had

TABLE 7.3. Number of Arenas of Experience of Technical Elite

No. of arenas	Arenas of ec.-tech. exp. prior to present position		Same with three gov't. arenas collapsed		Arenas of exp. incl. present position		No. of each w. additional full-time party exp. (nontech. positions)
	N	%	N	%	N	%	
1	8	15.7	15	29.4	1	1.9	0
2	26	51.0	32	62.8	26	51.0	7
3	14	27.4	4	7.8	15	29.4	4
4	3	5.9	0	0.0	9	17.7	2
Total	51	100.0	51	100.0	51	100.0	13

experience in more than one of the six major arenas of economic, technical, and scientific employment I have designated: the party apparatus; government ministries, central state secretariats, committees, offices, and administrations; central planning and agricultural commissions and the former *Volkswirtschaftsrat*;[34] regional and other government posts; academic and research institutions; and industry and state and collective farms. Even if the three arenas of the state bureaucracy are combined, over two-thirds of the 51 have worked in two or three of the four major economic-technical spheres. Thus, the diversity of experience recommended for leading cadres is by and large observed in practice. The absolute numbers of those with experience in each of the six arenas (Table 7.4) takes on added significance when we separate out members of the *top elite* among the 51; they are defined as those belonging to the SED Politburo (including candidates) or Secretariat, or ranking as members of the Presidium of the Council of Ministers.[35] There are 11 of them.

Thirteen of the whole group of 51 have had some experience in industry and 1 on a farm collective; 11 of the former have worked in state factories (VEBs) or *Kombinats*. Only 2 of the 11 (Kurt Fichtner and Herbert Weiz) belong to the top elite, but most of the rest are important government ministers. Two of those with industrial experience were VVB directors after these were made economic (rather than administrative) institutions under the New Economic System; in view of the significance ascribed to these positions in the official press for some years, the low number advancing to higher posts is surprising. Seventeen others of the 47 have worked in academic institutions and research bodies, but in several cases their present job either is academic or is one most logically filled by such a person. Werner Jarowinsky, who taught at Humboldt University from 1954 to 1958, and Günter Kleiber, who was an *Assistent* for four years, are the only representatives of this group in the top elite.

Aside from several who were former ministers, 18 have worked

---

[34] The National Economic Council was the central government organ for short-term planning and direction of industry between 1961 and 1965; it replaced sections of the State Planning Commission and the industrial ministries for this period.

[35] Margarete Müller, though a Politburo candidate, is viewed by many as a decorative "token woman" in the SED leadership and thus is not included in this narrower group. See Förtsch, *Die SED*, p. 121.

TABLE 7.4. Prior Occupational Experience of Technical Elite by Arena

Arena		N (51)	Percentage	Top elite N (11)
1	Party technical-economic functions	21	41.2	4
2	State ministries, secretariats, etc.	23	45.1	8
3	Planning Commission, VWR, LWR	19	37.3	6
4	Regional and other state positions	20	39.2	6
	2–4 (All state economic-technical funct.)	**39**	**76.5**	**11**
5	Academic functions	17	33.4	2
6	Industry/agriculture	14	27.4	2
7	Full-time nontechnical party functions	13	25.5	5

in government ministries, 10 below the level of state secretary or deputy minister. Five of these belong presently to the top leaders; a sixth and seventh have been deputy ministers, and an eighth a minister. Only Georg Ewald, Günter Mittag, and Gerhard Schürer in the top group do not have experience in a ministry. Seventeen of the total number have had prior experience in the State Planning Commission or the now-defunct *Volkswirtschaftsrat,* and 2 more in the Agricultural Council; 6 (Kurt Fichtner, Walter Halbritter, Günter Mittag, Alfred Neumann, Gerhard Schürer, Herbert Weiz) are in the top elite. A total of 13 (4 top elite) have worked in regional government posts and 4 (1 top elite) in regional party posts with primarily economic-technical responsibilities. Three of the top elite have worked in the Central Committee apparatus (Walter Halbritter, Günter Mittag, Gerhard Schürer), while 5 at one time held nontechnical party jobs as their primary posts (Georg Ewald, Werner Jarowinsky, Alfred Neumann, Günter Kleiber, and, probably, Walter Halbritter).

To sum up, experience in economic ministries and in industrial planning and directing organs is most frequently the path to the DDR's economic leadership. (The *Volkswirtschaftsrat,* which had short-term planning responsibilities and also replaced the industrial ministries in day-to-day economic leadership, in effect bridged the gap between the two.) With the exception of Georg Ewald, all members of the top elite went through one or the other; and only 16 of the entire 51 are without prior experience in either. While about 40 percent have experience in economic or technical roles in the party, and 30 percent in each case in regional government, industry, and academic and research institutions, these are of decreasing significance, in the order given, in producing top leadership. It is not surprising that the ministries and planning commission should be so important as routes to strategic elite positions since they, along with the Central Committee apparatus, are much more likely to be directly involved in aspects of policy making and thus more consistently visible to the SED's leaders than those in the other three arenas. Nevertheless, the great variety of career patterns leading to the elite suggests that the SED is willing to recruit leadership talent wherever it appears, so long as it is coupled with early and long party membership.

"RECRUITMENT" AND "COOPTATION"

Frederic J. Fleron, Jr., has made a useful distinction between the "cooptation" and "recruitment" of experts to leading positions in the Soviet Union. The distinction rests on whether the officials in question were brought into the political elite only after some years in a specialized professional position (coopted), or rather entered the political elite, though in technical or economic roles, very early in their careers (recruited). It is Fleron's assumption that the first group, but not the second, "probably established very close professional-vocational ties outside the political elite" and that this fact has consequences for their political attitudes and behavior.[36] The assumption, as Fleron grants, is essentially untested, and it is plausible that even the "recruited" party experts share numerous values with the external professional-vocational constituency, in somewhat the way that Western bureaucrats are said to absorb the outlooks and values of those they are charged with regulating.[37] Nevertheless, the distinction remains an important one, and I have sought to classify the members of the DDR's technical elite according to it.

The basis of the classification of the 51 is their primary activ-

[36] Frederic J. Fleron, Jr., "Representation of Career Types in the Soviet Political Leadership," in R. Barry Farrell, ed., *Political Leadership in Eastern Europe and the Soviet Union* (Chicago: Aldine, 1970), pp. 123, 138. Fleron's concept of "cooptation" is based on Philip Selznick, *TVA and the Grass Roots* (New York: Harper & Row, 1949), pp. 13–16.
[37] On this point, see Jerry F. Hough, "The Party *Apparatchiki*," in Skilling and Griffiths, eds., *Interest Groups*, pp. 72–87.

TABLE 7.5. Recruitment and Cooptation into the Technical Elite

	Top leaders		Entire elite	
Older generation	1		7	
(Party veterans)		(1)		(4)
(Coopted after 1945)		(0)		(3)
Recruited into party roles	5		17	
Recruited into state roles	2		8	
Coopted into state roles	1		11	
Mixed recruited/coopted	2		8	
Total	11		51	

ities until 1955 or the age of 35, whichever came later. Seven, born before 1916, began their careers well before 1945 and are thus of small concern here. I have grouped the remainder in four categories: those *recruited* into positions in the party apparatus or mass organizations at an early age; those recruited into positions in the state bureaucracy; those *coopted* into state positions after some years of experience elsewhere (largely in industry or academic institutions); and those mixing early experience inside and outside the party or state apparatus.[38] As Table 7.5 shows, only one-quarter of the 44 younger functionaries can be said to have been "coopted" from other careers; this number includes several present ministers brought from industry (Herbert Weiz, Rudi Georgi, Wolfgang Junker, Heinz Matthes, Günter Prey, Kurt Singhuber, Otfried Steger). Another 8, including 2 members of the top elite (Werner Jarowinsky and Wolfgang Rauchfuss) and other important figures, had mixed early career experiences.

The largest group—17 of the total of 44 and half of the top group, were recruited early into party jobs—sometimes as FDJ functionaries and often as employees of the Central Committee apparatus. Four of the Politburo members or candidates belong to this group; a fifth, Alfred Neumann, is a party veteran, and the other two (Werner Jarowinsky and Margarete Müller) have mixed early backgrounds, including important party responsibilities. Per-

---

[38] Fleron dichotomizes "recruited" and "coopted" officials for statistical purposes with the cutting point at seven years of professional experience. *Op. cit.*, p. 123. In the present context a better understanding of DDR elite structure is afforded by a fourfold categorization, distinguishing between party and state recruitment and identifying a "mixed" group.

haps the most difficult group to assess are the 8 who came early in their careers into diverse sections of the state bureaucracy. One might expect these men to stand somewhere between the recruited party and coopted government officials in their socialization experiences and political outlooks.

But, to repeat, evidence that establishes any linkage between early career experience and political outlook or behavior is fragmentary at best.[39] On the one hand, it should be remembered that even the coopted tend to have been early party members[40] and may have called attention to themselves by part-time political activism which our classification necessarily overlooks. And, on the other hand, the most imaginative and, on occasion, dissident DDR technical officials in the past have tended to have deep and long-standing party roots (see next chapter). Probably the most that can be confidently said is that the presence of 25 percent "coopted" and additional "mixed" functionaries in the leadership group guarantees the entrance of the economically "rational" outlook and pragmatic style described earlier as typical of the technical intelligentsia as a whole.

The career pattern data does make evident some of the ways in which the characteristics of the technical strategic elite depart from those of the broader stratum from which they come. They are distinguished by a range of political education, involvement, and experience that at its most modest far exceeds that of the ordinary technician; the variety of their professional experience and, so far as can be judged, the quality of their professional talents, also set them apart. The fact that 20 (see Table 7.2) have earned doctor's degrees[41] shows them to be a highly educated elite in comparison with the rest of the technical intelligentsia (as well as with party leaders in other spheres).

[39] On the numerous problems of inferring elite political attitudes from any sort of social background data, see Dankwart Rustow, "The Study of Elites: Who's Who, When, and How," *World Politics*, XVIII (July 1966), 691–717; Donald D. Searing, "The Comparative Study of Elite Socialization," *Comparative Political Studies*, I (January 1969), 471–500.

[40] Six entered between 1946 and 1953; it may be significant, however, that the date of entrance of the other five (and in one case, party membership itself) is unknown; of those recruited through the party, the entrance date of only two of seventeen is unknown, and eleven were members by 1948.

[41] While some of the twenty were awarded the degree after having risen to leadership positions, in no case does the award appear to have been merely honorary.

The decisive questions, however, of how closely the orientations of the elite correspond to those of the stratum from which they came and to what extent its members perceive themselves as "representing" the views and interests of that stratum remain. They can only be finally answered on the basis of data on the effects of elite socialization and on the attitudes they themselves have directly or indirectly expressed.[42] The latter is available in somewhat fragmentary form and will be discussed in Chapters 8, 9, and 10. Anticipating those chapters, we shall find members of the technical strategic elite subject to cross-pressures between the demands of their professional backgrounds and their political roles. The supposition that their postures often reflect their broader occupational links and thus sometimes mirror the attitudes of less elevated technicians finds some confirmation. But these postures, I shall argue, have not for the most part proven seriously dysfunctional for the existing pattern of rule.

[42] Carl Beck and associates are beginning to examine systematically the published statements of East European leaders in an effort to ascertain their "perceptions and images" of leadership roles and policy questions. Given the variety of propaganda and other functions such communications serve, the difficulties of using official publications for revealing "real" attitudes are formidable. See Carl Beck, "Career Characteristics of East European Leadership," in Farrell, ed., *Political Leadership,* pp. 162, 193–194; cf. also Erik P. Hoffmann, "Communication Theory and the Study of Soviet Politics," in Frederic J. Fleron, Jr., ed., *Communist Studies and the Social Sciences* (New York: Rand McNally, 1969), pp. 379–396.

8

REPRESENTATION IN THE
PARTY LEADERSHIP

The comrades will have noticed that at the Sixth Party Congress changes in the composition of the party leadership have been made in connection with the approval of the program and statute. In order that the Central Committee correctly carry out the decisions of the Congress, it was necessary to elect the most experienced comrades with the greatest professional expertise and the closest attachment to the working class and the people as members and candidates of the Central Committee, the highest leadership organ in the Republic. That is why the number of skilled workers, engineers, scientists, and creative artists, who have especially proven themselves in the construction of socialism and command great theoretical and practical knowledge, has grown on the Central Committee. Changes also took place in the election of the Politburo. Today the majority of Politburo members and candidates is made up of comrades who for practical purposes are active in the leadership of the economy. Thus, the personal unity of political-ideological and economic and cultural leadership is guaranteed. The implementation of the production principle in the party organs has led to the recruitment of additional comrades who are good Marxist-Leninists and at the same time real experts.

WALTER ULBRICHT, at Economic Conference, June 1963[1]

THE POLITICAL ELITE of the DDR initially contained almost no technical specialists. Positions of influence were manned primarily by veterans of the pre-Hitler Communist Party (KPD), together with those Socialists who had proven sufficiently malleable to survive in the leadership after the merger of the two old parties

[1] Walter Ulbricht, "Das neue ökonomische System der Planung und Leitung der Volkswirtschaft in der Praxis," Die Wirtschaft (June 28, 1963), pp. 5–6.

into the SED in 1946. Most members of this elite were of working class origins and with limited education. They had made their mark in the party through loyal service in the apparatus,[2] trade union work,[3] newspaper and ideological activities,[4] clandestine or military assignments on behalf of the illegal KPD or the Comintern,[5] wartime activity in the Moscow-based "National Committee for a Free Germany," [6] or combinations of these. Some were veterans from the earliest days of the party; a few had joined it only shortly before Hitler's seizure of power. Most of the Socialists had been party functionaries or professional politicians in the Weimar Republic.[7]

In the preceding chapter I sought to delimit the strategic elite of technical intelligentsia by identifying those positions in party and state whose incumbents appeared to have some substantial influence over economic policy making. There I analyzed the career patterns of members of the entire technical strategic elite, as they moved within and between both governmental and party hierarchies. In this chapter my primary concern is with the representation of the technical intelligentsia within the leading organs of the SED. Determination of the major lines of policy in the DDR is of course regarded as the province of the party and in practice is made within the Politburo, a body presently containing sixteen members plus seven candidates who do not enjoy formal voting privileges.[8] At the head of the SED's large administrative apparatus stands the Secretariat, at present with ten members, each (excepting Erich Honecker) responsible for a specialized sector of party work; the divisions of the Secretariat roughly parallel those of the

[2] For example, Walter Ulbricht, Hermann Matern, Erich Honecker.
[3] For example, Herbert Warnke.
[4] For example, Fred Oelssner, Franz Dahlem, Rudolf Herrnstadt.
[5] For example, Wilhelm Zaisser, Ernst Wollweber, Erich Mielke, Heinrich Rau.
[6] For example, Anton Ackermann, Lothar Bolz.
[7] See Thomas A. Baylis, "East Germany's Rulers: A Study in the Evolution of Totalitarian Leadership," unpublished Master's thesis (Berkeley: University of California, 1961).
[8] It is not improbable that many decisions are really made by smaller informal groups within the Politburo; there are indications, for example, that the decision to force full collectivization of the countryside in 1961 was taken without the knowledge of the full body. See Ernst Richert, *Macht ohne Mandat* (Köln and Opladen: Westdeutscher Verlag, 1963), pp. 61–62. For a discussion of decision-making procedures in the SED Politburo, see Wolfgang Leonhard, *The Kremlin Since Stalin* (New York: Praeger, 1962), pp. 4–5.

state administration. As a body the Secretariat meets at least once weekly; it is to be assumed that its presentations to the Politburo (to which nine of its ten members belong) give it an important de facto share in policy making, despite its formal status as an implementing body. The Secretariat and the apparatus ranged under it, and, to a lesser extent, the governmental Council of Ministers and the state bureaucracy enjoy their political influence by virtue of their specialized knowledge and experience in the day-to-day administration and control of a complex social and economic order. As in other modern industrial societies, the line between policy determination and implementation is indistinct in the DDR, and informed advice is frequently tantamount to decision.[9]

In this chapter I will use the membership of the SED Central Committee as a representative grouping in order to illustrate the shifting composition of the political elite. While scholars have often analyzed Communist Central Committees for this purpose,[10] their use demands justification, for as a body the committee only rarely exercises important powers, although it is more than, in Richert's words, a "declamation and acclamation organ." [11] Un-

[9] The best discussion of the distribution of power in party and state organs in the DDR is in Ernst Richert, *op. cit.*, esp. Chaps. 2 and 4; see also Eckart Förtsch, *Die SED* (Stuttgart: W. Kohlhammer Verlag, 1969), pp. 55–60; Carola Stern, *Die SED: Ein Handbuch über Aufbau, Organisation, und Funktion des Parteiapparates* ([Köln]: Verlag für Politik und Wirtschaft, [1954]). The close overlapping between Secretariat and Politburo membership is a departure from earlier SED practice and the example of the CPSU, where in 1970 only five of the ten party secretaries were members (three) or candidates (two) of the Politburo.

[10] The most detailed study of the East German Central Committee is in Peter Christian Ludz, *Parteielite im Wandel* (Köln and Opladen: Westdeutscher Verlag, 1968), Chap. 3. On the Soviet Union and Eastern Europe, see Frederic J. Fleron, Jr., "Career Types in the Soviet Political Leadership," in R. Barry Farrell, ed., *Political Leadership in Eastern Europe and the Soviet Union* (Chicago: Aldine, 1970), pp. 108–139, and works cited there; Michael P. Gehlen, "The Soviet *Apparatchiki*," in *ibid.*, pp. 140–156; Carl Beck, "Career Characteristics of East European Leadership," in *ibid.*, pp. 157–194; Michael P. Gehlen and Michael McBride, "The Soviet Central Committee: An Elite Analysis," *American Political Science Review*, LXII (December 1968), 1232–1241.

[11] Richert, *op. cit.*, p. 30. Open opposition to the party "line" or its leadership appears to have broken out only rarely in Central Committee plenums, as in the 1956–1957 ferment. Carola Stern's evaluation of committee meetings is, however, worth quoting: "Much more strongly than [Party Congresses and Conferences], they have the character of work sessions in which experiences are compared and, with the feeling of being 'among themselves,' discussions are comparatively more realistic and frank than at the party congresses, where the discussion speakers are determined

like the *Volkskammer* and the party congress, it is also not intended to mirror closely the composition of DDR society; in the committee elected in 1971 there were only 3 workers not holding significant positions of authority,[12] and only 25 women out of 135 full members and 54 candidates. The committee does have a representative character but one representative of groups within the leadership. It is representative of groups, in Jean-Paul Picaper's perceptive characterization, "in the course of evolution," which together constitute a "refracted image" expressing the tension between the existing elite structure and the "political will of the party." [13] The committee is a pool from which members of the top organs are drawn; membership is an emblem of having arrived, but it is also an incentive to the individual to prove himself worthy of the highest positions of responsibility. This is particularly true of the candidates, who are normally either advanced to full membership or dropped within two "terms" (the periods between party

---

beforehand and as a rule speeches written out and approved word-for-word by the regional party bureau are read from the page. The unpublished protocols of Central Committee meetings . . . which have reached the West reveal that the members and candidates of the Central Committee discuss in part very critically—although never in fundamental contradiction to the party line—difficulties in their areas of work, the mood of the population, the degree of plan fulfillment, the situation in the LPGs, MTSs [machine tractor stations], etc., during the plenary sessions. Thus, Central Committee meetings seem to have some importance for the instruction of Politburo and Secretariat members on the real situation in East Germany." Carola Stern, *Porträt einer bolschewistischen Partei* (Köln: Verlag für Politik und Wirtschaft, 1957), pp. 268–269. Förtsch, *op. cit.*, p. 110, contends that the Central Committee "is enlisted more and more in the preparation and discussion of decisions." Ludz, *op. cit.*, pp. 94ff., sees a great expansion of the committee's functions in recent years as a "coordination, transformation, and consultation body."

[12] On the 1967 committee there were no workers, but some proletarian flavor was maintained through the inclusion of an occasional untutored plant party secretary; Adolf Hennecke, the DDR's Stakhanov (but now a "scientific assistant" in the Ministry for Raw Materials); and two foremen (positions officially regarded as belonging to the technical intelligentsia). In 1971 one worker was added as a full member and two as candidates.

[13] Jean-Paul Picaper, "Le Parti communiste en Allemagne de l'Est: Evolution de sa physionomie et de ses fonctions," *Revue Française de Science Politique*, XVI (February 1966), 47. I have modified Picaper's formulation by applying his comments to elites instead of to "society" more generally. John A. Armstrong points out that the importance of the Soviet Union's Central Committee lies in its presenting a "sociological representation of the Soviet ruling strata." *Ideology, Politics, and Government in the Soviet Union* (New York: Praeger, 1962), pp. 65–66. Richert sees the committee as "image and symbol of the party line," which seems to me an oversimplification. *Op. cit.*, p. 29.

congresses). It hence reflects the top leadership's view of its own future composition but also concessions to the importance of different intraparty groups. In providing such group representation, it is a critical instrument of inner-party legitimacy; its periodic closed meetings lend an authority to party decisions that the congresses, which meet only every four years and whose rehearsed character is open for all to see, do not. Virtually all ranking figures of the party belonged to the 1971 Central Committee; these included all members of the Politburo and Secretariat and all first secretaries of the fifteen regional party organizations; all of the twelve SED members in the Presidium of the Council of Ministers (the four representatives of the satellite "bourgeois" parties of course did not belong); the heads of the principal mass organizations; and a variety of prominent figures from industry, agriculture, the universities, the arts, education, and the party apparatus. It is worth noting that thirteen members of the Council of Ministers (nine SED) did *not* belong. In summary, selection to the committee is utilized to reward, represent, and recruit members of the political elite and to spur them on to greater accomplishment, a complex amalgam of functions which together make it a particularly appropriate body for studying the evolution of the character of leadership.

My basis for classification of members of the committee differs somewhat from those usually employed and thus requires explanation. I have categorized members strictly according to the functions they performed at the time of the election of the committee in question, that is, the time of the party congress,[14] leaving out of account their previous experience and education.[15] Those assigned to the category of economic functionary include those dealing primarily with technical, scientific, and economic matters *within the party apparatus and the government;* this seems to me to give a more accurate portrait of the dimensions of the technical strategic

[14] Except that where a change in function virtually accompanies selection (as it frequently does), I have used the new function as the basis of classification.

[15] Fleron, *op. cit.,* pp. 116–117, argues that classification according to formal position is apt to be misleading (for example, when a veteran manager is coopted into the party apparatus); I attempt to minimize that difficulty by placing less emphasis on the particular hierarchy to which a man belongs and more on the function he performs (economic, ideological, etc.).

elite within the committee than would confining the classification
to factory managers, academics, and the like.[16] I have separated
functionaries concerned with agitation and propaganda from the
main group of party functionaries or *apparatchiki*,[17] and I have
likewise treated officials of the mass organizations as a distinct
group, although by and large they may be expected to align themselves closely with the men of the apparatus. The classification
"other governmental functionaries" is largely residual, including
primarily foreign affairs specialists, administrators of social services and the legal system, and regional and local government officials; police and military officials are listed separately. Educational
officials are grouped with members of the cultural intelligentsia.
"Workers" include only those whose primary occupation at the
time of election was some type of manual labor.

The purpose of this chapter is not limited to examining the
changing numerical proportions of different groups within the
Central Committee and other party leadership bodies. I regard it
as even more important to understand the qualitative changes in
the composition and character of the elite, for example, as reflected in the rising educational level of the economic functionaries and the fluctuating representation of subgroups among them.
I will also touch on some of the events that led to these changes
and present brief biographical sketches of a few of the more influential and symbolic figures of the elite.

[16] This explains the discrepancy between my figures and those of Ludz, *op. cit.*,
pp. 186–199. Ludz subsequently distinguishes between economic functionaries in
"narrower" and "broader" senses (p. 224). The disadvantage of a "broader" usage,
like mine, is that it somewhat increases the subjective element in classification.

[17] Those classified as *apparatchiki*, then, are principally first (and sometimes
second) secretaries on regional and local levels and within enterprises, specialists for
organizational and cadre work on all levels, and Central Committee apparatus officials whose functions are not identified as economic or agitational. This narrower
conception resolves some, though not all, of the problems raised by Jerry F. Hough
in his important essay, "The Party *Apparatchiki*," in H. Gordon Skilling and
Franklyn Griffiths, eds., *Interest Groups in Soviet Politics* (Princeton: Princeton
University Press, 1971), pp. 47–92. Hough argues essentially that the Soviet *apparatchiki*, including the first secretaries, must be regarded not as one unified group
but as several, with distinctive sets of outlooks and interests often closer to those
of the groups they regulate and control than to one another's. While the present
classification recognizes this distinction for economic and ideological specialists
within the apparatus, it does not do so for first secretaries. It should be noted that
SED first secretaries, unlike their Soviet counterparts, usually have not had any
advanced engineering or agricultural education or experience; many have, however,
been trained in higher party schools.

1950–1954: The Third Central Committee

On the Central Committee elected in 1950, the first after the establishment of the DDR, only 6 members (out of 51) and 6 candidate members (out of 30) could be identified as economic functionaries (see Table 8.2). Of the full members in this group the three most prominent were Heinrich Rau, Bruno Leuschner, and Willi Stoph. Rau and Leuschner were chairman and vice chairman of the State Planning Commission whereas Stoph headed the Central Committee's division for economic policy; none had received any formal technical, economic, or scientific education, although Leuschner had had commercial training. Gerda Bauer and Kurt Vieweg were agricultural functionaries; the latter had been schooled in agricultural economics and was later (1956) to receive a doctor's degree in that field. The sixth member, Friedrich Leutwein, was rector of the Freiburg Mining Academy; he was not reelected in 1954. Of the candidates, 4 were untrained agricultural functionaries; 1 was a foreman and initiator of an activist movement for high-speed lathe work. The sixth, Willy Rumpf, State Secretary in the Finance Ministry, had been trained in the field of insurance. The only economic functionary on the Politburo (9 members, 6 candidates) also chosen in 1950 was Rau; Stoph and Vieweg belonged to the eleven-member SED Secretariat.

The Central Committee was dominated by veteran functionaries from the KPD (*Kommunistische Partei Deutschlands*, Communist Party) and SPD (*Sozialdemokratische Partei Deutschlands*, Social Democratic Party) serving in positions in the party apparatus or the state leadership; nineteen of the fifty-one full members had been born before the turn of the century. Only a handful had received more than formal elementary education although several had been given extensive ideological schooling in Moscow.[18] So far as I can establish, only four had studied at universities.[19] There can be little question that the SED was led at this time almost exclusively by *apparatchiki* long on experience in working class politics, clandestine operations, and party organization, but lack-

[18] I am grateful to Jean-Paul Picaper for providing helpful information on the social origins, ages, and education of some Central Committee members.

[19] Friedrich Leutwin, Kurt Vieweg, Karl Steinhoff (a jurist), and the poet Johannes R. Becher.

ing a sophisticated understanding of the requisites of economic development. Their guidebook for economic policy was the experience of the Soviet Union and the directives of the Russian occupiers.

From within the leadership ranks, however, economic specialists developed, responding to the necessity of getting the war-battered East German economy into motion. The most important of these were brought together in the German Economic Commission (*Deutsche Wirtschaftskommission,* DWK), created by the Soviet Military Administration in June 1947 as the first central "government" for East Germany. The DWK combined the several specialized "Central Administrations" dealing with economic affairs and was charged with such matters as the coordination of the East German economy, hastening the delivery of reparations, and preparing the Two-Year Plan for 1949–1950—all of course under Soviet supervision.[20] The chairman of the DWK was Heinrich Rau, two of his vice chairmen Bruno Leuschner and Fritz Selbmann. Rau had been a member of the KPD from its founding and from 1920 to 1932 was secretary of the Agriculture Division of its Central Committee (his father had been a farmer); in addition to a variety of other party jobs dealing with agriculture, he had been commander of the 11th International Brigade in the Spanish Civil War. From 1946 to 1948 he was economics minister in the *Land* government of Brandenburg.[21] Leuschner, whose previous relevant experience was confined to his commercial studies, became head of the economic division of the KPD-SED Central Committee in 1945 and, according to Schenk, was charged by the Soviets with building the DWK and was its first, unofficial chairman.[22] Fritz Selbmann, another veteran KPD functionary (regional party director in Saxony, *Reichstag* delegate), turned to economic problems only in 1946 when he was appointed Saxony's minister for economics and economic planning.[23] He was reputed to be self-confident and inde-

[20] Stefan Doernberg, *Kurze Geschichte der DDR* (Berlin: Dietz Verlag, 1965), pp. 128–131; *SBZ von 1945 bis 1954* (Bonn and Berlin: Bundesministerium für gesamtdeutsche Fragen, 1961), pp. 54, 68–69.

[21] *SBZ-Biographie* (Bonn and Berlin: Bundesministerium für gesamtdeutsche Fragen, 1964), pp. 404–405.

[22] *Ibid.*, pp. 214–215; Fritz Schenk, *Im Vorzimmer der Diktatur* (Köln: Kiepenheuer & Witsch, 1962), pp. 113–114.

[23] *SBZ-Biographie,* p. 326.

pendent, and the remark was attributed to him that the East Germans had not gotten rid of the brown strait jacket in order to be forced into a red one.[24] Still another important figure, one of the few with extensive formal education in economics, was Margarete Wittkowski, who had studied national economy in Switzerland and England, and during the Nazi period had worked with Harry Pollitt, the English Communist leader, for the Comintern. She helped develop the planning apparatus in the DWK, where, according to Schenk, she took charge of the "practical work" underlying the more public performances of Rau, Selbmann, and Leuschner. "Her word was at least as much regarded in the apparatus as those of the three top leaders; to be sure she spoke not as loudly but with far more precision and expertise." [25]

It is perhaps significant that all four were to come into conflict with the party leadership, but none were permanently removed from important economic positions, a measure of their value to the regime. Max Gustav Lange and his co-authors observed early that in spite of their lack of formal training, Rau, Leuschner, and Selbmann had effectively "worked themselves into" their new responsibilities.[26] They were not, however, united in their views of the economy; Leuschner himself composed the denunciation of Rau which led to his replacement of the latter as head of the State Planning Commission in 1952. According to Schenk, Leuschner charged that in its previous work the commission had interfered too often in the spheres of other organs—ministries, *Länder* bodies, and factories—and thus burdened itself with too much "ballast" to provide effective economic leadership. Rau was attacked personally for his domineering leadership style, his failure to attend most commission meetings (which he called only "sporadically" in any case), his arrogance, and his refusal to pay attention to criticism. Schenk regards Leuschner's document as astonishingly critical and "realistic" by DDR standards; for this reason, he says, it was kept strictly secret, but it brought about Rau's removal and the implementation of Leuschner's (in fact the Soviets') reform

[24] Ernst Richert, *Das zweite Deutschland* (Gütersloh: Sigbert Mohn Verlag, 1964), pp. 59–60.
[25] Schenk, *op. cit.*, pp. 267–268; *SBZ-Biographie*, p. 388.
[26] Max Gustav Lange, Ernst Richert, and Otto Stammer, "Das Problem der 'Neuen Intelligenz' in der Sowjetischen Besatzungszone," in *Veritas, Iustitia, Libertas* (Berlin: Colloquium Verlag, 1954), p. 241.

proposals.[27] Leuschner's critique is especially interesting because its tone anticipates that of the New Economic System some eleven years later; it represents an argument for economically rationalized rather than "administrative" leadership.

Other party economic functionaries fell into conflict with the dominant group around Ulbricht. In 1951 Margarete Wittkowski was demoted to the unimportant position of vice chairman of the Consumer Cooperative Association as part of the purges following the "anti-Zionist" trials in Eastern Europe and directed against Jews and those who had spent the Nazi years in the West.[28] Fritz Selbmann (by now Minister of Heavy Industry) was censured at the beginning of 1952 by the Politburo for ignoring warnings about mistakes in the construction of the model iron works Eisenhütten-kombinat-Ost.[29] In May 1953 Kurt Vieweg, until then Central Committee Secretary for Agriculture, was removed from his post because of "illness"; that more was involved is indicated by the fact that he was subsequently dropped from committee membership as well.[30] While we have no direct evidence to that effect, it is plausible in the light of the later difficulties of Selbmann and Vieweg that both were involved in disputes over economic policy, in the latter case, probably concerning the regime's efforts at forcing the pace of farm collectivization.

The strikes and demonstrations of June 17, 1953, and their consequences revealed additional *Schwankungen* ("waverings") among the economic functionaries. Rau, in his public statements after the uprising, joined Prime Minister Otto Grotewohl and the editor Rudolf Herrnstadt in being more ready to admit the mistakes of party policy and to promise effective countermeasures than those around Ulbricht;[31] subsequently, he was accused of "swaying" in his support of the dictator when Herrnstadt and the state security minister Wilhelm Zaisser sought to overthrow him.[32] Selbmann has also been identified as a possible sympathizer with the Zaisser-

---

[27] Schenk, *op. cit.*, pp. 100–102.   [28] *Ibid.*, p. 268.

[29] *SBZ von 1945 bis 1954*, pp. 176–177.

[30] Martin Jänicke, *Der dritte Weg* (Köln: Neuer Deutscher Verlag, 1964), p. 37; Stern, *Die SED*, p. 79.

[31] Stern, *Porträt*, pp. 161–162.

[32] The charge was circulated only internally, however, and Rau kept his membership in the Politburo. Jänicke, *op. cit.*, pp. 36, 229, fn. 77.

Herrnstadt group,[33] who appear to have favored some sort of slow-down in the socialization of the DDR economy.[34] Leuschner managed to remain aloof from the intrigues, as was his wont, and was rewarded by being made a Politburo candidate.[35]

1954–1958: The Rise and Fall of the Managerialists

At the Fourth Party Congress in 1954 forty-one economic functionaries were placed on the Central Committee, in proportion to the total members and candidates double the number of 1950. Nearly half (18), however, were agricultural functionaries—mostly collective farm (*Landwirtschaftliche Produktionsgenossenschaft*, LPG) chairmen, Farmers' Mutual Aid Association (*Verein der gegenseitige Bauernhilfe*, VdgB) officers, and local party officials. For the first time, nine VEB managers were elected to the committee; at least two, however, were veteran Communists, and several others were young activists or party workers with limited or no technical training. One exception, and thereby a model for the future, was Wolfgang Schirmer, then thirty-four years old and the manager of the Leuna chemical works "Walter Ulbricht." Schirmer had received a doctor's degree in 1949 and joined the SED only in 1952. His counterpart for the farming sector was Erich Rübensam, thirty-two, a Doctor of Agriculture, who held the post of Deputy Minister of Agriculture and Forestry. Several older Communists-turned-economic functionaries joined the committee as well: Selbmann, Gerhart Ziller, Margarete Wittkowski, Ernst Lange, and Erwin Kramer.

Ziller, moreover, had been placed on the SED Secretariat in 1953 and given responsibility for economic policy. Leuschner and Rau were the only experienced economic functionaries on the Politburo, excluding Stoph, who had by this time turned his attention to the new East German army. The functionary Erich

---

[33] Joachim Schultz, *Der Funktionär in der Einheitspartei* (Stuttgart and Düsseldorf: Ring Verlag, 1956), p. 115.

[34] At least that would seem to be the implication of the otherwise unelaborated charge of the Central Committee that the insurgents' economic "platform" would have meant a "restoration of capitalism" in the DDR. Stern, *Porträt*, p. 165; see also Doernberg, *Kurze Geschichte*, pp. 241–242.

[35] Schenk, *Im Vorzimmer*, p. 213.

Mückenberger took over responsibility for agricultural policy on both leading party bodies.

It appears that the theoretical seeds of the "managerialist" opposition to Ulbricht, which was to end in the purges of 1958, were planted in 1954 and 1955, although evidence of actual collusion between the principals is lacking. The catalytic agent was the growing interest of the chief SED ideologist, Fred Oelssner, in economic questions, possibly as a reflection of the argument over heavy versus light industry in the Soviet Union.[36] Oelssner, who had had his differences with Ulbricht in the past,[37] gave the chief address at a March 1955 "theoretical conference" of the Institute for Economic Sciences, where he conducted a class. The conference was noteworthy for bringing party leaders Oelssner and Selbmann together with academic economists—Behrens, Vieweg, Kohlmey— who were later to be labeled "revisionists" and whose heretical views were already in the process of discussion. While Oelssner sharply differed with the Behrens program for greatly decentralizing the DDR economy and was in fact the leading advocate of a highly "dirigistic" [38] approach, he agreed with him on the question of the "law of value" and on the criticism of the arbitrary fixing of prices by the state in violation of that law. Like Behrens he argued that the law of value applied not only to capitalist but also to socialist society in the period of transition to communism. Selbmann put the practical implications bluntly: "For years we have violated—I would almost say systematically—certain economic laws, and there can surely be no doubt that that must have its consequences sometime and somewhere." [39] Oelssner also supported the view of Vieweg that "exaggerated overcentralization" of agriculture and policies discriminating against the private farmer (the regime was at that moment seeking to accelerate col-

---

[36] Jänicke, *op. cit.*, p. 41.

[37] In 1952 Ulbricht sharply criticized the ideological work carried out under his direction; in 1953 he apparently served as liaison man between the Politburo and Moscow and, after the June 17 uprising, had criticized the "norm" policy— Ulbricht's—which had provoked it. Horst Duhnke, *Stalinismus in Deutschland* ([Köln]: Verlag für Politik und Wirtschaft, [1955]), p. 212; Hans Schimanski, "Die Revolution im Glaspalast," *SBZ-Archiv*, IX (February 28, 1956), 150–154.

[38] See Richert, *Macht ohne Mandat*, p. 144, fn. 35.

[39] Quoted in Jänicke, p. 63. See also Peter Christian Ludz, "Revisionistische Konzeptionen von 1956/1957 in der 'DDR,'" *Moderne Welt*, II, No. 4 (1960–1961), 356, fn. 9.

lectivization by such means) were equally in violation of the law of value.[40]

At about this time Oelssner lost his Secretariat post, perhaps as part of the SED's formal abandonment of the "New Course," and was made a vice premier, heading the Commission for Questions of the Production and Supply of Consumer Goods. Here he joined Selbmann (Commission for Industry and Transportation) and Scholz (Commission for Agriculture), who were also vice premiers and, like him, "thoroughly professionally oriented pragmatists." [41] In April 1957, they were brought together with Rau (Foreign Trade) and Rumpf (Finance Minister) in an Economic Council of the Council of Ministers, led by Leuschner. For the first time in the DDR, Richert says, "a genuine economic cabinet" had been established, which could decide "really all questions of planning and execution in all economic sectors with unity and—what was above all the point—speed." [42] Gerhart Ziller, Central Committee Secretary for Economic Policy, also met regularly with the council, as, evidently, did the Planning Commission's Kurt Gregor and Margarete Wittkowski (who had returned to it in 1954).[43] With the exception of Rumpf and possibly Rau (who had a long-standing personal animosity against Selbmann), all shared a realistic, pragmatic approach to the economy:[44] as Oelssner was said to have expressed it, the conviction that economic problems could be solved only by economic, not political, means.

The dedication of the members of the council to economic rationality led several of them to seek to further it politically. A series of conflicts, first over the appropriate economic response to the unrest of late 1956, then over the size of plan targets and the application of Khrushchev's *Sovnarkhozy* scheme to the DDR, erupted between this group and the supporters of Ulbricht.[45] Whether the struggle of Selbmann, Oelssner, and Ziller would have ended with their defeat had the dispute remained one purely of economic policy is uncertain; in fact it became entangled with personal animosities among the principals and ultimately with the attempt of the cadres chief Karl Schirdewan and the head of the

[40] Jänicke, *op. cit.*, pp. 62–66.
[41] Richert, *Macht ohne Mandat*, p. 131.
[42] *Ibid.*
[43] Schenk, *op. cit.*, p. 316.
[44] Richert, *Macht ohne Mandat*, pp. 131–132.
[45] See Chap. 9, below.

police Ernst Wollweber to overthrow Ulbricht. We do not know the extent, if any, of the collusion between the two groups; the publicly aired charges against them went no further than to suggest that Oelssner had defended Schirdewan and Wollweber's "provocations" and utilized them to carry on his own attack on the leadership.[46] Ziller may have been more directly involved; at a party reception at Wismut in December 1957, he supposedly announced somewhat drunkenly that at the next Central Committee Plenum a group would rise against Ulbricht and force through a new party program. He also was said to have tried to enlist the functionary Karl Mewis in his plans. These reports reached Ulbricht, and Ziller shot himself on December 14.[47]

In a recent official history Selbmann and Oelssner are not even mentioned in connection with the "Schirdewan-Wollweber-Ziller" affair.[48] Selbmann, however, has been said to have participated in the anti-Ulbricht remarks at Wismut;[49] at the Thirty-Fifth Plenum, under attack, he angrily remarked that during the war "some [like Selbmann] sat in prison, in concentration camps; others [like Ulbricht] spoke over the radio." Albert Norden, replying on behalf of Ulbricht, attacked Selbmann for "often" being "presumptuous, arrogant, personally insulting, and uncomradely." [50] The principal charge against Selbmann, however, was that he was guilty of "managerialism" (*Managertum*). "For Fritz Selbmann," Norden said, "the new era is not socialism and communism, but the new technology and atom power." [51]

It is probable that the attacks on "managerialism" which were to dot the DDR press for the next months both reflected a genuine fear of a technocratic elite's developing its own group interests in opposition to the political line of the *apparatchiki* and also were a convenient stick for beating Selbmann and Oelssner. Thus, in mid-February the Wismut (!) party organization attacked Selb-

---

[46] See esp. Erich Honecker, Politburo Report at 35th Plenum, *Neues Deutschland* (hereafter cited as *ND*) (February 8, 1958), p. 5; discussion speeches of Otto Grotewohl, Heinrich Rau, *ND* (February 25, 1958), p. 3; Albert Norden, Franz Dahlem, *ND* (February 26, 1958), p. 3.

[47] Jänicke, *Der dritte Weg*, p. 90; Herbert Prauss, *doch es war nicht die Wahrheit* (Berlin: Morus-Verlag, 1960), pp. 256–257.

[48] Doernberg, *Kurze Geschichte*, pp. 319–320.

[49] Jänicke, *op. cit.*, p. 239, fn. 101.   [50] *ND* (February 26, 1958), p. 3.

[51] *Ibid.*

mann for allegedly crediting the success of the Wismut uranium mining works to his "personal activity" and suggesting that "the development of socialist industry ought to be above all the business of 'industrial managers.' " [52] A March *Neues Deutschland* article used Selbmann to exemplify the dangers of *Managertum* in the VVBs:

> They attempt to lead without the workers and often take a politically neutral position toward the vital questions of society. In their opinion only the ability of the plant manager, or at most the divisional managers, determines the results of the factory's work. They do not believe that the workers can also understand complicated economic questions when they are correctly explained.
>
> It is well known that leading comrades, too, like Comrade Selbmann, loved to speak of their factories and to push their own merits into the foreground. It fitted this attitude that Comrade Selbmann when he visited plants only rarely found his way to the party organization. Thus it is not surprising that in the proposals on the creation of VVBs Comrade Selbmann made in the commission established by the 32nd Central Committee Plenum for the preparation for reorganization of the state apparatus, the role of the workers and their unions was almost completely absent.[53]

In Richert's view, such charges, insofar as they reflected Selbmann's repeatedly expressed aversion to party interference in the economy, his skepticism about the usefulness of "mass initiative," and his insistence on the value of competent, trained management for economic development, were quite accurate. Yet these views helped to make him the economic leader with the "most resonance" among both factory managers and workers.[54]

Selbmann lost his seat on the Central Committee at the July party congress, and two months later his removal as deputy premier was confirmed. He performed self-criticism at the party congress and again in March 1959, and until 1964 served as vice chairman

---

[52] *ND* (February 20, 1958), quoted in *SBZ von 1957 bis 1958* (Bonn and Berlin: Bundesministerium für gesamtdeutsche Fragen, 1960), p. 192.

[53] Karl-Ernst Reuter, "VVB kontra Managertum," *ND* (March 7, 1958), p. 3.

[54] Richert, *Macht ohne Mandat*, p. 132; Richert, *"Sozialistische Universität"* (Berlin: Colloquium Verlag, 1967), pp. 163–164. Richert suggests that Selbmann and Oelssner were skeptical of decentralization and "mass initiative," in part because they doubted the abilities of the lower cadres.

first of the Planning Commission and then of the *Volkswirtschafts-rat* (VWR).[55] Oelssner lost his seat on the Politburo and was stripped of his government positions; he became head of the Institute for Economic Sciences. His self-criticism came only in September 1959; in it he emphasized that he had not belonged to the Schirdewan group but acknowledged that his agricultural proposals had been "opportunistic" and harmful and praised Ulbricht's defense of the "general line of the party." [56] Kurt Vieweg fled to the West and, on his return, was arrested. Margarete Wittkowski was reduced from full membership to candidate of the Central Committee; in 1961, however, she became a vice chairman of the Council of Ministers (responsible for consumer goods and trade) and in 1963 was returned to full Central Committee membership. Another putative supporter of the "managerialists," Paul Scholz (who had joined Oelssner in wanting to halt forced collectivization), was not punished in any visible way.[57] An extensive purge of *Bezirk* party officials, including eleven secretaries responsible for Economics or Agriculture, and the removal of numerous plant directors on charges of *Managertum* followed, though there is no evidence that they had any direct connection to Selbmann or Oelssner.[58]

In February 1958 the Economic Council was dissolved and a "super" Planning Commission created, incorporating the old industrial ministries and coopting a variety of ministers and other high state officials as members. Leuschner remained the head of the commission, and his enhanced authority made him nearly an economic czar, one of the most powerful figures in the DDR.[59]

---

[55] "Erklärung des Genossen Fritz Selbmann," *Neuer Weg*, XIV, No. 19 (1959), reprinted in *SBZ-Archiv*, X (October 10, 1959), 301–302; *SBZ-Biographie*, p. 326. Selbmann subsequently became active in the Writers' League and in 1969 published a volume of memoirs.

[56] "Erklärung des Genossen Fred Oelssner," *Neuer Weg*, XIV, No. 21 (1959), reprinted in *SBZ-Archiv*, X (November 10, 1959), 333; *SBZ-Biographie*, p. 258.

[57] See Richert, *Macht ohne Mandat*, p. 132. Scholz stepped down as a vice chairman of the Council of Ministers in 1967 at the age of sixty-five.

[58] See Jänicke, *Der dritte Weg*, pp. 93–94, 185; Jänicke also points to the number of economic and agricultural functionaries dropped from the Central Committee at the Fifth Party Congress, but these do not seem to be much in excess of normal turnover in that body (p. 91).

[59] *SBZ von 1957 bis 1958*, pp. 192–193; Schenk, *Im Vorzimmer*, pp. 331–332; Richert, *Macht ohne Mandat*, pp. 133–134. Leuschner's authority was, as Richert

By all reports he was one of the most "capable, illusion-free" men of the regime;[60] his remark at the Sixth Party Congress that party workers should acknowledge "we do not live in a seventh socialist heaven" was characteristic of his realism.[61] According to his adviser Schenk, he was a loyal, believing Communist, but also a pragmatist with little regard for party ritual or dogmatic functionaries. He favored liberalization of the economic system and reacted with enthusiasm to developments in Poland and the Soviet Union which appeared to promise it. Yet he was always quick to accept the decisions of the Ulbricht leadership and to suppress his own opinions, remaining aloof from the unrest of 1953 and 1956 and free from implicating association with the insurgents of 1953 and 1957.[62] This did not prevent him from losing his planning commission post in 1961 (see below) and being "kicked upstairs" as coordinator of the economy and, later, delegate to COMECON (Council for Mutual Economic Assistance). He died in February 1965.

1958–1963: THE EMERGENCE OF A NEW GENERATION

The purges of the "managerialists" by no means marked a decline in the strength of economic specialists in party and government roles; even the principals Selbmann and Oelssner remained in significant if less important posts, and most of the other experienced functionaries remained in their jobs. The purges did, however, begin the breakthrough to prominence of a new generation of technical experts, most of whom reached maturity shortly before or after the collapse of Hitler's Germany and who had received their advanced training under Communist auspices.[63] These were rep-

---

argues, substantially restricted by other aspects of the reorganization, which in some measure was imitative of the Khrushchev reforms: his lack of control over the non-industrial areas of the economy, the creation of regional economic councils, with responsibilities both to the commission and to the regional governments, etc.

[60] Richert, *Macht ohne Mandat*, pp. 61–62, 130.

[61] Sozialistischen Einheitspartei Deutschlands, VI. Parteitag, *Diskussionsreden über die schriftliche vorgelegte Berichte, über das Programm der SED und über das Referat des Genossen Walter Ulbricht* (Berlin: Dietz Verlag, 1963), p. 112.

[62] See Schenk, *op. cit.*, pp. 114, 276–277, 302–315, and *passim*.

[63] Ludz also suggests that the purge of Schirdewan's protégés on the *Bezirk* level of the SED accelerated the upward mobility of party specialists. *Parteielite*, p. 64.

resentatives of the DDR's "New Intelligentsia," and, unlike their predecessors, had technical, economic, or scientific diplomas and sometimes doctoral degrees.

The Fifth Party Congress (1958), held in the shadow of the Oelssner-Selbmann purge, brought a number of these well-educated cadres to the Central Committee. They included the physicist Robert Rompe and the deputy director of the Zeiss works Herbert Weiz, who in 1962 received his doctorate and became State Secretary for Research Technology. The most important additions, however, were the two Central Committee candidates Erich Apel and Günter Mittag. Apel was born in 1917 into a working class family and was trained as an engineer. His activities during the war are clouded in some secrecy, but it is reported that he worked on V-rockets at Peenemünde, from which the conquering Russians took him along with other technicians to the Soviet Union. Here he continued to work as an engineer, returning to the DDR only in 1952. In 1953 he was made Deputy Minister of Machine Building, in 1955 Minister of Heavy Machine Building; he joined the SED only in 1957, a year before becoming head of the Politburo's Economic Commission. In 1960 he was awarded a doctor's degree and a year later was made a candidate member of the Politburo and Secretary of the Central Committee for Economic Affairs. In January 1962 he succeeded Karl Mewis as head of the State Planning Commission.[64] Apel was often identified in the West as a pragmatist; one example in this mode might be his discussion speech at the Sixth Party Congress, which stressed questions of economic rationalization, devoted relatively few words to the obligatory propaganda, and gave more attention to problems than successes.[65] Other more extensive (and uncritical) ideological pronouncements can be found, however. They led Richert to the conclusion that Apel was politically "naïve" and "completely . . . misunderst[ood]" Leninism.[66] While Richert's conclusion that Apel was thus willing to leave "politics" to the *apparatchiki*, whom he regarded as the "experts" for that field, proved in part mistaken, his fundamental concern was undoubtedly for economic rational-

---

[64] *Frankfurter Allgemeine Zeitung* (December 7, 1965), p. 2; *ibid.* (December 8, 1965), p. 4; *SBZ-Biographie*, p. 16.

[65] See discussion speech in Erich Honecker, *Das Parteistatut der Sozialistischen Einheitspartei Deutschlands* (Berlin: Dietz Verlag, 1963), esp. pp. 58–63.

[66] Richert, *Macht ohne Mandat*, pp. 115–116, 139–140.

ity, and his ideological statements have at best tangential relevance to that concern.[67]

Günter Mittag was nineteen at the war's end, nine years younger than Apel, and received a more thorough ideological education than Apel did; in this he is more typical of the younger generation of leading technicians. A railroad inspector, he joined the SED in the year of its founding, and in 1951 went to work for the Central Committee. He received his doctorate from the Institute of Transport Science (Dresden) in 1958 and became Apel's assistant in the Politburo Economic Commission; in that year he came to prominence as a harsh critic of the "managerialists" of the Selbmann stripe.[68] After a brief period in the *Volkswirtschaftsrat,* he succeeded Apel as Central Committee Secretary for Economic Affairs and under NES became head of the central SED Bureau for Industry and Construction. In spite of his inauspicious entrance to prominence, he too was commonly identified with the economic pragmatists.[69] He worked closely with Apel in the development of the New Economic System and had as his special task formulating the role of the party in it. He repeatedy exhorted party functionaries to assert leadership in the promotion of economic rationalization, where necessary against the will of economic functionaries who for one reason or another were reluctant to accept innovation. In one characteristic passage he argued:

a very important side of the political-ideological work of the party organizations consists of patiently analyzing mistakes, eliminating their causes, and helping people step by step to *develop an economic way of thinking* and to learn to *observe the requirements of objective economic laws* in all their activity, and thus to wage a determined struggle for the implementation of the decisions of our party.[70]

[67] *Ibid.,* pp. 139–140, fn. 128, cites an article favoring an economic orientation contradicting certain party policies which are supported with equal fervor. Such contradictions are hardly unusual in the official pronouncements of SED leaders, however, and might be interpreted as a skillful effort to maintain fundamental principles of economic rationality intact while weathering the unfavorable political storms of that period (late 1961—see also below).

[68] See Günter Mittag, "Die Aufgaben der Parteiorganisationen in den Vereinigungen Volkseigener Betriebe," *Einheit,* XIII (August 1958), 1138–1147. For biographical data see *SBZ-Biographie,* p. 240.

[69] Richert, for example, cites his "extremely heretical" views published in *Einheit,* XV (May 1960) on the advantages of capitalist competition in forcing up the quality of the goods produced. *Macht ohne Mandat,* p. 143.

[70] Günter Mittag, "Wir brauchen jetzt ein durchdachtes System der ökonomischen Leitung," *Die Wirtschaft* (January 28, 1963), p. 6.

This view of the role of the party must be coupled with his observation elsewhere that "the class struggle . . . in the German Democratic Republic is carried out today above all in the field of production." [71] For Mittag, the party was to become first of all an instrument of economic development.

1963–1971: THE ECONOMIC REFORMERS

The largest and best-qualified representation of the technical strategic elite to date (see Tables 8.1 and 8.4) entered the Central Committee following the Sixth Congress (1963) where the groundwork for the New Economic System was laid. Thirty-eight economic functionaries were elected to full membership (out of 121) and twenty-eight more—nearly half the total—were made candidate members. They included nine plant managers and three general directors of VVBs; five officials of the Planning Commission and National Economic Council; and eleven members of the Council of Ministers, Deputy Ministers, and State Secretaries. Perhaps the most striking statistic concerns their education: Some 60 percent had university degrees or other advanced training, a jump of more than 20 percent over 1958. At least fourteen held the doctorate. These figures, it should be noted, are minimum ones, since in a few cases no definite information on education was available. The new prominence of members of the technical intelligentsia on the committee was fully intentional, as Ulbricht's remarks at the Economic Conference, quoted at the head of this chapter, reveal. They were placed there to lend authority to the NES reforms; but precisely the fact that their presence was thought necessary to this purpose is indicative of their expanded importance.

Among the most important of the new technicians entering the committee in 1963 were Gerhard Schürer, once head of the Central Committee's Division of Planning and Finance, from 1962 a vice chairman of the Planning Commission, and now chairman; Werner Jarowinsky, a doctor of economics who had taught on the Humboldt University faculty and from 1961 had been DDR State Secretary and Deputy Minister for Trade and Supply; Julius Bal-

---

[71] Günter Mittag, *Fragen der Parteiarbeit nach dem Produktionsprinzip in Industrie und Bauwesen* (Berlin: Dietz Verlag, 1963), p. 126.

kow, Minister for Foreign and Inter-German Trade; Günter Wyschofsky, a chemist who also moved from heading a division of the Central Committee to a vice chairmanship of the Planning Commission; Siegbert Löschau, Schirmer's successor at the head of the VEB Leuna "Walter Ulbricht"; and Horst Sölle, then Deputy Trade Minister. These men were believed to share the pragmatic outlook of Apel and Mittag. All were young, excepting Balkow, who was a prewar SPD member and had participated in a Communist resistance group during the war; the others averaged under thirty-seven at the time of the Sixth Congress. All had become party members by 1948, and all but Balkow and Jarowinsky worked in the Central Committee apparatus early in their careers. Jarowinsky came to be regarded as the technicians' "most intellectually considerable spokesman" by Richert, who attributed to him the view that the party needed to adapt itself to a "new functionalism." [72]

The experience in the Central Committee of many of these young technicians makes it difficult to accept the sharp dichotomy drawn by Richert between the "old Communists" who became economic experts and the new men he labels as "Nur-Wirtschaftler," at least insofar as it is based on the political and ideological naïveté of the latter.[73] One might expect the older group to be more intense in its dedication to achieving a successful Communist society and to have a somewhat broader view of the DDR's problems and of the realities of power within the regime, owing to their pre-1945 experiences. The younger leaders would presumably be more career-oriented and in that sense opportunistic, and yet less able in their own thought processes to escape the narrow confines of the ideological system inculcated in them. Consequently, the former might be more willing to expose themselves politically and to risk challenging the presently dominant rulers than the latter, provided they were persuaded that it was necessary for the success of Communism. This is speculation; but to date the open rebels in the higher ranks have in fact usually been veteran Communists. The case of Apel, however, suggests that this rule is not invariable, and, in their zeal for reform, the younger

---

[72] Ernst Richert, "Ulbricht and After," *Survey* (October, 1966), p. 155.
[73] Richert, *Macht ohne Mandat*, pp. 139–140, fn. 128.

TABLE 8.1. Composition of Central Committee According to Function Performed

	Party congress																	
	III (1950)			IV (1954)			V (1958)			VI (1963)			VII (1967)			VIII (1971)		
	M[a]	C[b]	T[c]	M	C	T	M	C	T	M	C	T	M	C	T	M	C	T
Economic-technical functionaries N:	6	6	12	27	14	41	28	17	45	38	28	66	40	21	61	39	22	61
%:[d]	11.8	20.7	15.0	30.0	36.8	32.0	25.9	42.5	30.4	31.4	46.7	36.5	30.5	42.0	33.7	28.9	40.7	32.3
(Agricultural functionaries) (N)	(1)	(3)	(4)	(10)	(8)	(18)	(7)	(6)	(13)	(10)	(7)	(17)	(10)	(6)	(16)	(11)	(5)	(16)
(Scientists) (N)	(2)	(0)	(2)	(1)	(0)	(1)	(3)	(0)	(3)	(1)	(3)	(4)	(2)	(0)	(2)	(2)	(0)	(2)
Party bureaucrats N:	18	8	26	16	6	22	30	7	37	29	9	38	33	10	43	36	7	43
%:	35.4	27.6	32.5	17.8	15.8	17.2	27.8	17.5	25.0	24.0	15.0	21.0	25.2	20.0	23.8	26.7	13.0	22.8
Agitprop functionaries N:	4	1	5	3	3	6	9	1	10	11	1	12	20	2	22	15	2	17
%:	7.8	3.4	6.2	3.3	7.9	4.7	8.3	2.5	6.8	9.1	1.7	6.6	15.3	4.0	12.2	11.1	3.7	9.0
Educational-cultural personnel N:	2	1	3	9	3	12	6	5	11	11	9	20	10	7	17	12	9	21
%:	3.9	3.4	3.8	10.0	7.9	9.4	5.6	12.5	7.4	9.1	15.0	11.1	7.6	14.0	9.4	8.9	16.7	11.1
Functionaries of mass organizations N:	4	7	11	10	5	15	11	4	15	10	6	16	10	4	14	9	6	15
%:	7.8	24.1	13.8	11.2	13.2	11.7	10.2	10.0	10.1	8.3	10.0	8.8	7.6	8.0	7.7	6.7	11.1	7.9
Police-military officials N:	5	1	6	7	2	9	8	2	10	5	3	8	5	2	7	5	2	7
%:	9.8	3.5	7.5	7.8	5.3	7.0	7.4	5.0	6.8	4.1	5.0	4.4	3.8	4.0	3.9	3.7	3.7	3.7
Other state officials N:	12	2	14	12	4	16	14	4	18	16	3	19	13	4	17	18	4	22
%:	23.6	6.9	17.5	13.3	10.5	12.5	13.0	10.0	12.2	13.3	5.0	10.5	9.9	8.0	9.4	13.3	7.4	11.6

Workers	N:	0	3	3	6	1	7	2	0	2	1	1	2	0	0	0	0	1	2	3
	%:	0	10.4	3.8	6.7	2.6	5.5	1.9	0	1.4	0.8	1.7	1.1	0	0	0	0	0.7	3.7	1.6
No information	N:	0	1	1	1	6	7	3	4	7	0	0	0	0	0	0	0	0	0	0
Totals	N:	51	30	81	91	44	135	111	44	155	121	60	181	131	50	181	135	54	189
	%:	100.1	100.0	100.1	100.1	100.0	100.1	100.1	100.0	100.1	100.1	100.0	100.0	99.9	100.0	100.1	100.0	100.0	100.0

[a] M = members.   [b] C = candidates.   [c] T = total.   [d] Percentages exclude those on whom no information was available.

Sources: This table and Tables 8.2, 8.3, and 8.4 are based on *SBZ-Biographie*, 1961, 1964; *Wer ist Wer in der SBZ?* (Berlin-Zehlendorf: Verlag für internationalen Kulturaustausch, 1958); *SBZ von A bis Z* (Bonn: Deutscher Bundes-Verlag, 1963, 1965, 1966), 8th-10th editions; *Handbuch der Volkskammer*, 3. Wahlperiode (Berlin: Kongress Verlag, 1959); *Neues Deutschland* (July 25, 1950), p. 1; *ibid.* (April 7, 1954), p. 2; *ibid.* (July 17, 1958), p. 3; *ibid.* (January 27, 1963), p. 5; *ibid.* (April 23, 1967), reprinted in *SBZ-Archiv*, XVIII, No. 9 (1967), 148-152; *ibid.* (June 20, 1971), pp. 4-5. Ludz, *Parteielite, passim;* files of Institut für Politische Wissenschaft, Berlin; *Die Volkskammer der Deutschen Demokratischen Republik*, 5. Wahlperiode (Berlin: Staatsverlag der DDR, 1967); *ibid.*, 6. Wahlperiode (Berlin: Staatsverlag der DDR, 1972); *A bis Z* (Bonn: Deutscher Bundes-Verlag, 1969).

TABLE 8.2. Composition of SED Central Committees (Members + Candidates) by Function Performed (Percentages)[a]

	Party congress					
Function	III (1950)	IV (1954)	V (1958)	VI (1963)	VII (1967)	VIII (1971)
Economic-technical	15.0	32.0	30.4	36.5	33.7	32.3
Party bureaucratic	32.5	17.2	25.0	21.0	23.8	22.8
Agitprop	6.2	4.7	6.8	6.6	12.2	9.0
Culture-education	3.8	9.4	7.4	11.1	9.4	11.1
Mass organizations	13.8	11.7	10.1	8.8	7.7	7.9
Police-military	7.5	7.0	6.8	4.4	3.9	3.7
Other state	17.5	12.5	12.2	10.5	9.4	11.6
Workers	3.8	5.5	1.4	1.1	0.0	1.6

[a] Summary version of Table 8.1.
Source: See Table 8.1.

functionaries have the advantage of not being so burdened by the legacy of Stalinism and the old KPD as their senior colleagues have been.

The representation of technicians on the Central Committees elected in 1967 and 1971 dropped only slightly from the numerical high point of 1963. Within this group, the only dramatic change in the 1967 committee was the increase from eleven to eighteen of the number of ministers, deputy ministers, and state secretaries, due largely to the dissolution of the National Economic Council and the reinstatement of the industrial ministries. In 1971 the absolute number of technical specialists represented remained unchanged at sixty-one while the committee as a whole was slightly enlarged; three of the technicians were retired "party veterans," however, and two were foremen and might plausibly have been placed in another category. Only one of the VVB general directors, once touted as the central figures of the economic reforms, remained on the committee. The educational qualifications of the technical functionaries continued to rise modestly on both committees; by 1971 two-thirds had received an advanced education in a university, higher party school, or technical school.

It is worth remarking that since 1950, technical specialists have been much better represented among the nonvoting Central Committee candidates than among the voting full members. Since 1958,

TABLE 8.3. Central Committee Economic Functionaries by Category—
Total members and candidates[a]

Function	Party congress					
	III (1950)	IV (1954)	V (1958)	VI (1963)	VII (1967)	VIII (1971)
Members of Council of Ministers, deputy ministers, state secs.	2 (1)	4 (2)	5 (2)	11 (2)	18 (5)	16 (5)
Leading officials of State Planning Comm., Nat'l. Ec. Council	1 (0)	2 (0)	2 (1)	5 (2)	1 (0)	1 (0)
Lower functionaries in ministries, SPC, VWR	0	1 (0)	2 (0)	2 (1)	2 (1)	1 (0)
Central Committee secretaries and other CC functionaries	3 (1)	3 (1)	4 (3)	5 (2)	5 (1)	6 (1)
Regional state economic functionaries	1 (1)	0	2 (2)	3 (1)	2 (1)	1 (0)
Regional party economic functionaries	0	2 (1)	1 (1)	3 (1)	4 (3)	5 (3)
Plant managers	0	9 (3)	7 (2)	9 (5)	8 (4)	7 (4)
VVB general directors	0	0	0	3 (1)	3 (1)	1 (0)
Other factory officials	1 (1)	2 (0)	7 (1)	5 (2)	3 (1)	6 (6)
Collective or state farm chairmen	0	10 (3)	8 (3)	10 (5)	9 (3)	6 (2)
Functionaries of Farmers' Mutual Aid Association (VdgB)	3 (2)	4 (3)	2 (1)	2 (0)	1 (0)	1 (0)
Scientists, institute directors	1 (0)	3 (1)	5 (1)	6 (4)	4 (0)	4 (0)
Other	0	1 (0)	0	2 (2)	1 (1)	6 (1)
Totals	12 (6)	41 (14)	45 (17)	66 (28)	61 (21)	61 (22)

[a] Candidates in parentheses.
Source: See Appendix 2 and sources for Table 8.1.

this disproportion has also characterized educational and cultural figures while party organization men and ideological functionaries have been consistently strongly overrepresented among the full members. In 1971, over 40 percent of the candidates but only 29 percent of the full members were technical and economic specialists; the corresponding figures for party and ideological functionaries together were 17 percent of the candidates and 38 percent of the full members. While it would be an error to stress the disparity

TABLE 8.4. Advanced Education Among Central
Committee Economic Functionaries[a]

	Party congress					
	III (1950)	IV (1954)	V (1958)	VI (1963)	VII (1967)	VIII (1971)
All members and candidates						
Total N	12	41	45	66	61	61
N with advanced education	3	10	17	40	39	41
% with advanced education	25.0	24.4	37.8	60.6	63.9	67.2
N with university degrees	0	2	4	20	22	24
N with other advanced education	2	3	5	6	7	6
N with doctoral degrees	1	5	8	14	10	11
Full members only						
Total N	6	27	27	38	40	39
N with university degrees	0	2	2	8	14	13
N with other advanced education	2	2	5	5	7	5
N with doctoral degrees	1	3	4	9	8	7
Candidate members only						
Total N	6	14	17	28	21	22
N with university degrees	0	0	2	12	8	11
N with other advanced education	0	1	0	1	0	1
N with doctoral degrees	0	2	4	5	2	4

[a] Figures given are for the highest level of education attained by members of each group.
Source: See Appendix 2 and sources for Table 8.1.

excessively, since formal voting in the Central Committee rarely if ever has much meaning, the relative disadvantage suffered by the technical intelligentsia suggests the prominent advisory and even decorative element in their representation.

Thus, the considerable changes of style and lesser ones of policy introduced by the Honecker regime after the replacement of Walter Ulbricht as SED First Secretary have been accompanied by a remarkable continuity of personnel. This stability without doubt reflects Honecker's cautious approach to the transition process and also suggests that the balance of group influences within the SED leadership that emerged after the first, heady phase of economic reform has tended to rigidify. The composition of the SED Politburo and Secretariat confirms the rigidity.

Politburo and Secretariat

Membership on the Central Committee, as I stated, does not carry great influence in itself although it is an indicator of having achieved influence elsewhere. Members of the technical elite sitting on the Politburo or the Secretariat, on the other hand, do participate directly in regime decision making. Following the selection of a new Politburo after the Sixth Congress, Ulbricht declared that a "majority" of that body's members and candidates were "comrades who for practical purposes (*praktisch*) are active in the leadership of the economy." [74] Such a conclusion could only have been reached by including among the majority Ulbricht himself, the (then) premier and vice premier Grotewohl and Stoph, respectively, and the trade union functionary Warnke, all of whom indeed had responsibilities including substantial portions of economic policy. None of these men could be considered to belong to the technical intelligentsia, however, or indeed to have much expertise in economic matters. Neither could Alfred Neumann, a veteran *apparatchik* entrusted with heading the National Economic Council, or the agricultural functionary Grüneberg.

As Table 8.5 shows, at no time have Politburo members and candidates with primarily economic and technical responsibilities approached commanding a majority of that body, and the number of those with professional education and experience has been still smaller. Since 1963, the year of the economic reforms, technical functionaries have constituted a minority of between 7 and 9 of

[74] See quote at head of this chapter. It should be noted that by the time of this speech the agricultural specialist Dr. Karl-Heinz Bartsch had already been expelled from his position as Politburo candidate for concealing his membership in the Waffen-SS.

TABLE 8.5 Economic-Technical Representation in SED Politfuro
and Secretariat 1950–1971

	Politburo			Politburo candidates			Secretariat		
Year[a]	Total members	Those w. ec.-tech. resp.	Those w. ec.-tech. training	Total members	Those w. ec.-tech. resp.	Those w. ec.-tech. training	Total members	Those w. ec.-tech. resp.	Those w. ec.-tech. training
1950	9	1	0	6	0	0	11	2	0
1954	9	1	0	5	2	0	6	2	1
1958	13	4	0	8	1	0	8	2	0
1963	14	2	0	9	7	5	7	2	1
1967	15	3	1	6	5	4	10	3	2
1971	16	2	1	7	5	4	10	3	2

[a] Members elected at party congress of years listed.

Source: See sources cited in Table 8.2; also Karl Wilhelm Fricke, "Honeckers Mannschaft," *Deutschland Archiv,* IV (September 1971), 962–967.

the 21 to 23 members and candidates; no more than 5 have been trained professionals. The professionals have consistently been limited to nonvoting, candidate membership. In the history of the SED, only one trained technical specialist, Mittag, has ever become a full member of the Politburo.[75]

After the deaths of Apel and Leuschner in 1965, only Mittag and Jarowinsky, then both candidates, remained as full-blown representatives of the technical strategic elite, although they enjoyed the apparent sympathy of two other candidates, the agricultural specialists Georg Ewald and Margarete Müller.[76] Mittag and Grüneberg were subsequently elevated to full membership, and following the Seventh SED Congress (1967), two more young economic

[75] Figures compiled by R. Barry Farrell indicate that in 1967 the DDR ranked, with Czechoslovakia, at the bottom of the five most developed Soviet bloc states in percentage of Politburo members holding university degrees or the equivalent, and led only Poland in the percentage of members possessing some technical specialization or experience. R. Barry Farrell, "Top Political Leadership in Eastern Europe," in Farrell, ed., *Political Leadership,* pp. 96–99.

[76] Georg Ewald, whose only advanced education has been in the higher party school, is nonetheless regarded as an able, pragmatic professional; Richert identifies him as one of the designers of the New Economic System. Ernst Richert, *Die DDR-Elite* (Hamburg: Rowohlt Verlag, 1968), pp. 65–66, 105. Margarete Müller is a collective farm chairman with a diploma in agriculture from the University of Leningrad; as suggested above (Chap. 7, fn. 35), she may serve largely a decorative function in the Politburo.

functionaries were added as candidates: the director of the Office of Prices Halbritter, and the State Secretary for Electronic Data Processing Kleiber. Between the Seventh and Eighth Congresses two full members died, and at the Eighth Congress (1971) an additional full member and candidate member were added. None of these openings were filled by technical specialists, and Ewald, Halbritter, Jarowinsky, Kleiber, and Müller remained candidates, surrounded by a still larger number of party bureaucrats and ideologists. Three of the four new men appointed are in their early forties and are probably seen as an organizational and ideological counterweight to the technicians among the younger generation of the SED's leadership. Two are regional first secretaries; one is a propaganda specialist; and the fourth, older man is a veteran military and police official.[77]

The situation on the Secretariat is much the same. Grüneberg is Secretary for Agriculture, Mittag for the Economy, and Jarowinsky for Trade and Supply. The remaining seven members[78] are all *apparatchiki* or specialists for ideology and propaganda. There has been a remarkable continuity in the membership of both Politburo and Secretariat since 1963.[79] Seventeen of the twenty-three members of the former still sit on the present body, and six of the seven secretaries, although three new secretaries have been added. Five of the six who left the Politburo did so only through death; the sixth was expelled for concealing his membership in the SS. The only secretary to leave has been Ulbricht. Thus, in the DDR's period of economic reform and modernization the leading party bodies have remained consistently and firmly in the hands of the *apparat* men and the ideologists. The economic specialists have been given hardly more than token representation, sufficient to provide an input of needed technical expertise but of little direct significance as a power factor. Ludz's "institutional-

[77] The regional first secretaries are Werner Krolikowski (born 1928) and Harry Tisch (born 1927), and the propaganda specialist is Werner Lamberz (born 1929). The fourth addition is the veteran police and military official Erich Mielke. Krolikowski and Lamberz are full members, Tisch and Mielke candidates.

[78] Including Horst Dohlus, a party organization specialist named to replace Ulbricht at the Eighth Congress.

[79] See Förtsch, *Die SED*, pp. 122–123. There has been a similar continuity in the Soviet leadership since Khrushchev's removal. The case of Poland, where massive renewals of the leadership followed the student upheavals of 1968 and the retirement of Gomulka at the end of 1970, presents an instructive contrast.

ized counter-elite" of specialists[80] remains a feeble minority at the centers of decision making, even if we assume them to articulate a distinctive set of perspectives there.

It is also not implausible to believe that some measure of attitudinal cooptation may take place among those members of the technical strategic elite rising to the Politburo and Secretariat. The case of Mittag may be instructive. Since his elevation to full Politburo membership in 1966 he has become (at least publicly) one of the most vocal party spokesmen on behalf of the strengthening of party authority, the strict application of democratic centralism to the economy, and the meticulous study of the example of the Soviet Union. He has harshly attacked "twaddle about self-administration" or "decentralization" and its advocates, condemned those who looked to the West for economic models, and demanded the "intensive study" of Marxism-Leninism by the technical intelligentsia.[81] While Mittag's earlier reputation in the West as an innovative technocrat was doubtless overdrawn (he first came to prominence, as I noted, through his attacks on the "managerialists" after the 1958 purge), the change in tone of his pronouncements from the early days of the New Economic System is nonetheless unmistakable.

The domination of the Politburo and Secretariat by party bureaucrats and ideologists is thrown into special relief when we consider the composition of the Council of Ministers (as of December 1971), which, particularly with the abolition of the National Economic Council and the reduction in importance of the State Planning Commission, has been given primary responsibility for directing the economy.[82] Of the council's thirty-nine members, nineteen are ministers with economic responsibilities, five are vice chairmen without portfolios who rose to prominence as economic

---

[80] Ludz, *Parteielite,* pp. 43–44 and *passim.*

[81] See especially Mittag's "Meisterung der Ökonomie ist für uns Klassenkampf," *ND* (October 27, 1968), p. 4; *idem., Die Durchführung des Volkswirtschaftsplanes im Jahre 1970* (Berlin: Dietz Verlag, 1970). See also Kurt Erdmann, "Neue Wirtschaftsmassnahmen ab 1. Januar 1968," *Deutschland Archiv,* I (May 1968), 206–207; Achim Beyer and Rüdiger Mann, "Dr. Mittag und die Wirtschaftspolitik der SED," *Aktuelle Information des Instituts für Gesellschaft und Wissenschaft in Mitteldeutschland,* No. 5 (Erlangen, 1968)

[82] See fn. 28, Chap. 7, above. The membership of the Council of Ministers constituted after the November 1971 *Volkskammer* elections is given in *Deutschland Archiv,* IV (December 1971), 1340.

functionaries, and another is head of the State Planning Commission. Two of the nineteen are representatives of the "bourgeois" parties, Manfred Flegel and Werner Titel, who have degrees in economics. Thus, together, twenty-five members—nearly two-thirds —of the council represent the economic sector of the government. The same dominance is reflected on the council's Presidium, eleven of whose sixteen members (nine of the twelve SED members) are economic specialists.[83] Willi Stoph, the chairman, and Alfred Neumann, a vice chairman, are both *apparatchiks* with some background of economic experience, and while Neumann is also an *apparatchik* in spirit, Stoph has frequently been identified as an able pragmatist and sympathizer with the economic experts.[84] Only Horst Sindermann is an entirely unambiguous spokesman for the party apparatus on the Presidium. Thus, we are left with a curious dualism both in composition and function between an "economic" Council of Ministers and a "political" Politburo and Secretariat.

ADVISORY ROLES

Direct influence through participation in basic policy decisions shades off gradually into indirect influence through advising. The leading administrative instruments of party and state—the divisions of the SED Secretariat and the specialized ministries—combine advisory with implementing roles, even while their chiefs may exercise a more direct voice in policy making. Both, moreover, contain within them advisory bodies bringing outside "practitioners" and academics, often with scientific and technical specialties, into association with bureaucratic officials. The ministries thus have more or less permanent "advisory councils" (*Beiräte*) and establish ad hoc committees from time to time for specific problem areas; they may also call large conferences of practitioners

[83] The four "bourgeois" members of the Presidium are Werner Titel, Manfred Flegel, and the Ministers of Posts and Justice Rudolph Schulze and Kurt Wünsche. Their influence must be assumed to be highly limited, given their lack of access to leading SED bodies and the function their appointments are intended to serve: providing nominal representation in the government to their parties, which are joined to the SED in the National Front.

[84] See Werner Barm, "Stophs Zeit kommt noch," *Die Zeit* (March 13, 1970), reprinted in part in *Deutschland Archiv*, III (April 1970), 412; Peter Christian Ludz, "The SED Leadership in Transition," *Problems of Communism* (May–June 1970), pp. 29–30.

in particular branches of the economy.[85] Broader economic conferences are sometimes called by both the Council of Ministers
and the Central Committee.[86] Numerous standing and temporary
commissions and working groups of the Central Committee also
serve advisory purposes and include in their membership Central
Committee secretaries, full-time employees of the committee apparatus, representatives of the state bureaucracy, and outside specialists. Little publicity is given the creation and work of the commissions, but in some cases they appear to have taken over the
direction or supervision of government organs in corresponding
fields. Thus, the Economic Commission, headed for some years by
Ulbricht himself and later by Apel, watched over economic policy
until its dissolution in 1962 in favor of Bureaus for Industry and
Agriculture.[87]

A number of advisory structures have emerged for guiding the
development of scientific and technical research. At the center of
them is the Research Council, a body of some sixty leading scientists created in 1957 to guide the State Planning Commission in
research planning and to provide some direction and coordination
for the great variety of research facilities in the DDR.[88] The underlying purpose in the creation of the council was to facilitate
the efficient application of scientific discovery to economic development, a concern reflected by the division of its 140 "working
groups" into categories corresponding to branches of the economy.
The Research Council comprises a DDR scientific elite whose
prestige evidently lends it substantial authority; the Council of
Ministers, an East German source tells us, does not pass the state
research plan without the Research Council's approval or agree
to any expenditure for research without consulting it.[89] There is,

---

[85] Richert, *Macht ohne Mandat*, pp. 160–162.

[86] Ludz, *Parteielite*, pp. 103–114.

[87] See Richert, *Macht ohne Mandat*, pp. 32–35; Förtsch, *op. cit.*, p. 106; Stern,
Porträt, p. 276; *SBZ von A bis Z*, 1963, p. 536; *Die SED: Historische Entwicklung,
ideologische Grundlagen, Programm und Organization* ([Bonn]: Bundesministerium
für gesamtdeutsche Fragen [1967]), pp. 74–75.

[88] See Renate Rausch, "Förderung und Organisation der Forschung in der DDR,"
in Peter Christian Ludz, ed., *Studien und Materialien zur Soziologie der DDR*
(Köln and Opladen: Westdeutscher Verlag, 1964), pp. 263–284, esp. pp. 271–274;
also Vladimir Slamecka, *Science in East Germany* (New York and London: Columbia
University Press, 1963), pp. 7–8.

[89] Hans Reinhold, "Über die führende Rolle der Arbeiterklasse auf geistigem
Gebiet," in *Sozialismus und Intelligenz*, p. 110.

however, no evidence that the council has utilized its power to promote the interests of the scientific community in conflict with other groups or the party leadership, for example, to moderate the demand for scientific results immediately applicable to production.[90]

The importance of economic research facilities and academic economists in advising the DDR's leadership became particularly obvious in the conceptions underlying the New Economic System, which required a fundamental intellectual departure from Stalinist economics. The Institute of Economic Sciences, a branch of the Academy of Sciences, was the center of development of such ideas by men like Kohlmey (while head of the institute also a chief adviser to the Central Committee apparatus),[91] Behrens, and Oelssner, all of whom fell out of favor when first advocating them but later were quietly rehabilitated. The rector of the *Hochschule für Ökonomie,* Alfred Lange, worked closely with Apel and Mittag and has been identified as one of the chief contributors to the theoretical foundation of NES;[92] another important figure is Helmut Koziolek, the director of the Central Institute for Socialist Economic Leadership, who formerly headed the Economic Research Institute and helped create the important Advisory Council for Economic Research, both adjuncts of the State Planning Commission.[93]

A final category of advisers are the personal *Referenten* to leading SED figures, such as Dr. Wolfgang Berger, for many years Ulbricht's economic adviser. The influence of such men—and this is true in some degree for the more institutionalized advisory roles as well—is impossible to generalize, depending as it does on the abilities, personalities, and role conceptions of both advisor and advised. Although technical experts man a great number of such positions, their power in them suffers from the important limitation of being defined, in fact, as advisory. A similar limitation restricts technicians with principal administrative responsibilities; their power is substantial in day-to-day operations but remains sub-

[90] Rausch, *op. cit.,* p. 274. See also above, Chap. 4.

[91] Richert, *"Sozialistische Universität,"* p. 161.

[92] *Frankfurter Allgemeine Zeitung* (December 7, 1965), p. 2; see also Richert, *Macht ohne Mandat,* p. 134.

[93] See Peter Christian Ludz, "Bildungsstätte für zentrale Führungskräfte," *SBZ-Archiv,* XVII, No. 15 (1966), 231.

ject to withdrawal. There comes a point in human organizations where delegated or advisory authority becomes sufficiently institutionalized that it can no longer be taken away; in other cases, it may be recaptured only at the risk of substantial economic or other losses. The SED's leaders, by retaining firm control over the commanding heights of party power and by maintaining a great degree of organizational fluidity elsewhere, have so far prevented the first, higher level of institutionalization; they have not, as we shall see, entirely avoided the dangers of the second.

We have observed in this chapter the steady growth of representation of highly educated technical specialists in the Central Committee and the Council of Ministers since 1950. But at the centers of policy making the technicians have been kept numerically weakest and the *apparatchiki* have remained strongest. Moreover, those "representatives" of the technical strategic elite in the Politburo and Secretariat are subject to continuing pressures not to be genuine representatives of group interests at all, but men who share with their *apparatchik* counterparts a commitment to a conservative vision of the party's leading role and a loyalty to collective leadership decisions.

There are costs to maintaining such an arrangement, of course. The sharp discrepancy between the composition of the lower echelons of the political elite and that of the decision makers proper is a potential source of severe tensions. Particularly in times of economic failure, the disparate makeup of the two is likely to be reflected in policy disagreements, based on divergent group perspectives and interests. We shall see numerous instances of such disagreements in the next two chapters. We shall find that the SED's commitment to economic modernization, while real enough and unquestionably necessary for its survival, is inevitably circumscribed by the hoary Leninist question of "Who-Whom?", the question of party power.

9

TECHNICIANS AND POLICY I:
THE CONFLICT OF PRIORITIES

> The struggle between the two social systems cannot, however, be decided by administrative means, even if these have a certain role to play during the entire transition period, but first of all by economic means. . . .
>
> FRITZ BEHRENS, 1956 [1]

> There can be no political-ideological work detached from the demands of reality. Political-ideological work is always tied to the concrete tasks of the class struggle, which today is carried out in the German Democratic Republic above all in the arena of production.
>
> GÜNTER MITTAG, 1963 [2]

THE FINAL test of the political influence of any group lies not in the presence of its members in decision-making bodies (which might conceivably be merely decorative) but in the degree to which they are able to affect actual policy outcomes. Political science has yet to devise fully satisfactory methods of measuring such group or individual influence although the methodological controversies provoked by the community power studies and the group approach to politics have helped clarify some of the virtues and disabilities of rival modes of analysis.[3] Even in polities where direct observation of portions of the decision-making process is

---

[1] Fritz Behrens, "Zum Problem der Ausnutzung ökonomischer Gesetze in der Übergangsperiode," in *Zur ökonomischen Theorie und Politik in der Übergangsperiode, Wirtschaftswissenschaft*, V (3. Sonderheft, 1957), 115.

[2] Günter Mittag, *Fragen der Parteiarbeit nach dem Produktionsprinzip in Industrie und Bauwesen* (Berlin: Dietz Verlag, 1963), p. 126.

[3] For a recent survey, see Douglas M. Fox, "Whither Community Power Studies," *Polity*, III (Summer 1971), 576–585.

feasible, it is difficult to attribute a given policy definitively to the influence of any particular group. In Communist systems, where decision making is largely concealed from external view and relevant influential groups are seldom formally organized or even unambiguously defined, the difficulties are still greater.[4]

The approach most readily available to students of Communist systems rests essentially on the subjective inference of a causal relationship between group interests and policies where no direct link can be shown. In this approach, the policies decided upon are examined to see to what degree they appear to reflect the demands and interests, articulated or not, of the group in question and particularly to see whether they represent a change in the group's favor. A second, more direct possibility—where appropriate data are available—is to study the public elements of discussion and argument leading to a given set of decisions to see whether group representatives appeared to initiate and support them, oppose them, or remain silent.[5] Of course, in Communist systems public advocacy does not always mirror private conviction; the analysis of such statements often requires the arcane tools and interpretive methods of the Kremlinologist. Finally, the environment of assumptions in which decision making takes place—the question of what issues are permitted to be raised at all and in what terms— may be studied to see whether it favors or greatly limits the group. As critics of the "nondecision" approach have noted, the existence of such an environment is not amenable to ready empirical demonstration.[6]

Although each of these three approaches thus has its difficulties, the simultaneous use of all provides internal correctives for at least some of them. My examination of DDR economic policies from 1956 to the present seeks to employ all three strategies, but the nature of the available DDR materials makes emphasis on the

[4] Franklyn Griffiths, "A Tendency Analysis of Soviet Policy-Making," in H. Gordon Skilling and Franklyn Griffiths, eds., *Interest Groups in Soviet Politics* (Princeton: Princeton University Press, 1971), pp. 344–346.

[5] Cf. Robert A. Dahl, *Who Governs?* (New Haven: Yale University Press, 1961); also his "Critique of the Ruling Elite Model," *American Political Science Review*, LII (June 1958), 463–469.

[6] Cf. Peter Bachrach and Morton S. Baratz, "Two Faces of Power," *American Political Science Review*, LVI (December 1962), 947–952; Raymond E. Wolfinger, "Nondecisions and the Study of Local Politics," *ibid.*, LXV (December 1971), 1063–1080; Frederick W. Frey, "Comment," and Wolfinger, "Rejoinder," *ibid.*, 1081–1104.

first unavoidable. I shall attempt to show the changes in the influence of the technical strategic elite by examining the development of regime policy together with what sketchy and ambiguous evidence is available concerning the posture of the leading figures on particular issues. I will also argue that the very issues raised in internal policy disputes (the third approach above) suggests the enhanced influence of representatives of the technical intelligentsia.

The record of East German politics since 1956 may be viewed as one of continuing conflict, sometimes latent, sometimes overt, between policies justified by the requirements of "politics"—that is, dogmatic ideology and traditional power considerations—and others answering to the perceived demands of economic rationality. With few exceptions, politics emerged victorious from each of these encounters until the adoption of the New Economic System at the Sixth SED Congress (1963). Then the situation became more blurred: Economic reform itself became the ground on which the struggle continued.

THE HERESY OF FRITZ BEHRENS

The prehistory of the New Economic System really begins with the 1956 heresy of the economist Fritz Behrens, a veteran Communist, at that time dean of the Leipzig economics faculty, head of the DDR's Central Statistical Office and a vice chairman of the State Planning Commission. Taking advantage of the relative intellectual freedom that flourished in the DDR that year, Behrens put forward a series of proposals which, while similar in many respects to those later made by the Soviet economist Evsei Liberman[7] and to parts of the New Economic System itself, went beyond the detailing of economic reforms to their underlying political and ideological implications. Therein lies their importance, for they constituted the rudiments of an ideological platform for the adherents of economic rationalization—the only one, before or since, which has been quite so self-consciously spelled out.

Behrens proposed a sweeping decentralization of the DDR econ-

---

[7] The beginnings of Liberman's own advocacy of economic reforms centering on the use of profit as a criterion of success date to about the same time. Richard W. Judy, "The Economists," in Skilling and Griffiths, eds., *op. cit.*, pp. 234–235.

omy which would grant individual factories a broad measure of autonomy and encourage the "initiative" of the workers, while limiting the central planning organs to the determination of desirable economic "proportions" and the use of the "economic levers" of prices, credit, and so on for achieving them. The individual factories would operate on the basis of rigorous "economic cost accounting," with their success to be judged principally according to the criterion of profitability. Price reform would be central to the success of this scheme. Prices should be based fundamentally, Behrens argued, on the "law of value" (*Wertgesetz*), reflecting, in his view, both the expenditure of labor in production and demand for the product. He proposed a threefold division of prices, one group of which would be fixed, a second flexible above a legal minimum, and a third—for consumer goods—flexible below a legal maximum.

Most of these proposals, even to the slogans of "economic levers" and "economic cost accounting," became DDR policy eight years later; the clearest exception is the price scheme, which, however, resembles that subsequently adopted in Czechoslovakia and Hungary.[8] The significance of Behrens' argument, however, is that he justified economic reform by an unorthodox interpretation of the Marxist theories of the state and of "spontaneity" and "consciousness," coupled with a specific critique of conditions in the DDR. These proved entirely unacceptable to the party leadership, which denounced them as "revisionist."

Behrens pointed to a fundamental contradiction emerging in the period of transition to socialism: that "between the form of state direction of the economy and the *content* of the rapidly developing economic substructure."[9] Experience had shown that a socialist economy could rest only on "the resourcefulness, the initiative, and the creativity of the working masses," and, therefore, a "centrally administered economy on a socialist basis" was "impossible."[10] While strong central direction could be justified in the initial stages of the transition period, the "development of the social forces of production, driven by the new relations of pro-

---

[8] Werner Bröll, "Die Wirtschaftsreformen der DDR im RGW-Vergleich," *Deutschland Archiv*, IV (July 1971), 710–712. See also Karl C. Thalheim and Hans-Hermann Höhmann, *Wirtschaftsreformen in Osteuropa* (Köln: Verlag Wissenschaft und Politik, 1968).

[9] Behrens, "Zum Problem," p. 116.   [10] *Ibid.*, p. 109.

duction," soon had to be accompanied by a "process of the gradual decentralization of the direction of state and economy and the gradual dismantling (*Abbau*) of central direction [and] its replacement by economic policies based on the utilization of economic laws." [11] "Dismantling" was viewed by Behrens as a partial manifestation of the "withering away of the state." [12] He rejected the Stalinist view that the state must be strengthened because the class struggle is intensified in the transition period; in any case, conditions in Eastern Europe in the era of peaceful competition differed from those under Stalin in the USSR. Even while some (for example, military) functions had to remain centralized, the "economic-organizational" and "cultural-educative" functions (ironically, Stalinist categories) need not be.[13] "The belief," he insisted, "that the state can do everything and that every matter, even the most private, must be controlled and directed by the state is not socialist, but 'Prussian,' that is, Junker-monopolistic." [14]

In the DDR, Behrens maintained, overcentralization and the heavy-handedness of the bureaucracy had slowed down economic growth: On the one hand, discontinuities in production had harmed work productivity, driven up labor costs, and lowered the quality of output; on the other, useless surpluses (*Überplanbestände*) and excessive purchasing power existed side by side in the consumer sector.[15] The bureaucracy showered directives upon the factories in such quantity as to weaken rather than strengthen effective control. The "ideological reflex" in the face of these difficulties was to blame them on "enemy agent activity and sabotage" and to seek to cure bureaucratism by agitation rather than by getting at the structural causes of the problem.[16] Bureaucratism was maintained in the DDR by the false belief that "consciousness" among the masses precluded their "spontaneity" and that the latter was equivalent to "anarchy." In fact, consciousness and spontaneity formed a dialectical unity, and only an economic system permitting worker spontaneity and serving their "material interest" was appropriate to socialism. Indeed, state planning, he remarked, must not consist of commands from above but rather be the "organizational unification of the will of the workers." [17]

[11] *Ibid.*, p. 112.
[13] *Ibid.*, pp. 130–132.
[15] *Ibid.*, p. 118.
[17] *Ibid.*, pp. 128–129, 125.

[12] *Ibid.*, p. 117.
[14] *Ibid.*, p. 125.
[16] *Ibid.*, pp. 122–123, 130.

Behrens' theses and those of his younger co-worker Arne Benary[18] thus openly assaulted the principle of highly centralized political control with both economic reasoning and an interpretation of Marxism much at variance with official doctrine. The regime leaders, with the cautionary examples of Poland and Hungary immediately before them and seeing shadows of the Yugoslav experiment with workers' councils, reacted with alacrity. Behrens, Benary, and the chief of their institute Günther Kohlmey were sharply attacked by Ulbricht and others at the Thirtieth Central Committee Plenum at the end of January 1957; the Behrens and Benary articles appeared in print only later, embedded in lengthy refutations.[19] Their publication had apparently been demanded by the committee, whose members wanted to see the objects of denunciation.[20]

The attack centered on the Behrens-Benary interpretation of the *Wertgesetz*, which was said to invite a return to the "anarchy of the capitalist market economy," [21] on their theory of spontaneity, and on their view of the diminishing role of state power. All were seen, quite correctly, as a threat to strong centralized party control; as the party euphemism put it, they reflected an "underestimation of the significance of political power for the working class." [22] It was noted that Behrens and Benary ignored the "leading role of the Marxist-Leninist party," a consequence of their "individualist-anarchist" spontaneity theory; socialist production, however, demanded a "maximum of organization and discipline," the duty of the party.[23] At the present historical stage, not the "withering away" but the consolidation (*Festigung*) of the socialist state was demanded. The hoary warnings about capitalist encirclement were trotted out, and Behrens was charged with

[18] Benary, "Zur Grundproblemen der politischen Ökonomie des Sozialismus in der Übergangsperiode," in *Zur ökonomischen Theorie*, 62–94.
[19] See "Das 30. Plenum und dit Wirtschaftswissenschaftler," *Wirtschaftswissenschaft*, V (February–March, 1957), 161–165; also Martin Jänicke, *Der dritte Weg* (Köln: Neuer Deutscher Verlag, 1964), pp. 104–105.
[20] Jänicke, *op. cit.*, p. 105, citing Fritz Schenk.
[21] Karl Kampfert, "Gegen das Aufkommen revisionistischer Auffassungen in der Wirtschaftswissenschaft," in *Zur ökonomischen Theorie*, 8.
[22] *Ibid.*, p. 3.
[23] *Ibid.*, pp. 9–10; Fred Oelssner, "Staat und Ökonomie in der Übergangsperiode," revised manuscript of speech at 30th Plenum, *Wirtschaftswissenschaft*, V (April–May 1957), 325; "Mitarbeiter des Instituts für Wirtschaftswissenschaften distanzieren sich von revisionistischen Auffassungen," *Wirtschaftswissenschaft*, V, No. 3 (1957), 446.

minimizing the operations of "imperialist espionage and sabotage organizations." [24]

The continuing attack upon Behrens and Benary, a characteristic mixture of ideological refutation and ad hominem suggestions about the usefulness of their doctrines to "international reaction," finally produced the obligatory formal recantations. At the third Universities Conference (March 1958) one speaker noted the great influence of Behrens on his students and the DDR's youth and asked: "Comrade Behrens, were you aware that in October 1956, while the events in Poland and Hungary were developing, while here the enemy was attempting to do everything to weaken and attack our republic, [your] article could be the banner for the concentration of all elements who are against the republic, that your article was the platform for Harich and others?" [25] On this occasion Behrens admitted his arguments were "objectively" revisionistic and that "even if I still maintained them" they had been overtaken by "developments" in the DDR and the Soviet Union (the Khrushchev reforms?).[26] The ambiguity of this statement was recognized, and in 1960, with Benary, he issued a more thorough self-criticism.[27]

ECONOMIC POLICY, 1956–1961

Fred Oelssner had delivered one of the speeches assaulting Behrens at the Thirtieth Plenum; but his address revealed a great deal of agreement with some of Behrens' fundamental premises and a like awareness of the economic requirements conditioning economic policy:

> The state authority, the government, the ministries, or indeed the party, which determine economic policy, are thus not independent in their decisions; they may not make their decisions arbitrarily but

[24] Kampfert, *op. cit.*, pp. 7–8 and *passim.*

[25] Robert Naumann, "Hand in Hand mit der Arbeiterklasse," *Neues Deutschland* (hereafter cited as *ND*) (March 4, 1958), p. 5.

[26] Fritz Behrens, "Meine Konzeption war revisionistisch," *ND* (March 4, 1958), p. 5.

[27] "Erklärung des Genossen Professor Dr. Fritz Behrens. Erklärung des Genossen Arne Benary," *Neuer Weg*, XV, No. 9 (1960), 650–652. In his statement Benary acknowledged the influence of the Hungarian philosopher Georg Lukacs on his thought.

must take account of the economic facts and laws. When they don't do that, they will cause great damage. That is the other side of the relationship between state authority and economics. It is not less dangerous to ignore the economic bases of economic policy than to minimize the role of state authority.[28]

Oelssner went on to criticize the frequent tendency to push economic facts aside when they did not correspond to "theoretical" preconceptions: "Let me merely remind you how we handled our economic plans even a year ago. Once the plan had been determined, then nothing could be changed, even when its premises were known to have long become untenable. Only in the fall of 1956 did we move away from this unrealistic method and carry through the principle that the plan is not an icon which one can only pray to but an instrument of our economic policy." [29] That acceptance of this principle was still less than complete was made clear by Oelssner's long list of specific criticisms of DDR planning and its failure to utilize the law of value adequately. It is apparent that Oelssner was fighting simultaneously a two-front war: against Behrens (with whom he had a quite genuine disagreement over decentralization) and, more importantly, against Ulbricht and his economically conservative allies.

Other events of 1956 also stimulated leading economic functionaries to the advocacy of reform. Schenk reports that members of the Planning Commission, including Leuschner, followed with great enthusiasm the pronouncements of Gomulka on the "cult of personality" and his frank criticisms of the direction of the Polish economy. The unrest among the workers at Leuna (see Chapter 6 above) brought strong expressions of sympathy in particular from Selbmann; to mollify it a workers' conference was held, at which the formation of workers' committees and an attack on "bureaucratism" were to be announced and Leuschner was to give a speech candidly admitting the difficulties of the DDR economy. It was hoped that this would provide the impetus to a series of substantial reforms, but at the last moment the committees were stripped of any administrative authority and Leuschner's speech was stripped of its franker sections and pushed back to the end of the con-

---

[28] Oelssner, *op. cit.*, pp. 326–327.   [29] *Ibid.*, pp. 327–328.

ference. Leuschner later entertained similar hopes that Khrushchev's decentralization of the Soviet economy would provoke meaningful reforms in the DDR; here he was again disappointed.[30]

Oelssner had used the crisis days of November to deliver a frank speech on the shortage of consumer goods in the economy and had proposed that weak or unprofitable collective farms be dissolved.[31] At his Thirtieth Plenum speech at the end of January 1957, he pleaded for greater realism, including close attention to the law of value: "We are far from having overcome the method of shoving aside unpleasant facts with the remark, 'the figures aren't right,' instead of analyzing things basically and carrying out the necessary measures at the right time." [32] At the same conference, Leuschner demanded greater freedom from "political, dogmatic, and uneconomic" restrictions on the private sector of the economy, whose health was vital to the whole.[33]

Oelssner denounced with particular vigor what elsewhere he termed "plan fetishism," the tendency to regard the plan as sacrosanct and unchangeable; his conviction took practical form when, at the Thirty-third Plenum in the fall of 1957, he successfully joined with Selbmann, Rau, Ziller, and Leuschner in what was later charged to have been a "bitter struggle" to reduce the plan targets against the will of Ulbricht.[34] Matters came to a head, however, at the same plenum in the discussion of Ulbricht's proposal to apply Khrushchev's scheme for decentralization to economic "regions" (*Sovnarkhozy*) somewhat mechanically to the DDR. This Oelssner characterized as a "reversion to the premonopolistic stage of capitalism";[35] Selbmann (allegedly) added that "for us

[30] Fritz Schenk, *Im Vorzimmer der Diktatur* (Köln: Kiepenheuer & Witsch, 1962), pp. 306–316.
[31] Heinrich Rau, discussion speech at 35th Plenum, *ND* (February 25, 1958), p. 3.
[32] Oelssner, *op. cit.*, pp. 327, 331.
[33] *SBZ von 1957 bis 1958* (Bonn and Berlin: Bundesministerium für gesamtdeutsche Fragen, 1960), pp. 32–34.
[34] See Jänicke, *Der dritte Weg*, pp. 87, 92; Ernst Richert, *Macht ohne Mandat* (Köln and Opladen: Westdeutscher Verlag, 1963), p. 119, fn. 57. In December 1956 the CPSU Central Committee had decided to lower the production targets of the Soviet Five-Year Plan. It also established an economic "superministry" apparently similar to the Economic Council created in April 1957 in the DDR. Jeremy R. Azrael, "The Managers," in R. Barry Farrell, ed., *Political Leadership in Eastern Europe and the Soviet Union* (Chicago: Aldine, 1970), p. 239.
[35] Erich Honecker, Politburo report at 35th Plenum, *ND* (February 8, 1958), p. 5.

it makes no difference what is now being done in the Soviet Union" [36] although he did propose additional authority be given directly to the factories.[37] Ziller apparently shared their view.[38]

From March 1957 to February 1958, the DDR's leading economic pragmatists, including Oelssner, Selbmann, Ziller, and Leuschner, enjoyed an extraordinary organizational vantage point in the powerful Economic Council, which was responsible for all economic decisions save the most fundamental ones taken by the Politburo itself. The crushing of the personal opposition to Ulbricht and the broad ideological attack on "managerialism" [39] was quickly followed by the council's dissolution. This defeat for the economic pragmatists, while temporary and partial, opened the way for a series of policy initiatives of doubtful economic utility.

After completing the purges, Ulbricht carried out his own economic reorganization in partial imitation of the Soviet model. The central economic ministries were dissolved, certain planning functions were assigned to regional bodies, and power at the center was concentrated in the Planning Commission under Leuschner, who had avoided lending the "managerialists" open support in spite of his sympathy with their outlook. It was at this time that the seventy-plus *Vereinigungen Volkseigner Betriebe* (VVBs), each administratively responsible for a particular branch of the economy, regional "economic councils," and *Kreis* (district) planning commissions were created, producing what Richert terms a "godless confusion of competencies." [40] Confusion, however, did not basically transform control, and day-to-day direction of the economy remained largely in the province of economic pragmatists (who also dominated the Central Committee Economic Commission, created in 1958).[41]

Fundamental policy, however, continued to be determined by political considerations: Its focus became the *ökonomische Hauptaufgabe*, the overtaking of the Federal Republic in per capita

---

[36] Hans Schimanski, "Die Revolution im Glaspalast," *SBZ-Archiv*, IX (February 28, 1958), 153–154.
[37] Jänicke, *op. cit.*, p. 88.
[38] See also Ernst Richert, *"Sozialistische Universität"* (Berlin: Colloquium Verlag, 1967), pp. 162–164.
[39] See Chap. 8.   [40] Richert, *op. cit.*, pp. 133–134.
[41] *Ibid.*, pp. 128–129, 134.

consumption of all important goods and commodities by 1961.[42]
This program, with its initial emphasis on the expansion of consumer goods production, housing, and the like, followed a similar
pronouncement (vis-à-vis the United States) by Khrushchev in the
USSR, and was accompanied by new pressures for recognition of
the DDR and the neutralizing of West Berlin. Ulbricht hoped
thereby to establish the identity and viability of the DDR by
simultaneously liquidating the Berlin "show window" and increasing his state's economic attractiveness. The *Hauptaufgabe,* however, could only be achieved by sacrificing basic industrial development to present consumption, a reversal of the classical Bolshevik
pattern, a contradiction of the then current five-year plan (which
was duly replaced by a new seven-year plan), and probably a severe
obstacle to economic integration in COMECON.[43] There is no
evidence of opposition to these policies by high economic officials
in spite of their patent irrationality; perhaps the urge of the
"managerialists" was still too close at hand.

Achieving the *ökonomische Hauptaufgabe* would have been
problematic under the best of circumstances. In early 1960, however, Ulbricht decided to complete the collectivization of the
countryside and forced the remaining one-half of the country's
agricultural acreage into the "socialist sector" in the astonishingly
short time of three months. Circumstantial evidence, as well as
economic logic, suggests that collectivization was carried out only
in the face of opposition from the Planning Commission and
Minister-President Grotewohl.[44] Immediately before the collectivization drive, several agricultural officials, regional party secretaries, and Grotewohl himself had renounced the use of force in
bringing farmers into the collectives. At the Eighth Central Com-

[42] A resolution of the Fifth SED Congress (July 1958) stated: "This task is the
share of our republic in the worldwide struggle for peaceful coexistence and for
the peaceful competition between the socialist and capitalist social order, in which
the superiority of our socialist order will be demonstrated. The *ökonomische
Hauptaufgabe* therefore has a profound political and social content. . . ." Reprinted in Hermann Weber, ed., *Der deutsche Kommunismus: Dokumente* (Köln:
Kiepenheuer & Witsch, 1963), pp. 622–623.

[43] See Richert, *op. cit.,* pp. 55–57, 144–145, for an excellent discussion of these
problems.

[44] *Ibid.* has assembled the evidence on this point on pp. 60–62, esp. fn. 179; see
also Jänicke, *Der dritte Weg,* pp. 166–168; Carola Stern, "Ulbrichts Dorffabrik,"
SBZ-Archiv, XI, No. 9 (1960), 130.

mittee Plenum, summoned only toward the close of the campaign, the Planning Commission official Helmut Wunderlich and the party secretary of the Magdeburg district Alois Pisnik both expressed their surprise at developments. Since Pisnik was a candidate of the Politburo, it may well be that even this body was not consulted before the campaign was initiated. Leuschner publicly praised collectivization for enhancing the control of the planners but added that it would require much greater immediate investment in agricultural machinery, buildings, and fertilizers, which "naturally will and must have consequences for the other branches of the economy." [45] The short-run consequences for the goal of raising living standards could hardly have been anything but negative; the stagnation of farm production and the sudden growth of the refugee stream provoked by the collectivization campaign assured that result. By January 1961 it was admitted that some of the goals of the *Hauptaufgabe* would have to be postponed, and in March, while the planners revised the targets of the seven-year plan downward, Ulbricht admitted in effect that the *Hauptaufgabe* would have to give way indefinitely to the prior need to expand work productivity.[46] A new slogan emerged: "One cannot live in 1961 at the level one intends to work in 1965." [47]

The primacy of politics over economics enjoyed still another dubious triumph with the initiation of *Aktion Störfreimachung*, a program designed to free the DDR's economy from dependence on trade with West Germany. The program was announced in September 1960 in response to a West German threat to pull out of the interzonal trade agreement; it received additional impetus in 1961 from the developing Berlin crisis and the ultimate erection of the Wall. *Störfreimachung* required that thousands of items previously imported be put into East German production and that other facilities be converted to permit the utilization of materials and equipment from the Soviet Union and Eastern Europe. Members of the State Planning Commission and the VVBs and fac-

---

[45] Bruno Leuschner, discussion speech at Eighth Central Committee Plenum, *ND* (April 6, 1960), reprinted in *SBZ-Archiv*, XI, No. 8 (1960), 126–127.

[46] See Ali Wiesner, "Ökonomische Hauptaufgabe von der Tagesordung abgesetzt," *SBZ-Archiv*, XII, No. 5 (1961), 74; Hans Schimanski, "Die 12. Tagung des ZK der SED," *SBZ-Archiv*, XII, No. 7 (1961), 106.

[47] Ulbricht at the Fourteenth Central Committee Plenum, *ND* (December 26 and 28, 1961), reprinted in *SBZ-Archiv*, XII, No. 24 (1961), 388.

tories opposed this unrealistic attempt at partial autarky, as a later speech by the veteran functionary Karl Mewis, as well as other evidence, revealed.[48] The reason was without doubt the immense economic cost: Some 1,500 items in the chemical industry alone, wrote the Central Committee economist Alfred Lange, would have to be newly produced at home or imported from socialist neighbors; a "temporary" drop in work productivity—theretofore the chief concern of DDR economic policy—would be inevitable.[49]

In July 1961 Leuschner left the Planning Commission to become "coordinator" of the entire economy and subsequently DDR delegate to COMECON. This dubious promotion accompanied the rejection of the economic plan worked out under his direction on the grounds that it took too little account of the demands of *Störfreimachung*.[50] It was followed by the division of the commission into two sections, each of which was entrusted to a veteran *apparatchik* without technical experience. Mewis—notorious for his leading role in the collectivization drive—became head of the shrunken commission proper, now dealing only with long-term planning, while Alfred Neumann was made chairman of the National Economic Council, responsible for current planning and the direction of industry. Both Mewis and Neumann subsequently criticized the old commission for its "confused leadership principles";[51] later Mewis attacked "the wanderers between two worlds, whom we had in the economy and still have. . . ."[52] In mid-1962, however, *Aktion Störfreimachung* was quietly dropped; six months after that, so was Mewis.

It is undoubtedly significant that the two leading planning positions were occupied by loyal *apparatchiki* at the time of the construction of the Wall. The burgeoning East-to-West refugee

[48] Richert, *Macht ohne Mandat*, p. 58. See also Jänicke, *op. cit.*, p. 256, fns. 71, 73; Alfred Schnelzki, "Eng mit den Angehörigen der Intelligenz verbunden," *Neuer Weg*, XVIII, No. 1 (1963), 7–8.

[49] Lange's article—"Probleme der Umstellung der Volkswirtschaft der Deutschen Demokratischen Republik," *Wirtschaftswissenschaft*, IX (July 1961)—nevertheless defends the necessity for *Störfreimachung*. Fritz Schenk, " 'Störfreimachung' der Zonenwirtschaft," *SBZ-Archiv*, XII, No. 19 (1961), 301–303.

[50] Richert, *op. cit.*, p. 124.

[51] Fritz Schenk, "Konzil der Wirtschaftsbürokraten," *SBZ-Archiv*, XII, No. 21 (1961), 329–330.

[52] Jänicke, *op. cit.*, p. 174.

stream entailed economic costs of a degree that the regime could
no longer tolerate, particularly the heavy loss of trained technical
specialists. Yet if the fundamental justification for the Wall was
economic, the resurgent refugee problem itself—which only two
years earlier had seemed to be declining to manageable proportions—was largely the consequence of the "politically" inspired
policies of rapid collectivization and, to a lesser degree, *Störfreimachung*. In the absence of direct evidence, it must be sur-
mised that members of the technical strategic elite viewed the
Wall with, at best, mixed emotions. Ironically, however, the Wall
shortly was to open the way to genuine economic reform. The
concrete blocks and barbed wire deprived the SED of its time-
honored alibi for economic failures: currency manipulation and
economic sabotage by Western agents moving undetected across
the "open border." To maintain its legitimacy in the eyes of its
Soviet protector, the SED leadership had no remaining alternative
to economic success. Such success, it became rapidly clear, could not
be obtained through the dogged insistence on the fundamental
wisdom of the practices and methods of Stalinist economics.

In the critical decisions of the 1956–1963 period, then, "political" considerations consistently triumphed over economic ones. It
would be an error, however, to regard these years as ones of im-
potence for the technicians. Their numbers in prominent positions in party and state increased; even when the Planning Commission was divided and placed under the leadership of political
functionaries, the advisers and staff immediately below them remained largely unchanged. In these years demands for technological rationalization crept increasingly into party rhetoric; and the
very fact that the crucial issues I have discussed could be formulated as a choice between political and rational economic alternatives testifies to the growing influence of the second perspective.
Perhaps unconsciously, the ground was being prepared for the
New Economic System.

10

TECHNICIANS AND POLICY II:
THE AMBIGUITIES OF ECONOMIC REFORM

> Everyone there, writers, scientists, white collar employees,
> workers, all look with fascination to the new economic policy.
> The one group hopes it will bring more liberality (or better, less
> dogmatism), the other that it will make their regime more pro-
> ficient and thus more popular.
>
> MARION GRÄFIN DÖNHOFF, after 1964 visit to DDR [1]

> Now there are some comrades, among them economic function-
> aries, who express the view that the economic system has failed
> to prove itself. . . .
>
> PAUL VERNER, Politburo report to Fourteenth
> Central Committee Plenum, December 1970[2]

THE New Economic System (NES) was introduced in 1963; the
next eight years saw the elaboration and then the modification of its reforms, ending in the abandonment of the most politically significant of them. The examination of these events will
allow us to sharpen our perspective on both the possibilities and
limitations of the influence of the technical strategic elite in a
mature Communist society. At the time of their adoption, the NES
reforms represented the most sweeping departure yet attempted in
Eastern Europe, excluding Yugoslavia, from the received principles of a highly centralized "command" economy. They resembled, with some modifications, the proposals of Liberman, which

[1] Marion Gräfin Dönhoff, Rudolf Walter Leonhardt, and Theo Sommer, *Reise in
ein fernes Land* (Hamburg: Die Zeit Bücher, 1964), p. 24.
[2] *Neues Deutschland* (hereafter cited as *ND*) (December 10, 1970), reprinted in
part in *Deutschland Archiv*, IV (January 1971), 95.

had been the center of a lively debate in the Soviet press in the fall
of 1962, and had then been turned over to economic research
bodies for further study and recommendations. In many respects
they also resembled the economic heresies of Behrens, stripped of
their political implications. Belying its Stalinist reputation, the
SED had placed itself in the vanguard of Communist economic
innovation. At the same time it supported the reforms with a
broad reorientation of the official ideology and a massive effort to
mobilize all social groups on its behalf, going far beyond the agitation and propaganda campaigns which customarily accompany
important Communist policy innovations.[3]

The introduction of NES represented the greatest apparent triumph of the views of the technical elite up to that time; in spite
of incomplete information, it becomes important to explore the
question of why and how it was adopted. Five elements, all inter-
related, must be considered: the position of Ulbricht, pressures
from the Soviet leadership, the DDR's economic difficulties, the
innovative economic proposals discussed in both the Soviet Union
and the DDR, and important changes of personnel within the East
German economic leadership. First, it must be stressed that from
the beginning Ulbricht placed himself strongly on the side of economic reform and, in the subsequent internal conflict between
economic innovators and administrative conservatives, for some
time clearly favored the former.[4] His motivations may only be
guessed at; it should be recorded that he spent the entire month
of August 1962 "vacationing" in the Soviet Union and that the
Soviet discussions of economic reform, the CPSU's new program
adopted at the Twenty-Second Congress, and Khrushchev's reform
of the parent party's organization all played a considerable role in
the rhetoric preceding and accompanying the Sixth SED Congress
(January 1963). Ulbricht and the Soviet leadership shared a common interest in freeing the DDR from its economic difficulties:
the former for reasons of personal power, the latter because of the
commitment of its prestige in the Berlin question and the im-

[3] Sections of this chapter are taken from my article "Economic Reform as Ideology:
East Germany's New Economic System," *Comparative Politics*, III (January 1971),
211–229.
[4] This is the view of Carola Stern, among others, in her *Ulbricht: Eine politische
Biographie* (Köln: Kiepenheuer & Witsch, 1963), p. 263.

portance of the DDR to the Soviet Union's and COMECON's own economic development. It is also entirely plausible that the Soviet leaders saw in the DDR a useful experimental laboratory for testing "Libermanism" prior to its introduction at home, just as they had first tried out the "New Course" in the DDR in 1953.[5]

The death of *Störfreimachung* in 1962 may be taken as symbolic of a recognition of the failure of previous DDR economic policy. Total growth had slowed, agricultural production had dropped, investment had fallen drastically behind plan figures, and the DDR suffered from serious economic disproportions.[6] Economic crisis doubtless speeded the fall of Mewis and enhanced the influence of the younger generation of technicians. In mid-1962 Erich Apel moved to the Council of Ministers—he was to replace Mewis at the head of the Planning Commission in December—while Günter Mittag became Central Committee economic secretary. It seems probable that these, together with Leuschner, were in a particularly favorable position to promote measures of economic rationalization, given the evident failure of Mewis and Neumann.

Liberman's "Profit-Plan-Premium" was published in the DDR toward the end of September and was followed by the reprinting of some of the Soviet discussion it inspired. Ulbricht himself briefly described Liberman's proposals in his speech at the Seventeenth Central Committee Plenum (October 3–5) and urged: "Our economists and planners should carefully follow and evaluate this discussion. At the same time they should develop their own conceptions in order that there can be a fruitful exchange at the conference of economists which is coming shortly. The broad public discussion of important economic questions in the Soviet Union

[5] See the speculation to this effect in Joachim Nawrocki, "Vom NÖS zum Computer-Stalinismus," *Deutschland Archiv*, IV (April 1971), 348. There is little direct evidence on the nature and degree of Soviet influence over DDR domestic policy decisions, of course. The frequency and timing of visits between high officials of the two countries and the degree of coincidence of their ideological themes and policy actions are useful but circumstantial indicators which cannot distinguish between Soviet coercion and the effects of close basic ideological affinity and perceived mutual interest.

[6] See, for example, Ernst Richert, *Macht ohne Mandat* (Köln and Opladen: Westdeutscher Verlag, 1963), p. 146. Wolfgang Berger and Otto Reinhold, in their *Zu den wissenschaftlichen Grundlagen des neuen ökonomischen Systems der Planung und Leitung* (Berlin: Dietz Verlag, 1966), pp. 15–18, describe the last two problems with considerable candor but blame them on the machinations of the West.

underscores the growing role of economists and planners." [7] In response to this flattering invitation, leading academic economists and functionaries wrote numerous articles for the professional publications *Die Wirtschaft, Wirtschaftswissenschaft,* and *Deutsche Finanzwirtschaft,* as well as for the ideological journal *Einheit,* and the party organ *Neues Deutschland;* their general tone was favorable.[8] Among the proponents of Libermanism were the present Politburo candidate and head of the Office of Prices Walter Halbritter, the financial economist Herbert Wolf, and, not surprisingly, Fritz Behrens. Behrens, who was interviewed after having returned from a lecture tour in the Soviet Union, did not conceal his enthusiasm for proposals which resembled some of his own earlier heresies.[9] Another former heretic, Jürgen Kuczynski, had delivered himself of an attack on the old economic practices even before the Liberman discussion, in August.[10]

At the moment Liberman's proposals were being tabled in the Soviet Union, it became clear that they would be adopted in the DDR. In November the draft program of the SED, containing important elements of the New Economic System, was published; on December 7–8 the Liberman discussion continued at the economists' conference mentioned earlier by Ulbricht.[11] The essentials of the System were spelled out at the Sixth Party Congress in January,[12] and a working group of economists and "practitioners"

[7] Walter Ulbricht, "Die Vorbereitung des VI. Parteitages der Sozialistischen Einheitspartei Deutschlands," in his *Dem VI. Parteitag entgegen* (Berlin: Dietz Verlag, 1962), p. 38. My emphasis.

[8] See Karl C. Thalheim, *Die Wirtschaft der Sowjetzone in Krise und Umbau* (Berlin: Duncker & Humblot, 1964), pp. 62–64; Richert, *op. cit.,* pp. 147–148. Thalheim says that, as in the Soviet Union, the economic "practitioners" were more enthusiastic than the "theoreticians." It has also been noted that the tenor of discussion as a whole was more favorable than in the Soviet Union, suggesting that the fundamental decision may already have been made. Fritz Schenk, *Das rote Wirtschaftswunder* (Stuttgart: Seewald Verlag, 1969), p. 94.

[9] Interview with Fritz Behrens, "Planung-Rentabilität-Initiative," *Sonntag* (November 18, 1962), reprinted in *SBZ-Archiv,* XIV, Nos. 1–2 (1963), 29–30.

[10] *ND* (August 24, 1962), cited in Martin Jänicke, *Der dritte Weg* (Köln: Neuer Deutscher Verlag, 1964), p. 178.

[11] Berger and Reinhold, *op. cit.,* in an official account of the origins of NES, stress the "collective" effort led by a working group of the Central Committee commission in charge of developing the draft program, made up principally of economic functionaries of the Central Committee apparatus. It is noted that "the theory and practice of allied socialist states" was analyzed, and credit is specifically given to Liberman's work (pp. 22–25).

[12] Walter Ulbricht, *Das Programm des Sozialismus und die geschichtliche Aufgabe der Sozialistischen Einheitspartei Deutschlands* (Berlin: Dietz Verlag, 1963). It has

was assigned to develop detailed proposals. They are said to have proceeded "very timorously" until "representatives of the Central Committee" gave the "green light for a radical, comprehensive, and complex solution of the problem" and inspired them to go at their work with "ardent zeal." [13] Beginning in January many of the proposed reforms were tested experimentally in four VVBs and ten individual factories. After a giant conference of managers and economic functionaries in June, the Council of Ministers published a lengthy set of directives putting NES in relatively definitive form.[14]

All this makes it evident that economists and party and state technical officials had a continuing influence in the discussion and detailed construction of the New Economic System.[15] What remains uncertain is whether they actually were responsible for its adoption. They functioned, clearly, as a pressure group in favor of Libermanism; men like Apel, Mittag, and Leuschner were all in strategic positions for influencing Ulbricht; yet the possibility cannot be excluded that the critical and decisive pressure came from the Soviet leadership. Without the presence of the technical specialists in strategic roles, the New Economic System could not practicably have been introduced or implemented; but it is not clear that their demands for economic rationality had to be satisfied in 1963 any more than in earlier years. Of course, the DDR's economic difficulties proved an invaluable ally in this case to their influence; but by its nature such an ally is neither reliable nor permanent.

---

been noticed that some passages of this Sixth Congress speech seem to have been taken almost word for word from Liberman. Thalheim, *op. cit.*, p. 64.

[13] Berger and Reinhold, *op. cit.*, pp. 25–27. This passage would appear to suggest that the extent of the reforms remained a matter of dispute until well into 1963.

[14] Ulbricht, "Das neue ökonomische System der Planung und Leitung der Volkswirtschaft in der Praxis," *Die Wirtschaft* (June 28, 1963), pp. 1–21; *Richtlinie für das neue ökonomische System der Planung und Leitung der Volkswirtschaft* (Berlin: Dietz Verlag, 1963).

[15] Berger and Reinhold (*op. cit.*) note that ten "comrades" received the award "Banner of Work" for their participation in developing the NES, including Apel and Mittag. Of the rest, several were connected with the Central Committee's Division of Planning and Finance while "only" three did not belong to the party apparatus. Richert names Apel, Mittag, Jarowinsky, Ewald, Wolfgang Berger, and Margarete Wittkowski as some of the creators of NES. Ernst Richert, *Die DDR-Elite* (Hamburg: Rowohlt Verlag, 1968), p. 105. Another source identifies the rector of the *Hochschule für Ökonomie*, Alfred Lange, as one of the principal theoretical contributors. *Frankfurter Allgemeine Zeitung* (December 7, 1965), p. 2.

THE CONTENT OF REFORM

The reforms themselves may be described briefly; their main elements have since become familiar through their adoption elsewhere in the East European bloc.[16] Essentially, the New Economic System undertook a cautious departure from the customary highly centralized, administrative methods of Communist economic planning, decision making, and control, in order to increase productivity and technological innovation while retaining the basic form of a directively planned economy. It sought to do this by introducing marketlike devices for allocating resources and stimulating performance, though no real market, and by reorganizing the economy in such a way that every question might be "dealt with at the level at which it can be decided and resolved most competently (*am sachkundigsten*)."[17] The first strategy centered on the development of a closed system of interlocking economic "levers," marketlike indicators for evaluating the performance of economic units, including price, cost, profit, and sales; the most important of these was to be the profit of the individual factories and the new "socialist concerns," the VVBs.[18] In order to make profit a reliable indicator, the rationalization of costs through a comprehensive reform of prices was required; it was undertaken in several stages. For the same reason, an interest-like charge on plant and equipment (*Produktionsfondsabgabe*) was introduced. At the same time the emphasis on individual material incentives was increased; for the first time managerial personnel were compensated by "performance-determined" wages and premiums.

The second broad area of reform was the reorganization of the structures of economic decision making and control in both party and government so as to devolve responsibility on lower-ranking officials, most importantly factory and VVB directors. The VVBs, initially administrative bodies, were converted into "economic"

---

[16] The basic East German document setting forth the NES reforms is the *Richtlinie*; a Western account is Gert Leptin, "Das 'Neue ökonomische System' Mitteldeutschlands," in Karl C. Thalheim and Hans-Hermann Höhmann, eds., *Wirtschaftsreformen in Osteuropa* (Köln: Verlag Wissenschaft und Politik, 1968), pp. 100–130.

[17] *Richtlinie*, p. 17.

[18] The VVBs (*Vereinigungen Volkseigener Betriebe*) are organs responsible for all the firms in a particular branch of industry, for example, VVB potash, VVB shoes, VVB ship construction. There are now over one hundred.

organs with profit-and-loss accounting and major responsibility for investment, sales, planning, and the distribution of incentives. "In principle" new investment was to be financed out of the profits of the VVB or individual VEB or through credit extended by the state bank and expected to be repaid out of future profits.[19] The general directors of the VVBs were identified in early NES rhetoric as the critical figures of the reforms, but the responsibilities of individual plant managers were also enlarged and appear to have grown relatively more important with time. Party control functions were shifted from distant and/or untutored *apparatchiki* to party economic specialists closer to the managers in terms both of outlook and of bureaucratic distance. Untutored party officials were urged to "qualify" themselves in appropriate technical and economic disciplines, and special schooling was provided to that end in the hope of transforming the potential frictions between economic and party functionaries into cooperation based on mutual interests and goals.[20]

THE IDEOLOGY OF REFORM

The NES reforms were lent additional authority and political significance through the elaboration of an ideology justifying them. This ideology served in part as an instrument for winning, or deepening, legitimacy among the stratum of technical intelligentsia and the population as a whole; at the same time, it created openings for unintended interpretations and undesired inferences of broader social and political liberalization. In the past the DDR had quite justifiably stressed its ideological fidelity to the Soviet Union but never its ideological originality. It is striking, then, that after its adoption, the New Economic System was proudly claimed as "an important contribution of the German Socialist Unity Party to Marxist-Leninist theory." [21]

---

[19] Walter Ulbricht, "Probleme des Perspektivplanes bis 1970," *ND* (December 18, 1965), reprinted in part in *SBZ-Archiv*, XVII, Nos. 1–2 (1966), 26–31; XVII, No. 3 (1966), 42–48. See p. 30.

[20] "It is no longer acceptable," Ulbricht remarked at the Sixth Congress, "that a mason be party secretary in an electronic building elements factory or that a printer be party secretary in a large construction company." *Das Programm*, p. 243.

[21] This is the subtitle of the book by Berger and Reinhold; see also Uwe-Jens

Perhaps the most authoritative ideological formulation was provided by Apel and Mittag in a book published in 1964.[22] They began with the assertion that the "technical revolution" must indeed be regarded as a genuine revolution based upon a qualitative transformation of the forces of production. The New Economic System was the means by which the development of these forces and the welfare of the people could best be served during the construction of socialism. The surmounting in a socialist society, as foreseen by Marx, of the contradiction between the social character of production and the private appropriation of its output eliminated the major obstacle to the full development of the new productive forces; but this development demanded also the emergence of unified, scientific, and economically rational leadership of production and research. The movement of technology from mechanization to automation and the introduction of electronic data processing were important elements of the revolution. Through them man was said to receive "a qualitatively new position in the work process; he is freed not only from heavy manual labor but also from the routine mental activity tied to the continuous control and direction of production, and new horizons in creative activity open up." [23] The determination of the SED, therefore, to push forward the technical revolution was no arbitrary, "subjective" decision but reflected the "objective economic lawfulness of the steady further development of the productive forces." [24]

On the critical question of the decentralization of authority, Apel and Mittag were less direct, but the ideological importance they give it is clear in their discussion of "scientific leadership." The focal point of this discussion was the new role of the general directors of the VVBs, who were called the "key figures" of NES. They repeated Ulbricht's call for economic officials distinguished by their "enthusiasm for responsibility, creativity, and boldness" and urged the general directors to make decisions themselves

---

Heuer, *Demokratie und Recht im neuen ökonomischen System der Planung und Leitung der Volkswirtschaft* (Berlin: Staatsverlag der DDR, 1965).

[22] Erich Apel and Günter Mittag, *Wissenschaftliche Führungstätigkeit: Neue Rolle der VVB* (Berlin: Dietz Verlag, 1964).

[23] *Ibid.*, p. 12.   [24] *Ibid.*, p. 13.

rather than, as before, shoving them upstairs.[25] Other writings on NES urged individual factory managers to show more creative initiative and take more responsibility, and Mittag echoed a common theme in remarking that "an oversize administrative apparatus and a kind of leadership based predominantly on orders and decrees in questions of detail is no longer necessary." [26] The enthronement of the "socialist leadership personality" on the intermediate levels as a role model, joined to the numerous general attacks on "bureaucratism" and the more specific ones on the interference of the National Economic Council (then the central administrative body above the VVBs), was perhaps the most appealing element of NES to the young technical intelligentsia. It seemed to promise a significant redistribution of economic authority in favor of the managerial "practitioners" at the plant or VVB levels, even though terms like "decentralization" were scrupulously avoided.

The implications of the Apel-Mittag argument were developed most remarkably by Uwe-Jens Heuer in the book discussed in Chapter 6, which treated decentralization as the very core of NES. Heuer, in emphasizing the need for "self-organization" of the subsystems of the economy, not merely as a source of greater efficiency but also of genuine socialist democracy, thereby gave to NES a political dimension which otherwise remained largely implicit. The New Economic System became, in Heuer's treatment, an organizational instrument which, suitably anchored in socialist law, could satisfy the "democratic needs" of the working masses by allowing them a measure of influence over their own work lives.[27] The language of cybernetics, then fashionable in the East bloc, and arguments asserting the economic disutility of centralized bureaucratic planning were joined to reflections on interest conflict and alienation under socialism rather like then-current and later discussions in Czechoslovakia. Heuer's work, unlike Apel and Mittag's, never had the authoritative character associated with writ-

---

[25] *Ibid.*, pp. 23–24; the Ulbricht quote is from his *Die Durchführung der ökonomischen Politik im Planjahr 1964,* speech at Fifth Plenum of SED Central Committee (Berlin: Dietz Verlag, 1964), pp. 31–32.

[26] Günter Mittag, "Wir brauchen jetzt ein durchdachtes System der ökonomischen Leitung," *Die Wirtschaft* (January 28, 1963), pp. 6–7.

[27] Heuer, *op. cit.,* pp. 98–114, 162–181, and *passim.*

ings of Politburo members and was sharply criticized after publication; but the willingness of the DDR leadership to permit its publication at all is a measure of the pressures felt at that time for ideological rejuvenation and the willingness to use the NES as an instrument to that end.[28]

The range of NES's impact was also extended temporarily by the implied redefinition of the role of the party accompanying its reorganization according to the "production principle." [29] It was insisted that in the present stage of the DDR's development the critical problem of socialism was an economic one, which had to be solved by economic means. Accordingly, the promotion of economic rationalization was seen as a primary "political" task of the party. Indeed, Mittag's writings during this period characteristically treated the party as hardly more than a propagandist and a mobilizer for NES. "The most effective political argument in the long run," he observed in 1963, are "economic facts." [30]

It is not surprising that the ideology of NES should have proven so attractive a source of justification to a regime which had so long suffered from a legitimacy lag, whether that ideology was expressed in the more detailed rationalization of Apel and Mittag or, as it more often was, through a series of endlessly repeated slogans: "technical revolution," "thinking economically," "scientific leadership," "economic levers," "what profits the society must also profit the individual factory and the workers in it." [31] The New Economic System as ideology had about it the appeal of the scientific and the modern, and the promise of material well-being was surely a more effective theme than ritualistic phrases about the class struggle and the imperialist enemy; yet it was at least nominally integrated into Marxism-Leninism. The technical intelligentsia, which in large measure had been indifferent toward the

[28] In many respects the work on cybernetics of the philosopher Georg Klaus, whom Ludz designates as the DDR's "authoritative ideologist of technocracy," was similar in its social and political implications to that of Heuer; Klaus, however, was more reluctant to spell them out explicitly. See Peter Christian Ludz, *Parteielite im Wandel* (Köln and Opladen: Westdeutscher Verlag, 1968), pp. 294ff.

[29] That is, along functional lines rather than strictly geographical subdivisions ("territorial principle"). The distinction follows a similar one made in the Soviet Union.

[30] Mittag, *op. cit.*, p. 6.

[31] The last slogan was borrowed without acknowledgment from Liberman.

traditional ideology, was given with NES a strong apparent stake in the success of the regime. It is also quite clear that the ideological mobilization accompanying NES was an extremely useful instrument for overcoming the inertia and the vested interests of a variety of functionaries threatened by the reforms. The very breadth of NES's appeal, however, meant that diverse elements were willing to garb themselves in its slogans, and the consequence was a serious blurring of its meaning and a confusion of politics and economics.

Party members were thus urged to press the cause of economic rationalization as part of their political duties while failures in economic performance were laid to the "ideological" omissions of state and factory functionaries. Party officials were pressed to "qualify" themselves in economic or technical subjects on pain of losing their positions; economic functionaries were urged almost as frequently, though with less success, to exert "political" leadership and to study the Marxian classics. Ulbricht, in seeking to create a new type of leader both economically skilled and politically faithful, hoped without doubt to outflank the possible emergence of a self-conscious technocratic elite that might choose to rebel against, or to ignore, the inherited ideology and its guardians. In the same way, the ideologization of NES and the blurring of politics and economics were probably also meant to prevent any emergence of conflicting policy priorities along political/economic lines, as well as to "capture" for the SED any credit for economic success. Whatever the intent, however, the ambiguity thus produced did not eliminate rival groups but permitted them to mask diverse purposes under the same slogans.[32]

In particular, it permitted the technicians to press economic reforms in political guises. The new emphasis of party dogma on the economic slogans of innovation, rationalization, cybernation, managerial responsibility, and the like allowed technical specialists to

---

[32] The question of the meaning of the "primacy of politics" over economics, asserted by Lenin in a 1921 article, has come up frequently in recent DDR discussions. Heuer (*op. cit.*) treats it as simply implying that politics cannot be separated from economics and cites another remark by Lenin that the "nature of Soviet power" is that "political tasks take a subordinate place to economic tasks" (pp. 151–155). But cf. Rolf Sieber and Günter Söder, *Politik und Ökonomie im sozialistischen Gesellschaftssystem* (Berlin: Dietz Verlag, 1970).

pursue their professional interests in the name of political enthusiasm.[33] Also, the technical education given to many party functionaries made them more likely to be allies who understood the
problems and needs of the economic experts than the untrained
and suspicious dogmatists of an earlier day. Moreover, the organizational reforms of NES, particularly those vesting principal party
control over economic institutions in the specialists of the "Bureaus of Industry and Construction" (which were created both
within the Politburo and at the district and local levels of party
leadership), permitted the technical specialists more operational
independence than they had ever enjoyed before.[34]

POLITICAL CONSEQUENCES

Reforms in any directively planned economy can rarely be without
political implications although these need not invariably be in a
"liberalizing" direction. Where, however, reforms include the decentralization of economic decision making and the creation of opportunities for managerial innovation and experimentation, they
must carry with them some slackening of central party control;
what are introduced as measures of administrative convenience
may harden into a permanent reallocation of political power.
When substantive reforms are legitimated by a recasting of the
official ideology, such a reallocation is further encouraged. Moreover, the conscious elevation of the status of technical specialists as
"key figures" in the transformation of the social order lends them
potential power and invites them to challenge restrictions traditionally placed on them. In 1956 Behrens had eagerly acknowledged the political consequences of his own proposals for economic
reform; he anticipated the partial dismantling of central state di-

[33] Welles Hangen quotes the production manager of a VVB: " 'Do you find your
party work bothersome?' I asked. 'No, not nowadays,' he answered without hesita-
tion. 'There's been a big improvement in recent years. Now they devote more
attention to economic questions and less to the origin of man and other philosophical
questions. The main thing is to get rid of the old dogmatists and bring up younger
men.' " *The Muted Revolution* (New York: Knopf, 1966), p. 89.

[34] Ludz (*op. cit.*) stresses the relatively substantial autonomy initially granted the
bureaus and sees their creation as an attempt to integrate a type of "functional
authority" into the party structure. The bureaus were made responsible for directing the work of the party units in VVBs, factories, and other economic institutions
(pp. 78–81).

rection, constituting the first stages of the "withering away of the state." [35] Similarly, Heuer warned in his 1965 book against the belief "that the New Economic System can be implemented only in planning, technical, and economic terms without regarding the political and social consequences." [36]

Ulbricht and those around him were not unaware of these dangers and sought to prevent the new reforms from undermining party control. At the outset they sought to make the limitations upon NES clear by explicitly disassociating it from Behrens' proposals:

> We seek therefore precisely the opposite of what certain revisionist elements once wanted. They would have resulted in the weakening and undermining of socialist state authority through a questionable "self-administration" of the economy and the factory. Our system of planning and leadership . . . has been shaped so that economic laws can be utilized better than before in the period of the comprehensive construction of socialism. More exact leadership from above without petty tutelage with the simultaneous unfolding of the democratic cooperation of the workers.[37]

It was argued that NES strengthened the principle of democratic centralism by freeing the leading organs from the burden of detail and permitting them to concentrate on fundamental policy matters; economic "automatism" was rejected.[38] Herbert Wolf went so far as to contend that NES was in part a response to unwanted instances of economic "spontaneity" resulting from overcentralization.[39] Such arguments, along with the conscientious attempts to distinguish socialist *Gewinn* from capitalist *Profit* [40] and to deny any affinity of the NES reforms to the market economy, were of

---

[35] See above, Chap. 9.

[36] Heuer, *Demokratie und Recht*, p. 187. One might also cite the conclusion of the Czech economic reformers at the beginning of 1968 that their "New Economic Model" could not be effectively implemented without basic political reforms which would loosen the grip of conservative party bureaucrats.

[37] Walter Ulbricht, *Das Programm*, p. 95.

[38] Walter Ulbricht, "Das neue ökonomische System," pp. 3, 6; also Ulbricht, *Antwort auf aktuelle politische und ökonomische Fragen*, speech at Seventh Plenum of the SED Central Committee, December 2–5, 1964 (Berlin: Dietz Verlag, 1964), pp. 22–29; Günter Mittag, "Zur planmässigen Anwendung der ökonomischen Hebel," *Die Wirtschaft* (April 15, 1963), pp. 15–18.

[39] Hans-Dieter Schulz, "Die Hoffnung Heisst 'Nöspl,'" *Die Zeit* (April 30, 1965), p. 36.

[40] See Ulbricht, *Antwort*, p. 40.

course in part ex post facto ideological rationalizations. But they reflected as well the genuine fear that economic reform might spill over and impair central party control or ideological rigor, that Behrens indeed might have been right. Such a fear found expression in the words of the regime writer who sharply refuted the notion that the "closed system of economic levers" might constitute "a sort of market mechanism or automatism"; many, he complained, even believed "that through these levers all ideological questions have become virtually meaningless." [41] It also explains the tortuous efforts to assert the centrality of economic tasks in the "present epoch" without fully abandoning the doctrine of the "primacy of politics over economics." [42]

Nevertheless, the first months of the New Economic System brought with them a number of problems, most notably a degree of autonomy on the part of the Bureaus of Industry and Construction and an "economization" of the work of factory party cells that the Politburo majority felt obliged to counter. It did so by strengthening party control mechanisms and giving new emphasis to "ideological" work in the traditional sense.[43] In early 1964 countervailing sectors for ideology were created within the bureaus, a central Commission for Party and Organization Questions was erected, and the Ideological Commission was strengthened. At a Central Comittee meeting in December, Kurt Hager, Secretary for Ideology, complained that while, earlier, economic questions had been neglected in favor of more general political propaganda, now ideological work had been shunted partially into the background.[44] Ulbricht agreed and noted that "our party is not an 'economic party' in the narrow sense." [45] Honecker, even then the presumptive heir to Ulbricht, charged that meetings of factory party cells "are in some cases being conducted like production meetings," and an article pursuing this theme demanded that such meetings turn their attention from detailed questions of plan fulfillment

[41] "Was heisst denn ökonomisch denken? Aufzeichnungen eines Gesprächs mit Klaus Korn," *Forum*, No. 22 (1963), p. 2.

[42] See, for example, Richard Herber, "Zur Leitung der Parteiarbeit nach dem Produktionsprinzip," *Einheit*, XVIII (May 1963), 3–4.

[43] See the excellent discussion in Ludz, *Parteielite*, pp. 141–145.

[44] Kurt Hager, *Bericht des Politbüros an die 7. Tagung des Zentralkomitees der SED* (Berlin: Dietz Verlag, 1964), pp. 20–21.

[45] Ulbricht, *Antwort*, pp. 21, 30.

and technological improvements to a broader view integrating the performance of economic tasks with "the clarification of the basic questions of our party and government policy." [46] These measures obviously proved insufficient, for in the course of 1966 the Bureaus were quietly dissolved, and the very term "production principle" was subsequently stricken from the party statute.

Two additional unwanted by-products of NES were dealt with at the Eleventh Plenum in December 1965, held just after the dramatic suicide of Erich Apel. One was "egoistic" behavior by some VVBs and factories, which allegedly utilized the new economic mechanisms to further their narrowly conceived self-interest. The SED sought to meet the problem by better integrating the planning process and returning the financial oversight of the VEBs from the VVBs to the Finance Ministry. The second by-product was the desire of some economic functionaries to orient the DDR's trade more to the West, based on the economic argument that it would be better able to supply the requirements of the NES reforms, but obviously fraught with political implications as well.[47] The imposition of a five-year Soviet-DDR trade agreement and the suicide of Apel, apparently in protest, effectively put an end to such proposals.[48]

They also seem to have marked a symbolic turning point in the fortunes of the technical strategic elite in the SED leadership. Apel was by no means typical of the group of leading party specialists I described in an earlier chapter. Unlike most of them, he had joined the SED very late (1957) and appears to have had little prior "political" experience, although we do not know the details of his long residence in the Soviet Union. In Fleron's terms, he

[46] Gerhard Schulz, "Gedanken zur Rolle der Parteiversammlungen," *Einheit*, XX, No. 2 (1965), 11–12. Similar complaints emerged in the Soviet Union at about the same time. See Erik P. Hoffmann, "Role Conflict and Ambiguity in the Communist Party of the Soviet Union," in Roger E. Kanet, ed., *The Behavioral Revolution and Communist Studies* (New York: Free Press, 1971), Chap. 9. Hoffmann notes a shift in the emphasis of CPSU ideological work from "production propaganda" under Khrushchev to "moral incentives" under Brezhnev/Kosygin.

[47] Again, the parallel to Czechoslovakia suggests itself.

[48] See Hangen, *The Muted Revolution*, pp. 3–9; Rene Bayer, "Der Tod des Technokraten," *Die Zeit* (N. Am. edition) (December 14, 1965), p. 3. While many of the rumors surrounding Apel's death are not credible, the attacks upon the Planning Commission at the Eleventh Plenum and the extravagant justifications given for the pact lend credence to the assumption that its signing provided the immediate impetus for his act.

was close to a pure "coopted" type, the only one ever to reach so prominent a position in the SED leadership. He was a neighbor and friend of Robert Havemann's and reportedly discussed the latter's dissident ideas and writings with him.[49] Richert has termed Apel "fully indifferent" to and "naive" in matters of ideology; the latter is probably more just a judgment than the former.[50]

Apel apparently regarded the very success of the NES to be at stake in the dispute over the Soviet trade agreement. The pact tied over one-half the DDR's trade for the years 1966–1970 to the Soviet Union, reportedly on disadvantageous terms.[51] Apel, it is supposed, wished to transfer much of the DDR's trade westward, where it would be possible to obtain more of the sophisticated machinery and equipment needed by East German industry; he fought an extended battle over the issue with Ulbricht, who insisted that the DDR's political dependence on the USSR left no other choice but compliance with its demands. Apel's suicide—an act one would not expect of a more conventional and experienced Communist—was followed within a few hours by signature of the agreement.[52]

The entire episode makes it clear that the Soviet Union was not willing to sacrifice its own economic interests to East German economic reform and that Ulbricht was equally unwilling to sacrifice his special relationship to the Soviet Union on that altar. Subse-

[49] Hangen, *op. cit.*, pp. 8–9; interview.

[50] Richert, *Macht ohne Mandat*, pp. 134–135, 139–140.

[51] Hangen (*op. cit.*) reports, for example, that the DDR was required to deliver over 300 ships to the Soviet Union at "at least" 30 percent below world market prices, and pipes at 40 percent below, and to purchase Russian crude oil and pig iron at nearly twice the world price. An alleged "secret protocol" requiring the DDR to make up shortages in earlier promised deliveries was also said to be a critical element in the dispute over the agreement (pp. 4–5). Cf., however, the extremely skeptical account of Joachim Nawrocki, who argues persuasively that there is little firm evidence to support the view that the agreement was unfavorable to the DDR. *Das geplante Wunder* (Hamburg: Christian Wegner Verlag, 1967), pp. 172–184.

[52] In addition to the sources already cited, see *Frankfurter Allgemeine Zeitung* (December 7, 1965), p. 2; *ibid.* (December 8, 1965), pp. 1, 4; *ibid.* (December 9, 1965), pp. 1, 5; *ibid.* (December 10, 1965), p. 1; *ibid.* (December 13, 1965), p. 3; *ibid.* (December 29, 1965), p. 3; *ibid.* (December 30, 1965), p. 1; *ibid.* (December 31, 1965), p. 1; Rene Bayer, "Rätselraten um ein Testament," *Die Zeit* (N. Am. edition) (January 11, 1966), p. 4. It is worthy of note that Ulbricht traveled to the Soviet Union in September 1966 reportedly to protest the same price discrimination involved in the Apel affair. Hansjakob Stehle, "Ulbricht drängt im Kreml," *Die Zeit* (N. Am. edition) (September 13, 1966), p. 1.

quent personnel policies have made it quite apparent that no more Apels are to be permitted at the top of the party. It is worth noting, for example, that Gerhard Schürer, named as Apel's successor, is a graduate of the higher party schools of both the SED and CPSU, apart from being an experienced planner; also, that he has not been given the added authority of membership on the Politburo or Secretariat. Events at the Eleventh Plenum suggest that the Apel affair left a broader distrust among the party bureaucrats of the technical strategic elite and their reform program in its wake. Apel, who had been given a state funeral with full honors ten days before the plenum, was not criticized by name; the Planning Commission, however, was charged with having fallen behind in the adoption of modern planning methods and particularly with having failed to resist the "frequently unreal" demands of individual branches of the economy in favor of the more general interests of society. It was the duty of the chairman of the commission to maintain "balance" in the economy and, where necessary, to say "a decisive 'no' " to parochial demands that would upset it. Ulbricht showed himself particularly concerned over the lag in national income growth and demanded the steering of investments into areas which would improve it.[53]

Nevertheless, he proclaimed 1966 as the beginning of the second stage of NES, to include the completion of price reform, the partial introduction of the *Produktionsfondsabgabe,* and heightened emphasis on the internal financing of investment by the VVBs and VEBs—all important components of genuine rationalization. The major organizational reform accompanying the plenum—the abolition of the National Economic Council and its replacement by nine industrial ministries—could also be viewed positively by the technicians. The council was criticized again for overproduction of paperwork and for trying to decide all questions itself.[54] Alfred Neumann was made Minister for Material Economy, still an important post, but all of the other eight new ministries were put in the hands of managers or economic experts.

[53] Walter Ulbricht, "Probleme," esp. p. 44. See also Fritz Schenk, "Die zweite Etappe der Planlosigkeit," *SBZ-Archiv,* XVII, Nos. 1–2 (1966), 1–2; Peter Christian Ludz, "East Germany: The Old and the New," *East Europe* (April 1966), pp. 23–27.
[54] Ulbricht, "Probleme," p. 46.

RETRENCHMENT

Thus, in spite of its unwanted ideological and practical consequences the New Economic System was not immediately abandoned. Its growing success in stimulating the economy and its
usefulness as an instrument of legitimacy demanded that it be retained in some form. At the same time any erosive implications
it might have for the supremacy of central party control had to be
excised. The solution was to restate the basic ideological conception underlying economic reform in such a way as to reinforce
political centralization rather than the reverse and, simultaneously,
so to revise the content of the reforms themselves as to leave them
empty of significance as a launching platform for more basic social
change.

The vehicle for this reformulation was the explication of the
concept of "system" as a justification for centralized party dominance in all sectors of society, including the economy.[55] Ulbricht's
speech at the Seventh Party Congress (1967)[56] laid down the out-
lines of this strategy. The phrase "New Economic System" was
submerged in the expression, the "Developed Social System of
Socialism," the "core" of which was said to be the "Economic System of Socialism." The Developed Social System was characterized
by the interdependence of all its parts, including the economic
system, the institutions of "socialist democracy," the educational
system, socialist morality, the standard of living, and the system of
national defense. As a result, the social system had to be consciously structured to take account of these interdependencies; so
did each subsystem. Therefore, the emphasis in the "economic
system of socialism" was no longer upon decentralization of authority, the encouragement of initiative on the lower levels, and
the operational flexibility necessary to permit the economy to respond to "economic levers," but rather upon the "rational struc-
turing" and especially the "scientific planning" of the economy,
under the leadership of the SED. These themes were by no means

---

[55] See Hans-Dietrich Sander, "Lenin und die Selbstverständniskrise der Partei,"
Deutschland Archiv, III (May 1970), 553–554.

[56] Walter Ulbricht, *Die gesellschaftliche Entwicklung in der Deutschen Demokratischen Republik bis zur Vollendung des Sozialismus* (Berlin: Dietz Verlag,
1967).

entirely new; they built upon selected arguments that had already been present in some interpretations of NES, but now these were claimed to be the essence of the reforms. The term "New Economic System" was now applied to a broader range of phenomena, including social insurance and cultural policy, apparently as a loose synonym for the introduction of efficiency criteria. "New Economic System" thus increasingly became an "empty formula" [57] and shortly fell into complete disuse.

Such a verbal transformation did not by itself solve the practical question of how much centralization or decentralization was indeed to be permitted. For a time regime pronouncements revealed a decided uncertainty, perhaps reflecting internal disagreement, on this question. Ulbricht's own formulation sought to bridge the gap dialectically: "Central state planning and direction of the basic questions of the social process as a whole is to be organically tied to the self-responsible planning and directing activity of socialist goods producers on the one hand and to the self-responsible regulation of societal life through the local organs of state authority on the other hand." [58] Characteristically, this ambiguous formula was repeatedly quoted by DDR writers in 1968 and 1969 as the agitational pendulum swung still further toward an emphasis on central control and party and state authority.

The emasculation of the New Economic System was accelerated particularly in response to what the DDR leadership viewed as the cautionary example of Czechoslovakia. It is hard to avoid the conclusion that the frightened and intense hostility with which the regime reacted to the Czech experiments in some part reflected the perception that the DDR's own reforms might contain within them precisely the same threat to party authority that seemed to be emerging in Prague. Party spokesmen hastened to draw a sharp distinction between the DDR's economic system and the Czech

---

[57] This term (*Leerformel*), borrowed from Ernst Topitsch, is used by Ludz to describe the process by which Communist ideological expressions are progressively expanded in applicability and simultaneously emptied of substance. See Peter Christian Ludz, "Entwurf einer soziologischen Theorie totalitär verfasster Gesellschaft" in Ludz, ed., *Studien und Materialien zur Soziologie der DDR* (Köln and Opladen: Westdeutscher Verlag, 1964), pp. 34ff. See also Alfred G. Meyer, "The Functions of Ideology in the Soviet Political System," *Soviet Studies*, XVII (January 1966), 273–285.

[58] Ulbricht, *Die gesellschaftliche Entwicklung*, p. 130.

"socialist market economy"; the Czech schemes and their authors were denounced with an atavistic fervor and with arguments reminiscent of the Stalin era. Simultaneously, the East German advocates of a broadly interpreted social application of NES, including Behrens and Heuer, were charged with revisionism.[59] Günter Mittag was one of the most outspoken participants in this dismal assault.

In comparing "twaddle about self-administration" unfavorably to the virtues of the "socialist planned economy" carried out "according to the principle of democratic centralism by the socialist state authority," [60] Mittag struck the major themes of other official pronouncements on the question. "Self-administration" (*Selbstverwaltung*) was condemned as bourgeois and linked to Western efforts at ideological diversion; at the same time, "self-responsibility" (*Eigenverantwortung*), always subordinate to "scientific socialist planning and leadership," was praised.[61] Central planning once again became a primary authority symbol and sometimes was accorded almost lyrical treatment. "The 1971 Economic Plan," one later article asserted, "is the law of the state and the political and moral commandment of our action. It is the expression of the total social requirements and mutual interests of our worker and peasant state." [62]

---

[59] On Heuer and Behrens, see the perceptive article by Rudolf Schwarzenbach, "Zentrale staatliche Leitung und Eigenverantwortung im Gesellschaftssystem der DDR," *Deutschland Archiv*, II (February 1969), 144–146. Mittag launched a lengthy and bitter attack against Günther Kohlmey, an economist also implicated in the 1957 Behrens controversy, for slighting the role of the party in his writings and using concepts allegedly borrowed from West German economists. See Mittag, "Meisterung der Ökonomie ist für uns Klassenkampf," *ND* (October 27, 1968), p. 4.

[60] See Kurt Erdmann, "Neue Wirtschaftsmassnahmen ab 1. Januar 1968," *Deutschland Archiv*, I (May 1968), 206–207. On similar lines see Hans Luft, Harry Nick, and Gerhard Schulz, "Sozialistische Planwirtschaft—Lebensgrundlage der sozialistischen Gesellschaft," *Einheit*, XXIII, No. 6 (1968), 692–704.

[61] Walter Ulbricht, "Die Rolle des sozialistischen Staates bei der Gestaltung des entwickelten gesellschaftlichen Systems des Sozialismus," *ND* (October 16, 1968), reprinted in part in *Deutschland Archiv*, I (November 1968), 847–857. It has been noted that the revised edition of Ulbricht's collected speeches on the economic reforms omitted a section entitled "A Certain Self-Regulation on the Basis of the Plan." Kurt Erdmann, "Das Ende des Neuen Ökonomischen Systems," *Deutschland Archiv*, I (December 1968), 999.

[62] Horst Bley, Fritz Schellhorn, and Kurt Walter, "Plan- und Arbeitsdisziplin—Gebot hoher Effektivität," *Einheit*, XXVI, No. 1 (1971), 38. In another article the plan is called, ostensibly following Lenin, a "second party program." "Mitgliederversammlung—inhaltsreich und erzieherisch," *Neuer Weg*, XXVI, No. 2 (1971), 50. A Council of Ministers decision of December 1, 1970, announced that the "role and

The special importance of planning in post-NES ideology lay in the technological rationale it provided for the concomitant emphases on democratic centralism, the growing responsibilities of the state, and the necessary expansion and strengthening of the leading role of the party. These themes—in some ways reminiscent of Stalin's notorious doctrine that the dictatorship of the proletariat would have to be made continually stronger until the moment of its withering away—were sounded with growing regularity after 1966 and especially following the Czechoslovak events. Thus the textbook *The Political Economy of Socialism*[63] explained the growing significance of the party by its "scientifically grounded foresight" concerning the paths of social, cultural, and technological development, which permitted it to lead the necessary, "conscious molding *(Gestaltung)*" of socialist society. A second justification was the continuing "world-wide class struggle" and the threat of West German imperialism. The party had to "above all and with highest priority fulfill its political responsibility in the area of economic development," for political power could only be "maintained, consolidated and further expanded when it is manifested and developed as economic power." [64] On similar grounds the economic role of the state, the "highest and most comprehensive form of societal organization and coordination," also had to expand, "even after the triumph of socialist relations of production." [65]

---

authority of the plan" was to be "elevated" in 1971. Cited in Nawrocki, "Vom NÖS," p. 348.

[63] *Politische Ökonomie des Sozialismus und ihre Anwendung in der DDR* (Berlin: Dietz Verlag, 1969). Following the removal of Ulbricht, this text, extravagantly celebrated in the last period of his rule, was criticized as "not free from errors" by the veteran ideologist Kurt Hager. See Joachim Nawrocki, "Verfehlte Wirtschaftspolitik belastet DDR-Wirtschaft," *Deutschland Archiv*, IV (November 1971), 1123–1124. It remains, however, the most comprehensive and important source for contemporary DDR economic doctrine.

[64] *Politische Ökonomie*, pp. 194–196. For similar sentiments see Günter Söder, "Die führende Rolle der Partei und das neue ökonomische System der Planung und Leitung," *Einheit*, XXI, No. 11 (1966), 1372–1380; Georg Ebert, Gerhard Koch, Fred Mathe, Harry Mielke, "Theoretische Grundfragen der Führungsrolle der marxistisch-leninistischen Partei in der sozialistischen Planwirtschaft," *Einheit*, XXIV, No. 2 (1969), 131–143; Werner Lamberz, "Die Führende Rolle der Arbeiterklasse in der DDR," *Forum*, No. 7 (1970), pp. 8–9.

[65] *Politische Ökonomie*, pp. 200–202. See also Ulbricht, "Die Rolle," pp. 847–849; Gerhard Schürer, "Die Rolle des Staates auf ökonomischen Gebiet," *Die Wirtschaft* (May 22, 1969), pp. 8–10.

The rhetoric of planning and expanded state and party authority came increasingly to be complemented by a second rhetoric,
that of mass participation and "socialist democracy." [66] While the
discussion of these themes, fully appropriate to classical Marxian
doctrine and much of the socialist tradition,[67] has never been entirely absent from DDR ideology, in the late 1960s they were
stressed frequently and in a "dialectical" relationship to the first
set of themes. Thus, Ulbricht argued, "The *advantages of socialism*
consist in the inseparable and efficacious unification of the comprehensive, energetic *participation* of working people in the solution of social tasks and the direction of the economy, with the
broad scientific *planning* and rational organization of economic
and general social development of the state as a whole." [68] These
two apparently inconsistent principles were joined under the serv-
iceable banner of "democratic centralism," which was said to make
possible the dialectical unity of centralized economic leadership
and the "creative" participation and initiative of the individual,
especially at his place of work.[69] In fact, the DDR in common
with other contemporary East European states offers a great pan-
oply of institutionalized opportunities for participation, though
most of them have only consultative or advisory functions and can
be argued to serve largely manipulative purposes. Whatever the
reality, however, the use of a mixed rhetoric of centralization and
participatory democracy appeared to be an attempt to find a satisfactory legitimizing ideology as a substitute for the New Economic
System. Among its virtues was the retention of the aura of economic, scientific, and technical rationality of NES and at least
some of its appeal to the technical intelligentsia.

In the fall of 1970 the reforms themselves were emptied of most
of their remaining substance. The hard winter of 1969–1970 had
been followed by a poor harvest, a massive energy crisis, serious
bottlenecks in transportation and construction, and embarrassing
shortages of basic consumer items. The planners in their modern-

[66] See my "East Germany: In Quest of Legitimacy," *Problems of Communism*
(March–April 1972), pp. 46–55.
[67] See Reinhard Bendix, *Work and Authority in Industry* (New York: Harper
Torchbooks, 1963), pp. 3–4.
[68] Ulbricht, *Die gesellschaftliche Entwicklung*, p. 129. Emphasis of "participation"
and "planning" is mine.
[69] *Politische Ökonomie*, p. 38; Hanna Wolf, "Die SED—eine leninistische Kampfpartei," *Einheit*, XXVI, No. 5 (1971), 506–508.

izing ambitions had evidently allowed too narrow a margin for error, and the resulting economic "disproportions" furnished party conservatives the excuse for a final quiet assault on the remainder of the reform program. In its wake, the SED returned most of the powers of decision making and control that had been delegated to individual enterprises back to the central ministries.[70]

Thus, the authority of plant managers to make their own investment decisions was sharply curtailed, and their flexibility in internal financial administration very nearly eliminated.[71] Numerous factories were "concentrated" into *Kombinate,* directly responsible to one of the industrial ministries, which naturally reduced the importance of the VVBs; according to Honecker, the *Kombinate* by mid-1971 were producing over one-third of the output of the major DDR enterprises.[72] A large number of new or revised performance indices were introduced for evaluating plan fulfillment. They covered such diverse matters as growth in work productivity, the use of raw materials and energy, the composition of the work force, the reduction of administrative costs, and the profitability of exported goods, and were necessarily only imperfectly coordinated with one another. Reports on their fulfillment were required monthly in some instances and quarterly in others.[73] The significance of profit as an overarching indicator of economic performance was criticized ideologically and, as a practical matter, undermined not only by the proliferation of other indices but by policies requiring the return of one-half of "unplanned" profit to the state and sharply restricting the use of the remainder.[74] Taken

[70] See Angela Scherzinger-Rüger, "Gegenwärtige Probleme der Jahresplanung in der DDR," *Deutschland Archiv,* V (September 1972), 920–932; Kurt Erdmann, "Das Ende," pp. 998–1001; *idem.,* "Ökonomisches System 1971—Atempause oder neuer Kurs," *Deutschland Archiv,* IV (February 1971), 172–175; Konstantin Pritzel, "Warum Revision des NÖS?" *Deutschland Archiv,* IV (April 1971), 342–345; Nawrocki, "Vom NÖS," pp. 345–348. See also Ernst Richert, "Trend zur Entsachlichung in der SED–Führung?" *Deutschland Archiv,* II (May 1969), 484–492.

[71] "Konsolidierung durch Wachstumsverzicht?" *Deutschland Archiv,* IV (February 1971), 182–183; Erdmann, "Neue Wirtschaftsmassnahmen," p. 203.

[72] Honecker, *Bericht des Zentralkomitees an den VIII. Parteitag der SED* (Berlin: Dietz Verlag, 1971), p. 55.

[73] See Heinz-Werner Hübner, "Wie erreichen wir eine höhere Stabilität des Volkswirtschaftsplanes 1971?" *Die Wirtschaft* (January 27, 1971), pp. 4–5; see also Erdmann, "Ökonomisches System," pp. 173–175; Scherzinger-Rüger, *op. cit.,* pp. 921–927.

[74] In the words of a DDR source, "profit as a standard for judging the performance of factories and *Kombinate* [may] not be valued more highly than the fulfillment of the material indices of the plan and the increase of planned work produc-

together, these measures amounted to an emphatic recentralization
of economic control and raised the spectre of a "paper flood" rival-
ing that existing prior to 1963.[75] While a few technical elements
of the reforms remained in effect, it had become evident that the
DDR's new economic model was no longer Libermanism but
rather "computopia." [76]

The Economy and the Intelligentsia After Ulbricht

The reduction of economic reform to hardly more than a cult of
technological change and efficiency stripped of any liberalizing
implications was largely completed by the time of Walter Ulbricht's enforced retirement as SED First Secretary at the beginning of May 1971. The new leadership collective under Erich
Honecker was still more dominated by party ideology and organization men than its predecessors. It brought with it a new style
in its pronouncements on the economy: sober and realistic in tone,
but conservative in substance. The extravagant rhetoric of Ulbricht's last years about the "Developed Social System of Socialism" was consciously eschewed, and the attempt to transport verbally the "technological revolution" into every corner of DDR
society was ridiculed.[77] The formula chosen to deal with the newly
acknowledged economic difficulties was the tried one of greater
party control and ideological exhortation, coupled with the mobilization of voluntary labor and self-sacrifice to close the most
critical gaps.

The most striking characteristic of the early Honecker period—
apart from the new Western policy of the regime, whose inspiration was undoubtedly largely external—was the rhetorical return
to the ideal of a purer and more genuinely proletarian socialism.

---

tivity." "Wie soll es in der Jahresplanung weitergehen?" *Die Wirtschaft*, No. 48
(1971), p. 6, cited in Deutscher Bundestag, 6. Wahlperiode, *Materialien zum Bericht
zur Lage der Nation 1972* (Bonn, 1972), p. 114. See also Scherzinger-Rüger, *op. cit.*,
pp. 923–924.

[75] One chief bookkeeper of a VEB for heavy machine building complains: "In
the third quarter of 1971 we had to report 4,000 indices, 1,500 of them monthly and
2,500 once in the quarter. . . . Every quarter we report on savings in 425 material
categories." Cited in Scherzinger-Rüger, *op. cit.*, p. 927, fn. 55.

[76] See Alexander Eckstein, "Economic Development and Political Change in
Communist Systems," *World Politics*, XXII (July 1970), 492–493.

[77] See Honecker, *op. cit., passim;* New York *Times* (Sept. 22, 1971), p. 2.

The SED proclaimed anew the superior ideological status of the working class as leading force and chief beneficiary of socialist society, to the apparent disadvantage of the intelligentsia; party leaders gave the needs of the worker-as-consumer the attention once lavished on the imperatives of production; and the regime stressed the cultural and psychological dimensions of the socialist personality in addition to its more narrowly economic virtues. Without question, Honecker's own background and inclinations quite genuinely favor his almost populist concern for the ordinary worker,[78] and many thoughtful citizens of the DDR share his distaste for the visible sectors of privilege that thrived under Ulbricht's "Developed Socialist System." Honecker's own predilections may also be reflected in those portions of the new rhetoric that seek to counterpoise "humanistic" values to technological ones. Lamberz, for example, has written: "The party fights against any narrow technicistic approach to the introduction of new technology. Machinery and equipment are not only devices for producing material goods; they are simultaneously the conditions of work for collectives and human beings, whose development they may either inhibit or encourage." [79] Or as Hager has put it: "Human beings don't exist for the sake of any sort of [technical or cybernetic] systems, but rather all our actions are meant for the sake of human beings." [80] This sort of language stands in self-conscious contrast to that of the late Ulbricht years and also serves as a new kind of legitimacy claim on the part of the orthodox party leadership that is not available to "soulless" technocrats.

Yet it is difficult not to notice that the concrete policies meant to carry out the new rhetoric have been modest both in scope and significance. The children of workers have enjoyed some uncertain favoritism in admission to the universities, and in some areas nonworkers have found entrance into the party virtually impossible. The FDGB has been upgraded and told to become a more vigorous representative of workers' interests; most of the small remaining private and half-government-owned manufacturing enterprises have been fully nationalized, although private retail stores

[78] See Harald Ludwig, "Die SED vor dem VIII. Parteitag," *Deutschland Archiv*, IV (June 1971), 589, 593–595.

[79] Werner Lamberz, "Partei und Massen," *Einheit*, XXVII, No. 7 (1972), 852.

[80] Kurt Hager, *Die entwickelte sozialistische Gesellschaft* (Berlin: Dietz Verlag, 1971), p. 27.

and artisans' workshops remain. As elsewhere in the Soviet bloc, the DDR's extravagant promises of burgeoning consumer benefits have been followed by only modest adjustments in the economic plan, and then by renewed complaints of severe shortages and underinvestment in the consumer sectors.[81]

The Honecker period has brought with it endless discussions of the proper role and class position of the intelligentsia under socialism, the relationship between the intelligentsia and the workers, and the dependence of science and technology—treated under NES as a critical "force of production"—on their relationship to the ideology of the working class. The working class is now self-consciously labeled the "chief" force of production in socialist society.[82] Even the harshest statements on this subject, however, have simultaneously warned against any "minimization" of the intelligentsia's importance. Thus, a profound ambivalence still characterizes the official view of the technical specialists. Lamberz, for example, in July 1972, attacked both "right" revisionism, which argues that the intelligentsia must take over the leadership of society, and "left" revisionism, which assigns to it merely a "subordinate significance" under socialism. Only through a close alliance of workers and intelligentsia, he argued, could the "organic linkage of the accomplishments of the scientific-technical revolution with the advantages of socialism" be achieved.[83] DDR leaders still appear to fear that the myth of the working class is a less effective source of legitimation than an economic progress which, in spite of themselves, they believe depends upon the technical experts.

No hard evidence has yet emerged on the attitudes of members of the technical strategic elite toward the gradual liquidation of the New Economic System after Erich Apel's death. But it is probably not an error to surmise two basic lines of development. The first and perhaps less exceptionable is an absolute decline in the technical specialists' influence on policy making; it reflects several factors. One is the more or less direct intervention of the Soviet Union

---

[81] See Werner Lamberz, "Aus dem Bericht des Politbüros an die 7. Tagung des Zentralkomitees der SED," *ND* (October 13, 1972), reprinted in part in *Deutschland Archiv*, V (December 1972), 1330–1331.

[82] See Hager, *op. cit.*, p. 23.

[83] Lamberz, "Partei und Massen," p. 849.

on several occasions, forcing (or persuading) the DDR to limit and finally abandon its efforts to create a distinctive economic program. The imposition of the 1965 trade pact, the promulgation of the Brezhnev doctrine of limited sovereignty, and the deposing of Ulbricht are benchmarks in this pattern of intervention. A second factor is a measure of disillusionment on the part of other DDR leaders with the outcome of the recommendations of the technical specialists, owing variously to the fear of political liberalization being smuggled into the DDR in the cloak of economic reform, a fear underlined by the Czechoslovak events, and a disappointment over the economic results of the reforms, particularly following the crisis of plan fulfillment in 1970 and the severe shortages of the winters of 1969–1970 and 1970–1971. A third element is the probably growing perception by party *apparatchiki* of the political challenge represented by the rise of the technical strategic elite and an effort to consolidate and better utilize their control of the Politburo and Secretariat in order to beat it back.

The second basic line of development is more speculative; it posits the division of the technical strategic elite into two "opinion groups,"[84] each of which itself contains more subtle differentiations. The first we may call the "decentralizers," the advocates of the more innovative vision of NES, who see the path to economic success in a relentless attack on "bureaucratism" and in the maximization of the creativity and initiative of lower-level economic actors. They have largely been quiet in the aftermath of the dismantling of the reforms, but their influence may be presumed to be present in the muted criticisms of the mounting tide of bureaucratic paper and the irrational economic behavior imposed on individual factories by central economic directives.[85] The second group is a mixture of instinctual conservatives and the "computopians," who believe economic rationality to be best

[84] See H. Gordon Skilling, "Interest Groups and Communist Politics," in Skilling and Franklyn Griffiths, eds., *Interest Groups in Soviet Politics* (Princeton: Princeton University Press, 1971), p. 25.

[85] Thus at the 7th Central Committee Plenum in October 1972 the minister for light industry Johann Wittik argued that existing state production criteria required plants to "decide against the production of items that are really needed (*bedarfsgerecht*)." In December it was announced that Wittik had been recalled from his post "in order to assume other responsibilities." See Hans-Dieter Schulz, "Neues NÖSPL nötig," *Deutschland Archiv*, V (November 1972), 1134–1137; "Personalien," *Deutschland Archiv*, V (December 1972), p. 1251.

served by a highly sophisticated form of centralized planning and control made feasible by a cybernetic systems perspective and the use of advanced techniques of data gathering, processing, and analysis (including, ultimately, computer simulation of market conditions).[86] Members of the second group, of course, find it much easier than the first to make their peace with the non-technicians in the party leadership and are more likely themselves to combine strong traditional ideological commitments with their professional ones. In the DDR's ideological climate in 1973 they are necessarily the more visible of the two groups and, undoubtedly, the more influential in economic policy making, although it is unlikely that even they are entirely sanguine about some elements of the retrenchment I have described.

The dichotomy between the two groups is of course an abstraction from a more complex reality, though I think there is reason to believe it reflects a genuine, politically potent if still not entirely conscious division. The dictates of economic rationality, it has often been noted, are far from unambiguous[87] and can be employed in justification of decentralization or computopia with virtually equal plausibility. It is improbable, I think, that having been admitted into the leadership as consultants, advisors, and even participants in decision making, the technical strategic elite will or can be turned out again. Their influence over policy as a group may be temporarily reduced but hardly eliminated; instead the locus of influence within the group is apt to fluctuate in response to perceptions of economic success, outside pressures, and shifts in the postures and composition of other leadership elements.

[86] See Pritzel, "Warum," p. 344; Nawrocki, "Vom NÖS," p. 348. This issue has been at the center of debate among economists and managers in the Soviet Union. See Jeremy R. Azrael, "The Managers," in R. Barry Farrell, ed., *Political Leadership in Eastern Europe and the Soviet Union* (Chicago: Aldine, 1970), p. 242.

[87] See, for example, Zbigniew Brzezinski and Samuel P. Huntington, *Political Power: USA/USSR* (New York: Viking Press, 1964), pp. 423-424; Peter Christian Ludz, "Politische Aspekte der kybernetischen Systemtheorie in der DDR," *Deutschland Archiv*, I (April 1968), 1-10.

CONCLUSION

> Technocracy is conservative ideologically . . . to the very degree that its objective progressiveness serves it as an alibi in its efforts to consolidate the existing system, to arbitrate its conflicts, and to absorb the anti-[regime] forces.
>
> ANDRÉ GORZ[1]

> It seemed to me that no understanding could be reached between Czech reformers and East German technocrats.
>
> Former Czech official recalling 1967 visit to DDR [2]

LET US review in summary form the principal findings of this study. Even before the formal creation of the German Democratic Republic, the SED leadership embarked on the building of a new stratum of technical intelligentsia, whose purpose was to provide the loyal expertise necessary to staff an expanding and modernizing economy and in a broader sense to strengthen the legitimacy of the Communist regime. Today the technical intelligentsia is the largest and most important professional stratum in the DDR; its training dominates the resources of East German higher education; its prestige and material rewards place it near the top of the East German social hierarchy. It cannot be said to enjoy the degree of organizational unity, group cohesion, or stratum consciousness that would make it a fully self-conscious actor in East German politics, but its members do share identifiable professional grievances and interests, centering on the resentment of petty bureaucratic "tutelage" from above, and a pragmatic or *sachlich* style that even casual visitors to the DDR have remarked upon. The political attitudes of the technical intelligentsia vary over a broad spectrum, but perhaps the most

---

[1] André Gorz, *Strategy for Labor* (Boston: Beacon Press, 1967), p. 123.
[2] Radoslav Selucký, "Das ostdeutsche Wunder," *Deutschland Archiv*, V (October 1972), p. 1075.

widespread is a relative indifference to politics and ideology, accompanied by the urge to "get on" with the accomplishment of professional tasks. While repeatedly expressing its distress over the technicians' apoliticalness, the SED leadership has tolerated it in practice. The regime has tacitly acknowledged that such a posture, by facilitating the improvement of economic performance, strengthens its legitimacy without creating serious and overt dysfunctional consequences.

Those recruited from the stratum of technical intelligentsia into the elite are of course subject to more exacting political standards than the rank and file, but they nevertheless appear to reflect in numerous ways the outlook of their "constituency." Long party membership is an essential criterion of recruitment, but extended party service is not, and over time the criteria of advanced education and unusual ability as tested in professional experience have come to equal if not outweigh political requirements. No single path leads to the economic-technical elite in the DDR; educational backgrounds vary, and most elite members have had experience in two or three of the four major arenas of economic activity. Economics has been the predominant field of study for those with advanced education, followed at a considerable distance by engineering and the natural sciences. The most frequent career line runs through the government ministries and planning bodies. A smaller proportion (some 40 percent) of the technical elite have worked in party technical and economic positions, and still fewer (about 30 percent each) in academic and industrial occupations.

The representation of the technical strategic elite in high party and government bodies grew steadily until the mid-1960s, reaching its zenith during the period of economic reform; since then it has suffered a very modest decline. The overall growth in numbers has been accompanied by a rise in educational attainments, an expansion in the representation of industrial vis-à-vis agricultural personnel, and the replacement of an older generation of officials by a younger one consciously educated as part of a new socialist intelligentsia after the establishment of Communist power. While the technical strategic elite has come to dominate the governmental Council of Ministers and holds one-third of the places on the SED Central Committee, it has been accorded little more than token membership in the critical party decision-making bodies, the Politburo and Secretariat. This imbalance must be understood to reflect a conscious intent on the part of the party organization men and ideologists to utilize the technicians' expertise and strengthen regime legitimacy while leaving the ultimate powers of political decision in their own hands.

The record of DDR economic policy since 1956 and the conflicts surrounding it testify to the persistence of this strategy. Three phases may be distinguished, roughly covering the years 1956–1962, 1963–1967, and 1968 to the present. In the first phase, conflicts over policy fell with remarkable clarity along a division between the evident dictates of economic rationality and the *apparatchiks'* perception of what was ideologically proven and politically expedient. In every case the "political" alternative was chosen, but the very fact that policy alternatives had come to be couched in such terms gave evidence of the rising influence of the technicians. In the second phase, the views of the technical strategic elite were apparently transformed into definitive policy with the introduction of the New Economic System reforms, which also enjoyed the support of critical elements among the non-specialist party leaders. The weight of an exogenous actor, the Soviet Union, made it difficult to assess the full extent of the technicians' influence, however. The third phase brought the abandonment of the most innovative elements of the reform program but a continuing rhetoric of efficiency and technological modernization. This phase reflects not only what I judge to be a temporary eclipse of the technicians' influence, but a growing, if still largely tacit, division in their own ranks between planning-oriented centralizers and the advocates of something like a socialist market economy.

In a short summary formula, the policy influence of the technical strategic elite can be said to be substantial, established, and partly institutionalized, but still uneven in its effectiveness and often divided in its thrust. The most important and effective of its members are not "technocrats" in the sense of being apolitical professionals who have somehow acquired governmental power, but politician-specialists with economic training and technical interests who have learned to adapt to a rapidly changing political environment and sometimes to manipulate it on behalf of their preferred goals. The direction of their influence is not uniform because they differ in the weight each gives to his "political" and "professional" sides and because even in their professional judgment they do not entirely agree on the measures most likely to maximize economic rationality. Overall, their presence has affected both the style and substance of East German political decision making, but in quiet ways often concealed by the official ideological communications medium. In a period of political retrenchment it is easy to underestimate their impact.

COMMUNIST MANAGERIALISM AND PARTY POWER

There remains the question of the implications of these findings for the evolution of political authority in East Germany and other Communist systems. The optimism among Western observers that greeted the rise of technical specialists in the ruling parties and governments of Eastern Europe in the early 1960s has not been fully justified by subsequent events.[3] No titanic struggles between technocrats and *apparatchiki* have taken place. The difference *between* these two groups have proven to be considerably more subtle and complex than was first postulated, in terms both of their functions and their political outlooks. Differences *within* the technical strategic elite, on the other hand, have taken on greater significance than was once realized. The relevance of *other* strategic elites in shaping the possibilities and limits of "technocratic" power has become more apparent. As a consequence, the managerial hypothesis has drawn the critical attention of numerous commentators. Much of their case is well taken; let us examine some representative arguments.

One of the most astute, if cautious, critics of the hypothesis as applied to the Soviet Union is Jeremy R. Azrael.[4] Among the Soviet managers, he agrees, there are to be found both "liberals"

[3] Peter Christian Ludz, *Parteielite im Wandel* (Köln and Opladen: Westdeutscher Verlag, 1968), presents the most subtle and elaborate case for the triumphant rise of an "institutionalized counter-elite" of experts in the DDR. In spite of its frequent qualification, Ludz's thesis can be seen in retrospect to have suffered from the excessive optimism of the period. Nevertheless, Ludz's insights into the nature of change in mature Communist societies have substantially influenced this chapter.

[4] Jeremy R. Azrael, *Managerial Power and Soviet Politics* (Cambridge: Harvard University Press, 1966).

and "technocrats." The former identify with the dissenting Soviet writers and favor some sort of an "open society on Western lines"; the latter, much more numerous, see a technical elite "predestined to rule the world in accord with the dictates of scientific rationality." [5] The great majority of the Soviet technical intelligentsia, however, belong to neither;[6] they are, rather, conservative and unquestioning, and a substantial number are loyal Marxist-Leninist activists, deeply committed to the fundamental principles of the Soviet systems. It is from the loyalists that the political elite is recruited while the liberals and technocrats avoid party membership and "flee" if possible into their technical specialties in order to avoid compromising their convictions.[7] The new managerial elite will thus be composed of political "organization men," and while they will indeed press for professional advantages— "operational autonomy and procedurally stabilized access to the policy process within their own spheres"—they will accept the decisions of the party apparatus. "Managerial power," then, is "both marginal and contingent," and is likely to be "used in the future, as it has in the past, for essentially functional, system-supporting goals." [8]

Zbigniew Brzezinski and Samuel P. Huntington put the matter in still stronger terms: The "conventional counterpoise" of managers and party leaders is "quite illusory." [9] Technological innovation is being seized upon by the party in order to develop new and more palatable techniques of social control based upon a close

---

[5] *Ibid.*, pp. 154–157.

[6] In a later article Azrael revises this formulation and argues that at least the younger managers hold predominantly technocratic and reformist values. Jeremy R. Azrael, "The Managers," in R. Barry Farrell, ed., *Political Leadership in Eastern Europe and the Soviet Union* (Chicago: Aldine, 1970), pp. 243–245.

[7] Azrael, *Managerial Power*, pp. 157–167.

[8] *Ibid.*, pp. 166–167, 173–174. Again, Azrael's later opinion is rather different and more consistent with the argument of this book. "Hence, the future course of Soviet political development is likely to see a curtailment of the political primacy of the Party *apparat* and the emergence of an increasingly rigorous and increasingly legitimate pluralistic politics in which the managers will be united on a number of important issues and will have an influential, though not decisive, voice in determining basic policy. This voice will not sound any clarion call of democratic freedom, and it will often echo politically conservative themes; but it will help drown out the harsher voices of reaction, and it may unwittingly enable the long-silent masses to recover their own capacity for independent speech and their capacity to articulate their own demands." "The Managers," p. 246.

[9] Zbigniew Brzezinski and Samuel P. Huntington, *Political Power: USA/USSR* (New York: Viking Press, 1964), p. 168.

partnership between specialists and political leaders.[10] In a later, more subtle version of this argument, Huntington admits that the division of labor between the two groups may express itself in conflict but insists that such conflict masks an essential complementarity. "A complex society," he argues, "requires both increased functional autonomy for managerial specialists *and* increased political authority for the central political leadership." The leadership and control functions of the party apparatus make it "as essential to the system as the expert bureaucracy." [11]

A similar case has been made with some persuasiveness for the DDR by Jean-Paul Picaper:

> This would be a failure if, as is sometimes claimed, there existed an animosity between the "politicians" and the "experts" in the ruling machinery of the apparatus. Certainly such tensions exist, but a fusion has already been largely accomplished. It is clear that there is no "lobby of experts" in the SED. On the contrary, there is a certain complementarity between them and the "politicians." The quality which allows the admission of the "experts" into the ruling circle is precisely their competence, which is what distinguishes them from the "politicians." The difference between the two groups unites them rather than separates them. Since the political function itself tends to become a special vocation, the division of labor is enhanced. The party claims to see the "perspectives" of things; the experts, often charged with the responsibility for immense industrial investments, are more prudent, even conservative. Moreover, the party offers the young industrial managers a legitimation of their power in the factory and assures them of the docility of the working force through the subterfuge of a "leadership of men" propagandized in association with elements of social psychology. For the feeling of their authority characterizes the "experts" as much as the "politicians." In East Germany the "experts" are not a liberal element. Their reformism is limited to the desire to obtain good economic results, but it does not at all resemble a program of political opposition. Like all men of the party, they resist on the whole any initiative not coming from themselves. In some measure there exists a common ideology between the two groups which the party seeks to reinforce by linking to-

[10] *Ibid.*, pp. 121–125, 423–424.
[11] Samuel P. Huntington, "Social and Institutional Dynamics of One-Party Systems," in Huntington and Clement H. Moore, eds., *Authoritarian Politics in Modern Society* (New York: Basic Books, 1970), p. 33.

gether the political and economic-technical training of the young cadres in common institutes.[12]

A young West German writer on the DDR, Hans-Werner Prahl, has put the argument in more dialectical language. He sees the emergence of a "functional exchange relationship" between the party leadership and rising intelligentsia groups although like Huntington he grants the existence of shifting forms of conflict between specialized expertise and bureaucratic control. These conflicts he views as essentially integrative and supportive of the system; to be sure, the party leaders must "change the forms of their assertion and development of power" and utilize "feedback principles" to take account of the "dynamic of progress." This does not mean the development of a "technocracy," however, but an ongoing process of successful adaptation. As he puts it, there is a "change of style" without any "change of principle." [13]

While the four representative critiques I have described are far from identical, they are in rough agreement on the central proposition that the technical strategic elite and the *apparatchiki* are partners in power rather than rivals for it; insofar as conflict exists between them, it is functional for maintaining the system. In part, the complementarity of the two groups is explained by pointing to the socialization and recruitment process members of the technical elite undergo. In part, it is ascribed to the critical "political" functions performed by the *apparatchiki* either for the society as a whole or, more narrowly, in assuring the authority and status of the technicians.

Azrael puts the case most strongly for the effectiveness of formal and informal socialization in inducting Soviet technical students into the complex of approved political values; it is those who have been most successfully taught, he goes on to suggest, who are considered for more responsible positions. However, there is a second side to Soviet bloc socialization: Not only are Communist political norms inculcated but also, less consciously, rational technical-economic values which come with the emphasis of the schools on technical subjects, the stress of propaganda on eco-

---

[12] Jean-Paul Picaper, "Le Parti communist en Allemagne de l'Est," *Revue Fran-çaise de Science Politique,* XVI (February 1966), 44–45.

[13] Hans-Werner Prahl, "Intelligenz- und Elitegruppen in der DDR Gesellschaft," *Deutschland Archiv,* III (February 1970), 128–134.

nomic modernization, and the prestige and material rewards given to technical occupations.[14] Our evidence indicates that at least in the DDR the crudeness of political indoctrination tends to foster a mix of skepticism and loyalty; a generalized commitment to "socialism" and hostility to the social order of the Federal Republic are accompanied by the suspicion that the DDR's socialism is unnecessarily dogmatic and heavy-handed. In some measure there can be said to be a flight from the formal Marxist-Leninist value system to one informed by the celebration of technical and economic rationality. For a young elite growing up in isolation from openly competitive political practices and from democratic ideology, a quasi-technocratic value system is undoubtedly a more plausible alternative to the official doctrine than some variant of "liberalism." When the official ideology becomes itself blurred by technological language, as it did in the period of the NES, technical specialists are apt to find it still easier to meet the requirements of political loyalty and rise to positions of some prominence. It is only in a period of retrenchment and the "purification" of the received ideology that the tensions between it and quasi-technocratic values are likely to reemerge. Such a conflict characterized the early months of Honecker's leadership of the SED, but it brought no extensive personnel changes among the technical elite and seemed to have the character of a brief ideological interlude without long-term consequences.

The second part of the antimanagerial argument, that the party *apparatchiki* perform indispensable "political" functions which complement those of the technicians, cannot be fully dealt with within the framework of this book. But it appears flawed in at least three ways. It does not specify with any precision what these necessary political functions are and why it is only the *apparatchiki* that are able to perform them. It assumes rather than demonstrates that the importance of the party as the primary organizer and mobilizer of society and the repository of political legitimacy will not be diluted. It also tends to assume a degree of unity within the party apparatus that may not exist in reality and to neglect the political role of groups falling outside the rigid

[14] On this point see Günter Bartsch, "Die Kommunisten und das Generationsproblem," *Osteuropa*, XIV (May 1964), 332–336.

apparatchik/technocrat dichotomy. None of these assumptions is unassailable. The case of Yugoslavia, at the least, suggests that the party's accustomed role in Communist societies is not inviolable and that critical leadership and control functions may come to rest in hands other than the *apparatchiki's*. The assumption of the unity of the apparatus has been persuasively criticized by writers on the Soviet Union,[15] and studies of Communist "group politics" reveal a much more complex and multidimensional pattern of conflict than the dichotomic view would allow.[16] All these suggest that political functions may quite conceivably gravitate to state organs, local governments, the military, or elsewhere. The party apparatus is politically indispensable only by its own ideological definition and maintains its position only by stolidly reasserting a Leninist dogma whose relevance to advanced societies is by no means easy to demonstrate.

TECHNOCRATS AS POLITICIANS

As the interest group approach to Communist politics suggests, the problem of "technocratic" participation in power is partly a problem of coalition politics; such participation depends on alliances with other elite groups and individuals. We can best understand this dependence and its implications if we briefly examine some of the political characteristics built into the technocratic role, considered as an ideal type. To begin with, as numerous critics have emphasized, there is nothing inherently "democratic" about the technocratic outlook. The argument that political decisions can, and ought to, be made on rationally calculable grounds and thus should be placed in the hands of the specialist carries as its corollary the belief that popular election, the pulling and tugging of pressure groups, and backroom bargaining are out of place in an orderly society. The technocratic viewpoint is thus said to be fundamentally antidemocratic and indeed antipolitical: It holds "politics" responsible for the ills of the social order and reviles the politician as a corrupt and self-serving figure lacking the

[15] See Jerry F. Hough, "The Party *Apparatchiki*," in H. Gordon Skilling and Franklyn Griffiths, eds., *Interest Groups in Soviet Politics* (Princeton: Princeton University Press, 1971), pp. 47–92.
[16] See Skilling and Griffiths, eds., *op. cit., passim.*

knowledge requisite to making the decisions assigned to him.[17] Rational "technocratic" policy making would indeed seem to be able to function well only in an authoritarian framework, free from the conflicting pressures of a sundry multitude of political petitioners.

Yet the political posture of the technical intelligentsia of any society is not rigidly fixed but varies with the character of the regime and its own relationship to it. In a society with democratic institutions, an intensely dissatisfied technological stratum is apt to favor an authoritarian alternative which will enhance its own effectiveness and curb the irrational behavior of the "politicians." But where political irrationality can be laid at the door of the entrenched functionaries of a single ruling party, technocratic resistance is more likely to push—"objectively," as the Marxists say—in a liberalizing direction.[18] The differing political implications that technocratic influence may contain reflect the banal but not always appreciated truth that fundamental political choices are not in fact reducible to simple technical problems. Lurking behind every technocratic doctrine is a series of silent assumptions regarding the principles that ought to guide policy. F. F. Ridley has suggested that in France "technocrats" tend to favor public expenditure over private consumption, to be "anti-materialist," and, in economic matters, to be "anti-individualist." [19] One can readily imagine other technocrats in a different cultural setting favoring neo-capitalistic values. Thus, while technocrats agree in advocating the authority of expertise in politics and the purging of the "irrational," their posture in a given political context will depend upon just where they believe the finger of expertise ought to point. That, in turn, can vary over a wide range depending on the political and sociological environment.

While the technocratic phenomenon in itself suggests no unambiguous directions for policy, it imposes limitations on the means by which specialists may achieve political influence. The hostility of the (ideal) technocrat to politics would appear in

[17] See Bernard Crick, *In Defence of Politics* (Baltimore: Penguin Books, 1964), Chap. 5.

[18] Azrael notes that the "anti-authoritarianism" of the young Soviet managers "is more situational than philosophic." "The Managers," p. 244.

[19] F. F. Ridley, "French Technocracy and Comparative Government," *Political Studies*, XIV (February 1966), 44–45.

principle to be seriously disabling. Unwilling to bend to the customary tactics of political struggle (and here it does not matter whether the setting is democratic or authoritarian), he all but deprives himself of the possibility of directly achieving power. His only plausible route to influence becomes that of cooptation from above.

The members of the DDR's technical strategic elite are, I have noted, hardly pure "technocrats" in this sense. Their expertise is necessarily combined with the political adroitness required for survival in an organizational setting based on Leninist and Stalinist precepts. Only a minority, as I noted, are literally "coopted" from outside the party or government organs; the rest have spent most of their careers in official ranks, although largely in economic and technical roles. Nevertheless, they are coopted in the broader sense of being selected for elite positions from above, on the recommendation of cadre officials in the *apparat;* they do appear to be frequently impatient with, and occasionally naive about, "politics"; and they have little by way of a common organizational base. Hence, they are in need of allies if they are to implement their policy preferences and reinforce and expand their influence. Where technicians seem to have won significant victories in Eastern Europe—in Czechoslovakia in late 1967, in Poland at the end of 1970, and in the DDR itself in the period of economic reform—they have done so only in coalition with other groups or powerful individuals.

In 1963 the DDR's technical strategic elite enjoyed the influential patronage of Walter Ulbricht and the quieter good will of elements in the Soviet Union on behalf of its program of economic reform. As in the other two instances cited, the severe difficulties of the economy, perceived as a threat to regime authority, created temporary allies for the reform-minded technicians and permitted them their brief triumph. More permanent coalition partners are harder to acquire and keep, especially when, as in the DDR, the technical elite has failed to capture those leading political positions which would allow it to secure and reinforce its influence.

The alliance whose absence in the DDR has perhaps been the most glaring is the one between the technicians and leading members of the cultural intelligentsia, which was a vital ingredient of the Czech upheaval. It is from playwrights, film directors, novelists, philosophers, and poets that the most eloquent and persistent expressions of dissent have come in the DDR; yet, although watched with great attention in the West, their impact on regime policy has been at best marginal. Huntington notes the ability of an astute Communist leadership to play off the demands of the technical elite against those of the cultural elite as a means of controlling dissent.[20] Whether consciously or not, such a strategy has been pursued with success in the DDR—perhaps most dramatically illustrated at the Eleventh Central Committee Plenum in 1965, when renewed (although qualified) support for the NES accompanied a harsh intensification of party control over culture. Perhaps this only goes to illustrate how fortuitous an alliance between technical and cultural intelligentsias normally is, given the divergence of the interests of the two and the much greater policy relevance of the former in the eyes of the party bureaucrats and of the technicians themselves.

ADAPTATION AND LEGITIMACY

Like any large organization, a Communist party and regime must continually adapt in order to survive. In the 1960s the SED's mode of rule was unquestionably modified to meet the demands of economic modernization and a changing international environment.[21] There are, however, in the terminology of Philip Selznick, both "static" and "dynamic" forms of adaptation. That is, the changes made may remain essentially routine ones not fundamentally affecting the character of leadership and authority or, alternatively, constitute "character-defining" commitments reaching the "organization's capacity to control its own future be-

[20] Huntington, "Social and Institutional Dynamics," p. 37. "The managers' demands are usually concrete and limited; those of the intellectuals more diffuse and general. To grant the demands of the intellectuals would be to jeopardize the authority of the political elite and perhaps even the stability of the entire system. To grant the demands of the managerial elites for functional autonomy is to improve the efficiency and performance of the system without posing any real threat to the position of the political leadership." It should be evident by now that I do not agree with the last sentence.

[21] See Ludz, *Parteielite, passim.*

havior." [22] The price of bringing members of the technical intelligentsia into the DDR's political elite and of making concessions to their policy desires undoubtedly has been some dilution of the integrity and coherence of the political elite, which for an organization viewing itself as a Leninist "combat party" is of utmost significance.[23]

It is argued by the antimanagerialist critics, in effect, that the concessions made have been trivial and that the DDR's technical specialists have won only subordinate powers facilitating at best static adaptation. They thus remain no more than a docile, well-integrated pressure group loyally supporting the existing system with their specialized skills—a contention underlined by the peaceful burial of the DDR's economic reforms of the middle 1960s. At this writing, we are indeed witnessing in the DDR the reassertion of the claim to total hegemony on the part of the men of the party apparatus. This claim, I believe, is not likely to be honored over the long run; since at least 1956 it has persisted only in tension with an emerging elite pluralism.[24] It is surely correct, as Azrael suggests, that even in the darkest days of Stalinism, Communism was never so monolithic as it was believed to be in the West;[25] a variety of groups within the system energetically and often viciously competed for the favor of the dictator and his close associates. But accompanying the diminution of the power of the single leader himself, Communist group rivalries have become less those of jealous courtiers and more those of semi-permanent interest aggregations. There is some confirmation here of Suzanne Keller's proposition, noted in Chapter 7, that the growth in numbers, specialization, and interdependence of strategic elites in advanced societies tends to place limits on the arbitrary, monocratic exercise of power. However, it remains important to emphasize that the competition of plural elites is by no means openly accepted in the DDR but instead

[22] Philip Selznick, *Leadership in Administration* (New York: Harper & Row, 1957), pp. 33–36. Selznick derives these terms from Erich Fromm's psychoanalytic categories.

[23] See *ibid.*, pp. 119ff.

[24] See Jerry F. Hough's model of "institutional pluralism" in "The Soviet System: Petrification or Pluralism," *Problems of Communism* (March–April 1972), pp. 25–45.

[25] Azrael, *Managerial Power,* pp. 177–188 and *passim.*

is often inhibited by the SED's monolithic organizational ideal
and by pressures for ideological uniformity.

This book has argued that the ambiguity in the structure of
elite power in the DDR rests in a broader sense on the shifting
bases of regime legitimacy. While there may be said to have
developed a generalized belief in the legitimacy of "socialism,"
it has never been fully extended to the hegemony of the party or
to the rule of a particular set of leaders. For ordinary citizens
of East Germany, as elsewhere, socialism has first of all been understood in terms of concrete social benefits and the adherence
to broad principles of equality and social justice. The task of the
DDR's tireless propagandists has been to link these generalized
beliefs to acceptance of the leading role of the SED as the supposed embodiment of the power and will of the proletariat. For
many years party ideologists found their primary themes in the
history of German and Soviet revolutionary struggle, sharply
etched descriptions of the venality of the class enemy in the Federal Republic, and repeated citation of the successful example
of the Soviet Union. Such appeals produced only a disappointing
popular response in the face of such unyielding realities as the
visible lag in the standard of living behind the Federal Republic,
persistent shortages of basic consumer amenities, and resentment
at the clumsy intervention of party, police, and governmental
bureaucracies in almost every sector of life. It was only with the
introduction of appeals to economic rationality and modernization, reaching their height with the introduction of the New
Economic System, that a more promising path to legitimacy
was discovered. But then a new question became inescapable:
Whose authority did the new rhetoric actually support?

Azrael argues the weakness of managerial influence by asserting that "the apparat is still the principal custodian of the symbols of legitimacy";[26] I have tried to show that in the DDR it is
the guardian only of the old, quasi-charismatic symbols. While
it has sought to appropriate as well a legitimacy based on rational-
legal and performance criteria, it has been able to do so effectively
only by opening the political elite to other groups—particularly
but not only the technical intelligentsia—and by at least raising

[26] *Ibid.,* p. 169.

the possibility of some restrictions on its own powers (through "socialist legality," decentralization, new and expanded forms of political participation, etc.). The reforms of the New Economic System are illustrative: The apparatus bought an enhanced degree of acceptance at the price of strengthening the prestige and influence of a rival elite, devolving significant if secondary decision-making powers on managers and state bureaucrats and creating a mood for ideological as well as practical innovation which did not entirely halt at the boundaries it had set. The curtailment of the reforms and the self-conscious reemphasis of the party's leading role and the unity and authority of the ideology testify to the seriousness with which these centrifugal currents came to be regarded.

Nevertheless, the technological and consumer values the regime itself has popularized and the repeated ideological usage of material indices for measuring the DDR's success assure the technical strategic elite a continuing political influence and repeatedly if implicitly pose the basic legitimacy question. As is characteristic of most organizations, the SED denies the existence of intergroup conflict within its ranks and treats the problems that must be resolved as routine, day-to-day ones arising within a larger framework of ideological unity.[27] The recurrent proclamation of the goal of developing a new socialist man both technically skilled and ideologically devoted bears witness to this effort to paper over intergroup conflict; but our evidence suggests that the differences remain real ones with serious consequences for political behavior.

To argue that the shift in the basis of legitimacy that accompanied the NES is moving the DDR toward a form of elitist pluralism and ultimately toward a less autocratic political structure is not to assert that such a change is incapable of being halted or

[27] "Because of these consequences of bargaining, we predict that the organizational hierarchy will perceive (and react to) all conflict as though it were in fact individual rather than intergroup conflict. More specifically, we predict that almost all disputes in the organization will be defined as problems in analysis, that the initial reaction to conflict will be problem solving and persuasion, that such reactions will persist even when they appear to be inappropriate, that there will be a greater explicit emphasis on common goals where they do, and that bargaining (when it occurs) will frequently be concealed within an analytic framework." James G. March and Herbert A. Simon, *Organizations* (New York: Wiley, 1958), p. 131.

reversed, at least temporarily, or that if it is accomplished it will be entirely desirable from the standpoint of Western liberalism. Any established elite has substantial resources available for clinging to its power even when its accustomed base of legitimacy has begun to shrink. As we have seen in the DDR, it may seek with some success to appropriate for itself alternative legitimacy sources. The presence of large numbers of technically experienced personnel on the Central Committee and in government ministries has not yet forced their admission into the ultimate decision-making organs in more than token numbers or prevented the rebureaucratization of economic decision making and the imposition of unyielding cultural and external policies which until recently exceeded in severity those of the Soviet Union itself. The meshing of the interests of the "centralizers" among the technical strategic elite and the leading party bureaucrats, while not complete, and the growing uses of the computer in the service of central social control further suggest that some sorts of elite pluralism may not bring liberalization in their train but instead a conservative form of oligarchy by coalition.

It also should be recalled that fundamental change in Communist authority relationships may not be exclusively or even primarily the consequence of changes in social and elite structure. The most dramatic instances of change we have observed in Communist systems have resulted from restiveness over economic failures, cultural ferment provoked by ill-timed censorship or repression or even insufficiently rapid liberalization, resurgent nationalism or regional particularism, disputes and rivalries among Communist leaders, or some combination of these. To an extent, these events themselves were conditioned by important changes among social strata and elites, but it would not be accurate to single out their impact as the overriding one.

Authority changes brought about by the rise of a new stratum and elite are apt to be profound over the long run but undramatic and incremental. Furthermore, the changes that have thus far taken place in the DDR have occurred within the arena of the party, to which all the relevant actors belong and which serves them as a symbol of overarching unity, however tenuous that may finally prove to be. The adherence of all relevant elites to the party, the existence of distinct "opinion groups" within individual elites, and the abhorrence of the ideology for "faction-alism" preclude a spectacular open power struggle in which rival groups are sharply delimited. If, and as, the "technocrats" increase their numbers and influence in the centers of political decision it will be by quiet and gradual steps, of which the participants them-selves will scarcely be aware. At least in the Soviet bloc the mana-gerial revolution will be no revolution at all but a barely visible process of alliance building, infiltration, and absorption.

APPENDIX 1

Central Committee Members, 1971,
Classified by Function Performed

Function	Members	Candidates
Economic-technical functionaries	Baum, Bruno	Arndt, Otto
	Böhm, Siegfried	Bialecki, Joachim
	Dallmann, Fritz	Biermann, Wolfgang
	Ermisch, Luise	Fichtner, Kurt
	Ewald, Georg	Gaudian, Werner
	Fischer, Martin	Geipel, Norbert
	Frohn, Werner	Georgi, Rudi
	Fuchs, Klaus	Hasse, Horst
	Grüneberg, Gerhard	Hoppe, Ilse
	Grünert, Bernhard	Kamps, Peter
	Halbritter, Walter	König, Otto
	Hennecke, Adolf	Lietz, Bruno
	Heynisch, Werner	Müller, Erich
	Jarowinski, Werner	Preuss, Hans-Joachim
	Junker, Wolfgang	Schomann, Kurt
	Kiesler, Bruno	Skibinski, Willi
	Kleiber, Günther	Sölle, Horst
	Kramer, Erwin	Sternberg, Frieda
	Mittag, Günter	Wappler, Erich
	Müller, Margarete	Weiss, Gerhard
	Neumann, Alfred	Wohllebe, Gert

Function	*Members*	*Candidates*
	Pöschel, Hermann	Wunderlich, Helmut
	Rauchfuss, Wolfgang	
	Rompe, Robert	
	Rübensam, Erich	
	Rumpf, Willy	
	Schürer, Gerhard	
	Steger, Otfried	
	Thoma, Karl	
	Tomczak, Hans-Joachim	
	Walther, Elisabeth	
	Weiz, Herbert	
	Wenig, Josef	
	Wittig, Heinz	
	Wittik, Hans	
	Wittkowski, Margarete	
	Wulf, Ernst	
	Wyschofsky, Günther	
	Ziegner, Heinz	
Party bureaucrats	Albrecht, Hans	Feist, Manfred
	Axen, Hermann	Hempel, Manfred
	Brasch, Horst	Hering, Werner
	Bräutigam, Alois	Klemm, Horst
	Chemnitzer, Johannes	Schönfelder, Heinz
	Dohlus, Horst	Weingart, Edith
	Felfe, Werner	Zschau, Ursula
	Frost, Gerhard	
	Geggel, Heinz	
	Heidenreich, Gerhard	
	Hertwig, Hans-Joachim	
	Holzmacher, Gerda	
	Honecker, Erich	
	Hörnig, Johannes	
	Juch, Heinz	
	Knolle, Rainer	
	Krolikowski, Werner	
	Lange, Ingeborg	
	Lorenz, Siegfried	
	Markowski, Paul	
	Mückenberger, Erich	
	Müller, Fritz	
	Naumann, Konrad	

Function	*Members*	*Candidates*
	Pisnik, Alois	
	Quandt, Bernhard	
	Rohde, Alfred	
	Roscher, Paul	
	Schumann, Horst	
	Sindermann, Horst	
	Tisch, Harry	
	Trautzch, Gisela	
	Ulbricht, Walter	
	Verner, Paul	
	Walde, Werner	
	Wittig, Werner	
	Ziegenhahn, Herbert	
Agitprop functionaries	Bauer, Roland	Heinrich, Eberhard
	Berg, Helene	Zellmer, Christa
	Brandt, Edith	
	Diehl, Ernst	
	Hager, Kurt	
	Lamberz, Werner	
	Lange, Marianne	
	Maron, Karl	
	Modrow, Hans	
	Neugebauer, Werner	
	Norden, Albert	
	Reinhold, Otto	
	Singer, Rudolf	
	Tiedke, Kurt	
	Wolf, Hanna	
Educational-cultural personnel	Abusch, Alexander	Böhme, Hans-Joachim
	Adameck, Heinrich	Lorenz, Werner
	Benjamin, Hilde	Mäde, Hans-Dieter
	Burghardt, Max	Mebel, Moritz
	Dahlem, Franz	Minetti, Hans-Peter
	Grundig, Lea	Neuner, Gerhart
	Honecker, Margot	Sakowski, Helmut
	Kayser, Karl	Wolfram, Gerhard
	Kurella, Alfred	Zimmering, Max
	Lange, Erich	
	Meyer, Ernst-Hermann	
	Seeger, Bernhard	

Function	*Members*	*Candidates*
Functionaries of mass organizations	Balkow, Julius Ewald, Manfred Funke, Otto Heintze, Horst Jahn, Günter Jendretzky, Hans Thiele, Ilse Töpfer, Johanna Warnke, Herbert	Beyreuther, Wolfgang Kirchhoff, Werner Krenz, Egon Kuron, Karl Müller, Fritz Thieme, Kurt
Police-military officials	Dickel, Friedrich Hoffmann, Karl-Heinz Kessler, Heinz Mielke, Erich Verner, Waldemar	Beater, Bruno Scheibe, Herbert
Other state officials	Baumann, Edith Ebert, Friedrich Fischer, Oskar Florin, Peter Gotsche, Otto Herrmann, Joachim Kern, Käthe Matthes, Heinz Menzel, Robert Mewis, Karl Rodenberg, Hans Rödiger, Kurt Stief, Albert Stoph, Willi Strauss, Paul Streit, Josef Warnke, Johannes Winzer, Otto	Bittner, Horst Fechner, Herbert Krolikowski, Herbert Zimmermann, Arnold
Workers	Storch, Hermann	Läbe, Hans Tamme, Irene

APPENDIX 2

Central Committee Economic Functionaries, 1971,
by Category and Education

Category	Members	Candidates
Members of Council of Ministers, Deputy Ministers, State Secs.	Böhm, Siegfried * Ewald, Georg (A) Halbritter, Walter* Junker, Wolfgang † Kleiber, Günther* Neumann, Alfred Rauchfuss, Wolfgang * Steger, Otfried † Weiz, Herbert** Wittik, Hans Wyschofsky, Günther*	Arndt, Otto* Fichtner, Kurt** Georgi, Rudi** Sölle, Horst* Weiss, Gerhard **
Leading officials of State Planning Comm., Nat'l. Ec. Council	Schürer, Gerhard *	
Lower functionaries in ministries, SPC, NEC	Hennecke, Adolf	
Central Committee Secretaries and other CC functionaries	Grüneberg, Gerhard (A) Jarowinski, Werner** Kiesler, Bruno (A) Mittag, Günter** Pöschel, Hermann	Wappler, Erich*
Regional state economic functionaries	Wittig, Heinz (A)	

Category	Members	Candidates
Regional party economic functionaries	Baum, Bruno Ziegner, Heinz (A) †	Geipel, Norbert (A) * Lietz, Bruno (A) * Skibinski, Willi (A) *
Plant managers	Ermisch, Luise † Frohn, Werner* Walther, Elisabeth	Bialecki, Joachim Biermann, Wolfgang Müller, Erich* Wunderlich, Helmut †
VVB general directors	Tomczak, Hans-Joachim	
Other factory		Gaudian, Werner* Kamps, Peter* König, Otto** Preuss, Hans-Joachim (F) Schomann, Kurt (F) Wohllebe, Gert
Collective or state farm chairmen	Dallmann, Fritz (A) Grünert, Bernhard (A) † Müller, Margarete (A)* Thoma, Karl (A)	Hasse, Horst (A)* Sternberg, Frieda (A)
Functionaries of Farmers' Mutual Aid Assoc. (VdgB)	Wulf, Ernst (A)*	
Scientists, institute directors	Fuchs, Klaus** Heynisch, Werner* Rompe, Robert** Rübensam, Erich (A)**	
Other	Fischer, Martin* Kramer, Erwin (V)* Rumpf, Willy (V) Wenig, Josef (V) Wittkowski, Margarete**	Hoppe, Ilse*

Key: (A) = agricultural functionary.
    (F) = foreman.
    (V) = "party veteran."
    * = university degree (*Diplom*).
    ** = doctorate.
    † = other higher education.

BIBLIOGRAPHY

ONLY THE longer and more significant periodical articles are cited independently. A list of all periodicals used is found at the end of sections I and II.

I. EAST GERMAN AND EAST EUROPEAN SOURCES

Apel, Erich, and Günter Mittag, *Ökonomische Gesetze des Sozialismus und neues ökonomisches System der Planung und Leitung der Volkswirtschaft.* Berlin: Dietz Verlag, 1964.
———, *Wissenschaftliche Führungstätigkeit: Neue Rolle der VVB.* Berlin: Dietz Verlag, 1964.
Armélin, Peter, "Zur Problematik des Betriebsklimas—Ergebnisse einer industrie-soziologischen Untersuchung," *Wirtschaftswissenschaft,* XIII (February 1965), 239–251.
"Die Bedeutung der Intelligenz beim Aufbau des Sozialismus," Central Committee statement. *Neues Deutschland* (May 24, 1953), pp. 3–4.
Behrens, Fritz, "Kritik der politischen Ökonomie und ökonomische Theorie des Sozialismus," in Walter Euchner and Alfred Schmidt, eds., *Kritik der politischen Ökonomie heute: 100 Jahre 'Kapital.'* Frankfurt: Europäische Verlagsanstalt, 1968.
Berger, Wolfgang, and Otto Reinhold, *Zu den wissenschaftlichen Grundlagen des neuen ökonomischen Systems der Planung und Leitung: Das neue ökonomische System—ein wichtiger Beitrag der Sozialistischen Einheitspartei Deutschlands zur marxistisch-leninistischen Theorie.* Berlin: Dietz Verlag, 1966.

Bley, Horst, Fritz Schellhorn, and Kurt Walter, "Plan- und Arbeitsdisziplin—Gebot hoher Effektivität," *Einheit,* XXVI, No. 1 (1971), 37–45.

Böhme, Hans-Joachim, "Das marxistisch-leninistische Grundlagenstudium—Kernstück der sozialistischen Erziehung der Studenten," *Das Hochschulwesen,* XX (January 1972), 3–8.

Doernberg, Stefan, *Die Geburt eines neuen Deutschlands: Die antifaschistisch-demokratische Umwälzung und die Entstehung der DDR.* Berlin: Rütten & Loening, 1959.

———, *Kurze Geschichte der DDR.* Berlin: Dietz Verlag, 1965.

Dohlus, Horst, "Die Erhöhung der Kampfkraft unserer marxistisch-leninistischen Partei," *Einheit,* XXVI, No. 1 (1971), 3–13.

"Das 30. Plenum und die Wirtschaftswissenschaftler," *Wirtschaftswissenschaft,* V (February-March 1957), 161–165.

Ebert, Georg, Gerhard Koch, Fred Mathe, and Harry Mielke, "Theoretische Grundfragen der Führungsrolle der marxistisch-leninistischen Partei in der sozialistischen Planwirtschaft," *Einheit,* XXIV, No. 2 (1969), 131–143.

Edlich, Heinz, and Lothar Hummel, "Alle Talente fördern, alle Fähigkeiten entwickeln," *Einheit,* XXVI, No. 1 (1971), 46–53.

Falke, Rainer, and Hans Modrow, *Auswahl und Entwicklung von Führungskadern.* Berlin: Staatsverlag der Deutschen Demokratischen Republik, 1967.

Das funktionelle Wirken der Bestandteile des neuen ökonomischen Systems der Planung und Leitung der Volkswirtschaft. Hrsgg. vom Büro für Industrie und Bauwesen beim Politbüro des Zentralkomitees der SED. Berlin: Dietz Verlag, 1964.

Gambke, Heinz, "Zu einigen Problemen der Bündnispolitik der SED mit der Intelligenz in der Periode des Sieges der sozialistischen Produktionsverhältnisse (1956–1961)," *Beiträge zur Geschichte der deutschen Arbeiterbewegung,* VIII, No. 1 (1966), 23–42.

"Gesetz über das einheitliche sozialistische Bildungssystem," in *Unser Bildungssystem—wichtiger Schritt auf dem Wege zur gebildeten Nation.* [Berlin]: Kanzlei des Staatsrates der Deutschen Demokratischen Republik, 1965, pp. 83–133.

Gilde, Werner, "Ideen muss man haben," *Forum,* No. 1 (1970), pp. 3–4.

Grundmann, Siegfried, "Intelligenz und Arbeiterklasse in unserer Zeit," *Technische Gemeinschaft* (May 1969), pp. 4–7.

"Grundsätze über die planmässige Entwicklung, Ausbildung, Erziehung, und Verteilung der Kader in den Partei-, Staats-, und Wirtschaftsorganen sowie den Massenorganisationen und auf dem Gebiet der Kultur und Volksbildung." Decision of Central Committee Secretariat, February 17, 1965, *Neuer Weg*, XX, No. 6 (1965), 337–343

Hager, Kurt, *Bericht des Politbüros an die 7. Tagung des Zentralkomitees der SED*. Berlin: Dietz Verlag, 1964.

———, *Die entwickelte sozialistische Gesellschaft*. Berlin: Dietz Verlag, 1971.

———, "Freie Bahn für die sozialistische Wissenschaft." Concluding speech at Third SED Universities Conference. *Neues Deutschland* (March 6, 1958), p. 4.

———, "Die Intelligenz und der V. Parteitag," *Einheit*, XIII (August 1958), 1122–1137.

———, "Der Kampf für die sozialistische Hochschule." *Referat* at Third SED Universities Conference. *Neues Deutschland* (March 1, 1958), p. 4.

———, "Partei und Wissenschaft," *Einheit*, XXI, No. 4 (1966), 439–450.

Handbuch der Volkskammer, 3. Wahlperiode. Berlin: Kongress Verlag, 1959.

Havemann, Robert, *Dialektik ohne Dogma? Naturwissenschaft und Weltanschauung*. Hamburg: Rowohlt Verlag, 1964.

———, "Meinungsstreit fördert die Wissenschaften," *Neues Deutschland* (July 8, 1956), Beilage, p. 3.

Herber, Richard, "Zur Leitung der Parteiarbeit nach dem Produktionsprinzip," *Einheit*, XVIII (May 1963), 3–16.

Herber, Richard, and Herbert Jung, *Wissenschaftliche Leitung und Entwicklung der Kader*. [Berlin]: Staatsverlag der Deutschen Demokratischen Republik [1964].

Heuer, Uwe-Jens, *Demokratie und Recht im neuen ökonomischen System der Planung und Leitung der Volkswirtschaft*. Berlin: Staatsverlag der Deutschen Demokratischen Republic, 1965.

———, "Gesellschaft und Demokratie," *Staat und Recht*, XVI, No. 6 (1967), 907–920

Honecker, Erich, *Bericht des Zentralkomitees an den VIII. Parteitag der SED*. Berlin: Dietz Verlag, 1971.

———, *Fragen von Wissenschaft und Politik in der sozialistischen Gesellschaft*. Berlin: Dietz Verlag, 1972.

———, *Das Parteistatut der Sozialistischen Einheitspartei Deutschlands. Referat* at Sixth SED Congress. Berlin: Dietz Verlag, 1963.

Humboldt-Universität zu Berlin, *Jahrbuch 1963*. Berlin: Humboldt Universität, 1964.

Hübner, Heinz-Werner, "Wie erreichen wir eine höhere Stabilität des Volkswirtschaftsplanes 1971?" *Die Wirtschaft* (January 27, 1971), pp. 4–5.

Kannegiesser, Karlheinz, "Leitungswissenschaftliche Probleme unter dem Gesichtspunkt der Kybernetik," *Staat und Recht*, XIV (October 1965), 1609–1622.

Karl-Marx-Universität Leipzig, *Studienführer 1969–1970*. Leipzig, 1969.

Korn, Klaus, and Werner Weigelt, "Was 100 000 Ingenieure leisten könnten: Probleme der sozialistischen Menschenführung," *Forum*, No. 7 (1963), pp. 3–5.

Kramer, Horst, "Wissenschaft und Partei," *Deutsche Zeitschrift für Philosophie*, XIV, No. 4 (1966), 434–449.

Lamberz, Werner, "Die führende Rolle der Arbeiterklasse in der DDR," *Forum*, No. 7 (1970), pp. 8–9.

———, "Partei und Massen," *Einheit*, XXVII, No. 7 (1972), 846–854.

Lenin, V. I., *Selected Works*. 3 vols. New York: International Publishers, 1967.

Ludz, Peter Christian, ed., *Soziologie und Marxismus in der Deutschen Demokratischen Republik*. 2 vols. Neuwied and Berlin: Luchterhand, 1972.

Luft, Hans, Harry Nick, and Gerhard Schultz, "Sozialistische Planwirtschaft—Lebensgrundlage der sozialistischen Gesellschaft," *Einheit*, XXIII, No. 6 (1968), 692–704.

Lungwitz, Kurt, *Über die Klassenstruktur in der Deutschen Demokratischen Republik: Eine sozialökonomische-statistische Untersuchung*. Berlin: Verlag die Wirtschaft, 1962.

Martin-Luther-Universität Halle-Wittenberg, *Personal- und Vorlesungsverzeichnis*. Herbstsemester, 1965–1966.

"Mitgliederversammlung—inhaltsreich und erzieherisch," *Neuer Weg*, XXVI, No. 2 (1971), 49–54.

Mittag, Günter, "Die Aufgaben der Parteiorganisationen in den Vereinigungen Volkseigener Betriebe," *Einheit*, XIII (August 1958), 1138–1147.

———, *Die Durchführung des Volkswirtschaftsplanes im Jahre 1970*. Referat at Thirteenth Plenum of SED Central Committee. Berlin: Dietz Verlag, 1970.

———, *Fragen der Parteiarbeit nach dem Produktionsprinzip in Industrie und Bauwesen*. Berlin: Dietz Verlag, 1963.

———, "Für ein festes Bündnis mit der Intelligenz," *Neuer Weg*, XIV, No. 19 (1959), 1253–1256.

———, "Meisterung der Ökonomie ist für uns Klassenkampf," *Neues Deutschland* (October 27, 1968), p. 4.

————, "Planerfüllung 1967 erfordert schöpferische Masseninitiative," *Neuer Weg,* XXII, No. 14 (1967), reprinted in part in *SBZ-Archiv,* XVIII, No. 15 (1967), 238–240.

————, "Zur planmässigen Anwendung der ökonomischen Hebel," *Die Wirtschaft* (April 15, 1963), pp. 15–18.

————, "Die schöpferische Arbeit der Partei bei der Gestaltung des sozialistischen Wirtschaftssystems," *Einheit,* XXI, No. 4 (1966), 466–475.

————, "Wir brauchen jetzt ein durchdachtes System der ökonomischen Leitung," *Die Wirtschaft* (January 28, 1963), pp. 6–7.

Nelles, Johannes, "Zu einigen Fragen der Leitung eines sozialistischen Grossbetriebes," *Einheit,* XVII (September 1962), 29–36.

Neumann, Alfred, *Der Volkswirtschaftsplan 1965 in der Industrie und die weitere Durchführung des neuen ökonomischen Systems der Planung und Leitung der Volkswirtschaft. Referat* at Seventh Plenum of SED Central Committee. Berlin: Dietz Verlag, 1964.

Zur ökonomischen Theorie und Politik in der Übergangsperiode. Wirtschaftswissenschaft, V (3. Sonderheft, 1957).

Oelssner, Fred, "Staat und Ökonomie in der Übergangsperiode." Revised manuscript of speech at Thirtieth Plenum of SED Central Committee. *Wirtschaftswissenschaft,* V (April–May 1957), 321–331.

Peschel, Horst, "Der Beitrag der Kammer der Technik zur weiteren allseitigen Stärkung der Deutschen Demokratischen Republik," *Technische Gemeinschaft* (April 1970), pp. 12–22.

Politische Ökonomie des Sozialismus und ihre Anwendung in der DDR. Berlin: Dietz Verlag, 1969.

"Die Qualifizierung der Werktätigen: Betriebsakadamien berichten," *Einheit,* XVIII (May 1963), 136–143.

Richtlinie für das neue ökonomische System der Planung und Leitung der Volkswirtschaft; Beschluss über die Anwendung der Grundsätze des neuen ökonomischen Systems der Planung und Leitung der Volkswirtschaft im Bauwesen. Decisions of the Presidium of the Council of Ministers, July 11, 1963, and June 16, 1953. Berlin: Dietz Verlag, 1963.

Schnelzki, Albert, "Eng mit den Angehörigen der Intelligenz verbunden," *Neuer Weg,* XVIII, No. 1 (1963), 7–10.

Schroeter, Alfred, "Den Mathematik-Unterricht an unseren Schulen verbessern," *Einheit,* XVII (September 1962), 91–100.

Schulz, Gerhard, "Gedanken zur Rolle der Parteiversammlungen," *Einheit,* XX, No. 2 (1965), 11–15.

————, "Die organische Verbindung der Errungenschaften der wissenschaftlich-technischen Revolution mit den Vorzügen des Sozialismus," *Einheit*, XXVII, No. 7 (1972), 876–886.

Schürer, Gerhard, "Die Rolle des Staates auf ökonomischen Gebiet," *Die Wirtschaft* (May 22, 1969), pp. 8–10.

"SED-Politbüro zur Reorganisation der Parteileitungen nach dem Produktionsprinzip." Politburo decision. *Neues Deutschland* (February 27, 1963), reprinted in *SBZ-Archiv*, XIV, No. 8 (1963), 122–123.

Sieber, Rolf, and Günter Söder, *Politik und Ökonomie im sozialistischen Gesellschaftssystem.* Berlin: Dietz Verlag, 1970.

Söder, Günter, "Die führende Rolle der Partei und das neue ökonomische System der Planung und Leitung," *Einheit*, XXI, No. 11 (1966), 1372–1380.

Sozialismus und Intelligenz: Erfahrungen aus der Zusammenarbeit zwischen Arbeiter und Angehörigen der Intelligenz. Published by the Institut für Gesellschaftwissenschaften der ZK der SED. Berlin: Dietz Verlag, 1960.

Sozialistische Einheitspartei Deutschlands, VI. Parteitag, *Beschluss des VI. Parteitages der SED über die Aufgaben im Transport und Nachrichtenwesen.* Berlin: Dietz Verlag, 1963.

Sozialistische Einheitspartei Deutschlands, VI. Parteitag, *Diskussionsreden über die schriftliche vorgelegten Berichte, über das Programm der SED und über das Referat des Genossen Walter Ulbricht.* Berlin: Dietz Verlag, 1963.

Der Staat sind wir: Beiträge zu Probleme der Entwicklung des sozialistischen Staatsbewusstseins in der DDR. Berlin: Dietz Verlag, 1960.

Stalin, J., *Problems of Leninism.* Moscow: Foreign Languages Publishing House, 1953.

Statistisches Jahrbuch der Deutschen Demokratischen Republik 1965 (1968, 1970). Hrsgg. von der Staatlichen Zentralverwaltung für Statistik. [Berlin]: Staatsverlag der Deutschen Demokratischen Republik, 1965, 1968, 1970.

Statistisches Taschenbuch der Deutschen Demokratischen Republik 1972. Hrsgg. von der Staatlichen Zentralverwaltung für Statistik. Berlin: Staatsverlag der Deutschen Demokratischen Republik, 1972.

"Statut der Kammer der Technik, mit die vom 5. KDT–Kongress beschlossenen Veränderungen," *Technische Gemeinschaft* (April 1970), pp. 55–59.

Statut der Sozialistischen Einheitspartei Deutschlands. Berlin: Dietz Verlag, 1968.

Steiner, Helmut, "Aufstiegschancen in der DDR," *Marxistische Blätter*, III, No. 6 (1965), 22–27.

Das Studium an der Universitäten, Hoch- und Fachschulen der Deutschen Demokratischen Republik; Verzeichnis der Fachrichtungen; Studienführer. Hrsgg. von Staatssekretariat für das Hoch- und Fachschulwesen. Berlin: Staatsverlag der Deutschen Demokratischen Republik, 1965.

Tessman, Kurt, "Technische Revolution und Sozialismus," *Einheit,* XX, No. 2 (1965), 15–22.

Ulbricht, Walter, *Antwort auf aktuelle politische und ökonomische Fragen.* Concluding speech of discussion over Politburo Report at the Seventh Plenum of the SED Central Committee. Berlin: Dietz Verlag, 1964.

———, *Die Durchführung der ökonomischen Politik im Planjahr 1964.* Speech at Fifth Plenum of SED Central Committee. Berlin: Dietz Verlag, 1964.

———, *Die gesellschaftliche Entwicklung in der Deutschen Demokratischen Republik bis zur Vollendung des Sozialismus.* Berlin: Dietz Verlag, 1967.

———, *Zur Geschichte der neuesten Zeit.* Vol. I. Berlin: Dietz Verlag, 1955.

———, "Die nationale Mission der Deutschen Demokratischen Republik und das geistige Schaffen in unserem Staat." *Referat* at Ninth Plenum of SED Central Committee. *Neues Deutschland* (April 28, 1965), pp. 3–9.

———, "Das neue ökonomische System der Planung und Leitung der Volkswirtschaft in der Praxis." *Referat* at Economic Conference of the SED Central Committee and the DDR Council of Ministers. *Die Wirtschaft* (June 28, 1963), pp. 1–21.

———, *Dem VI. Parteitag entgegen. Referat* at the Seventeenth Plenum of the SED Central Committee; speech at second plenary meeting of DDR Research Council. Berlin: Dietz Verlag, 1962.

———, "Probleme des Perspektivplanes bis 1970." *Referat* at Eleventh Central Committee Plenum. *Neues Deutschland* (December 18, 1965), reprinted in part in *SBZ-Archiv,* XVII, Nos. 1–2 (1966), 26–31; XVII, No. 3 (1966), 42–48.

———, *Das Programm des Sozialismus und die geschichtliche Aufgabe der Sozialistischen Einheitspartei Deutschlands; Schlusswort . . . ; Programm der Sozialistischen Einheitspartei Deutschlands. Referat* at Sixth SED Congress. Berlin: Dietz Verlag, 1963.

———, "Die Rolle des sozialistischen Staates bei der Gestaltung des entwickelten gesellschaftlichen Systems des Sozialismus," *Neues Deutschland* (October 16, 1968), reprinted in part in *Deutschland Archiv,* I (November 1968), 847–857.

Die Volkskammer der Deutschen Demokratischen Republik, 5. Wahlperiode. Berlin: Staatsverlag der Deutschen Demokratischen Republik, 1967.
Die Volkskammer der Deutschen Demokratischen Republik, 6. Wahl-
periode. Berlin: Staatsverlag der Deutschen Demokratischen Re-
publik, 1972.
Weber, Hermann, ed., *Der deutsche Kommunismus: Dokumente.*
Köln: Kiepenheuer & Witsch, 1963.
"Die Weiterführung der 3. Hochschulreform und die Entwicklung des
Hochschulwesens bis 1975." Beschluss des Staatsrates der Deut-
schen Demokratischen Republik vom 3. April 1969, *Forum,* No. 7
(1969), reprinted in *Deutschland Archiv,* II (May 1969), 509–528.
Wolf, Hanna, "Die SED—eine leninistische Kampfpartei," *Einheit,*
XXVI, No. 5 (1971), 503–515.
Wolf, Herbert F., "Zu einigen soziologischen Problemen der Vorbereit-
ung von Ingenieurstudenten auf di Leitungstätigkeit im Be-
trieb," *Jugendforschung,* No. 15 (1970), pp. 31–39.
Wörterbuch der Marxistisch-Leninistischen Soziologie. Berlin: Dietz
Verlag, 1969.
*Aus dem Wortprotokoll der 33. Tagung des Zentralkomitees der SED
vom 16.–19. Oktober 1967.* Photomechanische Wiedergabe. [Bonn:
Bundesministerium für gesamtdeutsche Fragen, 1957.]
Wyschofsky, Günther, and Karl-Heinz Schäfer, *Die Zusammenarbeit
mit der Intelligenz: Erfahrungen aus der chemischen Industrie.*
Berlin: Dietz Verlag, 1961.

PERIODICALS

Deutsche Zeitschrift für Philosophie (monthly).
Einheit (monthly). SED ideological journal.
Forum (biweekly). FDJ organ for students and young intelligentsia.
Das Hochschulwesen (monthly).
Jugendforschung (bimonthly). No longer published.
Magdeburger Volksstimme (daily).
Neuer Weg (biweekly). SED organ for party workers.
Neues Deutschland (daily). Official SED organ.
Sächsische Zeitung (daily).
Sonntag (weekly). Cultural newspaper.
Technische Gemeinschaft (monthly). Official KDT organ.
Tribüne (daily). Official trade union organ.
Die Wirtschaft (weekly).
Wirtschaftswissenschaft (monthly).

II. Western Sources on the DDR

A bis Z: Ein Taschen- und Nachschlagebuch über den anderen Teil Deutschlands. Published by the Bundesministerium für gesamtdeutsche Fragen. Bonn: Deutscher Bundes-Verlag, 1969.

Apel, Hans, *Ohne Begleiter.* Köln: Verlag Wissenschaft und Politik, 1965.

Auerbach, Ludwig, "Menschen in der Sowjetischen Besatzungszone VII. Die Intelligenzschicht in der Sowjetzone Deutschlands," *Werkhefte,* XVI (January, February, March 1962), 34–48, 80–88, 117–132.

Baylis, Thomas A., "East Germany: In Quest of Legitimacy." *Problems of Communism* (March-April 1972), pp. 46–55.

————, "East Germany's Rulers: A Study in the Evolution of Totalitarian Leadership." Unpublished Master's thesis. Berkeley: University of California, 1961.

————, "Economic Reform as Ideology: East Germany's New Economic System," *Comparative Politics,* III (January 1971), 211–229.

Bendix, Reinhard, *Work and Authority in Industry.* New York: Harper Torchbooks, 1963.

Bergsdorf, Wolfgang, "Abschied von Humboldt," *Deutschland Archiv,* III (April 1970), 371–374.

Bericht der Bundesregierung und Materialien zur Lage der Nation 1971. Bonn: Bundesministerium für innerdeutsche Beziehungen, 1971.

Beyer, Achim, and Rüdiger Mann, "Dr. Mittag und die Wirtschaftspolitik der SED." *Aktuelle Information des Instituts für Gesellschaft und Wissenschaft in Mitteldeutschland,* No. 5. Erlangen, 1968.

Blücher, Viggo Graf, *Industriearbeiterschaft in der Sowjetzone: Eine Untersuchung der Arbeiterschaft in der Volkseigenen Industrie der SBZ.* Stuttgart: Ferdinand Enke Verlag, 1959.

————, Strukturwandlung der Angestelltenschaft in der SBZ," *Deutsche Studien,* II (August 1964), 192–202.

Bosch, Werner, *Die Sozialstruktur in West- und Mitteldeutschland.* Bonn: Bundesministerium für gesamtdeutsche Fragen, 1958.

Brant, Stefan [Klaus Harpprecht], *Der Aufstand: Vorgeschichte, Geschichte und Deutung des 17. Juni 1953.* Stuttgart: Steingrüben Verlag, 1954.

Brokmeier, Peter, "Die FDJ und ihre neuen Aufgaben," *Deutschland Archiv,* III (February 1970), 135–142.

Bröll, Werner, "Über den Stand der Wirtschaftswissenschaften in der DDR," *Deutschland Archiv,* II (February 1969), 113–130.

———, "Die Wirtschaftsreformen der DDR im RGW-Vergleich." *Deutschland Archiv*, IV (July 1971), 701–720.

Buchow, Wolfgang, "Aktuelle Aspekte und Tendenzen der Hochschulreform in der DDR," *Deutschland Archiv*, I (June 1968), 239–254.

Castellan, Georges, *DDR: Allemagne de l'Est*. Paris: Editions du Seuil, 1955.

Croan, Melvin, "East German Revisionism: The Spectre and the Reality," in Leopold Labedz, ed., *Revisionism: Essays on the History of Marxist Ideas*. New York: Frederick A. Praeger, 1962.

Dahrendorf, Ralf, *Society and Democracy in Germany*. Garden City, N.Y.: Anchor Books, 1967.

Deutscher Bundestag, 6. Wahlperiode, *Materialien zum Bericht zur Lage der Nation 1972*. Bonn, 1972.

Dönhoff, Marion Gräfin, Rudolf Walter Leonhardt, and Theo Sommer, *Reise in ein fernes Land: Bericht über Kultur, Wirtschaft und Politik in der DDR*. Hamburg: Die Zeit Bücher, 1964.

Duhnke, Horst, *Stalinismus in Deutschland*. [Köln]: Verlag für Politik und Wirtschaft [1955].

Erdmann, Kurt, "Das Ende des Neuen Ökonomischen Systems," *Deutschland Archiv*, I (December 1968), 998–1001.

———, "Neue Wirtschaftsmassnahmen ab 1. Januar 1968," *Deutschland Archiv*, I (May 1968), 202–207.

———, "Das ökonomische System des Sozialismus," *SBZ-Archiv*, XVIII, No. 9 (1967), 133–137.

———, "Ökonomisches System 1971—Atempause oder neuer Kurs?" *Deutschland Archiv*, IV (February 1971), 172–175.

Forschungsbeirat für Fragen der Wiedervereinigung Deutschlands, *Vierter Tätigkeitsbericht, 1961–1965*. Bonn: Bundesministerium für gesamtdeutsche Fragen, 1965.

Förtsch, Eckart, *Die SED*. Stuttgart: W. Kohlhammer Verlag, 1969.

Fricke, Karl Wilhelm, "Honeckers Mannschaft," *Deutschland Archiv*, IV (September 1971), 961–967.

Grätz, Frank, "Wirtschaftsführer in Ost und West," *Deutschland Archiv*, IV (October 1971), 1026–1037.

Hangen, Welles, *The Muted Revolution*. New York: Alfred A. Knopf, 1966.

Hanhardt, Arthur M., Jr., "Political Socialization in the German Democratic Republic." Paper delivered at 1970 meeting of the American Political Science Association.

———, "Political Socialization in the German Democratic Republic II." Paper delivered at 1972 meeting of the American Political Science Association.

Hiob, Frank, *Aspekte der Wissenschaftspolitik in der SBZ*. Bonn: Bundesministerium für gesamtdeutsche Fragen, 1962.

Die Intelligenzschicht in der Sowjetzone Deutschlands. Compiled by Ludwig Auerbach and Viggo Graf Blücher. 3 vols., mimeographed. München: Infratest GmbH & Co., November 1960.

Jänicke, Martin, *Der dritte Weg: Die antistalinistische Opposition gegen Ulbricht seit 1953*. Köln: Neuer Deutscher Verlag, 1964.

Juraschek, Georg, "Zur Frage des sozialen Weltbildes jugendlicher Flüchtlinge aus der sowjetisch besetzten Zone Deutschlands," *Integration*, VII (May-June 1960), 101–114.

Kritik der politischen Ökonomie heute—100 Jahre "Kapital." Frankfurt and Wien: Europäische Verlagsanstalt, 1968.

Lange, Max Gustav, "Ausbildung und Erziehung der kommunistischen Partei- und Gewerkschaftsfunktionäre in der Sowjetischen Besatzungszone Deutschlands." Unpublished manuscript. [Berlin? 1957?].

———, *Wissenschaft im totalitären Staat*. Stuttgart and Düsseldorf: Ring Verlag, 1955.

Lange, Max Gustav, Ernst Richert, and Otto Stammer, "Das Problem der 'Neuen Intelligenz' in der Sowjetischen Besatzungszone," in *Veritas, Iustitia, Libertas: Festschrift zur 200-Jahrfeier der Columbia University, New York*. Berlin: Colloquium Verlag, 1954, pp. 191–246.

Leissner, Gustav, *Verwaltung und öffentlicher Dienst in der sowjetischen Besatzungszone Deutschlands: Eine kritische Würdigung aus gesamtdeutscher Sicht*. Stuttgart and Köln: W. Kohlhammer Verlag, 1961.

Leonhard, Wolfgang, *Child of the Revolution*. Chicago: Henry Regnery, 1958.

Leutwein, Alfred [Siegfried Mampel], *Die 'Technische Intelligenz' in der sowjetischen Besatzungszone*. Bonner Berichte aus Mittel- und Ostdeutschland. Bonn: Bundesministerium für gesamtdeutsche Fragen, 1953.

Lippmann, Heinz, "The Limits of Reform Communism," *Problems of Communism* (May-June 1970), pp. 15–23.

Ludwig, Harald, "Die SED vor dem VIII. Parteitag," *Deutschland Archiv*, IV (June 1971), 584–597.

Ludz, Peter Christian, "Bildungsstätte für zentrale Führungskräfte," *SBZ-Archiv*, XVII, No. 15 (1966), 230–232.

———, "Die 'DDR' im Jahre 1964," *Hinter dem eisernen Vorhang* (January 1965), pp. 11–18.

———, "Die 'DDR' nach dem VI. Parteitag der SED," *Hinter dem eisernen Vorhang* (April 1963), pp. 9–16.

————, "East Germany: The Old and the New," *East Europe* (April 1966), pp. 23–27.

————, *The German Democratic Republic from the Sixties to the Seventies: A Socio-Political Analysis.* [Cambridge]: Harvard University Center for International Affairs, 1970.

————, *Parteielite im Wandel: Funktionsaufbau, Sozialstruktur und Ideologie—eine empirisch-systematische Untersuchung.* Köln and Opladen: Westdeutscher Verlag, 1968.

————, "Politische Aspekte der kybernetischen Systemtheorie in der DDR," *Deutschland Archiv,* I (April 1968), 1–10.

————, "Produktionsprinzip versus Territorialprinzip: Probleme der Parteiorganisation im Rahmen des Neuen Ökonomischen Systems," *SBZ-Archiv,* XVI, Nos. 1–2 (1965), 5–9.

————, "Revisionistische Konzeptionen von 1956/1957 in der 'DDR,'" *Moderne Welt,* II, No. 4 (1960–1961), 353ff.

————, "The SED Leadership in Transition," *Problems of Communism* (May-June 1970), pp. 23–31.

————, ed., *Studien und Materialien zur Soziologie der DDR. Sonderheft 8 der Kölner Zeitschrift für Soziologie und Sozialpsychologie.* Köln and Opladen: Westdeutscher Verlag, 1964.

————, "Widersprüche im Neuen Ökonomischen System: Organisatorische Probleme der Erzeugnisgruppen," *SBZ-Archiv,* XV, No. 7 (1964), 101–104.

Mampel, Siegfried, "Der totalitär-sozialistische Staat als Unternehmer und Arbeitgeber: Gezeigt am Beispiel der Sowjetzone Deutschlands," *Deutsche Studien,* II (August 1964), 142–156.

"S. M." [Siegfried Mampel], "Widerstand gegen leistungsabhängige Gehälter," *Deutsche Fragen,* XI, No. 7 (1965), 128–129.

Müller, Karl Valentin, *Die Manager in der Sowjetzin: Eine empirische Untersuchung zur Soziologie der wirtschaftlichen und militärischen Führungsschicht in Mitteldeutschland.* Köln and Opladen: Westdeutscher Verlag, 1962.

Müller, Marianne, and Egon Erwin Müller, ". . . stürmt die Festung Wissenschaft!" *Die Sowjetisierung der mitteldeutschen Universitäten seit 1945.* Berlin-Dahlem: Colloquium Verlag, 1953.

Nawrocki, Joachim, "Über Autorität und Vernunft der Wirtschaftsplaner," *Deutschland Archiv,* IV (January 1971), 3–5.

————, *Das geplante Wunder: Leben und Wirtschaften im anderen Deutschland.* Hamburg: Christian Wegner Verlag, 1967.

————, "Vom NÖS zum Computer-Stalinismus," *Deutschland Archiv,* IV (April 1971), 345–348.

Nettl, J. P., *The Eastern Zone and Soviet Policy in Germany*. London: Cambridge University Press, 1951.

Picaper, Jean-Paul, "Le Parti communiste en Allemagne de l'Est: Evolution de sa physionomie et de ses fonctions," *Revue Française de Science Politique*, XVI (February 1966), 36–55.

———, "Le Parti Communiste en Allemagne de l'Est, 1945–1967." Unpublished doctoral dissertation. Faculté des Lettres et Sciences Humaines de l'Université de Strasbourg, 1967.

Prahl, Hans-Werner, "Intelligenz- und Elitegruppen in der DDR-Gesellschaft," *Deutschland Archiv*, III (February 1970), 128–134.

———, "Konfusion in der Klassentheorie," *Deutschland Archiv*, III (August 1970), 888–892.

Prauss, Herbert, *doch es war nicht die Wahrheit*. Berlin: Morus-Verlag, 1960.

Pritzel, Konstantin, "Zusammenarbeit DDR-UdSSR und die sozialistische Integration," *Deutschland Archiv*, V (August 1972), 818–827.

Richert, Ernst, *Die DDR-Elite*. Hamburg: Rowohlt Verlag, 1968.

———, *Macht ohne Mandat: Der Staatsapparat in der Sowjetischen Besatzungszone Deutschlands*. Zweite, erweiterte und überarbeitete Auflage. Köln and Opladen: Westdeutscher Verlag, 1963.

———, *"Sozialistische Universität": Die Hochschulpolitik der SED*. Berlin: Colloquium Verlag, 1967.

———, "Trend zur Entsachlichung in der SED-Führung?" *Deutschland Archiv*, II (May 1969), 484–492.

———, "Ulbricht and After," *Survey* (October 1966), pp. 153–164.

———, *Das zweite Deutschland: Ein Staat, der nicht sein darf*. Gütersloh: Sigbert Mohn Verlag, 1964.

Richert, Ernst, with Carola Stern and Peter Dietrich, *Agitation und Propaganda: Das System der publizistischen Massenführung in der Sowjetzone*. Berlin: Vahlen, 1958.

Rudolph, Irmhild, and Erhard Stölting, "Soziale Beziehungen im VEB im Spiegel betriebssoziologischer Forschung in der DDR," *Deutschland Archiv*, Sonderheft, III (October 1970), 113–120.

SBZ von A bis Z: Ein Taschen- und Nachschlagebuch über die Sowjetischen Besatzungszone Deutschlands. Published by Bundesministerium für gesamtdeutsche Fragen. 8th-10th editions. Bonn: Deutscher Bundes-Verlag, 1963, 1965, 1966.

SBZ-Biographie: Ein biographisches Nachschlagebuch über die Sowjetischen Besatzungszone Deutschlands. Zusammengestellt vom Untersuchungsausschuss Freiheitlicher Juristen Berlin. 1st edition,

3rd edition. Bonn and Berlin: Bundesministerium für gesamt-deutsche Fragen, 1961, 1964, 1965.

SBZ von 1945 bis 1954: Die Sowjetische Besatzungszone in den Jahren 1945–1954. Bonn and Berlin: Bundesministerium für gesamt-deutsche Fragen, 1961.

SBZ von 1955 bis 1956: Die Sowjetische Besatzungszone in den Jahren 1955–1956. Bonn and Berlin: Bundesministerium für gesamt-deutsche Fragen, 1958.

SBZ von 1957 bis 1958: Die Sowjetische Besatzungszone in den Jahren 1957–1958. Bonn and Berlin: Bundesministerium für gesamt-deutsche Fragen, 1960.

SBZ von 1959 bis 1960: Die Sowjetische Besatzungszone in den Jahren 1959–1960. Bonn and Berlin: Bundesministerium für gesamt-deutsche Fragen, 1964.

Schenk, Fritz, "Konzil der Wirtschaftsbürokraten," *SBZ-Archiv*, XII, No. 21 (1961), 329–332.

———, *Das rote Wirtschaftswunder: Die zentrale Planwirtschaft als Machtmittel der SED-Politik.* Stuttgart: Seewald Verlag, 1969.

———, " 'Störfreimachung' der Zonenwirtschaft," *SBZ-Archiv*, XII, No. 19 (1961), 301–303.

———, *Im Vorzimmer der Diktatur: 12 Jahre Pankow.* Köln: Kiepen-heuer & Witsch, 1962.

———, "Die zweite Etappe der Planlosigkeit," *SBZ-Archiv*, XVII, Nos. 1–2 (1966), 1–2.

Schimanski, Hans, "Parteiaufbau nach Produktionsprinzip: Die SED wird nach sowjetischem Muster reorganisiert," *SBZ-Archiv*, XIV, No. 8 (1963), 119–122.

———, "Die Revolution in Glaspalast," *SBZ-Archiv*, IX (February 28, 1958), 150–154.

———, "Die 12. Tagung des ZK der SED," *SBZ-Archiv*, XII, No. 7 (1961), 106–110.

Schultz, Joachim, *Der Funktionär in der Einheitspartei: Kaderpolitik und Bürokratisierung in der SED.* Stuttgart and Düsseldorf: Ring Verlag, 1956.

Schulz, Hans-Dieter, "Die Hoffnung heisst 'Nöspl.' " *Die Zeit* (April 30, 1965), p. 36.

———, "Neues NÖSPL nötig," *Deutschland Archiv*, V (November 1972), 1134–1137.

Schwarzenbach, Rudolf, "Zentrale staatliche Leitung und Eigenverant-wortung im Gesellschaftssystem der DDR," *Deutschland Archiv*, II (February 1969), 131–147.

Die SED: Historische Entwicklung, ideologische Grundlagen, Pro-

gramm und Organisation. [Bonn]: Bundesministerium für gesamtdeutsche Fragen, [1967].

Slamecka, Vladimir, *Science in East Germany*. New York and London: Columbia University Press, 1963.

Smith, Jean Edward, *Germany Beyond the Wall: People, Politics . . . and Prosperity*. Boston: Little, Brown, 1969.

Stammer, Otto, "Sozialstruktur und System der Werthaltungen der Sowjetischen Besatzungszone Deutschlands," *Schmollers Jahrbuch für Gesetzgebung, Verwaltung und Volkswirtschaft*, LXXVI, No. 1 (1956), 55–105.

Stern, Carola, *Porträt einer bolschewistischen Partei*. Köln: Verlag für Politik und Wirtschaft, 1957.

———, *Die SED: Ein Handbuch über Aufbau, Organisation, und Funktion des Parteiapparates*. [Köln]: Verlag für Politik und Wirtschaft, [1954].

———, *Ulbricht: Eine politische Biographie*. Köln: Kiepenheuer & Witsch, 1963.

———, "Ulbrichts Dorffabrik," *SBZ-Archiv*, XI, No. 9 (1960), 129–133.

Storbeck, Dietrich, *Sozialstrukturen in Mitteldeutschland: Eine sozialstatistische Bevölkerungsanalyse im gesamtdeutschen Vergleich*. Berlin: Duncker & Humblot, 1964.

Thalheim, Karl C., *Die Wirtschaft der Sowjetzone in Krise und Umbau*. Berlin: Duncker & Humblot, 1964.

Thalheim, Karl C., and Hans-Hermann Höhmann, *Wirtschaftsreformen in Osteuropa*. Köln: Verlag Wissenschaft und Politik, 1968.

Universitäten und Hochschulen in der Sowjetzone. Bonner Fachberichte aus der Sowjetzone. [Bonn]: Bundesministerium für gesamtdeutsche Fragen, 1964.

Wer ist Wer in der SBZ? Ein biographisches Handbuch. Berlin-Zehlendorf: Verlag für internationalen Kulturaustausch, 1958.

Wiesner, Ali, "Ökonomische Hauptaufgabe von der Tagesordnung abgesetzt," *SBZ-Archiv*, XII, No. 5 (1961), 74–77.

Von Wrangel, Georg, "Das staatliche Industriemanagement in der Sowjetunion und in der SBZ," *Deutsche Studien*, II (August 1964), 168–177.

Zimmermann, Hartmut, "Wandlungen der Leitungsstruktur des VEB in soziologischer Sicht," *Deutschland Archiv*, Sonderheft, III (October 1970), 98–112.

PERIODICALS

Deutschland Archiv (monthly).
East Europe (monthly).
Frankfurter Allgemeine Zeitung (daily).
Hinter dem eisernen Vorhang (monthly).
New York *Times* (daily).
Problems of Communism (bimonthly).
SBZ-Archiv (biweekly—superseded by *Deutschland Archiv*).
Survey (quarterly).
Die Zeit (weekly).

III. WESTERN SOURCES—GENERAL

Almond, Gabriel, and Sidney Verba, *The Civic Culture.* Boston: Little, Brown, 1965.
Armstrong, John A., *Ideology, Politics, and Government in the Soviet Union.* New York: Frederick A. Praeger, 1962.
———, "Sources of Administrative Behavior: Some Soviet and Western European Comparisons," *American Political Science Review,* LIX (September 1965), 643–655.
Aron, Raymond, *The Industrial Society.* New York: Frederick A. Praeger, 1967.
———, "Social Structure and the Ruling Class," *British Journal of Sociology,* I (March, June 1950), 1–16, 126–143.
Aspaturian, Vernon, "Social Structure and Political Power in the Soviet System," in H. Albinski and L. Pettit, eds., *European Political Processes.* Boston: Allyn and Bacon, 1968.
Azrael, Jeremy R., "Bringing up the New Soviet Man," *Problems of Communism* (May-June 1968), pp. 23–31.
———, *Managerial Power and Soviet Politics.* Cambridge: Harvard University Press, 1966.
———, "Soviet Union," in James S. Coleman, ed., *Education and Political Development.* Princeton: Princeton University Press, 1965, pp. 233–271.
Bachrach, Peter, *The Theory of Democratic Elitism.* Boston: Little, Brown, 1967.
Bachrach, Peter, and Morton S. Baratz, "Two Faces of Power," *American Political Science Review,* LVI (December 1962), 947–952.
Barber, Bernard, *Social Stratification.* New York: Harcourt, Brace, 1957.

Bartsch, Günter, "Die Kommunisten und das Generationsproblem," *Osteuropa*, XIV (May 1964), 329–340.

Beck, Carl, "Bureaucracy and Political Development in Eastern Europe," in Joseph La Palombara, ed., *Bureaucracy and Political Development*. Princeton: Princeton University Press, 1963, pp. 268–300.

Bell, Daniel, "Notes on the Post-Industrial Society," in Jack D. Douglas, ed., *The Technological Threat*. Englewood Cliffs, N.J.: Prentice-Hall, 1971, pp. 1–11.

Bendix, Reinhard, "The Cultural and Political Setting of Economic Rationality in Western and Eastern Europe," in Gregory Grossman ed., *Value and Plan*. Berkeley and Los Angeles: University of California Press, 1960, pp. 245–261.

———, *Max Weber: An Intellectual Portrait*. Garden City, N.Y.: Anchor Books, 1963.

Berliner, Joseph, *Factory and Manager in the USSR*. Cambridge: Harvard University Press, 1957.

Bottomore, T. B., *Elites and Society*. Harmondsworth, Eng.: Penguin Books, 1964.

Brzezinski, Zbigniew, and Samuel P. Huntington, *Political Power: USA/USSR*. New York: Viking Press, 1964.

Burnham, James, *The Managerial Revolution*. Bloomington: Indiana University Press, 1960.

Cole, G. D. H., *Studies in Class Structure*. London: Routledge & Kegan Paul, 1955.

Crick, Bernard, *In Defence of Politics*. Baltimore: Penguin Books, 1964.

Dahl, Robert A., "Critique of the Ruling Elite Model," *American Political Science Review*, LII (June 1958), 463–469.

———, *Modern Political Analysis*. Englewood Cliffs, N.J.: Prentice-Hall, 1963.

———, *Who Governs?* New Haven: Yale University Press, 1961.

Dahrendorf, Ralf, *Class and Class Conflict in Industrial Society*. Stanford: Stanford University Press, 1959.

Djilas, Milovan, *The New Class*. New York: Frederick A. Praeger, 1957.

Drucker, Peter F., *The New Society*. New York: Harper and Bros., 1950.

Eckstein, Alexander, "Economic Development and Political Change in Communist Systems," *World Politics*, XXII (July 1970), 475–495.

Edinger, Lewis J., ed., *Political Leadership in Industrialized Societies*. New York: John Wiley, 1967.

Edinger, Lewis J., and Donald D. Searing, "Social Background in Elite Analysis: A Methodological Inquiry," *American Political Science Review*, LXI (June 1967), 428–445.

Ellul, Jacques, *The Technological Society*. New York: Vintage, 1964.

Elsner, Henry, Jr., *The Technocrats: Prophets of Automation*. Syracuse: Syracuse University Press, 1967.

Farrell, R. Barry, ed., *Political Leadership in Eastern Europe and the Soviet Union*. Chicago: Aldine, 1970.

Ferkiss, Victor, *Technological Man*. New York: George Braziller, 1969.

Fleron, Frederic J., Jr., "Note on the Explication of the Concept 'Elite' in the Study of Soviet Politics," *Canadian Slavic Studies*, II (Spring 1968), 111–115.

Fleron, Frederic J., Jr., ed., *Communist Studies and the Social Sciences*. Chicago: Rand McNally, 1969.

Fleron, Frederic J., Jr., and Rita Mae Kelly, "Personality, Behavior, and Communist Ideology," *Soviet Studies*, XXI (January 1970), 297–313.

Fox, Douglas M., "Whither Community Power Studies," *Polity*, III (Summer 1971), 576–585.

Friedrich, Carl J., and Zbigniew Brzezinski, *Totalitarian Dictatorship and Autocracy*. Cambridge: Harvard University Press, 1956.

Friedrich, Carl J., Michael Curtis, and Benjamin Barber, *Totalitarianism in Perspective*. New York: Frederick A. Praeger, 1969.

Galbraith, John Kenneth, *The New Industrial State*. New York: Signet, 1967.

Gamarnikow, Michael, "The End of the Party Hack?" *East Europe* (November 1965), pp. 3–8.

Gehlen, Michael P., and Michael McBride, "The Soviet Central Committee: An Elite Analysis," *American Political Science Review*, LXII (December 1968), 1232–1241.

Gilpin, Robert, and Christopher Wright, eds., *Scientists and National Policy-Making*. New York: Columbia University Press, 1964.

Gorz, André, *Strategy for Labor*. Boston: Beacon Press, 1967.

Granick, David, *The Red Executive*. Garden City, N.Y.: Anchor Books, 1961.

Hough, Jerry F., *The Soviet Prefects: The Local Party Organs in Industrial Decision-Making*. Cambridge: Harvard University Press, 1969.

———, "The Soviet System: Petrification or Pluralism?" *Problems of Communism* (March-April 1972), pp. 25–45.

Huntington, Samuel P., and Clement H. Moore, eds., *Authoritarian*

Politics in Modern Society: The Dynamics of Established One-Party Systems. New York: Basic Books, 1970.

Ilchman, Warren, "Productivity, Administrative Reform, and Anti-Politics," in Ralph Braibanti, ed., *Political and Administrative Development.* Durham, N.C.: Duke University Press, 1969, pp. 472–526.

Johnson, Chalmers, ed., *Change in Communist Systems.* Stanford: Stanford University Press, 1970.

Kanet, Roger E., ed., *The Behavioral Revolution and Communist Studies.* New York: Free Press, 1971.

Kassof, Allen, "The Administered Society: Totalitarianism Without Terror," *World Politics,* XVI (July 1964), 558–575.

Keller, Suzanne, *Beyond the Ruling Class.* New York: Random House, 1963.

Kerr, Clark, John T. Dunlop, Frederick H. Harbison, and Charles A. Myers, *Industrialism and Industrial Man.* Cambridge: Harvard University Press, 1960.

Kornhauser, William, *The Politics of Mass Society.* Glencoe, Ill.: Free Press, 1959.

Lasswell, Harold D., and Abraham Kaplan, *Power and Society.* New Haven: Yale University Press, 1950.

Lasswell, Harold D., Daniel Lerner, and C. Easton Rothwell, *The Comparative Study of Elites.* Stanford: Stanford University Press, 1952.

Leonhard, Wolfgang, *The Kremlin Since Stalin.* New York: Frederick A. Praeger, 1962.

Linden, Carl A., *Khrushchev and the Soviet Leadership.* Baltimore: Johns Hopkins Press, 1966.

Lipset, Seymour M., and Reinhard Bendix, "Social Status and Social Structure: A Reexamination of Data and Interpretations," *British Journal of Sociology,* II (June, September 1951), 150–168, 230–254.

Lodge, Milton C., *Soviet Elite Attitudes Since Stalin.* Columbus, Ohio: Charles E. Merrill, 1969.

Mannheim, Karl, *Man and Society in an Age of Reconstruction.* London: Routledge & Kegan Paul, 1940.

March, James G., and Herbert A. Simon, *Organizations.* New York: John Wiley, 1958.

Marx and Engels on Politics and Philosophy, ed. Lewis Feuer. Garden City, N.Y.: Anchor Books, 1959.

Merritt, Richard L., *Systematic Approaches to Comparative Politics.* Chicago: Rand McNally, 1970.

Merton, Robert K., *et al.*, eds., *Reader in Bureaucracy*. Glencoe, Ill.: Free Press, 1952.

Meyer, Alfred G., "The Functions of Ideology in the Soviet Political System," *Soviet Studies*, XVII (January 1966), 273–285.

———, *The Soviet Political System*. New York: Random House, 1965.

———, "USSR, Incorporated," *Slavic Review*, XX (October 1961), 369–376.

Meynaud, Jean, *Technocracy*. London: Faber & Faber, 1968.

Mills, C. Wright, *The Power Elite*. New York: Oxford University Press, 1957.

Parry, Albert, *The New Class Divided: Science and Technology Versus Communism*. New York: Macmillan, 1966.

Ridley, F. F., "French Technocracy and Comparative Government," *Political Studies*, XIV (February 1966), 34–52.

Roszak, Theodore, *The Making of a Counter Culture*. Garden City, N.Y.: Anchor Books, 1969.

Rustow, Dankwart, "The Study of Elites: Who's Who's, When, and How," *World Politics*, XVIII (July 1966), 691–717.

Saint-Simon, Henri Comte de, *Selected Writings*, ed. F. M. H. Markham. Oxford: Basil Blackwell, 1952.

Sampson, Anthony, *The New Europeans*. London: Hodder & Stoughton, 1968.

Schaar, John, "Legitimacy in the Modern State," in Philip Green and Sanford Levinson, eds., *Power and Community*. New York: Vintage, 1970.

Schapiro, Leonard, "Collective Lack of Leadership," *Survey* (Winter-Spring 1969), pp. 193–200.

Schonfield, Andrew, *Modern Capitalism*. New York: Oxford University Press, 1965.

Schwartz, Joel J., and William R. Keech, "Group Influence and the Policy Process in the Soviet Union," *American Political Science Review*, LXII (September 1968), 840–851.

Searing, Donald D., "The Comparative Study of Elite Socialization," *Comparative Political Studies*, I (January 1969), 471–500.

Selznick, Philip, "Institutional Vulnerability in Mass Society," *American Journal of Sociology*, LVI (January 1951), 320–331.

———, *Leadership in Administration*. New York: Harper & Row, 1957.

Servan-Schreiber, Jean-Jacques, *The American Challenge*. New York: Atheneum, 1968.

Simirenko, Alex, "Ersatz Charisma: A Sociological Interpretation of Communist Countries," *Newsletter on Comparative Studies of Communism*, IV (August 1971), 3–15.

Skilling, H. Gordon, "Background to the Study of Political Opposition in Communist East Europe," *Government and Opposition,* III (Summer 1968), 294–324.

Skilling, H. Gordon, and Franklyn Griffiths, eds., *Interest Groups in Soviet Politics.* Princeton: Princeton University Press, 1971.

Statistisches Jahrbuch für die Bundesrepublik Deutschland 1969 (1970). Stuttgart: Kohlhammer, 1969, 1970.

Thompson, Victor A., *Modern Organization.* New York: Alfred A. Knopf, 1961.

Tucker, Robert C., "The Theory of Charismatic Leadership," in *Philosophers and Kings: Studies in Leadership. Daedalus* (Summer 1968), pp. 731–756.

Veblen, Thorstein, *The Engineers and the Price System.* New York: Harcourt, Brace, 1963.

Weber, Max, *From Max Weber: Essays in Sociology,* eds. Hans H. Gerth and C. Wright Mills. New York: Oxford University Press, 1958.

————, *Wirtschaft und Gesellschaft.* Studienausgabe, hrsgg. von Johannes Winckelmann. 2 vols. Köln: Kiepenheuer & Witsch, 1964.

Wolfinger, Raymond E., "Nondecisions and the Study of Local Politics"; Frederick W. Frey, "Comment"; Wolfinger, "Rejoinder." *American Political Science Review,* LXV (December 1971), 1063–1104.

Wolin, Sheldon S., *Politics and Vision: Continuity and Innovation in Western Political Thought.* Boston: Little, Brown, 1960.

INDEX